THE GERMAN 66TH REGIMENT

IN THE FIRST WORLD WAR

THE GERMAN 66TH REGIMENT

IN THE FIRST WORLD WAR

THE GERMAN PERSPECTIVE

OTTO KORFES
TRANSLATED BY TERENCE ZUBER

The
History
Press

The Regiments of the German Imperial Army during the Great War

Based on the unit war diaries

The Prussian Army

Volume 302

The 3rd Magdeburg Infantry Regiment Nr. 66

Oldenbourg i. O./ Berlin 1930

Gerhard Stalling. Founded 1798

The 3rd Magdeburg Infantry Regiment in the Great War

Written by veterans of the regiment using official records

and reports from officers and men of the regiment

Dr Otto Korfes, editor

Captain (inactive) and Archivist in the Reichsarchiv

With 1 map, 23 Sketches and 88 pencil drawings by E.R. Döbrich-Steglitz

Translated by

Terence Zuber

1930

Tradition Publishing Wilhelm Kolk/Berlin SW 48

For this series of unit histories the Reichsarchiv has made available the unit war diaries, including the annexes, according to an express regulation and a contract between the editor and the archive. The editor is solely responsible for the contents.

Reichsarchiv Section G

Responsible for the series 'The Regiments of the Imperial German Army'

First published 1930, this edition published 2016

The History Press
The Mill, Brimscombe Port
Stroud, Gloucestershire, GL5 2QG
www.thehistorypress.co.uk

Original text © Otto Korfes, 1930
Translation © Terence Zuber, 2016

The right of Terence Zuber to be identified as the Translator
of this work has been asserted in accordance with the
Copyright, Designs and Patents Act 1988.

British Library Cataloguing in Publication Data.
A catalogue record for this book is available from the British Library.

ISBN 978 0 7509 6200 1

Typeset in 11/13.5pt Bembo by The History Press
Printed and bound in Great Britain, by TJ International Ltd

Contents

The German Infantry Regiment

The basic tactical unit was the infantry company. The wartime strength of a German infantry company in 1914 was five officers and 260 NCOs and enlisted men. The company commander was usually a captain who was responsible for individual, NCO, and squad and platoon training, particularly individual marksmanship and small-unit fire tactics. The company was broken down into a small company command group and three platoons of about eighty men (in practice, sixty-four to seventy-two men), each platoon consisting of eight squads, each squad led by a sergeant or corporal.

The German non-commissioned officer corps was a particular strength of the German Army. Each peacetime German infantry battalion had between seventy-two and seventy-eight career NCOs, while a war-strength battalion had eighty-five NCOs (including four medical NCOs). These were men who had re-enlisted expressly to become non-commissioned officers. They were carefully selected and provided with excellent training by the company commander and army schools. Training of the individual soldier was in their hands. The company first sergeant, the 'mother of the company', held his position for a considerable period and enjoyed immense prestige and responsibility.

The company also included the combat trains, which consisted of the ammunition wagon and the mobile field kitchen, and the field trains, which included a company supply wagon and a rations wagon.

The German infantry battalion consisted of four infantry companies and the battalion headquarters: twenty-six officers and 1,054 NCOs and enlisted men. The battalion commander was usually a major, perhaps a lieutenant-colonel. He was assisted by the battalion adjutant, the most capable lieutenant in the battalion, who was the operations officer, and by a rations officer, in combat usually a reserve lieutenant, as well as a surgeon and a paymaster, who was also the NCO in charge of property. Each battalion had eight bicycle messengers, armed with carbines. The company trains were united under battalion control to form the battalion combat trains (four ammunition wagons, four mobile field kitchens, plus the battalion medical wagon) and the battalion field trains (battalion staff wagon, four company supply wagons, four rations wagons, one sundries – tobacco and similar personal use items – wagon, one battalion supply wagon), altogether nineteen vehicles, thirty-eight horses and forty-seven men.

On the march and in combat, the battalion combat trains stayed close to the battalion, but the field trains could be as far as a day's march behind.

The German infantry regiment was composed of three battalions and a machine-gun company: eighty-six officers, 3,304 NCOs and enlisted men, seventy-two vehicles and 233 horses. The regiment was the most important unit in the German army. The regimental commander was responsible for selecting and training the officer corps. The annual recruit, company and battalion inspections and range-firing exercises took place in his presence and largely under his control. Unit pride was directed principally towards the regiment and its history. The regimental commander was a lieutenant-colonel or colonel. The regimental staff consisted of three lieutenants: the adjutant (operations officer), an assistant operations officer and the leader of the field trains (which united all the battalion field trains), as well as the regimental surgeon. The regiment also had a large four-horse wagon with engineering tools: 1,200 small shovels, 275 large shovels, 288 pickaxes, 107 picks, sixty-six axes, thirty saws and ninety-six wire cutters. The regimental trains included seventy-two wagons, 165 EM and 210 horses. In theory, the field trains would catch up with the regiment when it billeted or bivouacked, but that rarely happened in mobile operations.

German regiments (with the exception of the Prussian Guard and the Bavarian Army) had two designations. The first was often geographical, in this case, 3rd Magdeburg. The second was its number in the Prussian Army, in this case 66th Infantry. Battalions were numbered with Roman numerals I, II, III, and referred to as I/ IR 66 (1st Battalion, Infantry Regiment 66). Companies were numbered consecutively within the battalions: the 1st, 2nd, 3rd and 4th companies always belonged to the I Battalion, 5th, 6th, 7th and 8th the II Battalion, 9th, 10th, 11th and 12th the III battalion. The 3rd Company, 1st Battalion, Infantry Regiment 66 was abbreviated 3/ I/ IR 66 or just 3/ 66. The same system applied to cavalry, artillery and engineers.

It was not possible to go beyond translating the regimental history and annotate or explain the background in German history, or the developments in German army doctrine, organisation or weaponry, which would have constituted a major work in itself.

Terence Zuber

Translator/Editor Notes

After the Great War, practically every combat-arms regiment in the German army, including reserve, and sometimes even combat replacement (Ersatz) units, produced a regimental history. Since the Reichsarchiv in Potsdam was destroyed, and the operational records of the Saxon archive lost (not in the bombing of Dresden, but apparently destroyed by the East German Communists), these regimental histories are the only records we have for the Prussian and Saxon armies, though the complete Bavarian archive exists, as do the Baden and Württemberg archives up to division level.

As a group, these are the best regimental histories ever written; indeed they are military histories of the first rank. They should be considered primary documents. They were generally based on the extensive unit records available: war diaries, after-action reports and the mass of administrative documents generated by trench warfare. I was able to see the storage area of the Bavarian army archive, and the quantity of Great War documents is astounding. The regimental histories were written by unit commanders up to the regimental level, adjutants (operations officers) and other leaders of the unit, sometimes working in conjunction. Some were professional soldiers, some reserve officers, which meant that in civilian life they belonged to the educated upper-middle class: university professors, lawyers, businessmen. We therefore get direct insight into what the leaders were doing and thinking. Moreover, these men had trained in evaluating military operations in peacetime: an after-action report would be written for each tactical training exercise and then reviewed and commented on in detail by the next two higher echelons of command. These books were written principally for the members of the unit and their families, so they were generally accurate. They also demonstrate the high level of tactical doctrinal sophistication in the German Army.

Quite a few regimental histories are among the best descriptions of tactical combat anywhere at any time, for example *Das 1. Badische Leib-Grenadier Regiment Nr. 109 im Weltkrieg 1914–1918* (The Baden 1st Household Grenadier Regiment Number 109 in the Great War 1914–1918, Karlsruhe 1927). It is 1,225 pages long, 705 pages describing the regiment's tactical operations, all on the Western Front. There are multiple authors. The maps are outstanding and there are lots of them. The rest of the book considers individual aspects in the development of tactical combat: doctrine, weapons, defensive positions, communications, gas, troop quarters, rations, combat and field trains, administration, medicine, chaplains, troop welfare and the replacement battalion. The breadth and attention to detail are unparalleled. If there is a shortcoming, it is that there are no first-person accounts. There is also little possibility of an English translation of such a huge work ever being published.

The history of Infantry Regiment 66 is, by the standards of German regimental histories, in the upper-middle range. It is 458 pages long, of which 382 describe operations; the remainder are tables with the positions occupied by officers and lists of the officers and men killed.

It would be hard to imagine anyone more qualified to edit this history than Otto Korfes. Korfes was a lieutenant in 5th Company 2nd Battalion Infantry Regiment 66 (which we will abbreviate 5/ II/ IR 66, or 5/ 66) at the beginning of the war. By October he was the regimental adjutant (operations officer). He was promoted to captain and for a relatively short time near the end of the war was commander of II/ 66, until he was wounded. After the war, Korfes joined the Reichsarchiv, which was charged with preserving the records of the German Army and writing the official history of the war, earning his PhD in History.

A particular strength of the book is the number of first-person accounts, which give invaluable individual insights. A weakness was that it was not properly edited: the English translation is better organised and much tighter than the German original. As the war goes on, the maps become less adequate; on the other hand, the war was by then being fought on a featureless moonscape. Since the German 1914–18, modern American and British NCO rank structures are so dissimilar, I have decided to translate them as follows:

Unteroffizier	Sergeant
Vicefeldwebel	Senior Sergeant
Feldwebel	First Sergeant/Master Sergeant

IR 66 was a good unit, but so were most of the infantry regiments in the German Army. For the meantime, IR 66 will stand for all German infantry regiments.

The purpose of this book is twofold. First, it is to acquaint anglophone readers with the war as the German soldier saw it, and as a German regiment fought it. The second is to interest German-speaking historians with the German regimental history, a heretofore badly underused and most valuable source material.

Key for the map sketches

1. Stellung   1st Position
2. Stellung   2nd Position

German terms

German dates are day/month/year: 3/6/14 is 3 June 1914

Ausgehoben Verteidigungdsstellung	Dug-in Position
Bewegungen	Movement
Clarière	Clearing in woods
Entfaltung	Deployment
Feind	Enemy
Lage	Situation
Laufgraben	Communications Trench
Mulde	Depression (in ground)
Nachm. (Nachmittag)	Morning
Neue Stellung	New Position
Schlacht	Battle
Schneise	Cut in woods
Stand	Time
Vorm. (Vormittag)	Morning
Zwischenstellung	Intermediate Position

Abbreviations

AK	Armeekorps	Army Corps
ID	Infanteriedivision	Infantry Division
RD	Reservedivision	Reserve Division
IR	Infanterieregiment	Infantry Regiment
RIR	Reserve Infanterieregiment	Reserve Infantry Regiment
FAR	Feldartillerieregiment	Field Artillery Regiment

Unit Designations

III/ 66	3rd Battalion, 66th Infantry Regiment
3/ 66	3rd Company, 66th Infantry Regiment
2/ FAR 4	2nd Battery, 4th Field Artillery Regiment

Glossary

AK	Armeekorps	Army Corps
Capt.	Captain	
FAR	Feldartillerie-regiment	Field Artillery Regiment
Fme	Ferme	Farm
FO	Forward Observer	
HKK 2	Heereskavalleriekorps 2	2nd Cavalry Corps
HQ	Headquarters	
ID	Infanteriedivision	Infantry Division
IR	Infanterie-regiment	Infantry Regiment
Landwehr	Territorial troops	
Lieut-col	Lieutenant-colonel	
Lt	Lieutenant	
MG	Machine Gun	
NCO	Non-commissioned Officer	
OHL	Oberste Heeresleitung	Senior German HQ
OP	Observation Post	
RD	Reservedivision	Reserve Division
Res.	Reserve	Reserve
RK	Reservekorps	Reserve Corps

FOREWORD

After Captain Lademann published a short regimental history, in 1922, the desire arose for a more detailed work. With the assistance of numerous members of the regiment, Captains Hermens, Korfes, Siegener, Winckler (Joachim) and Reserve First Lieutenants Borchert and Heine, and Reserve Lieutenant Wadepuhl have succeeded in describing the combat operations in detail. They have prevented exceptional deeds from being forgotten and preserved the names of worthy members of the regiment for posterity. Unfortunately, it was not possible to name all the brave men; they would fill an entire book. The names of the dead are included in a roll of honour.

This book can have no finer introduction than that written by Captain Lademann:

> Having already proven itself in two wars during the 54 years of its existence, in the summer of 1914 the 3rd Magdeburg Infantry Regiment deployed to the combat zone. For 51 months it fought continually on the Western Front, preserving its reputation and adding new laurels of victory to its standard. This small book will tell of the regiment's deeds. Men who wore the number 66 in the Great War will remember from this simple account the difficult days that the old regiment experienced and, in spite of everything, the good days too. He will relive the advance in the hot summer sun in 1914 and the difficult combat in villages, then the long periods of trench warfare and the bloody fight that has gone down in history as the Battle of the Somme. Once again the quiet positions in Alsace will appear before him. Once more he will remember the bitter days in May 1917 on the Chemin des Dames and the swampy Ailette valley. He will recall the great offensives of 1918 and the dark weeks that preceded the Armistice, and the End. He will march again on dusty country roads, sit by the light of a candle in the bomb-proof dugout, hear the rustle of the wind in the forested rest area and wade in the bottomless mud of the trenches.
>
> That is the purpose of this book, to reawaken our memories of the greatest days of our lives, and the memory of those who gave their lives.

A new bond will be tied between all those who fought shoulder to shoulder, and although the regiment no longer exists, may this contribute to the preservation of the spirit which inspired it until, with God's will, better times return.

Stoeklern zu Grünholzek, Colonel (Inactive)
Commander of Inf. Regt 66 1915–18

Schleusener, Lieutanant-Colonel (Inactive)
Chairman of the Association of Former Officers Inf. Regt 66

1
PRE-WAR HISTORY

Infantry-Regiment 66 (IR 66) was established by the Army Reorganisation which is associated with the name Kaiser Wilhelm, who laid the foundation of the greatness of both Prussia and Germany. The Prussian mobilisation in 1859, to support Austria–Hungary in its war against France and Piedmont, showed serious deficiencies in the Prussian Army; the then Prince Regent Wilhelm began a farsighted reorganisation. The youngest year groups of the Landwehr (National Guard) were retained on active duty. With men from the older year groups of the Ersatz (Replacement) Battalions and the Line regiments, they formed new units, called Landwehr Cadre Regiments. So, the Landwehr Regiment and elements of IR 26, who drew their recruits from the *Bezirke* (Counties) of Stendal, Burg and Neuhaldensleben, were formed by *Allerhöchste Kabinetts-Ordre* (Royal Order in Council) of 5 May 1860 into a 'combined infantry regiment', with its first commander, Colonel von Kirchbach, who would later win considerable fame. It was designated *3. Magdeburgisches Infanterie-Regiment Nr. 66* (3rd Magdeburg Infantry Regiment No. 66) in the *Allerhöchste Kabinetts-Ordre* of 4 July 1860.

The campaign against Austria in 1866 gave the young regiment its first opportunity to show its mettle in combat. When cannon fire announced the advance of the Elbe Army at the Battle of Münchengrätz, 13 Brigade was given the mission of driving the enemy from Musky Hill. While the first enemy shells landed (which fortunately caused no casualties), II/ 66 and Fusilier Battalion (III/ 66) advanced with a loud 'Hurrah!' and Regimental Bandmaster Schulz ordered the Prussian Anthem played. The regiment won undying fame in heavy fighting as an element of the 7th Infantry Division (7 ID) at the Battle of Königgrätz. The success was dearly bought, with fifteen officers and 476 enlisted men becoming casualties, after the 26th Infantry Regiment (IR 26) the heaviest casualties in the division. The reward for this quick and glorious campaign was the creation of an energetic and militarily powerful league of north German states under the leadership of the King of Prussia. The fruits of this victory, which promised a brilliant future, were due for the greatest part to the discipline and training of the Prussian army. In these, IR 66 showed that it was the equal of the older regiments, and added the laurels of victory to its young colours. This was reflected in the decorations that the king awarded the regiment: for the battalion standards, the combat ribbon to the 1866 Campaign Cross with silver tassels, surmounted by two upright swords. The standard of II/66, whose peak had been damaged by a shell, was given a silver ring with an inscription below the peak. In the following years of peace, the regiment trained energetically to maintain the edge it had gained in combat.

In the campaign of 1870–71 against France, it contributed significantly to the victory at Beaumont on 30 August 1870. Its mission was to allow the division to deploy out of the woods, which it accomplished with exceptional bravery. The losses, in only 90 minutes of combat, were terrible: ten officers, fourteen NCOs and III enlisted men dead, thirteen officers, forty NCOs and 439 men wounded – almost half the casualties suffered by the entire division. The regimental commander, Count Finkenstein, was wounded in the shoulder but remained in command, and during the pursuit was hit in the mouth and killed. The regiment won additional fame during the siege of Paris.

The heroic deeds of wartime were followed by quiet, unceasing work in peacetime. In 1872, the officers laid a granite tablet with the names of their fallen comrades at the cemetery at Beaumont. On 6 August 1875, a monument with the names of the fallen of both wars was unveiled in the courtyard of the Ravensburg Kaserne.

The regiment frequently had the opportunity to demonstrate its combat readiness to the Kaiser: in 1873 at Eisleben, 1876 at Merseburg and again in 1883 at the *Kaisermanöver* (Imperial Manoeuvres), for the last time in front of the venerable hero Kaiser of the great wars.

In 1885, the regiment held an unforgettable celebration of the 25th anniversary of its founding. Old comrades returned from all directions: the first commander, General Count von Kirchbach, was among the guests of honour.

The year 1888 brought deep mourning. On 9 March, shortly before his 91st birthday, death took the venerated hero Kaiser from Germany. After a few weeks, his son, Kaiser Friedrich, followed him. His lasting fame will be secured as much by the manner in which he unflinchingly bore his pain as by his generalship in battle. For the second time in the same year, the regiment formed ranks to swear its oath to its new warlord, Kaiser Wilhelm II.

In 1889, the Fusilier Battalion was designated III/ 66 and was issued black leather web gear (replacing white). The other two battalions had been re-equipped in 1887. In 1890, the regiment was issued the Model 1888 rifle, which led to the recall of many reservists for training with the new weapon. In 1891, the regiment participated in the *Kaisermanöver* as part of IV Corps, for the first time under Kaiser Wilhelm II.

In 1895, the regiment celebrated the 25th anniversary of its heroic battle at Beaumont. The regiment was at the Major Training Area at Loburg on 30 August. The brigade formed a square, the standards that were at Beaumont were decorated with oak-leaf garlands and the brigade commander gave a speech to commemorate the dead. The actual celebration was held on 26 September. By dint of hard work, the caserne courtyard was transformed into a richly decorated festival grounds. After the regiment had formed up, almost 1,100 veterans assembled on the Local Training Area, the *Schroteplatz* , and marched forward, organised in their old companies. After an address by Chaplain Dr Hermens, the regimental commander gave an impassioned speech, recalling the heroic deeds and the fallen, who were true to the soldier's oath they had taken, and laid a wreath at the war memorial. This was followed by the regiment and the veterans, many led by their old commanders, passing in review, then a banquet for the officers and veterans and celebrations by the individual battalions. The camaraderie and happy reunion with the old officers was clearly apparent at this festival. In November, the Grenadier March of the old von Bonin and von Kalckstein Regiments (1806) was given to the regiment as its march.

The commemorative festival gave reason to restore the weathered memorial at the Beaumont cemetery. The inscription was smoothed off and the only remaining ornamentation was an iron cross. The chain around the monument was replaced by a wrought-iron fence. An iron tablet with the names of the fallen officers and numbers of casualties was affixed to the middle.

In 1897, IV/ 66 was transferred to the newly formed Infantry Regiment 152. At the unveiling of the Kaiser Wilhelm Monument in Magdeburg on 25 August, the regiment passed in review in front of the Kaiser; 1/ 1/ 66 brought the garrison's standards out of the Headquarters to II/ 66, the Honour Company at the monument, and then replaced them there again. The barracks of III/ 66 were rebuilt with a second and sometimes third storeys, a welcome improvement.

In 1898, the regiment participated in the *Kaisermanöver* in Westphalia. The call for volunteers for the China expedition was warmly received and answered by an officer, a medical officer, seven NCOs and sixty-eight enlisted men.

The *Allerhöchste Kabinetts-Ordre* of 1 January 1900 directed that the tattered standards that had been carried in glorious battles be refurbished, so that in the summer of 1903 the three battalion standards received new bunting. They were ceremonially affixed to the standards and consecrated on 30 August, the anniversary of Beaumont, in the presence of the Kaiser and royal family in the Hall of Honour at Berlin. Present were the regimental commander, First Lieutenant Bonsac, the son of Captain Bonsac who had fallen at Beaumont, two lieutenants and three standard bearers. The new standards were given to the regiment by the Kaiser personally on the occasion of the *Kaiserparade* (parade at the *Kaisermanöver*) at the historic site of the Battle of Rossbach.

Since the death of General von Alvensleben in 1881, the regiment had no chief. In 1902, the regiment had the high honour that the King of Spain, Alfonso XIII, be named chief on the occasion of his coronation. The Kaiser named as head of the German delegation to the coronation at Madrid, Prince Albrecht of Prussia, accompanied by Colonel von Dehn-Rotfelser, who brought the king the uniform of the regiment. On the first anniversary of this day, 17 May 1903, the king sent as a present his life-size portrait wearing the regimental uniform. A special delegation first presented the portrait to the Kaiser, then it was brought to the regiment and hung in the Officer's Club.

On 9 November 1905, the regiment had the high honour to receive its chief personally. He first inspected the regiment and a delegation of former regimental commanders and then they passed in review. He watched combat training on the *Schroteplatz* LTA, followed by a tour of the barracks and breakfast in the Officer's Club.

The marriage of King Alfonso to Princess Ena of Battenberg, on 31 May 1906 in Madrid, was attended by a German delegation representing the Kaiser, led by Prince Albrecht, with Colonel Baron Digeon von Monteton in attendance. In a special audience, he extended to the king the best wishes of the regimental officer corps and gave as a wedding present a bronze statue of Sergeant Bieler, who was killed at Beaumont while carrying the standard of 11/ III/ 66.

In 1908, a solemn ceremony took place. The units that fought on the bloody fields of Beaumont erected a number of monuments to honour the fallen. Perhaps the most beautiful was that of our 13 Brigade and Field Artillery Regiment (FAR) 4. Significantly, it was placed where once IR 66 courageously attacked out of the woods. The not insignificant expense, 13,000 marks, was met by the Gera Association for the Maintenance of German War Graves in France and The Veteran's Associations of IR 26, IR 66 and 13 Brigade. It was dedicated on 12 October 1908 and put under the protection of the French government. Some seventy comrades from the participating regiments assembled to revisit the scene of that memorable day, including deputations from the veterans of IR 26 and IR 66 under the leadership of First Lieutenant of Landwehr (inactive) Engel. The journey continued to Sedan and a walk over the battlefield. In the autumn of 1908, the graves of the officers who had fallen at Beaumont were decorated with a new monument.

The regiment continually strove to maintain its old reputation for combat effectiveness, which it demonstrated by winning the *Kaiserpreis* (for the company with the best combat gunnery score in the corps). In 1898, it was won by 11/ 66, 1901 by 9/ 66, 1907, 1908 and 1909 by 1/ 66 and 1912 by 5/ 66.

An important addition to the combat power of the regiment took place on 1 October 1909: a Machine Gun Detachment was formed from personnel of the regiment and billeted in specially constructed buildings in the *Schroteplatz* Local Training Area. In 1911, it formed the Machine Gun Company under Captain Siegfried and was attached to III/ 66.

In the fall of 1912, the Reichstag authorised the creation of two new army corps, XX and XXI, which were established by the War Ministry on 1 October 1912. Shortly before the autumn manoeuvres, it was announced that the IV Corps was to give up four companies to XXI Corps. IR 66 was to give up one company, and the decision was taken to send 10/ 66. The entire company, down to the youngest recruit, was to be sent to the 10 *Lothringischen* (Lorraine) *Infanterie-Regiment* 174. The company commander, Captain Dallmer, had just been transferred to Magdeburg from there, so back he went. On 1 October 1912, after the *Kaisermanöver*, the oldest year-group of conscripts was released and the cadre and youngest year-group were sent to IR 174.

IR 66 could not look back on a long history, but its existence coincided with a period of incomparable progress for the German people. In this time, Germany, under the leadership of Prussia, took its rightful place in the world, the expression of which was the Emperor's Crown for the House of Hohenzollern.

The regiment had taken a significant role in the battles and sacrifices that led to this great success. Pride in this great past united the old comrades. It was the serious obligation of the younger generation to ensure that in the future the laurels of victory would continue to be attached to the regiment's standards.

2

WAR

July 1914 found the regiment in its garrison at Magdeburg, busy with its normal peacetime routine. It was scheduled to leave the city in September for the autumn manoeuvres.

There were dark clouds on the political horizon. The murder of the Austro-Hungarian Crown Prince by a Serbian fanatic forced Austria to take serious measures against Serbia. For years, the Entente had worked to encircle Germany and Austria–Hungary, which threatened to make war unavoidable. All German attempts to avoid war collapsed due to the Russian mobilisation. The Central Powers were also forced to mobilise, though they did so at the last possible moment.

At 1400 on 31 July the 'Period Preparatory to War' was announced by Imperial Order, and the seriousness of the situation became evident to every German. From long-slumbering national pride broke forth like a volcano the intense blaze of patriotism and self-sacrifice, in the most peace-loving and industrious people in the entire world. Instantly, German quarrels and discord vanished, and in the face of the foreign enemy all Germans recognised each other as true brothers and helpers. Those days of the end of July and the beginning of August 1914 made, for all those who experienced them, the deepest impression of their lives. The city of Magdeburg, normally sober and withdrawn in speech, took on an entirely different character. The seriousness of the situation made the citizens loquacious and active, ready to aid their neighbours and the Fatherland. In the evening, when the places of work were closed, fervent patriotic songs broke forth. Immeasurable masses of people, of all occupations and classes, moved together through the streets and became, out of love for the Fatherland, one people.

For the active-army soldiers, the normal duties continued. At 1630, armed guards, with live ammunition, were posted to watch the most important rail installations, particularly bridges. The feverish tension was broken at 1845 on 1 August by the order for general mobilisation. The following days were strenuous. The arriving reservists were assigned to companies and issued their combat uniforms, weapons and equipment, down to first aid dressings and identity disks. Ammunition was brought out of the bunkers, vehicles out of the sheds and horses requisitioned for wagon teams and mounted men. The war-strength companies (250 men) conducted road marches and combat training. In these days, one task followed the next, until every man was strained to breaking point. The regimental adjutant, the three battalion adjutants, the purser (property clerk), the regimental clerk, the battalion clerks, the company first sergeants and their clerks, the armourers and the orderlies did not get a moment's rest. The mobilisation calendar, carefully prepared with exactitude, did not need to be altered. Everything worked the way it was supposed to. On 6 August, IR 66 had completed its mobilisation. On the afternoon of 6 August, the regiment assembled on the *Schroteplatz* LTA for an unforgettable, sombre Holy Communion.

Unfortunately, the regiment had to detach a number of officers, NCOs and men to create new units. Some went to Reserve Infantry Regiment (RIR) 26, RIR 27, Brigade Ersatz (Replacement) Battalion 13 and other formations. The last peacetime regimental commander, Colonel von Dresler und Scharfenstein, assumed command of Reserve Infantry Brigade 13, and was replaced as regimental commander by the former commander of IR 153, Colonel Freiherr von Quadt-Wykradt und Hüchtenbruck. Lieutenant-colonel Ezettriz became the Ia (operations officer) General Staff officer on the IV Reserve Corps staff. Captain Evler became the 1st Adjutant on the same staff. Major Schmidt took over I/66 and Majors Jenke and Häusler became reserve battalion commanders. A lieutenant-colonel, five captains and seven lieutenants were also transferred. All active-duty First Sergeants and the clerks in the staff went in their assigned peacetime duty positions to the field.

On 8 August, the regiment loaded onto rail cars at the Magdeburg station. The battalion's march through the city was like a triumphal procession, past the citizens who thickly lined both sides of the street. Mothers, women and brides waved to the warriors going to the field with tears in their eyes, and accompanied them to the gates of the station. Fifes and drums played over the noise of the crowd and flowers decorated the uniforms. The long row of rail cars waited at the station.

The trains rolled to the west, a last farewell to the towers of Magdeburg, then came new countryside and new impressions. Everywhere young and old waved at the passing train, which passed through Braunschweig, then Hildesheim, over the Weser, through Westphalia, Düsseldorf and over the Rhine. In the early dark morning of 10 August, the train stopped in Jülich. After a short rest, the regiment foot-marched through Geilenkirchen, Waurichen, Puffendorf and the surrounding villages. Due to the proximity of the Dutch border, strong exterior security was posted. The border at Herzogenrath was guarded by NCO outposts from the regiment. 11 August was a rest day.

3

APPROACH MARCH

Our iv AK (*Armeekorps* – army corps) was assigned to the 1st Army under General von Kluck. The army assembled in the northern Rhineland and was to form the right flank of the German Army, crossing the Meuse north of Liège, marching through Louvain, Brussels and north France to envelop the left flank of the French Army, which would be held fast in an iron grip, as far as the Swiss border, by the other German armies. The route to Belgium led through Aachen. The 1st Army was able to begin movement a day earlier than planned. The route to be followed was immensely long. There were many enemies to defeat, and great fortresses blocked the way. Such a mission could only have been given to the magnificent German Army of 1914. IR 66 could be proud to be among the troops given such a glorious task.

At 0630 on 12 August, the regiment marched as part of 7 ID (*Infanteriedivision* – infantry division) towards Aachen. In Broich and the surrounding villages the battalions bivouacked closely packed together. The countryside was thick with troops. North and east of Aachen assembled ii, iv and iii AK. Behind them, iii and iv RK (*Reservekorps* – reserve corps) were unloading. By this time we knew that the march passed through Belgium. The free afternoon was used to once again check equipment, write letters home and to say goodbye to the cheerful German population. Everyone, soldiers and civilians alike, was in a serious, solemn mood. It was evident in the faces of all that they were completely prepared to give everything for the Fatherland, as the victors of Mülhausen (Mulhouse, Alsace, 9 August 1914), Lagarde (Gerden, Lorraine, 2 August 1914) and Badonviller (Lorraine, 12 August 1914) had done, of which we had just learned. All day long we heard the sound, like far-away thunder, of the guns at Liège.

Early on the morning of 13 August, just as the sun had come up, the division assembled and marched in burning heat to Aachen, arriving in the city just before noon, dusty and sweaty, but in perfect formation. Our reception by the population was indescribable: general jubilation, extravagant masses of flowers, refreshments and bread, sweets and fruit, given to the soldiers by pretty girls and women. No one expected this, the most wonderful reception that IV AK ever experienced, though we could not have known that yet. In the city we passed in review in front of the corps commander, Lieutenant-General Sixt von Armin. His quiet and serious face looked with satisfaction on the elite of the province of Saxony.

On the far side of the city was a valley that led to the border. The sun beat down without pity and dust filled the air. Another world appeared: lorries drove past from Liège, loaded with wounded, also Belgian prisoners. Our first view of the seriousness of war. Late in the afternoon the regiment reached Neutral-Moresnet and bivouacked in the village and the surrounding fields, tired but content. The village was quiet and peaceful, much as though we were still in Germany.

Early in the morning on 14 August, the regiment crossed the border into Belgium and suddenly everything changed. The villages were deserted: their inhabitants had fled or were in hiding in the houses. The roadblocks made from trees fallen across the road had been removed. There were signs on the houses, 'We took fire from this house'. The mayors and clergy had set the population in a panic, while failing to inform them correctly of the laws of war, and this was the reception they gave our border security force, troops fighting at Liège, and reconnaissance cavalry! As retribution, several houses had been burned down in the centre of the villages. Other signs said, 'This house must be protected!', evidence of the German sense of responsibility, which unfortunately only helped to preserve from punishment the few that had not participated in the combat.

The regiment marched in oppressive heat until, at 1600, it reached Dahlem and quartered there and in the surrounding area. The population was unquiet, and a search of the houses revealed weapons.

In the morning of 15 August, the regiment crossed the Meuse at Argentau on a pontoon bridge built by Engineer Battalion 4, with cannon fire echoing over to us from the isolated forts that still held out. Close nearby, the iron bridge destroyed by the Belgians stuck up out of the water. The crossing proceeded smoothly. That evening, the regiment reached Millen and Genoels-Eldern and quartered. The troops were fed from the mobile field kitchens: meat, vegetables and potatoes requisitioned from the surrounding area. There was seldom any bread.

The Flemish inhabitants were very accommodating, in contrast to the inhabitants of the cloister, who made a furtive impression. The ensuing nervousness led to fear of a night attack and in fact II/ 66, which was nearest to the cloister, was alerted.

Sunday 16 August brought an unexpected rest day which, after the exertions of the last week, was greeted with great joy. It was taken to allow the following two reserve corps to close up on the four (IX, III, IV AND II) first-line corps. At 1600, the first field church services were held in enemy territory. The regimental band then played patriotic tunes, and we all sang along. The 100 or so limited-duty men from IR 26 and 66 were each formed into a company to perform rail security under Captain Knaths (8/ 66). Lt Reich (Martin) took over command of 8/ 66.

At 0500 on 17 August, the regiment marched through Tongres, reaching Alken at 1600, where it quartered. Once again the inhabitants made an open and willing impression. We did not speak to each other in French, but were able to use *Plattdeutsch* (the north German dialect, similar to Dutch). Late in the afternoon, we unsuccessfully shot at an enemy aircraft.

Aerial reconnaissance reported strong Belgian forces behind the Gette River, so we had to assume we would soon engage the enemy. Everyone was eager to come to grips with him. The war had begun, but we had not yet seen combat.

4

Battle on the Geete

The Belgian Army had recovered from its initial shock and waited for French support in a dug-in position behind the Geete. General von Kluck decided that on 18 August he would attack the Belgians in front with the forward three corps, while II AK attacked their northern flank to cut them off from Fortress Antwerp.

The IV AK objective was Haelen. Early in the morning, all the troops were ready to march. Initially the division marched in column, with IR 66 as advance guard. East of Rummen, the brigade gave the order to deploy; II/ 66 was to march oriented on the Rummen-Hulsbeck road, III/ 66 south of the road, I/ 66 was corps reserve. Two battalions of IR 26 would advance on the left.

Movement began at 0800. Hussars rode in front of II/ 66; 6/ 66 under First Lieutenant Holscher was the advance guard, the point element was led by Lt Hermens. It advanced towards the Gette on a wonderful, arrow-straight road with deep roadside ditches, marching magnificently in the bright early morning sun which rose behind it. Left and right the road was lined with high poplars, whose crowns provided a shady roof. To both sides of the road were meadows, lined with wire to form individual enclosures. It looked like home, the Altmark north of Salzwedel.

Suddenly it cracked and whistled and popped in the trees. Rifle fire from forward! The hussars raced back. The column halted and moved to the ditches. Major Knauff stood quietly and easily on the road and gave his orders: we will attack! Initially, 6/ 66 would continue towards the Geete; 5/ 66 would deploy on the left of 6/ 66, cover the flank and attack; 7/ 66 and 8/ 66 would follow on both sides of the road. Lt Hermens' point was reinforced to platoon strength and advanced by bounds against an invisible enemy. The other two platoons

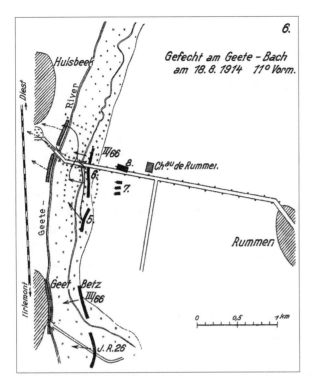

6.

*Gefecht am Geete - Bach
am 18. 8. 1914   11° Vorm.*

of 6/ 66, under Reserve Lieutenant Roebbling and Acting Officer Westphal, followed in support. Heavy rifle fire struck from the forest and bushes that lined the far side of the Geete. A broad water-filled ditch blocked the way, and could only be crossed by a road bridge. Lt Hermens was the first to spring forward, his men following after. The platoon closed to within 200m of the enemy and opened fire. While attempting to advance again, Lt Hermens was severely wounded by a bullet to the head and fell into a water-filled ditch. He was pulled out by Landwehr Sergeant Feldmann, who carried him out of the enemy fire. Trumpeter Wieblitz was killed by a bullet through the heart, the first fatal casualty in the regiment. Sergeant Ullmer assumed command, was hit by four bullets and put out of action.

The riflemen of 5/ 66 under Lt Korfes (the editor) had come level with 6/ 66 and fired diagonally into the enemy. 7 and 8/ 66 moved up, taking very little enemy fire. Lt Korfes crossed the water-filled ditch, taking the men of 6/ 66 with him. Suddenly they saw movement in the enemy position. As the enemy retreated to the west, under German pursuit fire, 5 and 6/ 66 crossed the Geete on tree trunks, then 7 and 8/ 66 followed on a bridge. III/ 66 crossed to the south, at Geet-Beetz, hardly under fire.

Weapons and pieces of uniforms of various Belgian units were found in the abandoned Belgian position. The first battle was over. On the horizon, a Belgian cavalry regiment could be seen disappearing over a ridge. Since the limit of advance in the division order was the Diest–Tirlemont rail line, the regiment linked up with I/ 27 on the right and IR 28 on the left. II and III/ 66 occupied an assembly area at the foot of the high ground on the west side of the Geete to cover the construction of a bridge. Men sent out to find water returned with red wine and champagne. The inhabitants said that the position had been held by 200 Guides (cavalry), which had relieved the Belgian 4th Infantry Regiment the previous day. Therefore, the main enemy force had abandoned the Geete position, so that IV AK was opposed only by rearguards without artillery, which were easily dealt with. It was unknown if the high ground to the front was occupied. Farther left and right, cannon fire could be heard, so there were German troops working to establish bridgeheads over the Geete. As the regiment waited for the bridge to be completed, a strange situation developed. Slowly and carefully, men, women and children moved down the high ground to the front, vigorously waving handkerchiefs, until they were within shouting distance. Encouraged by us, they approached more closely. They told us that the high ground was not occupied. We found it hard to believe that such a tactically strong position would not be held, but the fact that they went back to their homes argued for their honesty, as they did not fear being shelled by their countrymen. And in fact, reconnaissance found the terrain up to Cappellen free of the enemy. After 1/ 66 returned to the regiment at Geet-Beetz, it took over the advance guard and at 1430 the advance was renewed: it was fired on by cavalry and civilians. As darkness fell, the regiment quartered at Kersbeek-Miscom.

At 0800 on 19 August, the regiment assembled at Cappellen and moved out with 1/ 66 as advance guard. At Kieseghem, numerous skillfully sited defensive positions were found, reinforced by abbatis and wire and apparently abandoned in haste. In Lubeek, 1/ 66 was given forty prisoners by Hussar R 10, who were sent to the rear. The hussar patrols had been frequently fired on, once from a church with a Red Cross flag. The hostile attitude of the inhabitants, which frequently led to march columns or patrols being fired on, was cause enough for serious countermeasures. Therefore several burning villages were to be seen in all directions. Numerous footsore or straggling Belgians were brought in. The Belgian troops left uniforms, weapons and equipment on the side of the road, which gave proof that the Belgian Army was fleeing in panic. The misfortune that the irresponsible actions of the Belgian government had brought to pass was evident in seeing the large groups of refugees stopped in the fields to the side of the road: women, children and the old, clutching their few possessions. In several villages the inhabitants would come out in long processions with hands held high and waving white flags, in order to ask for mercy from the supposed German barbarians.

While resting 2km east of Louvain, the regiment was suddenly fired upon from houses and bushes by a Belgian lancer patrol. Captain Bonsac, 7/ 66, ordered a platoon to take up arms and charged forward at their head in the direction of the shooting: the enemy patrol was driven off. A number of prisoners were taken, as well as many completely exhausted horses. Aside from this patrol, the enemy was nowhere to be seen: apparently he had succeeded in withdrawing to Antwerp. Nevertheless, it was necessary to try to fix the Belgian Army in place or cut it off from Antwerp, so the entire 1st Army continued to advance rapidly.

During the afternoon, IV AK reached the gates of Louvain. After a long rest, at 1830 the order was given to march into the beautiful old city. The artillery was in position, aimed at the roofs. IR 66 was the lead regiment, II/ 66 the advance guard, and entered the city with the flags unfurled and band playing. The population thickly lined the streets and watched, sullen and silent. Singing the 'Watch on the Rhine' with a thundering voice, the troops marched in perfect order down the streets. That evening, the regiment quartered at Boverberg on the Louvain–Brussels road. I/ 66 established outpost security.

According to reports, the Belgian Army had left Brussels and was retreating to Antwerp. The division began the march at 0800 on 20 August with IR 66 the lead element. En route there was a rest for several hours while negotiations for the capitulation of Brussels and the march into the city were conducted. At about 1500, IV AK entered the Belgian capital. In front was Hussar R 10, followed by the regiment, the band leading, then III, II and I/ 66. A barricade had been erected at the entrance to the city, which the inhabitants were made to clear away. A few hundred metres beyond that, the corps passed in review before its commander, General Sixt von Arnim. The troops marched through beautiful Brussels in squad column, with fixed bayonets, singing, and to the sound of Prussian march music, the streets thickly lined with people. The populace was calm, and the Belgian national colours were frequently seen. Marching in step for 16km through the city in the burning August heat was fatiguing, but exhilarating. A great British newspaper wrote that the German troops had made a good impression, above all Infantry Regiments 66, 40 and 26. Only at the west side of the city was a normal march column formed and a stop to rest taken. III/ 66 remained as the garrison of Brussels and was attached to the 16 Infantry Brigade. I/ 66 quartered in Waasbroek and II/ 66 put outposts south-west of Brussels on the road to Hal. Rumours of a mass Belgian uprising made the rounds, and the highest degree of readiness was ordered. Danger seemed to lurk in the darkness. But all was quiet.

It was now certain that the Belgian Army was at Antwerp and III RK remained behind to provide security against the strong fortress. First Army left Brussels behind it and swung towards the French border and the 2nd Army near Maubeuge, where strong French resistance was expected. We now knew the British had landed, but not where and when we would find them. At 0730 on 21 August, 7 ID began the march, IR 26 advance guard, with IR 66 at the head of the main body, I/ 66 leading, followed by II/ 66 (with the MG Company) on the road Meilemerch–Vlesenbeeck–Elinghen, reaching Schamelbeek at 1630, where it quartered. The population was generally calmer.

On 22 August, the march continued in the same order through Enghein and Bassilly to La Cavée, where we quartered. During the march a British aircraft was brought down at Grandicq Farm by rifle and MG fire. This first contact made it likely that we would soon meet the British Army. The difficult marches made great demands on man and horse, but few dropped out and morale was excellent. The lack of bread was a disadvantage, and the field trains could not keep up with the combat troops.

5

MONS,
23–24 AUGUST 1914

On Sunday 23 August, we were supposed to make contact with the British. First Army ordered the continuation of the deeply echeloned march to the area north-west of Maubeuge. The regiment marched at 0700 as the lead element of the main body, order of march being II/ 66, I/ 66, MG Company, direction of march Chievres–Pommeroeul (15km west of the centre of Mons), when at 1500 the report arrived that the British held the Conde Canal north of Thulin. The division continued the march so as to engage the British that day. The advance guard, IR 26, was at the south side of Blois de Ville late in the afternoon when it was surprised by artillery fire from a position south of the canal. IR 26 attacked west of the main road to Thulin against the canal south of Ville-Pommeroeul. At 1930, II/ 66 was committed east of the road. There was heavy firing forward: IR 26 must have made serious contact. The desire to help our sister regiment and get to grips with the enemy motivated every man in the battalion. Just like in peacetime training, the battalion advanced in the growing darkness on a broad front from the rail line south of Ville-Pommeroul, accompanied by the MG platoon of Reserve Lieutenant Seldte. The battalion had to wade through several broad and deep water-filled ditches. For the smaller men, loaded with equipment, this wasn't easy, as the water came to their necks. The heavy MG and rifle fire from the front fortunately all went too high, and there were no casualties.

In spite of the difficult terrain, by 2000 the canal had been reached and contact with IR 26 established at the sugar factory (*Zuckerfabrik*). Res. Lt Seldte brought his MG into position on the roof of a farm building near the canal. I/ 66 was in division reserve on the rail level crossing east of Ville-Pommeroul, occasionally under enemy MG grazing fire, and at 2200 was moved forward to the north side of the sugar factory. In spite of their exhaustion, the troops were burning to get at the British. Since the bridge had been blown down by the British, the division bridge train and Engineer Battalion 4 were brought forward. At about midnight, Musketeer Hermann Voigtländer swam the canal and discovered that the British had withdrawn. At about 0130, II/ 66 crossed on pontoons. Because it was still dark and the situation uncertain, the battalion advanced only 400m and dug in, together with IR 26. The

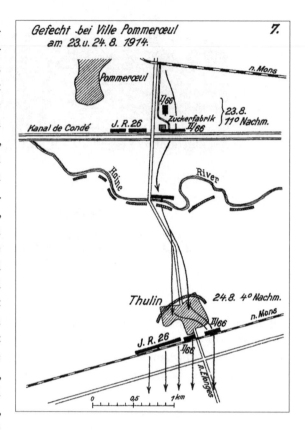

British had withdrawn to Thulin and to the south. As soon as dawn began to break, at 0500, II/ 66 crossed the Haine River and attacked towards Thulin. Lt Winckler and Res. Lt Borchert from 8/ 66 and Lt Fricke from 7/ 66 led the troops, who soon took heavy fire from the scattered farms. Thulin was vigorously defended by a small force. The advancing battalion took fire from almost all the houses, especially from a church on which hung a Red Cross flag. The troops attacked with determination and after a short fight, in which Res. Lt Borchert and elements of 8/ 66 distinguished themselves, the town was taken. The battalion had taken casualties: Reserve Sergeant Kunzmann was killed on his birthday. The attack continued under heavy fire to the rail embankment. According to the brigade order, this was the limit of advance. The fire soon died down. Withdrawing enemy cavalry was engaged with lively pursuit fire. IR 26 had also reached the rail embankment, and I/ 66 Thulin, which, because of the house-to-house fighting, was now partially in flames. After a good rest, which was for the most part undisturbed by the enemy, at 1320 the attack was resumed, with Elouges the objective for II/ 66, with I/ 66 to the right. The attack was supported by the entire division artillery, which took the heights west of Elouges, which were held by the enemy, under concentric fire. The riflemen went continually forward, just like in the training area, in spite of heavy long-range enemy artillery and small-arms fire. Soon the well-aimed shrapnel fire of Field Artillery Regiments (FAR) 4 and 40 smoked the enemy infantry out of his trenches and silenced the enemy artillery. At 1,000m range, the British infantry left their trenches in groups, effectively engaged by our pursuit fire. II/ 66 occupied Elouges. Once again we encountered civilians who took part in the fighting. IR 26 had come up on our right and crossed Quivrain–Elouges rail line. Numerous prisoners, MG, weapons and horses were captured. The two days had cost us three killed (from 8/ 66) and twenty-three wounded, including Res. Lt Borchert. The victorious troops rested from their exertions.

The battle was a complete success for 1st Army: all of the other corps had defeated the British, but sometimes only after difficult fighting. Air reconnaissance determined that they were retreating to the south-west. Captured enemy orders showed that we had been engaged with four infantry and a cavalry division: the mass of the British Army. For 25 August, the Army intended to pursue the British and cut off their retreat. IV and III AK would attack frontally over the line Qunaing–Angre–Athis, while II AK was to move south of Valenciennes to take the enemy in the flank.

The regiment assembled at the south-west side of Elouges at 0500 on 25 August, and at 0900 marched in the direction of Audregnies. The battlefield and the route of march showed the effect of our artillery and the extent of British losses: dead horses lying next to shot-up artillery caissons, abandoned vehicles, dead and wounded British troops being attended to by British medical personnel. These pictures, as well as the reports from the neighbouring corps, confirmed the fact that we had won a victory. Morale was raised even further when the news arrived that Namur had fallen. After a good rest at Angre, we crossed the Belgian–French border at Marchipont shouting 'Hurrah!'

During the march we passed by the old, demilitarised Fort Le Quesnoy and around 2300 reached Poix du Nord and Englefontaine, where we quartered. During the day, III/ 66 marched from Brussels and rejoined the regiment.

The advance guard of the 7 ID, 14 Brigade, fought that night against a British brigade in Landrecies. After elements of the main body engaged, the fight ended early on 26 August with a British withdrawal.

Air reconnaissance revealed that the enemy was in full retreat on three main roads, from Bavai to Le Cateau, Landrecies and Avesnes. On 26 August, the Army ordered a continuation of the pursuit by forced march to the south-west.

HKK 2 (*Heereskavalleriekorps 2* – 2nd Cavalry Corps) moved south from the area of Avesnes-les-Aubert (west of Solesmes) at 0430 with its three divisions on line, and after a short march made contact with strong British forces of all arms in the villages north of the Warnelle stream. This resulted in an hours-long fight for these villages, which were taken by the Cavalry Corps' Jäger Battalions. IV AK joined this battle at 0910.

8 ID had marched early in the day with its main body through Solesmes towards Viesly, without making contact, while IR 72 went ahead into Le Cateau, where shortly after 0600 it attacked a British battalion while it was forming up and took numerous prisoners. As it pushed on to the south side of Le Cateau, it engaged a strong enemy force on a hill 800m south of the rail line.

6

LE CATEAU, 26 AUGUST 1914

When it was reported, early in the morning, that the British were nearby, 7 ID alerted the troops. This time the advance guard mission fell to IR 66. At 0530, it marched through Croix to Forest, II/ 66 the point element, followed at a distance by III, then I/ 66. Everything went so quickly that there was hardly time to pass out the coffee. Everyone knew something serious was going to happen. At the south side of Forest, hussar patrols reported that the high ground west and south of Le Cateau was held by strong British forces. Division ordered 13 Brigade to attack Le Cateau and, to the west, 14 Brigade would envelop the enemy's right flank.

It was between 0800 and 0900 when the regimental commander, Colonel Freiherr von Quadt, ordered the regiment to deploy behind the Solesmes–Le Cateau rail line, with III/ 66 right of the Forest–Montay road, II left, I/ 66 with the attached MG Company in reserve behind the left flank. IR 26, following IR 66, would attack on the left through Le Cateau.

Events proceeded so fast that a careful execution of the order was impossible. The 6/ 66, under First Lieutenant Holscher, was far ahead of II/ 66 and had already crossed over the rail line and entered the village of Montay. Major Knauff quickly deployed II/ 66 and followed 6/ 66, whose Corporal Thormann had established that the enemy had left the high ground south of Montay. First Lt Holscher and Res. Lt Roebbling led the riflemen of 6/ 66 up the slope. The company had just reached the crest of the hill when it took heavy rifle fire and was pinned to the ground. Then the company took well-aimed shrapnel fire. It was the devil's own situation: the enemy was invisible, but his fire landed mercilessly amongst the riflemen. It took a considerable time until the binoculars of the company commander and Lieutenants Hesse and

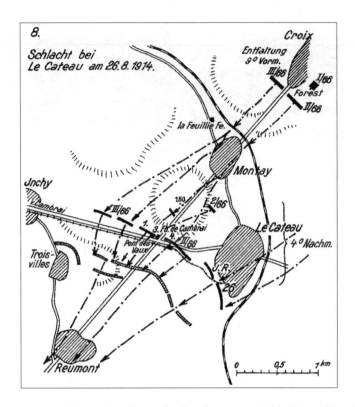

Roebbling succeeded in identifying the barely recognisable line of the British trenches on the high ground 400–600m south of the Le Cateau road. The enemy position was strongly held and well-concealed in the terrain, had a good field of fire and observation, supported by numerous artillery, and was capable of extended resistance.

In the meantime, Major Knauff and the other companies had run through Montay under artillery fire and saw 6/ 66 move over the crest of Hill 150, which was too far from the British position to conduct an effective firefight; the companies had to close the range. The terrain to the front offered essentially no cover, and was still completely exposed to the enemy artillery fire. The motto in peacetime training was 'Close with the enemy, cost what it may!', which the battalion now put into practise. The 5/ 66, under First Lieutenant Moeller, and 7/ 66, under Captain Bonsac, followed by 8/ 66, under Lt Redlich (Martin), crested the hill at a dead run, with bullets whizzing past and shrapnel bursting over their heads.

At the same time, Major Pagenstecher had thrown III/ 66 into the fight. While leaving Forest it had taken artillery fire, which 10/ 66, under Captain Ulfert, and 9/ 66, under Captain Niemeyer, had avoided by swinging to the west. They quickly moved through the western end of Montay. At the far end of the town they again took artillery fire, which caused the first casualties. The troops stopped for a short time, until the artillery shifted its fire, then 10/ 66 moved forward in long bounds. On the south-west-facing hillside, enemy fire forced it to ground. But they recognised the enemy line and returned fire. The 6/ 66, on the high ground to the left, felt the advance of 10/ 66 reduce the enemy fire. The 9/ 66 advanced using the terrain for cover. The then Lieutenant Siegener wrote:

> We were able to advance using the terrain as cover, first the reverse slope of a hill, then through low ground, where we deployed and went forward in skirmisher line. Infantry fire went harmlessly over our heads as we were completely under cover. We went along a hedge, then through more low ground; we had found the right place. To our left front was 10/66 in a firefight. We needed to make only a bound of 100m to come level with them. Then we crawled to the crest, but we could not see the enemy, though bullets were going past our ears. So we had to advance further. With one more bound we reached our firing position and saw the British on the other side of a row of poplars [the Le Cateau–Cambrai road] in trenches. We opened fire at 900m range; it was 1100. We lay in our position for hours and could have stayed hours more; an advance was out of the question. There was hot fire on both sides and it was interesting for the first time to see a firefight develop. There was a continual cracking, rattling, hissing and whistling; an indescribable noise that left nevertheless an unforgettable impression. Our people quickly took off their packs to use as rifle rests or began to dig skirmisher holes. There were few casualties.

The 12/ 66 followed: it had a tough time. The by now completely alert enemy concentrated its fire on the company right flank. Thanks to the leadership of Lt Goslich and Res. Lt Weck, the men stayed together and continued to advance in spite of the heavy enemy fire. The 12/ 66 extended the right flank and pulled 9/ 66 forward with it. Then it halted and opened fire. The 11/ 66 was the last company, and after crossing the open ground took cover behind 12/ 66. Soon elements of 11/ 66, under Res. Lt Mende, were moved forward into the firing line. Colonel Freiherr von Quadt moved forward onto Hill 150, behind which was 1/ 66 and the MG Company. They had moved through Montay under artillery fire, which they experienced for the first time. Under the firm control of their leaders, they passed through it in perfect order. There was uncertainty concerning the situation forward, so the orderly officer, Lt Korfes, went over the crest of Hill 150 to establish the friendly and enemy situation. Based on his report, 1/ 66 under Capt. Speichert and 3/ 66 under Capt. Paulus [*not* the future Field Marshal who surrendered the 6th Army at Stalingrad] were inserted between III and II/ 66. The battle was at its peak. Both companies took heavy artillery fire crossing the crest of the hill, which caused casualties.

Capt. Speichert was killed. But the companies continually moved forward. The MGs were committed; they were able to use the terrain more effectively than the infantry and came forward more easily. Res. Lt Seldte and Lt Redlich (Richard) moved their sections to the II/ 66 sector, Lt Blume to III/ 66.

The three companies on the left of II/ 66 had moved in long bounds over the crest, taking considerable casualties, then south down the slope to the deep cut in the Cambrai road, to within 400m of the well dug-in enemy. A terrible hours-long firefight began. Losses increased. The brave and lively First Lt von Moeller was killed, hit in the head, his platoon leader, Res. Lt Hoff, badly wounded. The MG of Lts Redlich and Seldte, who were soon joined by Capt. Siegfried, brought relief. Well-protected by their gun shields, they poured fire into the British line. The British fire would slacken for a time, then resume with the previous intensity. The MG of Lt Blume opened fire from the III/ 66 sector. The entire regiment was attempting to suppress the British fire so that it could assault: would it succeed? Worst off was 6/ 66, which was still pinned down on the bare slope of Hill 150. Res. Lt Roebbling wrote:

We were lying on a field of clover, on which there were still large stooks of cut grass. According to the tactics regulation, we should have gotten fire commands, but none came. Instead, I lay there and searched and searched with my binoculars, but saw nothing. In the meantime the bullets were whistling past us and slapping into the ground. The second man on my right cried out 'Adieu, Süssenbach (my corporal and range estimator) I've had it!' The answer came, 'Get over it, Busse, it can't be that bad!' – 'Be brave.' After a while he groaned, 'Ach, it's just my shoulder and ear. Take my rucksack off me, would you? It's pressing down on me.' Under a rain of bullets the good fellow crawled over and helped him, bedded him down in the hay. 'Süssenbach,' I said, 'bring me his rifle and a couple rounds!' [Roebbling addressed his corporal with the formal pronoun 'Sie', which was being quite polite], which he did. I was still unable to see anything to shoot at. On the right somebody said that they were in the road cutting and the right half of the platoon opened fire. I couldn't see anything in the road cut. Then all hell cut loose: exploding shrapnel! For the first time we heard the shells howling as they came toward us, then the explosion and shortly thereafter a rattling around us. It made a real impression on us, and dutifully we greeted every shrapnel by pressing our noses into the dirt until they couldn't go any further. Soon we would count four salvos of four shells, then a pause. Finally I saw something in my binoculars: 'Halfway up from the line of poplars, on a stubblefield, a trench! Range 800!'

In this hellish noise, a completely audible fire command is impossible. I was just happy to see that the men beside me heard me. My responsibilities were temporarily just about over, so I continued to observe and fired every so often, to calm my nerves. When the shrapnel permitted, I looked around. To the left and right there still aren't reinforcements: we have the entire concentric fire on us. To the left I see the company commander on a high pile of bricks. He has a wonderful, but very dangerous, location there. The pile of rocks positively attracts shrapnel shells. A hay rick in front is already burning. Now we get a new kind of shrapnel: previously they made white smoke, now it's red-brown, and smells distinctly of sealing wax. The explosion is louder and the rain of shrapnel balls is much thicker. 'Can't we go forward yet?' asks the impatient Busse. 'No, not yet! But reinforcements are coming up on the right!'

Sometimes, the enemy rifle fire isn't so intense, and neither is the shrapnel fire, and the pauses between salvoes are longer; we can stick our heads up. Finally we can think about advancing. I give the order to the left and receive the reply 'We're out of ammunition!' Wonderful! A rifle round hits the front sight of my rifle and the ricochet howls away vertically; it is as though my hand has been struck by a whip. The back of my hand is cut open, along with the vein behind my middle finger and the skin behind my three middle fingers. I'm bleeding nicely! For a second my nerves threaten to crack and I think about crawling back to the aid station. But what would happen here if they see the only officer pulling back? Under no circumstances! 'Süssenbach, patch me up!' The good man quickly had his wound dressing torn out and did a good job wrapping the wound. A crack goes by my ear and tears into my rucksack (later I count eighteen holes in my coat). Then more shrapnel: they shower down especially thickly, a pod of them falls five steps in front of us, bounces over our heads and lands noisily ten steps behind us. We collect shrapnel balls. We continually get reports of casualties, 'Sergeant Winnig has had his heel shot away.' 'Senior Sergeant Eule has been wounded in the chest and leg!' I say to myself, 'Hang on.' And really, it immediately began to get better. We can feel that the shrapnels are directed at us less and less, the enemy artillery has a longer line to shoot at. Then we see our own artillery landing in the enemy trenches. Now I can lift up my head and see a long skirmisher line on the rail embankment at Forest. Our artillery must be shooting brilliantly: we can see it clearly and feel it even more so. The enemy artillery fire is weaker and less accurate. If we had any ammunition, this would be the time to advance. Then we once again take incoming rifle fire and the reason becomes apparent. Elements of 10/ 66 enter our line, the long-awaited ammunition resupply is here, and the wonderful packets of ammunition are soon flying down the line. I wait until everyone has had time to hang the ammo belts around their necks. Now forwards. Just in time, as an artillery piece has set up right behind us and is drawing the enemy's attention: I'm envious of their beautiful gun shield, which completely protects them from small-arms fire.

The battery commander is behind the shield on the tower of his command wagon, the stereoscopic periscope just above the top edge. He is exposed at most for 5cm below the bottom edge of the shield. They have only fired two salvoes when shells begin landing: Hill 150 is just too good a target, too easily located on the map.

The long-awaited help comes at 1100. FAR 40, which had been firing from Forest, moved at a gallop through Montay and up the hill. It is a magnificent sight to see how the guns sweep forward. The batteries fan out behind the crest and open fire, causing the IR 66 men in front to hunker down. Then they see with satisfaction the effect on the British. The shells howl and then shrapnel bursts over the necks of the Tommies. All thirty-six guns of the division artillery are firing. How they roar and crack! The air above the British begins to smoke, their infantry and many artillery batteries both get their share. The IR 66 men no longer feel alone. Now the IR 26 men come out of Le Cateau and attack the British right flank. The faces of the battalion commanders relax: the worst is over. Major Knauff goes from company to company in the road cut. Major Schmidt is with 2 and 4/ 66. Major Pagenstecher was badly wounded as he went to the firing line with 11/ 66 and Capt. Schleusener had taken over command of the battalion.

But the assault can't begin yet. Lt Fricke attempted to do so in 7/ 66, swinging his sword in the air, and led his men forward. All who rose up with him were hit, Lt Fricke was killed, and with him Officer Cadet Roeggeln. Lt Seldte's MG hammer the enemy. In spite of the heavy fire, Capt. Bonsac tried to bring his company forward, in vain. Capt. Bonsac was killed, letting the same sabre fall that his father carried when he was killed leading 7/ 77 at Beaumont. The situation was similar in 5/ 66. Res. Lt Thierkopf wrote:

Twice the major ordered the assault. One squad that moved resolutely from the corner was shot down after ten paces. Only one sergeant crawled back. Then our artillery began flanking fire. From the left, our infantry advanced against the British. 'Lieutenant,' a musketeer called suddenly, 'they're waving white handkerchiefs over there. They want to surrender!' He was right, they had tied white handkerchiefs on the end of their rifles and continually waved them at us. 'Let's go, boys! Advance by bounds! Move out!' Everyone near me jumps up and storms forwards. Then we hear bullets humming past us, flanking fire from close range. One of my range estimators falls groaning, shot in the stomach. We press ourselves to the ground on the flat stubble. Behind a stook of grain I look through my binoculars, in vain. Nothing to see. We are completely in the open, served up on a platter, and around us is the continual humming of the bullets. Then suddenly I'm struck on the back, and thrown about. What was that? Was I hit? I quickly reorient myself on my stomach and begin to check my limbs, bringing my arms and legs to my body and stretching them out again, one after the other, like a spider in the web. Thank God, they all work, everything's OK. I start looking again through the binoculars. A shrapnel ball hits my sword-knot and smacks against my knee. Then I receive another blow on the back. Something warm is running down my arm: blood. That has to be checked out. I carefully pull myself up and walk upright and undisturbed through the British bullets to the road cut where a medic bandages my upper arm, which has been shot through.

The situation has improved on Hill 150, where 6/ 66 and elements of 10 and 3, under Res. Lt Moll, are still pinned down. The German artillery fire, now reinforced by the 15cm heavy howitzers of Foot Artillery R 4, finally allows them to advance. First Lt Holscher and Lt Hesse lead the riflemen forward. Res. Lt Roebbling followed. He wrote:

OK now: advance by bounds! Go! With two stops to catch our breath we move forward 75 metres to the edge of a field of sugar beets. We can't see a thing! The enemy has noticed us and concentrates his fire on us. He probably feels that we are the greatest danger to him. For our part, we try not to show ourselves. Our heads are no longer silhouetted against the sky, as they had been, and our field grey uniforms disappear in the green vegetation. This position is clearly better than the previous one: only occasionally does a bullet come to our line, the vast majority go far over us. The beet field must be 150 metres deep and goes gradually upwards. I give the command 'Crawl forwards!' It's an experiment, and it works! Everybody likes the fact that we can advance without drawing a lot of enemy fire. Of course, my left hand is terribly painful, and I can't carry a rifle with it, but I can use it to crawl, but nevertheless I'm in front of everybody else. I now have the impression that we're not drawing effective fire at all, and that the enemy fire is much too high. I lift my head and can't see the enemy trench: we're in dead ground. I am happy to yell this out to the troops, and at first carefully, then boldly they stand up. Now we go quickly forward in the low ground and can take our time cutting the wire fence around the meadows. Then we cross the road and the rail line. Artillery shells howl over our heads.

Behind 6/ 66, 4/ 66 under Capt. Trenk has joined the fight. Only 2/ 66 is in reserve. Ammunition was being expended at a rapid rate and one of its platoons is committed to carry it forward. Corporal Collet fearlessly brought ammunition up to the firing line, for which he was promoted to sergeant. The fight had begun at 0900, it was now 1400, and enemy resistance had not slackened. The

British even counter-attack, but they are either shot down or are driven back to their trenches. Then suddenly there is movement in the enemy front ranks: they raise their hands and wave white handkerchiefs, so that elements of IR 66 and 26 go forward to make them prisoner, only to be taken under effective MG fire from all sides. At the same time new British units and artillery appear. This trick enrages the advancing German infantry, and they open heavy MG and rifle fire: the British cannot reach their trenches, but run to the rear in panic flight. All the men and horses of an approaching battery are shot down by the MG of Lt Redlich and Res. Lt Seldte. The MG, as always, were really on the ball today, the guns of Res. Senior Sergeant Joschkowitz and Sergeants Ackermann and Velten are particularly outstanding. For another hour, and then another after that, our artillery, rifles and MG keep up the fire. II/ FAR 4 appears on the battlefield: another eighteen light howitzers, whose effect is easy to see. Their shells annihilate British batteries and trenches, and the British fire weakens. The British infantry is quieter and seems to have had enough. Colonel Freiherr von Quadt commits Capt. Bergansky's 2/ 66. The advancing company takes casualties, but arrives just in time to take part in the assault.

It is clear in the firing line that the British are weakening, especially on the right. Elements of 10/ 66 and 11/ 66 succeed in assaulting the nearest enemy trenches. Then 9/ 66 storms forward. Lt Siegener wrote:

Shortly before 1600 there was suddenly movement in the British position, and we can see them slowly falling back. Finally entire squads withdraw, and we begin a crazy rapid fire along the entire front. We can see the British take casualties the second they go back: entire squads are hit. Now we move forward, first by bounds, and then in continuous advance, in the face of artillery and small-arms fire. We take heavy casualties, but we are determined to close with the enemy. We reach the main road, double-time over it and take up a firing position.

In front of us 200 metres is a trench, still occupied. We want to take it under fire and then go over to the assault, but soon we see white flags, and men holding their hands up in surrender. An officer comes up to me and gives me his sword. But British troops to the rear continued to fire at us. I pointed this out to the officer and threatened to shoot him. He waved to the rear and the firing stopped.

The assault spread like an electric shock: the command 'Fix bayonets!' was given everywhere. What an effect that had! You could see it in everyone's face and eyes. It was 1600, and suddenly the battlefield was alive with charging skirmisher lines; both regiments went over to the assault, unstoppable, standards fluttered in the breeze, bugles sounded, swords glittered in the sun and shouts of

'Hurrah!' drowned out the guns. The assault wave was followed by the support companies, just like on the meadows back home. A magnificent, unforgettable scene! In places there was still strong enemy resistance. As the British infantry was retreating in mobs, one particularly bold battery poured a hail of shrapnel on the assault wave, and especially on the well-dispersed support columns: Lt Siegener and Res. Lt Kreidner were severely wounded. But there was no stopping the assault. The enemy was soon in general flight. While some escaped capture by running from haystack to haystack, others climbed out of their trenches and threw down their weapons. Res. Lt Roebbling wrote:

> As we came over the next piece of high ground, even the artillery fire stopped. To my left I can see our line assaulting, Capt. Bergansky swinging his sabre, and further to the left I think I can see Hesse and Westphal. In front of us white flags waving, and a row of brown uniforms appears. With raised hands they climb out of their trenches, continually waving handkerchiefs and holding their hands in the air, many supported by their comrades. Victory, praise God! We cry tears of joy. How beautiful, how wonderful! We've won, we've won! Lord God we thank you! Hesse and Westphal really are to the left, and approach me. Capt. Bergansky remains on the left with his men, in front of six caissons, all of them shouting 'Hurrah! Hurrah!' New streams of British continually appear, without weapons.

The assault was unstoppable. The enemy trenches were taken, the battery positions overrun and the advance continued to the Troisville–Reumont road. The battle was won, but the casualties were heavy. Five officers – among them three company commanders – seventy-five NCOs and men were dead on the battlefield; eighteen officers, 398 NCOs and men wounded. Seven wounded officers stayed with their units.

After the troops had reinforced their strength from the numerous cans of British meat they found, the regiment was reorganised and the advance continued. A battalion was formed out of the companies of Paulus (3/ 66), Redlich (MG Company) and Niemeyer (9/ 66), which marched at 1900 to Bertry, with 8/ 66 as advance guard under Lt Winckler. We assumed we would make contact during the advance, but that did not come to pass. For now the enemy had disappeared, leaving behind only a large number of wounded in the houses.

While 26 August had been a complete victory, the regiment had paid for it with heavy losses, recompensed by the capture of thirteen artillery pieces and 600 prisoners of war. Enemy losses in dead and wounded were extraordinarily heavy. It would become apparent that for a considerable period our enemy was incapable of engaging in combat. The British Army had defended itself bravely, but was unable to stand up to the German battalions.

7

CLARY

III and I/ 66 were quartered in Bertry, the dead-tired troops asleep in houses, barns, stalls and sheds. At the exit from the village, local security was provided by Lt Licht's platoon from 10/ 66. A squad had been pushed far forward from the edge of the village, and in front of that a two-man sentry. In spite of their exhaustion, they kept awake and peered into the night into which the British had disappeared. Acting Officer Voigt wrote:

At 0330, an enemy patrol approached the village. Musketeers Kokel and Gdezyk, who had just begun their sentry-go, called out a loud 'Halt! Who's there?' and locked and loaded their rifles, then recognised that these were enemy troops, and immediately shot one man and wounded another. Then an enemy detachment approached the sentries, and called out in bad German that they wanted to surrender. The sentries fell back to the squad, firing continually. Before they had gotten there, a British officer came through the garden outside the house that was serving as a guard room, called out 'Hände hoch! Ergebt euch!' (Hands up! Surrender!) into the well-lit room, fired his pistol, without hitting anyone, and stood in the door. Corporal Rosenhagen, who was standing immediately behind the door, answered with 'We don't give up so quickly!', took up his rifle and fired two rounds through the door: with a loud cry the officer fell to the ground mortally wounded, and died soon after. By now the company had been alerted, occupied the edge of the village and covered the surprised and motionless British with such effective fire that they soon surrendered. The company had the good fortune to capture in a few minutes a battalion commander, four officers and 298 enlisted men from three different regiments.

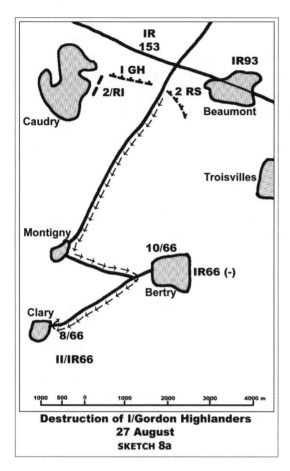

**Destruction of I/Gordon Highlanders
27 August
SKETCH 8a**

A large number of British lay dead or wounded on the ground. From 10/ 66, a sergeant and six Musketeers were wounded; two later died of wounds. Due to the alertness of the two sentries and the determined action of corporal Rosenhagen, the company was spared a disastrous surprise attack.

The security outposts of 1/ 66 also drove off British detachments. The shots resounded through the night and alerted the ɪɪ/ 66 security in Clary, a platoon of 8/ 66 under Lt Winckler, that had established two outposts. At about 0600, a group of eighty British under an officer approached one of the outposts and quickly surrendered. This caused Lt Winckler to alert the entire platoon. He wrote:

I went to the other outpost and stood at the exit from the village, which we had barricaded with carts and ladders. Suddenly I saw a long yellow column about 800 metres away, moving towards the village. That must be a battalion, I thought, and they all want to surrender! The column had deployed a point element, and farther to the right was a skirmisher line near a small house. As they got closer, we could see them waving white cloth and swinging their rifles. By now I had deployed the platoon on the edge of the village and manned the barricade. At first I considered whether we should let them come on, and then decided that we were too weak, and when they noticed this, they would overwhelm us. What was decisive was when, at 400 metres range, they deployed several squads while behind them another long skirmisher line appeared.

I gave the order to open fire. They were so close and thick it was not necessary to stipulate the range. The bullets slammed the approaching mass. An unforgettable scene! Over there, chaos. Some were hit and fell to the ground, others turned, fled and were shot down, or crawled into the sugar beet field. Soon we were getting heavy return fire. A reservist next to me was killed. My outstanding range estimator, Res. Corporal Teschner (killed in February 1915 at Arras), was severely wounded.

When the firing began the other two platoons of 8/ 66 were quickly committed to extend the line held by Winckler's platoon. The British had recovered from the initial shock and replied with a lively fire; soon a heavy firefight was under way. Major Knauff committed 5/ 66 and 6/ 66, and Capt. Siegfried brought the MG platoons of Res. Lts Seldte and Redlich into the fight. The artillery fired on the farm where a large group of British had fled. The British came under a hurricane of fire. Res. Lt Thierkopf wrote:

> Our company swarmed through the gardens and past the houses to the edge of the village in complete disorder. We took up positions behind the thick hedges, higher than a man, while bullets from an invisible enemy flew over our heads. I soon saw them in my binoculars, holding them with one hand, because the other was painful. There is a windmill by an isolated farm and, barely visible, movement in the sugar beet field front. The entire edge of the village begins to fire. Behind the corner of the house, the British supports appear by squads, one after the other. Machine guns open fire next to us. The first shell goes howling over our heads; that gives a wonderful feeling of security. Bam! A corner of the house flies into pieces, kicking up dust and smoke.

The battle lasted an hour, then the British ran out of strength. Major Knauff gave the order for the assault. Res. Lt Thierkopf described it:

> Our nerves were wound up to the breaking point. We had to advance, first over a wire fence! One of our musicians is already at work: the British wire cutters do good service. 'Attack by bounds! Move out!' Our MG are firing like crazy. We run through the sugar beets – hard work. The heavy knee-high leaves, wet with dew, slap against our legs. We reach the first trench: wounded groaning at the bottom. Two Tommies, [who] had been firing until the last minute, jump up and run for the rear – too late. We fire standing off-hand and shoot them down like rabbits: they fall head over heels. Then suddenly a multitude of raised arms appears, a sea of khaki, a mass of about 200 men, moving forwards together. Shocked, I raise my pistol, look around and see that near me are only an NCO and three or four men. They are advancing with levelled rifles, hoarsely shouting 'Hurrah!', their eyes wide, the whites showing, bloodshot. I, too, am full of rage, hate, anger. I quickly move behind the house and see a pile of shot-up,

bleeding humanity groaning there – I can't look and turn away. Behind the mill, several men are running away: we fire a few shots after them. Then I bring my prisoners back, a slow, miserable procession. They carefully carry their wounded by twos and threes. When I think back on it now, my heart is seized by compassion, but then my head and heart were full of anger, fire and death. I pushed them forward with my drawn sabre, 'Go on, men!'.

The day we defeated the British at Clary! Men from ten or eleven different regiments, artillerymen without cannons, officers and men, stragglers. With the blue-white-red cloth of national colours pinned under the regimental badges. Marching to Germany as prisoners.

The fight was over. Our losses were heavy. Among the seriously wounded was Capt. Siegfried, who was shot in the chest while standing at the edge of the village, observing the effectiveness of his MG. This brave and well-respected officer was replaced as MG Company commander by Lt Redlich (Richard). But the British losses were terrible. Their trenches were full of dead, and wounded covered the battlefield. We took 700 prisoners, including many officers.

At 1030, the march was resumed and at about 1600, the regiment reached Le Catelet, where it quartered. The British fired on a hussar patrol from a hospital protected by a Red Cross flag and killed a senior sergeant.

In its evaluation of the events on the Western Front to 27 August, the Reichsarchiv official history [*Der Weltkrieg* 1, 645ff.] said:

The armies smashed against each other in a massive collision. The offensive power of the German Army was superior, even when it was outnumbered. Seldom has an army with such combat power taken the field, especially in the attack, with such outstanding training, as the German mass army of the summer of 1914. In this million-man army there was, from the highest leader to the last soldier, only one thought, a passionate will to win, and one irresistible drive, forwards, attack the enemy! Capable tactical leaders directed this pent-up force into powerful blows against an enemy who was also attacking, often with superior numbers. The enemy was not only immediately thrown onto the defensive, but often overrun in the first shock. The German offensive spirit revealed the highest morale and power, such as was seen in practically no other battle in the war of movement on the Western Front. The allied enemies were defeated on the entire front and their combat power severely reduced. On 24 August, the French supreme commander, General Joffre, had to report to the War Minister that his massive offensive had failed completely, writing, 'On 23 August the French offensive in Belgium was brought to a halt. The reservations that I had already maintained in the last few days concerning the offensive combat power of French troops in open country have been confirmed … in spite of the numerical superiority secured by our leadership, our army corps did not show the offensive power that we had expected after our initial successes … we are now forced onto the defensive.'

The German Army had won an indisputable victory over a brave and numerically superior enemy, the German troops and leadership had accomplished great deeds, its offensive power was increased to the highest levels, while the enemy morale was crushed. But in spite of all this, there was no longed-for great decisive victory in the west.

On 27 August, 1st Army ordered the march on 28 August to the Somme River crossings on the road between Corbie and Nesle. All corps were to pursue and maintain contact with the enemy with cavalry and artillery, to increase his disorganisation and catch him crossing the Somme. IV AK was ordered to cross the Somme at Péronne.

8

THE BATTLE OF PÉRONNE

Once again the day was to be hot and bloody, as the regiment assembled on 28 August at the south side of Le Catelet. We knew that we were to pursue the British and that would require difficult forced marching. The regiment moved out to the south-west at 0800, eager and victorious, on the great highway that led to the Somme at Péronne. IR 26 was advance guard, IR 66 the lead element of the main body in the 7 ID march column, order of march II, I, III/ 66, sweating in the heat and covered in dust. The troops plodded on, it was noon, then afternoon, when suddenly rifle and artillery fire was heard to the front. The main body halted and the regimental commanders rode to the division staff, where they learned that the advance guard battalion of IR 26 had encountered strong resistance 2.5km north-east of Péronne. Major General Riedel ordered the attack with three columns that would converge on Péronne: on the right, to both sides of the Bussu–Péronne road, Column Faellingen (I and II/ 26); in the middle, to both sides of the road Bussu–Fbg (*Faubourg* – suburb) de Bretagne, Column von Quadt (I and II/ 66); left of that, Column Stumpff (III/ 26, III/ 66 and the artillery). We were surprised that we were being opposed by the French. We didn't know about them yet, and were interested to see how well they would fight.

Colonel von Quadt moved out his column (II, followed by I/ 66 and a platoon of field artillery) at 1630 from the south side of Bussu, in order to deploy in a wood to the west. The advance guard took strong and unexpected rifle fire. A few quick orders sufficed to move the companies from the road and into the protection of a wood to the south. I/ 66 had already moved south to an assembly area on the reverse slope of a hill. After analysing the situation, Major Schmidt deployed 2, 3 and 4/ 66, which advanced in open order towards the high ground.

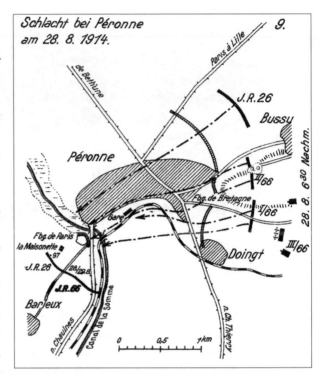

Schlacht bei Péronne am 28. 8. 1914.

In accordance with the regimental order, Major Knauff deployed 7 and 8/ 66 in the first line, 6/ 66 behind the left flank and 9/ 66 behind the centre. As Lt Winckler left the woods with 8/ 66, they took rifle fire. Moving quickly, they reached the high ground and, along with 7/ 66 on the right, led by Res. Lt Engel, opened fire at 800m against the enemy in the east side of Péronne. Tremendous fire hit both companies, but as on the previous two days, the fire commands were given and carried out calmly. The situation was not an easy one. While the enemy was well-hidden behind haystacks, our firing line was easily recognisable, so that we began to take painful losses. Company commanders Lt Redlich (Martin) and Res. Lt Amersdörffer had to commit their reserves, but this wasn't enough. Major Knauff sent 6/ 66 to extend the left flank and moved 5/ 66 to the west edge of the wood. Now there was firing on a broad front, as IR 26 had also reinforced the line. Colonel von Quast committed 1/ 66. 2 and 4/ 66 moved over the high ground and were immediately engaged in a serious firefight. The regimental commander also ordered the MG company commander, Lt Redlich (Richard), to engage the platoons of Lt Blume and Senior Sergeant Theuerkauf. They came forward at a gallop, through Bussu, while Lt Redlich found an overwatch position left of II/ 66. Res. Lt Seldte wrote:

> Right below them was the rail bridge over the Somme, and behind that the sea of houses in Péronne, surrounded by the old fortress wall. The enemy riflemen were easy to see with binoculars, in the sunken roads in front of Péronne which formed a half-circle parallel to the edge of the city, as far as the eye could see, whose heavy fire had already cost both regiments considerable casualties.

The MG went forward widely dispersed and soon four guns were pouring unexpected fire from a higher position oblique to the right into the French light infantry. This relieved the pressure on our infantry considerably. They were able to advance by bounds until they were 600m from the enemy, although the enemy fire had not been completely suppressed. The heat of the day and the exertions of the preceding days made themselves felt. But the example of the officers and NCOs pulled the men forward, though in spite of the MG fire and the troops' aggressiveness, it was still not possible to assault the enemy position.

General von Stumpff, the artillery officer leading the column to the left, which included III/ 66 under Capt. Schleusner, had a method. He held the infantry back and used it only to protect the guns. Without undue haste, he brought up his guns and howitzers, and once all were in position, he ordered them to shell the city, filled with supply units and troops, as well as the troops on the outskirts. A merry barking, humming and crashing began. The shells arched hissing into the city, filled to the brim with troops and supply vehicles and guns. The grey-black clouds rose up at the impact area, a wonderful sight for the attacking companies. After a quarter-hour's bombardment, Major Knauff thought that the enemy was getting cautious. He didn't wait, but turned to the battalion drummer next to him and ordered, 'Sound "Fix bayonets!"' It rose up, clear and demanding, and was repeated to the front, rear and by the neighbouring units. This signal had been imbued in the body and soul of the peacetime-trained troops, and immediately they began rapid fire on the enemy. The rearward lines moved forward, 5/ 66 under Lt Rieger and, in 1/ 66, 1 and 2/ 66. Suddenly the field was full of running skirmisher lines. Major Knauff drew his sword and ordered 'Charge!' to be sounded. His battalion drummer played it, and the other buglers repeated the signal. Res. Lt Thierkopf wrote:

> Charge! The trumpeters blast it out, the drummers ceaselessly beat out the assault march, stirring and spurring us on. The skirmisher lines rise like one man, the reserves, deployed in long lines, fly up out of their positions. The whole battalion goes on the assault together, with flying colours and hundreds of voices crying 'Hurrah!'. That's far more than the enemy can stand. We take the hedge, storm through farms and over the rail embankment. There are the first French dead, mountain troops in dark brown uniforms with their strange, floppy beret. Shots come from behind corners, out of windows, from the church tower. The first houses go up in flames – Péronne is on fire!

1 and II/ 66 advance continuously, the standards fluttering, a hole is shot through the bunting of the II/ 66 standard. With beating drums and blaring bugles, and

the troops shouting 'Hurrah!', the assault continues to the edge of the city. The enemy, French mountain troops, flee without firing. The assaulting infantry breaks into the deserted city, pushing the mountain infantry in front of them. The musketeers crowd around the first fountains they find and drink. But the halt is a short one.

At the southern side of Péronne, Major Knauff led elements of I and II along the rail embankment and through the rail station towards the Faubourg de Paris, with flags flying and without meeting any opposition. Other elements of 1/ 66 moved through the southern part of Péronne, when the point element of 4/ 66 under Lt Riep took fire from a barricade at the entrance to the Faubourg de Paris. Due to the energetic leadership of Capt. Trenk, the barricade was quickly taken. The standard of 1/ 66 was in danger, but saved by the colour party. There was resistance everywhere in the city. Res. Lt Thierkopf wrote:

> I collected whoever was around me and led them forward. On the far end of a long, narrow alley a disorganised mass of yelling men had stopped, drunk with combat and victory. It was still necessary to be careful! Ahead at a corner, where the alley curved, lay a handful of field grey – one with a fresh loaf of bread in his arm, completely covered in blood. They had put MGs on the bridge. No further advance is possible here. We stopped and reorganised the intermixed units.

It didn't take long until the last of the French mountain troops and Territorials disappeared from the city. It was dark and Péronne was burning: as the companies departed, the flames flew blood red towards the heavens, lighting the old city, which in this war will have an even more bitter fate.

After the MG Company and III/ 66 (which was not engaged) arrived, in the growing dark outposts were set, and the regiment dug in on the line La Maisonette (Hill 97) – a rail line two km south of the Faubourg de Paris – with II/ 66 on the right, right flank on the Barleux road, in contact with IR 26, to its left III/ 66, then I /66. Digging-in in the heavy, stony ground was in places not completed until 0400. The dead-tired troops slept in the position and were later fed from the field kitchens. The enemy, who according to the locals and prisoners was approaching from the south-west with strong forces, did not attempt anything during the night.

Our losses on this day were fifteen men killed (ten from II/ 66) and twenty-nine men wounded (twenty-five from II/ 66). The troops had once more performed superbly, and in spite of the increasing demands on their march and combat discipline, had shown that they carried a fine offensive spirit, and were capable of further decisive deeds against the heart of the enemy.

The fighting on 28 August gave 1st Army an indication that French forces were coming from the south and south-west to protect the beaten British and hold up our advance. They did not succeed, either on 28 August or on the following days. First Army continued the march, first to the south-west, and ruthlessly pushed aside all French resistance. It increased its march tempo, in order to force the retreating French and British to fight, or to overtake them.

The leadership could make unparalleled demands on the combat-experienced troops. The burning heat during the day and the very cool nights during the pursuit marches did not affect the morale of the troops at all, nor did the continual combat readiness during the meagre hours of rest. The leaders and troops gave their all with the thought that, by marching towards the enemy, they would assist their comrades in other units and bring the war to an end.

At 1000 on 29 August, the regiment marched as part of the main body to the south-west, and in the early hours of the afternoon reached Estrées (I and III/ 66) and Deniécourt (II/ 66), where the troops bivouacked either in the open or in buildings. The 8/ 66 was made division headquarters guard and bivouacked in the wonderful castle park at Deniécourt. The field trains, which the troops had not seen in weeks, arrived late in the afternoon. The well-deserved rest did not last long. At 2100, the troops were alerted and at 2330 began to march to Lihons.

The regiment occupied an assembly area north of Méharicourt between 0230 and 0530 due to the supposed approach of strong French forces from the south-west. The 13 Brigade deployed on both sides of the Méharicourt–Rounroy en Santerre road, IR 66 with its left flank on the road. After reconnaissance had shown that there was no enemy in the terrain south of Rouvroy, the march was then continued to the south. During a rest from 0830 until 1030 at Rosières en Santerre, a telegram from His Majesty the Kaiser to 1st Army was read and greeted with great joy and a 'Hurrah!' for our highest warlord. It said: 'After quick, decisive blows against Belgians, British and French, the 1st Army is nearing the heart of France. I extend to 1st Army my Imperial thanks and appreciation.' At 1700, the regiment quartered in Warwillers.

Once again the troops had a long day of marching. The exertions of the long marches were eased by the excellent rations. The inexhaustible agricultural resources of the area were able to meet the heavy demands in meat, potatoes and vegetables placed on it. There was, however, a shortage of bread and tobacco, because the field trains could not keep up with the troop units. The field post hardly ever appeared. The mobile field kitchens were indispensable. In peacetime exercises, when they were not used, the troops generally did not bother to cook their own meals. Now, the field kitchens provided warm food and coffee without any effort by the troops at all, often at exactly the right moment. When the unit had to move suddenly, the tough field soldiers, regardless of rank, accustomed themselves to pouring the meal they had just been issued back into the deep pot of the field kitchen, rather than having to sadly and with an empty stomach throw it away. At the next halt, they could resume their meal, with an even bigger appetite. Supplies of wine were everywhere, and contributed to maintaining the troops' health, while eating the unripe fruit was dangerous.

On this day, 30 August, 2nd Army fought the difficult Battle of St Quentin. To take the pressure off 2nd Army, and to cut off the retreat of the French forces opposing it, 1st Army decided to swing south. In the process it broke contact with the forces it had been pushing west and south-west. The 1st Army order said:

> It is necessary to exploit the success of the 2nd Army and cut off the enemy line of retreat. Once again exceptional marches are required.

The Reichsarchiv official history (*Der Weltkrieg* III, p. 193–4) said:

> Although the troops of the 1st Army had not taken a single rest day since the beginning of the advance, but rather had made almost superhuman forced marches, General von Kluck felt he was justified making further demands on the troops, which might bring a decisive end to the campaign. And the troops showed that they could meet the highest standards. Those that were weak or sick had already fallen out. Those that remained took up each new march, confidently and proudly, as a test.

The regiment marched at 0430 on 31 August as part of the main body, order of march III, I and II/ 66, and in extremely hot weather marched until 1600. II/ 66 quartered in Le Mareuil Lamotte, the rest of the regiment in Biermont. During the day, word arrived of the decisive German victory over the Russians at Tannenberg, which further motivated the troops not to stop until they, too, had won a decisive victory.

The troops had just begun to settle down when they were alerted. Detachments were sent forward to secure the bridges over the Aisne and Oise. II/ 66 marched at 2130, with 6/ 66 remaining behind to protect the artillery. To lighten the troop's load, the rucksacks were loaded onto requisitioned wagons. It arrived at 0100 at the crossroads north of Marest sur Matz and rested on the road in an uncomfortably cool night. At 0400, 8/ 66 was given the mission of relieving a hussar detachment at Choisy (between the Aisne and Oise). The company received a friendly reception along the way from the inhabitants, who thought they were British. It reached Choisy at 0730 and occupied the bridges. The remainder of II/ 66 (5 and 7/ 66) moved out at 0700, crossed the Oise and marched to Choisy, where it was joined by 6/ 66. The rest of the regiment marched at 2300 and crossed the Oise at Thourotte.

A task force under Colonel von Quadt and made up of a company each from IR 26, 27, 165, Engineer Battalion 4 and a battery from FAR 40, was loaded onto lorries and seized the bridges at Compiègne. It could not prevent the large bridge at the north-west side of the town from being blown up, probably by British cavalry.

After a good rest, the reassembled regiment crossed the Aisne late in the day at Choisy, where it was joined by 8/ 66. It marched through the wonderful oak and birch Forest of Compiègne on a good road, through Pierrefonds to Palsne. During the march, Capt. Knaths, riding in advance of his dissolved special railway guard detachment (begun 16 August), rejoined the regiment. The long-awaited bread was brought forward by a lorry supply column and distributed to the troops while they were in the forest. In general, the inhabitants took us for British and cheered. At 2300, the regiment quartered at Palesne and Morienval. It had been on its feet all night and the next day until deep into the night, having marched 50km. Dead tired, the regiment was soon asleep.

On the evening of 1 September, 1st Army HQ learned that the British Army was close at hand, and decided to attack it on 2 September. It was necessary once again to alert the resting troops. In consequence, at 0630 7 ID began the march and deployed, facing south, towards the woods to the east of Crépy en Valois and marched through it. IR 66, marching in the main body, was in the second line. It was a false alarm, the enemy had pulled back, and around midday the division assembled at Levignen. The troops were given a rest in the wonderful birch woods of the Blois du Roi, south of Crépy, in beautiful warm weather. The troops' morale rose because the general opinion was that the encirclement of Paris would begin soon and that by Christmas at the latest we'd be home. We continued the march to Boissy-Fresnoy and Betz. II and III/ 66 provided security and dug-in their positions on the line Boisy-Fresnoy–Betz, which in the heavy, stony ground, was not completed until midnight, the troops sleeping in the trenches. Nothing of significance happened during the night. I/ 66 provided security for the corps HQ at Crépy.

On 3 September, the regiment assembled at 0730 on the Nanteuil le Handouin–Betz road and marched south from Betz to the Ourcq River at Crouy sur Ourcq, where it was supposed to quarter, but the order arrived to march to the Marne. This began at 1300 in exceptionally hot weather. The area had not yet been touched by war. Hills covered by green woods, valleys by fruitful meadows and quiet villages, each succeeding the other, had their own charm for the troops as they continually marched forward.

During the early afternoon, a detachment made up of all the bicyclists in the division, and led by Lt Winckler, was sent forward to seize the Marne bridge at Méry, which was supposed to be held by a French cuirassier squadron. Instead, at 1900, they found there the Rathenow Hussars from III AK, who took the lead element of the detachment, 2/ FAR 4 under Capt. Gebhardt, with a platoon of 8/ 66 riding on the caissons, to be enemy and fired on them. The detachment succeeded in occupying the bridge, which the advance guard of the division crossed at midnight. The regiment quartered at Saacy and Citry, with III/ 66 providing security. It had been a hot and, because of the hilly terrain, particularly strenuous march day, during which the troops had once again put 50km behind them. That morning, while on the march, an enemy aircraft dropped a bomb on I/ 66, but no damage was done.

First Army had crossed the Marne. On its right flank was the great Fortress Paris, a mysterious threat. General von Kluck left IV RK, II AK and 2 KD to guard his flank while marching the rest of the army to the south-west to cut off the retreating enemy from Paris.

The day began on 4 September at 0730 with a long, monotonous march through Orly and Rebais. II/ 66, the advance guard, stopped at 1600 on the far side of Rebais to rest. III and I/ 66, at the front of the main body, stopped north of the city. The 10/ 66 received the mission to load up on requisitioned wagons and go past the advance guard and seize the crossing over the Grand Morin at St Siméon, during which an incident occurred recorded by Lt Berns, the adjutant of III/ 66:

> I was sent to Rebais to requisition wagons for a company, along with the company commander, Capt. Ulfert. He went into one farm and I into another. I was in the process of having a wagon emptied by the inhabitants when I heard horses nearby. I didn't pay any attention until I heard shots fired and saw, about ten paces away, eight to ten British and French cavalrymen riding in my direction and shooting. There was no question of offering resistance; I was a prisoner. I was forced to mount my horse and led to a nearby wood, where they took my money, watch, binoculars, letter case and the spike on my helmet. After about a half an hour – an eternity for me – the enemy patrol took lively fire from the approaching company, mounted up, and I had to go with them; a Frenchman held my reins. My horse was wounded. Now a wild ride began through the streets of the village, with me in the middle. Suddenly we took heavy fire from the flank. Behind me and next to me the enemy cavalrymen dropped dead; I was the only one not hit. I hit the Frenchman next to me hard – I was free, but I could not control my horse, who ran with the others. At the last minute I succeeded in turning the horse around. I raced into our rifle fire, swinging my arms, and the men raised their weapons into the air; I was saved! The Frenchman that had been leading my horse was now our prisoner, the others were dead or wounded. I got my sword and the spike on my helmet back, covered with British blood.

10/ 66 had been marching to Rebais when it suddenly took fire in the left flank from a wood. Two squads from 11/ 66 under Sergeant Wolff were deployed against the enemy. Sergeant Wolff was killed. The enemy was quickly silenced and the march resumed. The 10/ 66 and the regimental bicyclists under Sergeant Seemann appeared at just the right time to give the fleeing British cavalry an appropriate reception. A few quick rifle shots sufficed to put paid to most of the enemy cavalry. The rest – a captain and fifteen men – were captured.

That evening, 11/ 66 reached St Denis, 1/ 66 Montmogis and 111/ 66 St Siméon. The latter two battalions provided local security. During the night there were small engagements with French cavalry patrols that resulted in the capture of several French cuirassiers, which were wearing the historic peace-time uniforms: a polished helmet with black horsehair, blue coat and red pants.

On 5 September, 1st Army continued the pursuit. The regiment marched at 0730 with 11/ 66 as advance guard through St Siméon to Choisy (south-east of Coulommiers), and deployed. The artillery shelled the town and, after a short firefight with some French cavalry patrols, the town was taken. After a good rest, the march was resumed and the regiment bivouacked in Chevru and the surrounding area. 111/ 66 provided local security. No one had any idea that the long enemy withdrawal was about to end, that we had reached the southernmost point of our advance, and that enormous exertions were to be required of the regiment.

9

BATTLE ON THE MARNE AND OURCQ, 6–9 SEPTEMBER 1914

While the troops of the 1st, 2nd and 3rd Armies pursued the retreating French and British Armies, the French had moved corps to Paris and created a new army, in order to attack on 6 September against the German right flank. At the same time, the other French armies turned about and attacked. The IV RK, providing security against Paris, was the first to be engaged. It defended itself heroically, but was in serious difficulties. General von Kluck decided to bring back the corps that were south of the Marne and throw them against the enemy forces attacking from Paris.

IV AK turned around and, at 0830 on 6 September, marched back the same way it had come a few days previously. In the afternoon it reached Rebais, where it quartered. Cannon fire could be heard to the west for the entire day. The rest period gave the companies a welcome opportunity to conduct inspections and thoroughly clean the weapons, as though this was a peacetime manoeuvre. Since the last rest day had been 16 August, this one seemed well-deserved. In their imaginations the troops built castles in the sky, including rest and the encirclement of Paris, which was 64km away as the crow flies.

This idyllic peacetime manoeuvre disappeared at 1830, when the regiment was alerted; the division order said that IV RK and II AK were in heavy contact on the Ourcq against enemy forces advancing from Paris. At 2130, the march north towards the Marne began. The field trains and ration supply columns distributed canned vegetables and iron rations to the passing troops as they left Rebais, and then they too moved out at 0100, guarded by 6/66.

By now the troops were used to the unexpected and accommodated themselves to the unavoidable, the more so because the sound of cannon fire from the north-west signalled that our comrades and countrymen were in danger. There

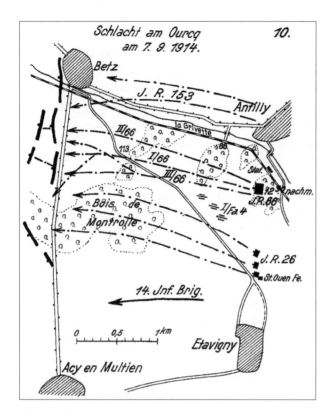

was no thought that we were conducting a retreat, though everyone noticed that 'We were already here once'. Leaden fatigue overcame everyone. The men slept standing up and staggered left and right. Men in the ranks stumbled, with his nose in the mess gear of the man in front. Every so often the cry went out 'Get the barrel of your weapon up!'. Officers dismounted from their horses and walked, in order not to go to sleep on the horse. At a short rest everyone lay where he stood onto the dust of the road. Soon the march was resumed; it took a lot of effort to get the column in motion again.

In an unbroken march, the regiment passed through Orly, Bussières, Méry (Marne) and Montreuil to Coulombs, which it reached at 0900. It was intended that we rest and eat here, but hardly had the rations been distributed than the order came: 'Get ready. We move out in two minutes.' Everyone gobbled down what he could and reluctantly threw the rest away. The day gradually became very hot. The regiment marched through Crouy to Rouvres. Numerous stragglers made their way to Rouvres and were collected by 6/ 66. At Rouvres, the regiment received the following order:

> 7 ID will deploy to the right of IV RK. IR 66 division reserve behind the right flank, in the area of Antilly. March to be conducted covered and concealed. IR 26 corps reserve.

The march continued with II/ 66 advance guard, without consideration for the ensuing straggling. Considering the necessity of bringing the regiment quickly into position, the motto was, 'Whoever falls out, falls out.' For hours the march went across beet and stubble fields in blazing heat. Our tongues stuck to the roof of our mouths. There were blackberries on the edge of a wood and finally – finally! – a spring, which we threw ourselves on with the last of our strength.

After a short period in an assembly area north of the rail line Mareuil sur Ourcq–Betz, in the woods south of Antilly, at 1200 the regiment was moved past the rail station south of Antilly, and closer to the division flank. Numerous small woods limited visibility, so at 1230 a thin skirmisher line from II/ 66 was sent towards the wood south of Point 88, about a kilometre south-west of Antilly. I/ 66 was to follow left of II/ 66, III/ 66 behind the middle of the regiment. This movement was conducted on the regiment's own initiative, on the assumption that anything could be hiding in the woods. It was unlikely that, while the battle could be heard raging south of the Bois de Montrolle (Montrolle Forest), the area north of it was free of enemy forces.

Our suspicions were quickly justified. The regimental and II/ 66 commanders reached the edge of the wood in advance of the skirmisher line. From here they could see beyond the Betz–Acy en Multien road. The entire plateau was covered with advancing enemy skirmisher lines; the leading elements had already crossed that road and were nearly to the Betz–Etavigny road. There could be no question that the enemy to our front was attacking.

The decision to attack was made at once, initially with II/ 66, with I/ 66 coming up as quickly as possible on the left. II/ 66 was able to open fire at 1300. The opposing French infantry visibly and suddenly came to a halt east of the Betz–Acy road, although the range was very long – 2,000m – and the effectiveness of our rifle fire could not have been great. We could observe French infantry attempting to reach the Bois de Montrolle. Major Knauff recognised that from his current position it would be difficult to stop the French, and sent 8/ 66 to the woods at Point 113 on the Betz–Etavigny road. A patrol led by Sergeant Nisse, 8/ 66, provided security for the right flank near Betz. It was about 1400. A short time later, Major Knauff followed with 5 and 7/ 66, which took heavy losses (6/ 66 still had not rejoined). There were no enemy forces in the wood.

The French artillery now covered the approach through the wood with shrapnel and high-explosive shells, and put I/ 66 under fire as it left the woods. In places it was devastatingly effective. A platoon of Res. Jäger Bn 4, which had attached itself to I/ 66, was entirely cut down by a salvo of shrapnel. The regimental staff on the woodline south-west of Point 88 had several men and horses wounded: Colonel von Quadt took a grazing wound. The brigade adjutant, Capt. Jaenisch, was severely wounded on the way to the IR 66 staff, so that the brigade commander, General von Schüssler, and his orderly officer arrived alone. To avoid this fire, whose effect on morale was worse than the casualties it caused, the companies of I/ 66 moved into the woods to the north, which would at least hide them from observation. The battalion continued its advance and occupied the position on the Betz–Etavigny road, and, intermixed with II/ 66, took up the firefight. III/ 66 was moving forward in the woods behind the right flank and in part also became intermixed with the other two battalions. The regiment stopped on the Betz–Etavigny road. The enemy artillery seemed to have focused on this area and succeeded in pinning the riflemen in the sunken roads. French priority of fire against I/ 66 was fully justified. IR 26 was in corps reserve and had several hours to get its men fed and give them some rest. IR 153 was coming up but was not engaged until 1530. Our artillery had taken the French infantry on the Betz–Acy road under fire. Colonel von Quast did not think it prudent to continue the attack unless there was a simultaneous attack against the Bois de Montrolle and Betz village, so he ordered, between 1400 and 1500, that the Betz–Etavigny road was not to be crossed, an order that never reached II/ 66.

At 1400, IR 26 saw IR 66 leave the wood south-west of Betz in a south-westerly direction, and IR 26 decided to attack into the Bois de Montrolle on its own initiative. By 1530, the three regiments had received an order from 13 Brigade for a coordinated attack: IR 26 to attack into the Bois de Montrolle, IR 153 Betz, while IR 66 was to resume its attack. Unfortunately, IR 66 would not get any artillery support: I/ FAR 4 had been assigned to support IR 66, and apparently was looking for IR 66 south of Antilly, when the regiment was already south-east of Betz. When it could not find IR 66, it supported IR 26 instead. But the IR 66 attack succeeded without artillery. The MG of Lt Blume and Senior Sergeant Teuerkauf were inserted in the line to provide fire support. The Betz–Etavigny road was crossed, but the left flank in particular had a hard time, because it was taking flanking fire from the Bois de Montrolle. As was often the case, the large wood drew the entire left flank of the regiment, so that elements of the regiment under Capt. Paulus, intermixed with elements of IR 26, attacked the Bois de Montrolle in a south-westerly direction. The advance was easier in the centre, with III/ 66 under Capt. Schleusener and I/ 66 under Major Schmidt. On the right, II/ 66, under Major Knauff, advanced with a strong right wing, which had contact with IR 153, and was conducting a serious firefight with French infantry. Several French batteries fired in desperation. When I/ FAR 4 took the entire Betz–Acy road under effective shrapnel fire, and, under instructions from Major Knauff, destroyed several French MG, the French infantry began to retreat from its position, first slowly, then faster, some into the Bois de Montrolle, some towards Villers-St-Genest, effectively engaged by our pursuit fire. The forward line – Res. Lt Thierkopf, as ever, in the lead – pursued and by 1630 had reached the Betz–Acy road. There was nothing more to be seen of the enemy infantry, aside from scattered fire out of the Bois de Montrolle. Against our centre and right flank, the French artillery, conducting rapid fire, expended an enormous quantity of shells to cover the retreat of their infantry. Although there were only a few batteries, the fire was so impressive that II/ 66 believed the battery was 200m to their front. In spite of an advance by Lt Wagner and 4/ 66, it was not possible to take these guns as long as the regiment was taking flanking fire from the north treeline of the Bois de Montrolle. An attempt to flank the French guns ordered by Major Knauff broke down in the face of French artillery fire.

No further advance was possible here. On the other hand, weak elements under Res. Lt Mende, who had been wounded several times, and Capt. Schleusner, were able to cross the Betz–Acy road and establish themselves 400m to the west of it. Mende's detachment was able to capture two enemy artillery forward observers and their telephones. The advance stopped here, too, in part because it had no support on either side. Only a few IR 26 men under Lt von Reuss joined up with Mende's group. Between the Bois de Montrolle and the regimental left flank was a 700m gap. Shortly before dark, other elements of the regiment succeeded in advancing a few hundred metres west of the road. Lt Licht, 10/ 66, attempted to capture a nearby French battery, but it was able to get away at the last minute.

In the course of the day we took a number of prisoners, among them a professor from Paris who was wearing black buttoned lacquer dress boots. They reported being moved that night from Paris to the front on lorries. The prisoners, and the French infantry in general, gave the impression of being exhausted, hungry and demoralised. This explains why their attack immediately stopped when they met resistance, and why they offered such weak defence. The only tough and effective opponent was the French artillery, whose intense defensive fire was able to bring our attack to a stop.

That evening, the regimental commander with his last reserve, two MG and two composite companies, was in the area of Point 113 on the Etavigny–Betz road. The left flank was composed of Detachment Mende, with Lt Blume and two MG, Lt Reuss from IR 26, about seventy men together, forming a 'hedgehog', an all-around defensive position 400m west of the Betz–Etavigny road in a small square wood. Two hundred metres to the north was Battalion Schleusener, about three companies strong, which had already dug in. Next was Detachment Schmidt, in contact with Battalion Knauff, which bent the flank back to the road, together about six companies strong. Somewhat to the south of the rail line we established contact with IR 153. We began, as much as possible, to reorganise the units. According to the division order, we were to defend in place and make contact with IR 26. During the night, the field kitchens were brought forward so that the troops could be fed. Many were so tired that they slept through the meal. The 6/ 66 rejoined the regiment. Morale was excellent: we felt that we had won a complete victory. Capt. Niemeyer drank a bottle of champagne with the other officer in his company, Res. Lt Reinhardt, with a toast that 'The war will be over in 14 days'. The losses on 7 September were fifteen men killed, eight officers and sixty-seven men wounded, with sixteen men missing.

The troops had once again performed superbly. From 2130 on 6 September, they had marched continually until they entered the fight at 1200 on 7 September, having covered about 60km. They then engaged in a difficult but victorious fight, and defended in the position they had won. The performance of the attacking regiments was acknowledged by the French. According to a description by a Frenchman named Courrière, the German troops attacking out of the woods by Betz and from the Bois de Montrolles presented an imposing picture (Captain Dollmann, *Die Schlacht vor Paris*, Stalling: Oldenbourg, 1928).

Lacking information concerning the actual situation on the front line, the corps headquarters ordered a withdrawal to yesterday's initial attack position, which reached the regiment at 0500 on 8 September and made the troops extremely angry. The order was sent to the battalions at 0630 and was obeyed slowly and reluctantly. Nobody could see any sense in the order: in the fighting on 7 September, the troops had gained a feeling of being completely superior to the enemy, in spite of the heavy artillery fire. Patrols had gone far forward and did not meet any opposition. Even the enemy artillery wasn't active. Acting Officer Collet (4/ 66) reported that Capt. Trenk told the battalion adjutant: 'Ride to brigade HQ and report to them that there are no enemy troops anywhere near Betz, the men of 4/ 66 are taking leisurely strolls, our patrols are scouring the area, there are no enemy forces far and wide and there will be no enemy attack.' After the adjutant came back for the third time and there was a sharp exchange of words, the withdrawal began at 0830.

At 0930, the regiment moved out, using the woods for concealment, and arrived south of Antilly and bivouacked in the small woods south and west of the rail station. Security elements had been left in the old positions and were withdrawn in the course of the afternoon to within 1,000m of the regiment. The regiment was brigade reserve; the day passed in complete quiet, and the enemy did nothing. The exertions of the previous day were forgotten in the beautiful sunshine. The regiment bivouacked in place, with the regimental staff in the Antilly rail station. An enemy attack that evening from the Bois de Montrolle against IR 26 collapsed in small-arms and artillery fire as soon as it left the wood.

The situation was unchanged on 9 September. The regiment rested in place until noon. At 1230, an order arrived for a renewed division attack, which excited everyone and removed the feeling of uncertainty. II and I/ 66 were division reserve and moved south to a position at St Ouen Fme (*Ferme* – farm, south of Antilly), with the corps, 7 ID and 13 Brigade HQs, while III/ 66 would be on the division right flank south of Betz. A medium-calibre French artillery battery was conducting a lively fire around the farm, without hitting anything. The attack was under way when it was stopped by higher headquarters. After waiting for several hours, at 1630 the completely unexpected order came to – withdraw. The division order to the regiment said:

> The army is swinging to the rear. IR 66 and 1/ FAR 4 will occupy a delaying position north-east of Antilly.

The battalions moved there independently. The regimental commander rode ahead, selected a position and the troops dug-in there. Security detachments occupied the bridges over the Grivette stream. The iron rations were cooked by the field kitchens and distributed, the ration wagons brought forward and bread passed out. The regimental staff set up at the sugar factory north-east of Antilly. The night was quiet and the enemy did not pursue.

The day of 9 September was a fatal one for the German people. The 1st Army situation had completely changed from that on 7 September. By bringing IX AK and 6 ID to the north flank, it was possible to conduct an enveloping attack, with a brigade of IV RK moving into the enemy rear. There was the prospect of a great victory. The French were already attempting to avoid the envelopment by fleeing to Paris. The 2nd Army's situation was also good. The gap between the 1st and 2nd Armies, which the British and French troops were entering, would not become dangerous if the 1st and 2nd Army attacks succeeded. *Der Weltkrieg* said (IV, p. 525):

> Then the OHL (*Oberste Heeresleitung*, the German HQ), which to this point had not intervened in the conduct of operations, unexpectedly did so, and in a manner fateful for the outcome of the battle.

OHL judged that the gap between 1st and 2nd Armies was so dangerous that on 9 September it ordered them to break off the battles on the Ourcq and Marne and fall back to a line from the west of Soissons to the east of Fismes. The leaders and troops obeyed the order to break off the victorious battle and retreat with great reluctance. The campaign begun so hopefully, full of marches and victories, was now at an end. The Reichsarchiv's words of praise for the troops' performance in the first weeks of the war deserve repeating (*Der Weltkrieg* IV, p. 542):

> There is no greater proof of the excellence of the German Army in 1914 than the fact that it was victorious on the decisive wing of the battle, in spite of unfortunate circumstances and great enemy superiority in numbers.

The Battle of the Frontiers had been won by martial enthusiasm and superior morale, along with a passionate determination to close with the enemy. The heavy casualties of these battles was followed by literally superhuman exertions and deprivations during weeks of pursuit. On the Marne the German troops had to find new sources of strength: a deeply rooted sense of duty, self-discipline, an iron will to win and a strong sense of responsibility, gave every man the strength to do his duty, even in the face of the most difficult situations.

The fate of the Army of 1914, which under such shocking circumstances saw the hard-won victory, which was almost in its grasp, torn away (and which even the enemy marvelled at) is a great tragedy. Fateful forces were at work on the Marne, which perhaps later generations will be able to comprehend, after our historical period of European state formation has concluded and the inner correlations and consequences can be uncovered.

10

RETREAT FROM THE MARNE, 10–12 SEPTEMBER 1914

The regiment remained overnight in the position north of Antilly. The morning of 10 September was overcast. French cavalry patrols were driven away from the bridge, and didn't reappear. The regiment soon received orders to march, and began movement at 0530 in the direction of Cuvergnon, field trains and III/ 66 leading; III/ 66 was then to dig-in to a delay position south of the town. The regiment left this position at 1600, marching through Ivors and Vauciennes to Largny, west of Villers-Cotterêts, where that evening the regiment occupied alarm quarters, with security at the entrances to the village. Once again, the night was quiet, with no sign of the enemy.

At 0700 on 11 September, we continued the march in a north-easterly direction through Haramont, Taillefontaine and Mortefontaine to Ferme de Pouy, 3km north of Mortefontaine. Field hospitals with a great number of wounded and supply units joined the column, leading to frequent halts in the march, so that it did not end until 0130, made more difficult by steep terrain and poor roads. To cap it all off, there were accidents with the wagons carrying the packs. The enemy pursuit was weak.

The regiment was ordered to dig-in at Ferme de Pouy, facing south, to the east of the Montigny–Mortefontaine road, to cover the Aisne crossing. II/ 66 linked up with II/ 26 on the right, and 5/ 66 prepared a sugar factory in front of the position for defence. The work was done in a heavy rain which lasted until evening. A battalion of IR 156 assisted in digging in. I/ 66 was initially in reserve, and at 1900 relieved III/ 66 in place, which went into division reserve at St Baudry.

Enemy cavalry and artillery had been reported approaching, and at 1800 they appeared. The brigade area and the Ferme were shelled heavily but ineffectively, except for hay ricks near the Ferme that were set on fire. 5/ 66 was pulled back to be regimental reserve. The artillery fire soon stopped and the regiment held its positions during the night.

Late in the evening, the order to withdraw to the Aisne arrived, and the combat trains of 1/ 66 and 11/ 66 were sent ahead at 2330, through St Bandry and Fontenoy to Bieuxy. The regiment (without 111/ 66) marched early on the morning of 12 September through Ressons-le-Long and Gargny to the bridge built by the engineers over the Aisne at Le Port (west of Fontenoy). The crossing was supposed to take place between 0400 and 0500, but delays several hours-long occurred due to overcrowded roads and the convergence of several columns at the crossing site. FAR 40 went into battery to protect the crossing. Slowly, the infantry crossed on foot bridges, vehicles on the bridges.

During the afternoon, the regiment, including the combat trains, marched through Fontenoy and Cuisy en Amont to Tartiers. The regiment rested and at 1500 received an order to move concealed to Cuisy-en-Almont. While 1/ 66 quartered there, the regimental staff and 11/ 66 in La Maison Bleue, after dark 111/ 66 went forward through Laval to Courtil, with security on the Aisne, to guard against enemy attempts to cross. Several hay ricks were set on fire to improve visibility in the pitch-dark night. Contact was maintained with IR 26 on the right in Osly and IR 93 on the left in Pommiers. The enemy had followed slowly and there was no combat. Enemy artillery fire had begun that afternoon but was ineffective. In view of the uncertain situation, the troops in Cuisy were held in readiness to move; one company of 11/ 66 was, in rotation, prepared to move immediately.

II

COMBAT ON THE AISNE, 13–27 SEPTEMBER 1914

On 13 September, the German right flank was north of the Aisne and expected that a fight was coming. The French, drunk with victory, thought they could deal with the Germans easily. They were mistaken, and ran into an unbreakable wall of fire. This was still manoeuvre warfare; a succession of offensive and defensive actions. But there were no longer any rapid, deep advances; the fighting was now restricted to the same limited area, which initially allowed the troops to get some rest, but in a few days led to deep dissatisfaction and impatience. It was now the beginning of autumn with cool rainy weather and the onset of diarrhoea, which affected everyone. This transition from advancing in the open field to years of holding out in soon-to-be firmly dug-in positions was not a happy memory for anyone.

A misty rain fell on the morning of 13 September. III/ 66 had spent the night shivering in its position on the Aisne. At dawn, it was withdrawn to the south-east of Leval, where it dug-in, supported by a MG platoon. Continual enemy movement towards the Aisne could be observed. The enemy had already crossed south of Fontenoy and Osly, and were taken under artillery fire. The enemy vigorously shelled the road from Laval to Cussy. In spite of that, the field post was delivered to III/ 66 by the regiment's automobile. II/ 66 dug-in south of Maison Bleue. After dark, III/ 66 was relieved by I/ 66; two companies of III/ 66 took quarters in Laval, the other two companies (the brigade reserve) in Maison Bleue, II/ 66 and the MG Company in a large farm.

On the morning of 14 September, 15 Brigade reported, and as it soon became clear, somewhat prematurely, that its right flank (IR 93) was being turned and asked for assistance. III/ 66 moved to Pommiers, while I/ 66 was to march to Vauxrezis as regimental reserve, but was diverted to Pommiers, to the

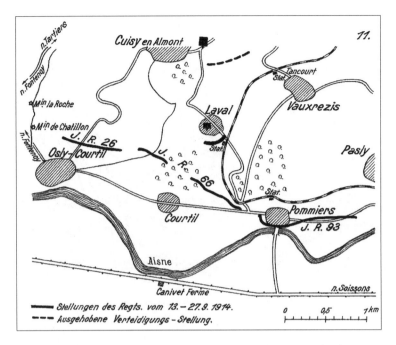

bend in the road south-east of Laval, and concealed in a wood. The situation in the IR 93 sector was completely quiet, as the enemy had withdrawn back over the Aisne. III/ 66 returned to quarter at Leval, I/ 66 maintained contact with IR 93 west of Pommiers. At 2000, after receiving its rations and bread, II/ 66 relieved I/ 66. The artillery fire that had covered the Cuisy–Pommiers road the entire day stopped after dark, so that the relief proceeded undisturbed. I/ 66 moved to Cuisy to become brigade reserve; II/ 66 pushed its position forward to near the crossroads north-west of Pommiers, with the left wing connecting with IR 93 at the road, front facing south and south-west. A MG platoon was attached. Strong patrols provided security as far as the Aisne. Contact was maintained with IR 26 at Osly and IR 93 at Canivet Fme.

At 0700, the artillery of both sides began firing again. II/ 66 remained in its positions, undisturbed. It was reported at 1300 that IR 26 was being attacked from Osly by enemy forces in brigade strength, and the regiment was ordered to attack towards Osly to flank them. At 1300, III/ 66 went forward to attack to the right of II/ 66, which had already committed 5/ 66. The enemy attack west of Osly broke down and the German artillery set fire to all the villages. There was a short firefight with weak enemy elements on the east edge of Osly. Any enemy forces in Courtil were cleaned out, and fire from Canivet Fme and the other side of the Aisne against the II/ 66 position was silenced. Our further advance was blocked by friendly artillery fire. When the regiment received the report from II/ 66 at 1730 that the area east of Osly was clear of the enemy, it ordered a return to the defensive position; after dark, III/ 66 would

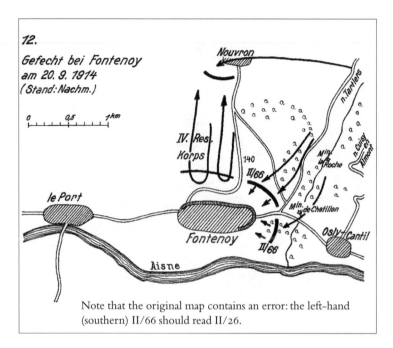

12.

Gefecht bei Fontenoy
am 20. 9. 1914
(Stand: Nachm.)

Note that the original map contains an error: the left-hand
(southern) II/66 should read II/26.

relieve II/ 66. During the withdrawal, 5/ 66 suddenly came under shrapnel
fire, which did not cause casualties. At 2045, II/ 66 quartered in Laval, but was
alerted at 2230 because the enemy threatened to break into the IR 26 position
and to the west of it. The battalion was not committed.

Trench warfare, with active patrolling and surprise shellings of the position,
roads and villages, became more and more pronounced. The front-line position was held by a battalion, which was relieved daily, and two MG platoons.
A brigade order at 2330 on 18 September extended the regiment's position
to the ridge that ran from Cuisy to Osly; 3/ 66, under Capt. Paulus, relieved
12/ 26 there at 0130.

A patrol led by Lt Licht (10/66) on 18 September found Osly free of enemy
forces, and was able to identify the location of two enemy batteries: Lt Licht was
awarded the Iron Cross 1 Class by corps order. On 19 September, Lt Licht led a
second patrol to Osly and was able to determine the positions of the batteries
more precisely. He returned with two wounded French prisoners and civilians.
On all Lt Licht's patrols, the two brothers, Senior Sergeant Franz Rauch and
Corporal Hans Rauch, distinguished themselves. Both were awarded the Iron
Cross. They were killed in the assault on Mercatel on 5 October 1914.

On 16 September, the first Iron Crosses were awarded for the battles of Le
Cateau and Péronne to officers, NCOs and men. As II/ 66 was standing in
formation in the church square of Cuisy on 18 September to receive the awards,
a shell landed in the 6/ 66 ranks and killed three men and wounded sixteen
more, including the company commander, Res. Lt Robbling.

On 19 September at 2030, the first 400 replacements arrived from Germany, just in time for a hard day of combat. After all the French attacks had been beaten back, General von Kluck decided to attack the enemy elements still on the north side of the Aisne on 20 September and throw them back into the river. The principal unit in the attack would be IV RK, with IV AK supporting by attacking Fontenoy. In the 7 ID sector, II/ 26 was given the mission of attacking at 0530 from the La Roche heights (north of Osly) towards Fontenoy to take the enemy in the flank. II/ 66 was to be at Vaugerins (east of Tartiers) at 0500 as division reserve; I/ 66 was in the defensive position, III/ 66 in Laval. At 1000, the commander of II/ 66, Major Knauff, received the following verbal order:

> The IV RK attack is not making progress. II/ 26 is south-east of Fontenoy. II/ 66, with two field artillery pieces attached, will move through Tartiers towards the high ground north-east of Fontenoy, occupy it and attack Fontenoy. II/ 26 is attached to you.

The battalion immediately moved out south-west towards Tartiers, where it was joined by a platoon from 2/ FAR 40. Major Knauff rode ahead and 3km south-west of Tartiers met the adjutant of II/ 26, Lt Hube. From Min la Roche, Major Knauff sent the following report to 7 ID:

> Due to the withdrawal of 7 RD, II/ 26 has pulled back to Min la Roche. The area between Min la Roche and the Fontenay Valley is continually under the fire of several light and heavy batteries, which cannot be silenced by our artillery. An advance against the heavily defended Fontenoy under this artillery fire will not succeed. I am going to establish communications with 7 RD and deploy II/ 66 and the two artillery pieces in an assembly area west of the path Nouvron–Osly, II/ 26 near Min la Roche, so that if 7 RD renews the attack the two battalions can attack the south and east sides of Fontenoy. Artillery fire support for the attack on Fontenoy as well as counter-battery fire is necessary.

At 1130, II/ 66 deployed west of the Tartiers–Fontenoy road and moved by long bounds towards the north-east edge of Fontenoy. It passed through the thickly wooded slopes, which were under artillery fire, and at 1330 reached the slope south of the Nouvron–Osly road, with the left flank opposite the north-east corner of Fontenoy. Contact was made with the left flank of 7 RD, elements of which (Jäger and infantry) pulled back from the direction of Fontenoy north-east into the wood. To the front of II/ 66 lay dead Germans and French. The French trenches were visible north and north-east of Fontenoy. II/ 26 reoccupied its old position south-east of Fontenoy.

On the basis of a new attack order, this time from corps, II/ 66 deployed in a south-westerly direction, but soon took fire from close range, in part into the flank. The right flank crossed the ridgeline south of Point 140 on the Nouvron–Fontenoy road. II/ 66 opened fire and advanced. The attack split up due to fire it was taking in various directions from a well-hidden enemy aided by the terrain. The intense firefight led to heavy casualties, as the troops of the engaged companies tried to close with the enemy. Here and there they succeeded in throwing the enemy out of his position. The fighting was desperate, as Res. Lt Thierkopf vividly described the fight of 5 and 6/ 66:

We were taking artillery shell and shrapnel fire like hail from the front, left and right. Clouds of dirt and stones were thrown up ... Major Knauff assembled the companies at the tip of a wood. With a half-platoon I was the first to take my chances and advance. I had barely moved into the open ground when I saw figures waving to the front, 'We need help, comrades!' We were taking fire into the left flank. Damn! I turned the left-flank squad in that direction, and ordered the others to push forward and, hiding behind a corn stook, gestured and yelled to the rear, trying to make myself understood. The bullets hummed like bees. Then I ran to the left flank squad, which was lying on the edge of a field, firing, and threw myself down there. The stubblefield sloped down to the edge of a wood, where the French were. I could hear their rounds hit the earth in front of me, throwing up a fountain of dirt with a hissing sound. Then next to me the squad leader, Sergeant Knop, jerked suddenly up, silently threw his arms in the air, then collapsed. If we didn't get help soon, we were all going to be shot down like targets. Then down below I heard cries of 'Hurrah!'. The French, startled, stood in a mass in a clearing in the wood, gesturing wildly and yelling. Somebody was attacking the French in the flank. I drew my sword and yelled 'Let's go!' and over the stubble ran the wild hunt, with bayonets gleaming. The French couldn't take it and they ran as though they had been swept away, with only their dead left behind. We ran past them and into the woods. We soon reached a clearing and once again the bullets whizzed around us. Our position ran perpendicular to the line of foxholes, so we could only occupy those at one end. It was clear to me we're not going any further; the companies were mixed together, and we were conscious that the French could launch a powerful counter-attack at any time. Then we would be taken in front and flank, because they were still firing like crazy from loopholes in the walls and the windows in the first houses of Fontenoy.

Lt Hesse and the men of 6/ 66 had succeeded, under heavy fire, in reaching the difficult, heavily wooded slope that fell to the valley and getting close to a

French trench. With cries of 'Hurrah!' and lowered bayonets, 6/ 66 threw itself on the French and put them to flight. They immediately began to pursue, but came under heavy flanking fire; Lt Hesse was killed, and the attack here also came to a halt. The entire battalion had been stopped, taking heavy artillery fire from the south bank of the Aisne, as well as both frontal and flanking rifle fire from Fontenoy, but held on, returning fire, for long, difficult hours.

Major Knauff evaluated the situation as follows: an attack on Fontenoy – whose walls and houses had been prepared for defence, and from which the French were keeping up a heavy fire, and were supported by an estimated several companies of reserves which had been identified in the town – was pointless without artillery support. It was not possible to determine if II/ 26 was also attacking: visual contact could not be established, sending a direct patrol through the close terrain was out of the question and sending a patrol in a loop to the rear would take too much time. Weak infantry and occasional MG fire could be heard to the west of the Nouvron–Fontenoy road, but that soon died down. The leader of the RIR 72 MG Company had ordered 8/ 66, on the battalion right flank, to protect his MG. The stream of wounded from IV RK moving to the rear through the woods reinforced the impression that an attack on the north side of Fontenoy could not be counted on, and IV RK drew heavy French artillery fire from the south and south-west onto the battalion. It was impossible to break off the fight during daylight. The forward companies were therefore ordered to fight a delaying action and, as far as possible, move the troops back to better positions. At 1515, the following division order arrived:

> Since 7 RD has apparently returned to its old positions, unless there are compelling reasons to the contrary, the attack by II/ 26 and II/ 66 should be called off. II/ 66 should withdraw in the direction of Tartiers.

It was difficult to get the order to the firing line, and all elements were not notified until 1800. The withdrawal was laborious. All the wounded that could be found were moved back. True comradeship saved the lives of many or prevented them from being captured. The battalion continued to take enemy fire. The evacuation of the ground that had been won continued calmly, but with clenched teeth. It was an evening full of horrible experiences. Res. Lt Thierkopf wrote:

> In a clearing in a slope that went down to the valley (above it there was a dark pine forest) I hear a loud moaning. Shouted warnings and more bullets force me to throw myself for a short time on the ground. I see what I had already suspected: they had run blindly into the open and the French, in the valley, had not waited in vain. My fine men lay there, next to each other, among

them our little Acting Officer Meyer. He had been shot in the back and could not move. But we can't wait here long: flat as a piece of paper, I wind through the grass, somewhat uphill from me Senior Sergeant Klaebe, and we make it! Concealed by the pine forest, I am able to stand erect. Behind a moss-covered large block of stone I hear a call: a sergeant stands up and holds out his hand: 'Help me, Lieutenant!' I pull him over to me, and he falls forward as though drunk, sheet-white, his hand where he has been shot in the chest, and disappears. The battalion assembles in a sunken road leading down to the valley. A few shots are fired from the treeline, then darkness falls. The French artillery begins to feel in our direction … howling and cracking, the shells went over our heads; the trees splinter.

Major Knauff assembled his companies, which were now very weak. Patrols were sent out once again to search the battlefield for wounded; a great many were found, but the dead could not be recovered. The 5/ 66 medic, Corporal Rosmanith, worked tirelessly, going forward again and again, paying no attention to the enemy fire. At 2115, the battalion withdrew through Tartiers to Les Vangerins. At Min la Roche, the Medical Company took the wounded. II/ 26 had also been able to break contact and withdraw to Tartiers. The fight had caused II/ 66 severe casualties: ten dead, forty-eight wounded and eighty-six missing. The naturally strong French defensive position, supported by heavy artillery fire, meant that for hours the situation was difficult and changed continually, but the troops showed both prudence and boldness in mastering it.

The other battalions had no rest either. When it became known that the IV RK attack had failed, III/ 66 was alerted, and marched quickly to occupy 7 RD trenches south of Nouvron. It thereby came under its last peacetime commander, Colonel Dresler und Scharfenstein, who greeted his old troops in a warm, fatherly fashion. The battalion remained in this position for several days, exposed to heavy enemy fire. After III/ 66 had left, I/ 66 assembled at Laval as a reserve. Only one company remained in the front-line position, reinforced by a MG platoon. I/ 66 was not committed, and during the night another company and MG platoon occupied the position. Patrols were sent to the Aisne. The enemy was quiet and inactive.

The unsuccessful day at Fontenoy was followed by the dull days at the beginning of trench warfare, made worse by the rainy weather, poor rations and complete absence of tobacco. The trenches in the damp Aisne valley had no protection against the weather, which led to dysentery-like illnesses.

On 21 September, the division commander visited II/ 66 and praised the men for their performance at Fontenoy. That afternoon, a patrol from 4/ 66, led by Senior Sergeant Thiemann, found no enemy forces south of Osly, on our side of the Aisne. Musketeer Skalecki swam the Aisne and identified French security positions. On 22 August, the expert patrol leader, Lt Licht, was killed in the trenches in front of Nouvron, shot in the stomach. The 13 Brigade came under the control of 8 ID, which ordered II/ 66 to move to Tancourt near Vauxrezis as division reserve. The brigade commander became so ill he had to relinquish command to the IR 66 commander, Colonel Freiherr von Quadt, with Major Knauff assuming command of the regiment.

On the evening of 24 September, the enemy attacked the corps left flank. II/ 66 was alerted to support Fusilier Regiment 36, and 7 and 8/ 66 marched to Pasly. They were, however, not engaged, and spent a rather cold night in the open. II/ 66 used the few days of rest for combat training and, for the replacements, refresher live-fire training on a specially constructed firing range. On 25 September, III/ 66 was relieved in its position at Nouvron by a mixed battalion from IR 165 and returned to 13 Brigade. Res. Lt Wodepuhl (then a one-year officer candidate in 12/ 66) remembered an amusing incident:

In the middle of September we were billeted in a farmyard in Cuisy. Two kilometres towards the enemy, separated from us by a deep meadow, were several small farms with chickens. The meadow was under continual enemy artillery fire. Regardless, the important thing was the chickens. If a man was willing to give his life for a couple bottles of wine, as later a comrade did in Blagny (he tried to get across a street to get to the wine, in spite of the fact that he knew it to be closely watched and covered by rifle fire), others were ready to put their lives on the line for a couple of chickens. So let's go! But we had to carry a ladder with us, to get over a five-metre high wall. Just like the fire department! One man on the front of the ladder, one behind. Two more to take over when the first team gets tired. 'Go!, Go!'. The French peasant gaped as our heads appeared above his wall. Now we had to barter. He wanted two francs for a chicken, but we were only willing to pay a mark. Two men negotiated, while the other three were already in the chicken coop and stuck ten chickens in a sack. We couldn't come to terms with the Frenchman, which was fine by us, because we had gotten them a lot more cheaply. When we parted company with him, the chickens were already down in the meadow. We left him the ladder as a small compensation, but the ingrate complained anyway. Now to prepare the chickens. Plucking them was too much work, so we skinned them like rabbits, which was quick and easy. Add leek, carrots, onion, potatoes and apple sauce. In a circle of friends in any decent *Gaststätte* today, such a dish would cost a minimum of three marks; then it only cost us a ladder. When we suddenly had to move to the position at Nouvron, we took the apple sauce along in the mess kit on our packs. Most of it ran out, but at least we hadn't thrown it away. The situation at Nouvron was, for that stage in the war, tricky. We lay for six days in a half-dug trench without bomb-proof shelters, and after we were relieved we were not a little proud of ourselves.

The day of 27 September, a Sunday, brought a break from the daily routine and gave us hope that the time of waiting was over and that the regiment could take an active part in the coming decisive actions. The IV AK was pulled out of the line. II/ 66 marched at 1500 to Juvigny to form the army reserve with two companies of Fusilier Regiment 36, a company of IR 93 and a battery from FAR 75, all under Major Knauff. At 2100, I/ 66 was relieved in place by RIR 66. The regiment (minus II/ 66) marched under Major Schmidt to Blérancourt.

12

THE BATTLE OF ARRAS

The Attack on the Villages, 28 September to 12 October 1914

After the retreat from the Marne, OHL was unable to resume the offensive. The first elements, transferred with 6th Army HQ from the left wing in Lorraine to the right in Flanders, had to be employed to plug holes in the defensive front. With the remaining elements, the OHL tried to conduct a large-scale attack, in conjunction with the right wing of 1st Army. After initial successes, on 27 September it was halted by strong enemy forces on the line Bapaume–Roye. The 6th Army right flank (XIV AK) was protected only by cavalry. The Guard Corps, IV AK and I Bavarian RK were pulled out of the line and marched to extend the 6th Army right flank. They were to attack north of Bapaume towards Arras against the flank of the French Army.

IV AK marched north on 28 August from the Aisne in two columns towards its assigned sectors in the 6th Army front. IR 66, as an element of 7 ID, reached Quesmy and Maucourt on 28 September and Mouchy–Lagache on 29 September. On 30 September, the regiment reached Péronne, which it had taken only four weeks previously. What disappointments lay behind us in these thirty days! The unbelievable marches, which in the end were in vain, the great battle on the Ourcq and the awful defensive battle on the Aisne, which every member of the regiment was happy to have left. After two days of marching, the faces were happier. The disgusting intestinal sickness had stopped. The clear autumn weather and renewed movement raised hopes. During the march on 30 September, there were continually shrapnel clouds and cannon fire on the western horizon, which did nothing to dampen the good mood. That evening the regiment reached Ligny-Tilloy. II/ 66, which had been in army reserve,

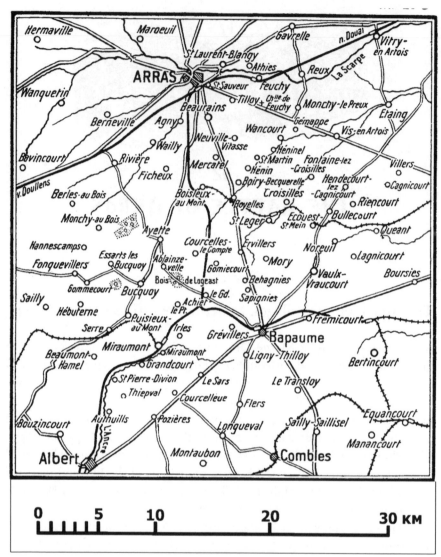

SCALE

marched for several days through Vézaponin and Ham, reaching Sailly-Saillisel on 30 September. Major Knauff resumed command of the regiment. Here, on the right flank of XIV RK, it wasn't so peaceful as on the march quarters of the last few days. Security had to be put out, because enemy forces were supposed to be advancing towards the German right flank. We expected to be in contact the next day.

On 1 October, 7 ID assembled at Bapaume, deployed an advance guard and moved in the direction of Frémicourt, Vaulx-Vraucourt, Ecoust St Mein. IR 66, order of march III, I, II, was at the front of the main body. A thin fog restricted visibility. At 1100, there was a halt at Ecoust St Martin. The advance guard was at Fontaine les Croisilles, in contact with enemy cavalry at Chérisy, which it drove off, but then hit resistance which brought the advance to a complete halt. The IV AK deployed to attack, initially with 7 ID committing 13 Brigade. IR 26 was to take Wancourt, IR 66 was to advance with I, III and the MG Company as far as Héninel and St Martin; by 1600, they had reached Fontaine. II/ 66, under Capt. Knaths, was division reserve. Lt Blume was transferred to IR 165 to be their MG Company commander: he was not happy to leave his company and the regiment.

The advance was preceded by a weak cavalry screen, which reported that the enemy occupied the villages: III/ 66 was ordered to probe towards them. Capt. Schleusener committed 11/ 66 under Res. First Lt Hagedorn against Héninel and 10/ 66 under Capt. Ulfert against St Martin. Major Knauff accompanied 10/ 66 mounted, along with Lt Redlich (Richard) and the regimental adjutant. As 10/ 66 passed over the protection of the high ground it took well-aimed artillery fire, which forced it to the ground. Major Knauff considered that attacking across the open slope down to the villages at the bottom was not very smart, so he ordered 10/ 66 to screen St Martin. He galloped back over the hill, followed by enemy fire, which wounded several of the staff horses. He had decided to take Héninel, using the entire regiment.

Capt. Schleusner sent out patrols to reconnoitre Héninel. A battalion bicyclist, Klinke from 9/ 66, had boldly ridden into Héninel, completely surprising the French, whom he thought were not very strong. It was now dusk, and Major Knauff decided to conduct a night attack, deploying III/ 66 to the left of the road to the village, I/ 66 to the right. The rifles were unloaded, bayonets fixed. When Major Knauff gave the signal, the village was to be assaulted, with the troops shouting 'Hurrah!' and the musicians playing the charge. The approach march proceeded in silence, no one said a word, only the weapons and mess kits clacked dully. The outline of the village appeared at the bottom of the hill, and it was quiet. Some wire around the enclosures had to be cut. Shouting and horns could be heard in the distance: IR 26 attacking Wancourt. Now it was our turn: a screaming mass of men charged forwards, reached the village, but not a shot was fired and there was no enemy to be seen. We later learned that the French had left shortly before our attack. Some houses were set on fire to provide illumination: we still couldn't believe that there were no French here. The units were disorganised by the charge, but quickly reassembled.

Major Knauff used the fact that the regiment was encouraged by its easy victory to send Capt. Schleusener with 9, 11 and 12/ 66 against St Martin, while I/ 66 occupied the north and west sides of Héninel. After an hour of dead

silence, first several shots
were heard from the
direction of St Martin,
then serious firing. Major
Knauff was at the edge of
the village, listening. He
trusted Capt. Schleusener
and was certain that he
would ask for help if necessary. In any case, in the
pitch-dark night it was not
clear where help should
be sent. In fact, III/ 66 had
accomplished its mission
with a bold attack. Capt.
Schleusener committed
all three companies, 12/ 66
under Res. Lt Weck along
the stream, 11/ 66 under
Res. First Lt Hagedorn
north of the road and 9/
66 under Capt. Niemeyer

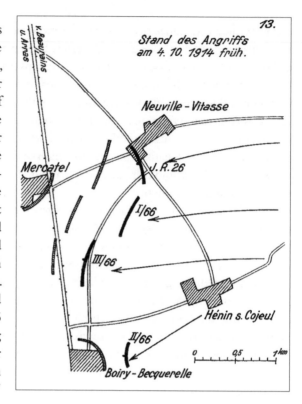

south of it. The attack from this direction surprised the enemy, who, after a short,
desperate resistance, was quickly overrun with a bayonet charge; those that did
not run away were captured. III/ 66 lost five dead and twenty-four wounded,
including Lt Hosmann. While still in contact with the enemy, III/ 66 prepared the
north and west sides of St Martin for defence, where the companies rested. This
relatively easy success would be followed by more difficult days.

IV AK was in a meeting engagement. The next day, 2 October, 8 ID would
attack on the right, 7 ID on the left, with IR 26 attacking in the north from
Wancourt towards Neuville-Vitasse and IR 66 in the south, towards Hénin,
with the right flank moving over the crossroads between Neuville and Hénin,
the Spiderweb. Initially, Major Knauff committed only 1/ 66 under Major
Schmidt; III/ 66, which was far to the front, would wait in St Martin until the
attack had reached its position. There was a heavy fog. The regimental staff
rode forward to the Spiderweb. Major Schmidt deployed 1, 3 and 4/ 66 south
of Neuville-Vitasse. The commander of the light howitzer section of FAR
40, Major de Greiff, arrived and asked for instructions for fire support. At this
point, there was no enemy to be seen, nor even the elements of 1/ 66 which
moved over the high ground. Patrols had taken fire, but the enemy's strength
and location were unclear.

Light wind blew off the fog and revealed the attack zone. The trees, houses and church tower of Neuville became clearly visible. There was small-arms fire from the right, which had to be IR 26 making contact. There was also fire from the other side of the high ground where the forward elements of I/ 66 were lying down. Major de Greiff's batteries took Neuville under fire. 'We want to give the town and church tower a good pounding' he said to his battery commanders.

Majors Knauff and de Greiff stood together on the high ground, observing with periscopic sights and binoculars; when shrapnel exploded over them everybody jumped back into a sunken road, which the French artillery held under continual fire. There was steady small-arms fire forward. Wounded moved to the rear, in the direction of Héninel, under their own power or being carried. From the high ground it was not possible to determine much about how the fight was going. Now and then individuals in the sugar beet fields and feedlots would jump up and rush forward, but it appeared that the enemy return fire was damned strong. The artillery tried to help, continually searching the terrain for the enemy infantry. While standing at noon by his periscopic sight, Major de Greiff was hit by shrapnel in the eye and killed.

A patrol under Corporal Helling from I/ 66 found the IR 26 firing line. Reinforcements from I/ 66 were therefore able to come forward and put very destructive flanking fire on the French, allowing the frontal attack to advance. The corporal said:

Since we had no contact with IR 26 on our right, Reserve Officer Candidate Weise sent Helling out on patrol with Musketeer Nowak II and another reservist. We moved out along a sunken road. The fog began to lift, so that it was possible to see about 100 metres. The patrol had hardly gone 300 metres when it saw three French riflemen in the sunken road. Our patrol gave a loud yell, advanced with levelled bayonets and the French quickly raised their hands. They were disarmed and the reservist led them back to the company. Apparently the French had waited for this historic moment in order to save their skins. Nowak and Helling went further on to the right. The fog had pretty much disappeared, but there still was no contact with IR 26. Both men were suddenly made aware of a sunken road 300 metres away, full of French infantry and several MG, conducting a heavy fire against IR 26 at Wancourt. An entire platoon of IR 26 lay in skirmisher line in an open field, mown down, as we later learned. Since we could easily put flanking fire on the sunken road, Nowak quickly went back to the company to get reinforcements. Sergeants Weise and Berth and their men came quickly, on command fired a salvo, followed by rapid fire. Surprised, the French fell into a wild panic. Many of them tried to run several hundred metres to high ground. It was like shooting hares. Many waved handkerchiefs in surrender. Practically none of them got away with a whole skin, because the sunken road was so packed that every round hit. We took thirty to forty prisoners, generally wounded. The majority were dead, being hit two to four times. We had one casualty, Sergeant Berth, who was hit by a ricochet in the chest. The fog had lifted completely and the sun shone down brightly on the battlefield, which stretched to the left and right for kilometres. From the deep sunken road, the French had been able to dominate the entire area and inflict heavy casualties, particularly since the fog prevented the artillery from firing in support, but the pressure was now off IR 26. Now the attack began along the entire line, the beginning of the six-day Battle of Arras.

Nowak and Helling were later awarded the Iron Cross II Class.

A patrol led by Res. Lt Seldte, and including the MG platoon of Staff Sergeant Theuerkauf and several squads of 4/ 66, had similar results. It began by driving off French troops in no-man's-land. Several French companies tried to attack from Neuville, but were cut down by MG fire.

1/ 66 made several bounds forward, but was so heavily shelled by French artillery that the advance brought exceptionally heavy casualties. Many sought cover in the numerous sunken roads, from where they conducted an intense firefight. At about 1300, Major Schmidt was able to report that his companies were gaining ground slowly but steadily. He extended the line on the left with an additional company. For the meantime, there was no reason for the regimental commander to intervene, so the regimental staff went to III/ 66 at St Martin.

Early that morning, Capt. Schleusener had received the order to hold in place, until 1/ 66 and IR 26 had come level to it. III/ 66 had therefore dug-in at the edge of St Martin behind hedges and walls and was in a firefight with enemy forces dug-in on the Héninel–Neuville road. 10/ 66 rejoined the battalion during the night. The village of Hénin to the left front prohibited any movement. But in order to prepare for the eventual attack, Major Knauff brought forward the uncommitted MG platoons. They moved down the road at a gallop, under artillery fire, and found overwatching positions under the roofs of the houses at the edge of town.

II/ 66, in reserve, had detached two companies to be corps HQ guard, which did not return until the next morning. The remaining two companies quartered in Fontaine with heavy security at the entrances to the village. To the left, IR 27, on the right wing of 14 Brigade, moving from the south, had unsuccessfully attacked Hénin, which the French had fortified. At 1300 on 2 October, the II/ 66 commander, Capt. Knaths, was ordered to march to Croisilles to support IR 27. When he reported at 1345 to Colonel von Below, the IR 27 commander, he was told to, 'Advance concealed and attack Hénin from the east. IR 27 is attacking from the south. Establish contact.' The battalion moved behind security elements. On the road 500m south of St Martin, the attack order was issued. The battalion deployed three companies in line in skirmisher order and advanced at 1600, taking fire, and passed through III/ 66, which was left and right of the St Martin–Hénin road, 500m from Hénin. On the right, 8/ 66 moved behind hedges and through roadside ditches to the entrance to the village, escaping the enemy fire and closing the distance quickly. The 5 and 7/ 66 had to advance by bounds over an open sugar beet field and took murderous fire, which became so strong that they were taking heavy casualties and no one dared lift their nose out of the field. Capt. Knaths committed elements of 6/ 66 and it suffered the same fate. A tremendous firefight developed. Lt Thesing from FAR 40 brought two guns forward. The brave gunners pushed their pieces down the road and blasted away at the houses from close range. With this fire support, 8/ 66 was able to break into the village. Houses caught fire and illuminated the gathering dusk. Now the French fire became unsteady. Capt. Knaths committed the last elements of the battalion and ordered the assault. Res. Lt Thierkopf wrote:

Finally! What's that? Men yelling 'Hurrah!'. Like devils, men come up from behind us over the sugar beet field with fixed bayonets, carrying all forward with them. Rifles are firing as though the gates of hell had opened, bullets whistle … Forwards, comrades, help has arrived. We are up on our feet, race forwards, I've drawn my sword and run with them, with only one thought: forwards into the crack and roar of the shells. Smack! Just as I lift my leg my calf is cut in half. I stumble, fall and am on the ground again.

Res. Lt Thierkopf, one of the bravest officers of 1914, who had already been wounded at Le Cateau, was hit twice more, and to the sorrow of the entire battalion, was no longer fit for combat. The young Officer Candidate Weber was killed. Capt. Knaths was wounded. But the assault succeeded, and 5, 7 and elements of 6/ 66 entered the burning village. But now the real fight began against brave, determined Alpine troops in each house and farmyard, with the church and its walled enclosure the centre of resistance. It was bitter street fighting; the French fired from under the roofs, from cellars and trees. Lt Theising's two guns from FAR 40 provided close-range fire support, and towards evening two platoons of MG entered the fight. The commander of 8/ 66 wrote:

The men were falling left and right, so I took the company into gardens to the right of the road and assembled it behind one of the first houses. Next to me, one of my recruits from 1913/ 14, Schröder, was wounded in the hand. At the same time I was hit in the upper left arm, and my capable range estimator, Corporal Knaust, patched me up. Now we went through the gardens. To make matters worse, we started taking fire from the high ground north of the village. The enemy withdrew to the south-west side of the village and prepared for a long fight by barricading himself in houses and behind walls. It was 1800 when Lt Rieger, the commander of 6/ 66, and I assembled part of the battalion behind a barn. We had heard that the battalion commander, Capt. Knaths, had been wounded in the foot during the assault. The units had become completely intermixed; we even had troops from IR 165. Anyone who was not wounded but unaccounted for was with 5 and 7/ 66 left of the road. A patrol sent forward by Lt Rieger came back literally with bloody noses, saying that they had gone only twenty metres before they were fired on from a heavily manned wall.

In spite of tough resistance, the attack made progress. Doors were broken down with rifle butts, holes made in walls and houses. Res. Senior Sergeant Joschkowitz succeeded in getting an MG and a handful of infantry into a house and put flanking fire on the thickly occupied wall, so that not an Alpine soldier escaped unharmed and the way was clear for our own infantry. As always, the fights in a village dissolved into individual actions. Success was only possible through a common determination to win. By 2300, the village had been cleared, with the exception of the north-western and south-western corners, the church and churchyard, which was heavily fortified. A continuation of the fight in the dark did not promise success. Since elements of IR 27 and IR 165 took part in the fight, there was an unnecessary concentration of troops. II/ 66 was therefore ordered to assemble at the entrance to the village. It dug in to the north of the village, ate supper and spent the night freezing, listening to occasional firing. The assault cost II/ 66 eighteen dead and seventy wounded. Capt. Paulus, previously the 3/ 66 commander, took over the battalion command. Battalion Surgeon Banke and his medical personnel worked through the night to bandage the many wounded.

The division order for 3 October called for a vigorous continuation of the attack. IR 26 was to take Neuville and the enemy position to the south of it. IR 66 was to attack between Hénin and Mercatel. For IR 66, this meant that I/ 66 had to come forward. That was not going to be easy, as it had to cross relatively open terrain to come up level with III/ 66. Slowly and with difficulty, continually taking casualties, it advanced. But by noon it was clear that the I/ 66 attack could last days unless a means were found to give it assistance.

Major Knauff and Capt. Schleusner used the morning to reconnoitre the enemy position. II/ 66 continued the attack in Hénin successfully. But it had enough to do in its own sector, and was unable to assist I/ 66. Capt. Lyons, who had just arrived with his battalion from IR 27, was asked to attack north from Hénin in order to take the French in the flank and run them out of their trenches. He did so, but came under flanking fire from the west himself, and Capt. Lyon's attack quickly came to a halt. Corporal Charles, 7/ 66, a tall former Foreign Legionnaire, ran from the cover of one tree to another to pull back wounded men.

Major Knauff recognised that, aside from Hénin, the attack threatened to come to a standstill. Since nothing could be done on the flanks, there was no other alternative to a frontal attack. Enemy trenches could be seen along the Hénin–Neuville road, the main point of the enemy resistance. Frequently, men could be seen going back to a hollow to get food and ammunition. The men of III/ 66 had been firing at the trenches and at any movement all day, along with the four MG of Lts Richard Redlich and Seldte, positioned in the attics of houses. The other two MG were with I/ 66. Major Knauff decided to break through here with III/ 66.

At the edge of the village, he discussed the attack with Capt. Schleusner. III/ 66 was to take the Hénin–Neuville road and the position behind it, putting pressure on the French to the north and those still in Hénin, and allowing I/ 66 to come forward and link up. The attack would be supported by the four MG and two artillery pieces. At the same time, II/ 66 and the 14 Brigade companies would increase the pressure in Hénin. Capt. Schleusner briefed his company commanders, the companies occupied an attack position at the edge of the village behind hedges and walls, and the guns set up on the north exit from St Martin. The barrels of the MG were pushed through the roof tiles of the houses. Capt. Schleusner called out, 'Niemeyer ready? Ulfert ready? Weck, Hagedorn ready?' When they replied in the affirmative, he said, 'Good, then in God's name, let's go!'

The companies moved into the open through lanes cut through the hedges and breaches made in the walls, and in a long bound moved 200m forward. The MG covered the trenches with intense fire, the canon put shrapnel after shrapnel over them and into the tops of the trees lining the road. The attack was carried forward with reckless daring. The lines of skirmishers advanced by bounds, lying down to fire, then springing forward fearlessly in the enemy fire. Many did not rise again, many went back to the rear with bloody wounds. One line reached the wire around a field, the wire cutters were quickly at work and the troops once again sprang up and ran forward. The enemy infantry recognised what was happening and fired rapidly, and the bullets chirped and sang and cracked. Two enemy batteries fired from the north-west on the edge of the village, and the fragments of the wall rose up in red clouds. Then they fired into the houses; the crew of one MG had just brought the gun down to ground level as a shell destroyed the roof. But the enemy fire support was too late. Lt Barnes came back to Major Knauff to report that the enemy position was completely in our hands and the enemy to our front had fled. The only further resistance was on the right flank, where Lt Borchert and men from 9 and 12/ 66 were engaged with the enemy in a destroyed mill. Thanks to the bravery of the officers and men of III/ 66, the attack had succeeded. But the losses were heavy, and three officers were wounded.

At the same time, II/ 66 had completed a difficult task in Hénin. Capt. Paulus had led it to the middle of the main road in the village, where he met elements of IR 165 and 1/ Engineer Battalion 4. The enemy still held part of the village, had dug himself in behind the sturdy wall of a park, barricaded the streets and put MG in the church tower. Early in the afternoon, 5 and 6/ 66 attacked the park wall, 7 and 8/ 66 were in reserve to the right of the road. An artillery piece set up on the street and fired at point-blank range at the church and houses. Officer Candidate Rossbach was killed by friendly fire from the gun as he ran to warn IR 165. Capt. Paulus ordered Lt Theising from FAR 40 to support the attack by directing the fire from his two guns against the church. The companies moved forward from house to house, through gardens and breaches quickly smashed through walls, taking fire from several directions. But now the battalion had the support of the engineers. Lt Dittmar, an engineer officer, described the house-to-house fight:

> The IR 66 men attacked to the right of the main street, IR 165 to the left. Each was reinforced by two squads of engineers, equipped with explosive charges from the company equipment wagon. With several charges strapped together, we were able to provide more effective support than previously. A charge blew a sufficiently large hole in the choir of the church. Another was set off in the wall of a stable. We went inside, carefully removed some roof tiles, and saw a few paces to the right a line of Frenchmen behind a garden wall, putting heavy fire against IR 66 men advancing on the Hénin–Neuville road. Our fire, at a range of twenty metres from the nearest Frenchman, caught them completely by surprise, forced them to flee at once. We pushed into the courtyard of a large farm and several shots were fired at us from the entrance gate. A massive dovecote in the courtyard gave us a certain amount of cover. Several engineers and IR 66 assault column followed me with fixed bayonets into the farm, which was empty. As we opened a window facing onto the street, we saw about fifty Alpine troops run from the wall of the churchyard into the last houses of the village. We fired until the barrels of our rifles glowed. It was an unforgettable picture: the brave sons of the Savoy Alps running in their steel-blue uniforms, big berets and short capes, not a stone's throw away from us. Several fell to our fire; a brave Frenchman crawled back to carry a badly wounded comrade, and we did not fire at him. The assault column following us, IR 66 and 165 men, stacked up in the narrow village

lane between the farm and the church. Other advancing elements cleared out the gardens and farms. Many prisoners were taken, from the 14th Alpine Battalion and 25th Infantry Regiment, generally big, bearded men, sons of the Alps and Brittany.

There was still a great deal of small-arms fire from the western part of the village. At 1930, Lt Winckler received an order for 8/ 66 to push through to the edge of the village. The company advanced along the main village street with fixed bayonets, illuminated by houses that had been set on fire. At the church they climbed over an abandoned barricade, beyond which the road divided left and right, and just 20m beyond that a heavily occupied barricade. Lt Winkler ordered 'Charge! Charge! Hurrah!', advanced a few paces and was hit in both legs and the elbow. Lying on the road, fully conscious, he yelled encouragement to his troops, 'Forwards, 8th Company!', and then was carried back by his range estimators. Res. Capt. Schroeder led both 7 and 8/ 66 to a successful conclusion of the fight, storming three barricades, reaching the west end of the village at 2330. The attack on 3 October cost the battalion four dead and twenty-one wounded.

During the course of the afternoon, I/ 66 also made progress. The 3/ 66 under Res. Lt Knickmeyer advanced the furthest. All the companies took heavy casualties. In 2/ 66, Officer Candidate Brandenstein was killed, in 1/ 66 Lt Henze was badly wounded. Late in the evening, the pressure from III/ 66 forced the enemy to evacuate the position in front and on the left flank of I/ 66, which was able to make contact with III/ 66 to its left.

At dusk, Major Knauff walked down the III/ 66 line, and decided to exploit the success of this difficult day by pursuing the defeated enemy with a night attack. The brigade commander approved and ordered IR 26 to also attack. Major Knauff ordered I/ 66 to attack at 2400, with III/ 66 joining in, making contact with 2/ 66, where the regimental staff would be. The regimental adjutant, Lt Korfes, described the attack:

The attack began at midnight on 4 October. The companies went quietly over the sugar beet fields. Suddenly the French signal to attack was sounded by clarions loud and clear in the night, then silenced by heavy rifle fire in the direction of Neuville. We hesitated for a moment, but since all was quiet in front of us, we continued to move forward. I was on the left flank of 2/ 66, in the middle of the company was Major Knauff, Capt. Bergansky and a platoon of IR 165 under Lt Krüger, the regiment's only reserve. When we reached III/ 66 on our left it moved out also, and I rejoined Major Knauff. We crossed the sunken Hénin–Neuville road at the mill ruin and continued the march. About 150 metres further on, we noticed that the skirmisher line had halted, and some incomprehensible shouts were heard. We moved forward and some men said, 'The French are in front of us' and others said, 'They want to surrender.' If we had advanced onto the French trenches at once, we would have avoided the unfortunate events that now followed. At the same instant we were hit by a wave of fire from the front and side at close range, not farther than 50m, that cut down a line of men. We immediately threw ourselves down, shaken and enraged that we had given the enemy a half a minute head start. Major Knauff and I were lying in the firing line, for now without a rifle. Knauff tried to get the men to go forwards, ordered a trumpeter to blow the charge, in vain: no voice could be heard over this din.

Our men fired into the darkness, without being able to see anything more than the enemy muzzle flashes. Capt. Bergansky's company lay with the right flank bent slightly back. They were also firing, but rarely in the right direction. I could also hear the two MG of Sergeant Theuerkauf begin to fire, probably in the wrong direction, too. If anything would help, it was to get Bergansky's men and the MG firing in the right direction, which Knauff set out to accomplish, sending the trumpeter lying next to him, but he was soon hit. Then he sent First Sergeant Schwerdt, who was lying quite close to us; he was shot in the heel. I jumped up in the direction where I thought Bergansky must be, threw myself down between two men, asked where Bergansky was, and was told he was off to the right. I soon found him and transmitted the regimental commander's order. He energetically raised himself up somewhat and in a clear and strong voice, as though he were conducting training at the Schroteplatz Local Training Area back home, yelled: 'Everybody here, Company Bergansky. Get up! Move!' He ran off into the darkness, which swallowed up him and his men.

Major Knauff and I lay next to each other, with First Sergeant Schwerdt and to the left and right several men. Everyone had a rifle and fired into the darkness. We tried to dig into the dirt with hands and elbows, and packed thick sugar beets on top of the thin soil. The spike on my helmet was shot off. Due to casualties, our fire was getting weaker, and first one MG was put out of action, then the other. If the enemy fire died down, groaning, screaming and cries for help could be heard.

It went on like this for hours. We waited for help from 1/ 66, which must be to the right with three companies, or III/ 66, which should have gone past us long ago, but we couldn't hear a thing. Finally, Major Knauff said: 'One of us has to get out of here and find some help, or in the daylight we're all dead.' I thought for a short while. The enemy fire seemed to be weaker to the left; perhaps the enemy position ended there. So to get out of the enemy fire as soon as possible I had to go left. A quick decision and I'm off, running behind our skirmisher line at a pace probably faster than I ever had before, and after 100 metres I'm out of the zone of fire. I later saw that a bullet had gone through my coat. I reached a steep slope and took a quick breather, then quickly back to the Neuville–Hénin sunken road, where I found 1/ 66.

After he had lost contact with 2/ 66, and due to the uncertain situation, Major Schmidt had kept 1, 3 and 4/ 66 in the sunken road. Major Schmidt immediately sent 4/ 66 under Capt. Trenk forward to support 2/ 66. Lt Wagner, with the leading troops of 4/ 66, took the enemy trenches in the flank and poured fire into them. At dawn, 2 and 4/ 66 assaulted the enemy trenches and took the rest of their garrison prisoner – about 200 men. Only now could the casualties in 2/ 66 be determined. The brave Capt. Bergansky had been killed, Res. Lt Mirre and First Sergeant Schwerdt severely wounded. The largest part of the company was dead or wounded. The MG Company had also taken heavy casualties. Both MG had been shot up, the platoon leader, Res. Senior Sergeant Theuerkauf, was killed, along with a gunner and several men, almost all of the rest of the crews wounded. The leader of the attached platoon from IR 165, Lt Krüger, was killed, along with many of his men.

The death of Capt. Bergansky was an irreplaceable loss for the regiment. His quiet and refined manner, his determined and energetic will, his intelligence and troop-leading ability, made him one of the most capable officers in the regiment. He could have served on a high-level staff, but he held it to be more honourable to lead his company in the field. In this conviction, that in the hour of greatest danger an officer belongs with his troops, he died as a paragon for all officers, an example for every member of the regiment.

The French had succeeded in pushing back into the village of Neuville. To protect the right flank and to support the heavily engaged IR 26, Major Schmidt found it necessary to swing 1 and 3/ 66 towards Neuville. He then put himself, along with Res. First Lt Laue, at the head of 1/ 66 and attacked the south side of Neuville. The bold attack succeeded in throwing out the French and occupying the southern part of Neuville. The company remained there the rest of the day, while IR 26 cleared out the village. In the morning, 3/ 66 extended to the south the line being held by 2 and 4/ 66 on the high ground; 2 and 3/ 66 were fused into one company under Res. Lt Knickmeyer.

Capt. Schleusener and III/ 66 had also won a significant success. He had attacked at the same time as 1/ 66 and initially met no resistance. After an 800m advance, they encountered an occupied enemy trench, which they assaulted and captured. They continued the attack into the dark night. A few hundred metres further on, at the side of a road, they overran a second trench, then a third; they had already taken several hundred prisoners. Confused French continually appeared, individually or in mobs, moving forwards or back. Schleusner stopped the battalion and had it dig-in just in front of Mercatel; the battalion was completely alone and further advance was pointless. During the night attack, Res. Lt Haack from 10/66 was killed. At dawn, it took fire from the rear; a French trench had been bypassed. Several NCOs and men of 11/66 attacked to the rear to deal with them, and these French, too, were captured. Sergeant Stackmann described the III/66 night attack:

Our attack was prepared in dead silence in order to surprise the French and break into his position without a shot being fired. Our approach in the quiet of the night must be detected sooner or later; because we had already shown ourselves to be very aggressive, we would have to assume that the French would be watching carefully. Regardless of how careful we were, there were going to be noises, perhaps from stumbling. The order to unload the weapons was carried out very reluctantly by the troops, because it would be a disadvantage if, when we conducted our assault, the French did not run away. Even in close quarters, a loaded rifle was quicker than a bayonet. After synchronising our watches, we began the attack on schedule, advancing at a walk as quietly as possible, cross-country in the direction of the assumed enemy position. Fifty to 100m in front of the Mercatel–Hénin road, we took heavy small-arms fire from the enemy position, which forced us to immediately fall flat on the ground. After a short time the fire died down; now there could be no delay, everywhere the order went up, 'Get up! Charge!', the musicians sounded the well-known assault signal and shouting 'Hurrah!' we went over the road and into the enemy in a roadside ditch deepened into a trench. When the first of the assaulting troops got to the trench, only a few of the French stood fast. They must not have had much ammunition left; I was advancing alone when I ran into a squad of French in the roadside ditch, and they didn't shoot but received me with outstretched bayonets; from their deep trench they could not accomplish anything with the bayonet. They probably thought it was dumb to surrender or run away from one man, so they remained in the defensive bayonet position, and I put a bullet from my pistol into each of them. At this point I thought it better to go back and get some help, but there was no one in the area. I assumed that by now the trench would be empty, so I went back and on closer inspection in the dark saw a Frenchman in the right corner who had enough courage to defend himself. I attempted to get at him with my sword, but he blocked all my cuts and thrusts with his bayonet. In the excitement I had forgotten to reload my pistol. There was nothing for it but to step back a few paces and put a strip of bullets into the magazine. By now the trench was pretty much in our possession. After I had crossed over the trench, I could see the French, recognisable in their red trousers, were moving off into the darkness. In the general noise, the voice of Sergeant Wesemann was easy to hear; it appeared that he was in close-quarters combat with someone. As I came closer I could see that he was wrestling with a determined Frenchman, and when Wesemann, who was quite strong, stumbled the Frenchman succeeded in actually getting on top him, and he could not get loose until the other soldiers pulled the Frenchman off him.

When we continued the advance we found the second-line trench empty. They had only begun work on it, it was only as deep as a shovel and in many places the earth had not even been broken. Apparently the French had been digging even as we had arrived. A little farther on, Sergeant Wesemann, some of his men and I came upon the middle of a short but deep sunken road running diagonally from left to right to our direction of advance. At the same time a number of our people somewhat to the left rear found an entrance to the sunken road. The French who had taken cover in the sunken road opened fire on our men in it, inflicting casualties; those of us on the top of the slope became aware of this when we heard the screaming and moaning of the wounded. Unfortunately, our men in the sunken road did not return the enemy fire; instead, they yelled to us that we were firing on them. I tried to climb into the sunken road and tell the men there the real situation. An enemy bullet went right past my left ear, and I was so disoriented by the air pressure and the loud crack that I dropped my pistol and only found it again after some searching in the sugar beet field in the dark. Once I got into the sunken road, I had to use personal example to convince the men of their error and get them to form up a firing line and open fire. We didn't fire long before the enemy fire stopped; they had probably decided to withdraw. When we continued the attack the next day, we found several French dead at the far exit from the sunken road. This was the limit of our advance for the night. The disorganised companies reassembled and we defended the position we had taken. We remained here the next day, though the situation was not particularly favourable. Just as we were moving into position (it had begun to get light) one of the men in our company, moving in front of me, was shot dead. At first we could not determine where the shot came from, because there was nothing to our front. We soon figured out that it had come from the rear, from one of the first trenches that we had overrun. We had not done a good job of clearing the position and a large number of French had hidden themselves there. Apparently they had played dead, because we had seen numerous French lying both inside and outside the trench. I myself had told the men not to shoot the bodies, because I just assumed that they were dead or wounded. I had no idea that they could be dangerous to us if we spared them. Now we were in a fine mess! As soon as anyone showed himself above the leaves of the sugar beets, he drew fire. Musketeer Schallat was carrying an artillery flag, which warned the artillery of our location. While he was trying to set it up he was shot in the arm. It was practically impossible to give effective return fire, as the enemy was in a deepened roadside ditch and difficult to see, while we stood out in shallow skirmisher holes in a sugar beet field, and were easy to see if we lifted our heads to look around. In order to camouflage ourselves, we fixed sugar beet leaves on our helmets. Since we were practically inactive, several enemy detachments got up the courage to advance by bounds. I doubt they intended to attack us, but rather to slip through our thin line and disappear. In so doing, they offered us good targets, and their intention remained an experiment. An open embankment on the road we had overrun was occupied by the enemy and we were able to take them under effective fire.

At dawn on 4 October, IR 26 was still fighting in Neuville, but elements that had arrived at the same level as 1/ 66 linked up, so that there was close co-ordination between the two regiments. Suddenly, thick march columns left Neuville moving through the valley towards Mercatel. Lts Redlich and Seldte brought their four MG into position immediately and opened a fire that could not have been more effective if they had been firing gunnery qualification at the Altengrabow Major Training Area against advancing cavalry targets. The MG were firing on thick columns at 800 to 1,000m range; their effectiveness was devastating and horrifying. The French scattered, some towards Mercatel, some uphill to the north, but the pitiless fire fell on them like hail. Many black dots lay immobile, and their number continually increased, until no movement was to be seen on the fields. Only a few reached Mercatel or the safety of the high ground. Weeks later, we found an immense mass grave here, dug by the medical company.

The French artillery soon extracted revenge for this blow, taking the high ground on which 2/ 66 had bled and where the MG position had been under fire for the entire day. The MG were soon brought to safety in the sunken road, but poor 4/ 66 and the remains of 2/ 66 were shelled terribly. They bravely bit their teeth together and held out for awful hours, but their nerves were strained to the limit. The French flat-trajectory artillery could not accomplish much against the sunken road.

III/ 66, lying far forward in front of Mercatel, also took heavy artillery fire. It had disarmed more French who had appeared to its rear and conducted a firefight against the edge of Mercatel. The French escaping from the MG fire towards Mercatel had to run in front of the right wing of the battalion at 800m range. The men of III/ 66 fired on these unfortunates with great success; many remained on the ground. 'Just like driving rabbits,' said Capt. Schleusner. 'I truly felt sorry for these poor fellows.'

The French occupied Mercatel and the road to Boiry-Becquerelle. III/ 66 was in an excellent attack position against Mercatel, but the French artillery fire prevented daytime movement. Therefore, in accordance with a brigade order, I/ 66 attacked Mercatel in coordination with IR 26 at dusk, at 1800, while III/ 66 attacked French troops on the Mercatel-Boyelles road. The IR 66 commander had already moved to the III/ 66 position; III/ 66 did not wait until I/ 66 came up to his level before he began the attack. The battalion immediately reached the road, but heavy flanking fire from Mercatel brought the advance to a halt, and Capt. Schleusner was severely wounded in the neck; a great loss for the regiment. Capt. Niemeyer assumed command of the battalion, and ordered it to dig in, with special attention being given to the direction of Mercatel.

I/ 66 and IR 26 had closed on the east side of Mercatel. The IR 26 attack along the Mercatel–Neuville road collapsed with severe losses. I/ 66 encountered such serious resistance just short of the vegetable gardens that it halted and dug-in there, although the left flank succeeded in linking up with III/ 66 on the road. Without artillery support, a continuation of the attack was impossible, but artillery could not fire at night, so the attack was put off until the next day.

At 0430 on 4 October, II/ 66 received the order to take Boiry-Becquerelle. The 7 and 8/ 66 deployed east of the village and moved out, but soon took fire into the left flank, which slowed progress until the flanking position was taken by IR 27 to the south. The commander of IR 27 ordered the battalion to march to Boyelles, where it quartered in a sugar factory. After 5/ 66 was committed, then 6/ 66 extended the 7/ 66 line to the right, the battalion attacked a trench 600m in front of Boiry, and took it along with forty prisoners. The elements of the battalion moving left of the road to the town found the way to Boiry open. Right of the road was a small wood containing enemy MG, which had to be cleared out. The skirmishers approached to within 200m by bounds, taking casualties, when the enemy left their position and disappeared in a deep sunken road, presumably in autos. The enemy evacuated Boiry, and soon began shelling the town. This day the battalion lost fifteen dead and forty-seven wounded, including the battalion adjutant, the brave and cheerful Lt Barnbeck, and the experienced Officer Candidates Jansen and Westpahl.

It dawned clear and friendly on 5 October. The general exhaustion as a consequence of the recent sleepless nights was taking its toll, and for several hours it was quiet. Only when our artillery began to fire from new positions did the regiment prepare to attack, with III/ 66 to form the *Schwerpunkt*. It was reinforced by 5 and 6/ IR 26 under Capt. Rausch, and Lt Seldte's MG platoon and two light howitzers from FAR 4 under Res. Lt Lindau. Major Knauff held the attached battalion Gruson from IR 165 as his reserve behind III/ 66. Heavy German artillery fire was directed at the village, which was covered in smoke. The French artillery answered. Capt. Rausch was ordered to soften up the south side of Mercatel. The direct artillery fire succeeded in blasting away the barricades and smoking out the French. MG fire drove them back into the houses, which were then shelled. The fire of the other batteries made their stay in the village ever more uncomfortable. At 1300, we observed a march column, apparently German, west of Mercatel moving north. Later we learned that this was II/ 66, which no longer had any enemy to its front. The order was given to carefully approach Mercatel. Several scouts crossed the road and moved towards the south side of Mercatel. Enemy resistance was weak. III/ 66 immediately advanced, joined by 5 and 6/ 26. The south side of Mercatel was assaulted with cries of 'Hurrah!' Now the companies of I/ 66 rose up, accompanied by those of IR 26. The French could not withstand this attack from the south and east. The French who did not flee promptly were captured, and by 1500 the entire village was occupied. The companies assembled and took a short breather. They found supplies of wine which were a welcome reinforcement. The French were not to be seen, aside from the many dead and wounded. II/ 66 was visible from the edge of the village, on a steep slope, being shelled severely.

The brigade and division staffs arrived in Mercatel and Capt. Holscher brought an order for IR 66 to continue the attack to Beaurains. It was 1700. The regiment was to attack west of the Mercatel–Beaurains road, while 8 ID attacked on east of it. IR 66 was composed of I, III/ 66 and the MG Company (four guns). The regiment would attack with I/ 66 on the right, III/ 66 on the left, MG following behind the left flank, along with Battalion Gruson from II/ 165 and II/ 26 under Capt. Rausch. The battalions occupied an attack position on the edge of the village. They were so understrength that they could form only a thin skirmisher line. The forward movement began while it was still daylight. Major Knauff moved with the regimental staff behind I/ 66. There was weak small-arms fire and a few artillery shells landed, but the advance was not delayed. Only when I/ 66 approached to within 200m of the southern

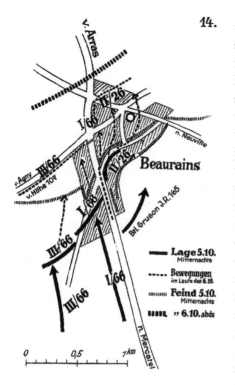

14.

tip of Beaurains did the fire become stronger, but a few rounds at close range from two light howitzers that had been brought forward quickly silenced it. I/ 66 advanced as far as the southern crossroads in Beaurains, where it came up to a thickly wooded park, took heavy small-arms fire and was stopped. Capt. Niemeyer and III/ 66 pushed beyond I/ 66 until flanking fire from the park forced it to stop, too. Acting Officer Couers (11/ III/ 66) was killed. The battalion dug in on a steep slope. Major Knauff was moving north on the main road, and at the entrance to the village met some men from Fusilier R 36, who reported that there were no enemy troops in the village. To the side some houses were burning, which provided illumination. At the southern crossroads, the regimental staff encountered French troops; Major Knauff and the adjutant, Lt Korfes, and their messengers, among them Corporal Hopfstock, 7/ 66, charged the startled French, shouting 'Hurrah!', and twenty French threw their weapons down and surrendered, while the rest fled into the darkness.

Heavy fire now came from a north-eastwards-leading side road, which made going over the crossroad impossible. The prisoners said that there were strong French forces in the village and that the troops at the southern side had probably fled. A company of IR 26 under First Lt Maenss arrived from the south on the main street, and Major Knauff oriented him on the situation. On the village street to the rear, a black clump of men appeared suddenly out of a farmyard: French or German, no one knew which. Several shouts back and forth, then they opened fire. Some of our men were hit, others opened fire. Major Knauff ordered the men to take cover, 'Right and left into the houses! Move!', and Maenss' company occupied the farms to both sides of the street, which could not be crossed because of the fire sweeping down it.

Major Knauff walked south-west out of the village on the road, taking Lt Berns with him. He recognised that taking Beaurains in the dark was going to be difficult, so he decided to surround the village. He ordered Capt. Rausch to attack along the main village street to the north, to relieve Maenss' company.

He then assembled elements of the regiment along with Gruson's to the south of Beaurains and moved north-east. II/ 26 would conduct the fight inside the village at the crossroads, I/ 66 was to penetrate into the park, III/ 66 would advance north, on the west of the village. He would move with Gruson's reinforced battalion around the village to the east. The enemy now had strong forces in the south part of the village and they kept up a heavy fire. A bullet hit Major Knauff in the neck, severing his jugular. He said to Lt Berns, 'I've been wounded', fell down and died.

Our regimental commander was dead! He was born to be a soldier and leader. Perceptive, clear-thinking, indomitably aggressive and personally brave. He identified completely with his battalion, II/ 66. He had no consideration for himself, and demanded high standards from his subordinates, who followed him blindly. He said to his battalion as it left garrison to go to war, 'My II Battalion! I am with you through thick and thin', and he carried out his word in the fullest and most serious meaning. At the end of September, he assumed command of the regiment and led it through the Battle of Arras. This difficult and costly fight showed his strength of will and heroic character in a post of great responsibility. Knauff's example inspired every man in the regiment. A few hours before his death, he was awarded the Iron Cross I Class as visible recognition of his deeds and those of the regiment. His death, in the middle of a difficult fight for the stubbornly defended Beaurains, struck the regiment hard. Every man mourned its leader.

Major Schmidt assumed command of the regiment, Capt. Trenk of I/ 66. Capt. Rausch and II/ 26 continued the fight on the main street, bringing Res. Lt Lindau's two light howitzers to the crossroads. Major Schmidt and Capt. Rausch discussed the situation. Capt. Rausch wanted to attack with his troops to the right of the village street, while IR 66 attacked to the left. No progress was made during the night and at midnight, division ordered a withdrawal from the village in order to shell it, but both Major Schmidt and Capt. Rausch refused to carry out the order.

II/ 66 marched at 1100 on 5 October as the advance guard for the 14 Brigade, from Boyelles towards Boisleux St Marc, where it deployed thin skirmisher lines and moved north. North-west of Mercatel it took heavy artillery fire for four hours. After dark, the enemy position was found, empty. The 6 and 7/ 66 were able to capture an enemy battery which was defended only with carbines. The battalion dug in to both sides of the Ayette–Arras road. It lost two men dead, eight wounded.

During the night, the battle everywhere came to a halt, and the exhausted officers and men got a few hours' sleep. With daylight on 6 October, the fight resumed. Capt. Rausch ordered the light howitzers to fire and, with Capt. Trenk, led the advance in the village by squads. The French withdrew slowly, defending each farmyard. I/ 66 gradually gained ground in the park and on the main street. A barricade on the main street had to be blown apart before the French would abandon it; that cost casualties and required considerable time. III/ 66 also advanced slowly west of Beaurains, delayed by enemy artillery fire, but effectively supported by the MG platoon of Res. Lt Seldte, as Sgt Velten described:

After we had reached the first houses we stayed to the left, grounded the MG and climbed up to the hay-and-straw loft of a large barn, in order to get a view of the terrain. We knocked out some roof tiles and, when it got lighter, we had an excellent field of observation and could see first individual enemy troops, then vehicles, mounted men and bicyclists. We quickly brought the MG up, placed them in the holes in the roof and opened continuous fire into the French flank. Our troops attacked the French from the east, and squad after squad of their troops left the cover of the houses and ran straight into our MG fire. But both guns began to have stoppages. It was not a question of a mistake on the part of the gunners. The guns fired slower and stuttered, and our platoon leader, Lt Seldte, cursed. It was frustrating: we had a wonderful target, an enemy column at 600m range, but were impotent because of stoppages we could not explain. The commander for the right gun was Sergeant Ackermann; I commanded the left gun. We furiously tried to rescue the honour of the platoon, bloodied our hands pulling the loading lever, tried every trick old MG men know, [but] nothing worked, neither Lt Seldte's anger nor our best intentions – the MG were jammed. Completely frustrated, the MG crews stood next to the guns, which apparently were on strike. According to the kindest of Lt Selde's orders, we should all go to the devil, that is, we slid down the worn steps of the hayloft with the MG. When everything was downstairs, the calm old soldier Reservist Gustav Breitner appeared with ammunition cases, late as usual. Then the shells came howling onto the roof of our hayloft and tiles, roof laths and dirt rained down on our heads. In spite of our anger, a satisfied chuckle went through the combat-experienced platoon, and even our furious platoon leader mentioned our undeserved good luck.

We could now establish the cause of our mysterious stoppages: years of dirt and dust lay deep on the floor of the hayloft, and because of our continuous fire had gotten through the ammunition belt and feeding mechanism into all the moving parts of the gun, and mixed with the gun oil and spent powder to form a thick paste that completely jammed the gun. After a thorough cleaning the guns were once again operational, but by now the French had disappeared. We were wiser for the experience and poorer for having failed to win a significant success. Or had the whim of the war god saved us from taking a devastating direct hit?

The north side of Beaurains was reached only in the course of the afternoon, where we could move rather freely; the French withdrew to the suburbs of Arras. Sectors were assigned for night defence: I/ 66 was positioned at the edge of the village to both sides of the main street; III/ 66 held the position it had reached during the day on the road Beaurains–Hill 107 (south-east of Agny); IR 26 was right of I/ 66 in the eastern part of Beaurains; II/ 26 returned to its regiment. Division pulled Battalion Gruson back to Mercatel.

On 6 October, II/ 66 put heavy fire on French troops being pushed out of Beaurains by III/ 66. During the afternoon, it advanced so boldly that it was well in front of the rest of the division and close to Agny, which was held by the French. It was then hit by heavy artillery fire, as well as MG fire from the rail embankment, and brought to a halt. II/ 66 took cover in favourably located sand pit and road ditches and dug-in, waiting for the rest of the division to arrive. There were numerous casualties, among them Officer Candidate Brenning, 5/ 66, buried by a shell: he was dug out with a broken thigh. The regiment spent the night of 6–7 October in its positions, disturbed only by French artillery harassing fire, which affected I/ 66 the most.

Higher headquarters intended to continue the attack on Arras, but soon gave it up. The next day, 7 October, was relatively quiet, with some artillery fire on the village. Lt Kleinert, the adjutant of I/ 66, was wounded by shell fragments while on the village street. Towards evening, II/ 66 was brought back to the Beaurains–Agny crossroads.

The division pulled 14 Brigade out of the line to relieve the right wing of the corps, 8 ID. IR 66 had to take over the 14 Brigade sector on the left wing of 7 ID; IR 26 assumed the IR 66 position. After dark, I/ 66 was relieved first, and marched through Guémappe to Wancourt to be division reserve. Then III/ 66 moved several hundred metres to the left, with its left flank on the main road at Point 107, the right halfway to Beaurains, where it linked up with IR 26. The battalion presented a shocking appearance: 300 men, wearing coats or with their coats over their shoulders, officers indistinguishable from the men, all unshaven and dirty. They moved in single file, their rifles slung around their necks. Almost every man carried on his back or shoulder a door or a couple of boards or planks, which they intended to use to build dugouts in the new position. The German soldier was a quick learner, and if he disliked digging-in in peacetime, he learned to do so under fire. For quite a while now, long shovels and pickaxes were to be seen, which had been found in the villages. The enemy fired a few shells in our direction. Immediately everyone lay on the ground and hid. II/ 66 deployed from the left of the main road to a deep railway cutting and found some foxholes that had already been started, which they deepened. III/ 66 had to dig their own. In the daylight, the troops were to be quiet and not move, so as not to draw fire. Major Schmidt, the commander of the

MG Company, Lt Redlich (Richard) and a MG platoon leader, Res. Lt Seldte, dug a hole in a pit behind the middle of the position, next to the road.

On the next day, 8 October, visibility extended from the position as far as Agny and beyond to the west of Arras. The enemy in our sector was quiet, but there were heavy troop concentrations arriving to the north and south of Arras, which our artillery fired on, though they were out of rifle and MG range. We had hoped that pressure from the Bavarians to the north of Arras would push the French to the south, but that did not occur. We took ineffective artillery fire, and the day passed uneventfully.

A brigade order arrived during the afternoon, stating that another attack was going to be made by 8 ID and the Prussian Guard in order to break through between Foncquevillers and Hébuterne. The staff of 13 Brigade and IR 66 were to be attached to 8 ID.

At dark, cavalrymen (mostly hussars) from 2 KD *(Kavalleriedivision* – Cavalry Division) arrived and crouched in the regiment's fighting positions, and II and III/ 66 marched off. The regiment was to quarter in Ayette, in order to march through Doucht to the woods to the west of there by early morning, which was the assembly area for the attack on Mouchy au Bois. IR 153 would attack on the right, IR 93 on the left, with heavy artillery support available. Since the enemy consisted of Territorial troops with little artillery, only weak resistance was expected. Major Schmidt dutifully reported to Colonel von Quadt, the brigade commander, that the troops were very tired and did not have the strength for a successful attack (II and III/ 66 together had only 600 men), but the order could not be changed. The regiment spent the rest of the night, only a few hours, somewhere in barns, at the best on straw.

At 0500, the regiment marched, with something less than a rosy attitude, to the concealed attack position on the west edge of a wood; the hussar security patrols posted there marched off. The village of Monchy au Bois was hidden behind a small hill and only the tops of the trees could be seen. At 0900, the artillery preparation began, with a higher expenditure of shells than usual, and we hoped that this time our attack would be adequately prepared.

Two companies of IR 26 arrived, led by Capt. Weisse, to be the sole regimental reserve. As ordered, the two battalions moved out at 1500, with II/ 66 on the left advancing directly on the village and III/ 66 on the right, and crossed the hill in a single long skirmisher line. They took weak small-arms and shrapnel fire, which did not stop the attack, and the skirmisher line entered the village or advanced to the right of it. The main street was full of dead horses, French dead in their red trousers, rubble and shell craters. Our losses were not light; Lt Goslich, a cheerful, brave young man, who to this point had only taken a bump on the head, was killed by a bullet to the head while advancing towards the village.

In the western part of the village, II/ 66 met continual rifle and MG fire. The commander of 5/ 66, First Lt Rochlitz, was surrounded and his troops had to cut their way through to him. The enemy still strongly held the church, where Capt. Paulus led the attack. Elements of IR 93 advanced along the road on the south edge of the village. Capt. Niemeyer bypassed the village, and was already west of it when he encountered heavy resistance. The neighbouring regiment on the right was at the same level. The regiment had gained a significant success, but the resistance of the Territorial troops was astounding, and we could see in their positions in the village that their casualties had been colossal, in addition to losing a large number of prisoners.

Given our casualties and the troop's exhaustion, a continuation of the attack to Berles au Bois offered no prospect of success. Capt. Niemeyer was ordered to stop and completely clear out the village. Capt. Paulus was given MG for support, IR 93 brought forward two artillery pieces, and the old game began once again. The French had to be shelled out of every garden, house or farm. But by now we had a lot of practise doing this, and the co-operation with IR 93 and the guns was effective. Nevertheless, the fight in the town lasted all night, and the village was not in our hands until morning. It had not been possible during the night to form a continuous line, and small groups gathered around their leader, some in the garden hedges, some in front of them. It was difficult to keep the security outposts awake. In front of the village, on the road to Berles au Bois, elements of III/ 66 under Lts Schulz, Kargill and Rahmlow had dug-in. Everyone was exhausted and they all must have gone to sleep, when suddenly the French appeared. They intended to retake the village with a night attack, and encountered Lt Schulz's men first and overran them. A few, including Lt Schulz, succeeded at the last second in running back to the village. Cargill and Rahmlow and many of their men were killed. The noise awakened the groups in the village, and a terrific fire began at close range, with every bullet hitting a target. The French disappeared as quietly as they had approached, with the only evidence of their night attack the silent dead or groaning wounded. 1/ and 4/ 66 arrived in Monchy, while 2 and 3/ 66 lay in the wood to the rear.

The French artillery seemed to have no doubts that Monchy au Bois had been lost, because from dawn on 10 October they began to merrily blast away at the village. There were still numerous civilians hiding in the cellars. A large portion of them had assembled in the schoolhouse under the leadership of a dynamic young schoolmistress. She resolutely appeared several times at the regimental HQ to ask for food and medical assistance for her charges. Regimental Surgeon Vial soon became a sort of village doctor. Our wounded, and the wounded French lying about, were not neglected, although the medical company had not succeeded in evacuating all of the wounded during the night.

At 1100, the positions of both battalions took heavy artillery fire, and strong concentrations of French troops at the mill between Monchy au Bois and Berles indicated that the enemy would attack. Our own attack would not be continued. The Prussian Guard had not been able to take Hébuterne, had evacuated Foncquevillers during the night, and the possession of Hassescamps was questionable and it would soon be evacuated. However, we securely held Monchy au Bois, and we did not want to give it up. Lt Redlich (Richard) set up the MG of Reserve Lt Seldte and Senior Sergeant Joschlowitz in the battalion positions, which awaited the enemy attack at the edge of the village. When the French tried to advance, they were met by annihilating fire, took heavy casualties and ran back, disappearing into Berles au Bois. There was no enemy to be seen between Monchy and Berles au Bois. The regiment, very reduced in numbers, was pleased by this success.

The shelling continued the entire day, became steadily stronger, and brought the regiment another heavy loss. The regimental staff and the MG Company were in a farmyard on the northern exit from the village which was hit by several shells in quick succession. Several NCOs and men were killed, some severely wounded, including Senior Sergeant Böning, or lightly wounded, including Reserve Lt Seldte and Senior Sergeant Joschkowitz. Nine horses were killed, and several lay in pieces on the ground. Unluckily, Lt Richard Redlich was severely wounded in the lower abdomen, and died the next day in indescribable pain, fighting to the last for his life. We mourned this outstanding officer for a considerable time, and have never forgotten this brave man and the best of comrades. The MG Company had taken such heavy casualties and so much equipment had been destroyed in the fights for St Martin and Mercatel that it was practically combat-ineffective.

First we treated the severely wounded. During this time, Senior Blacksmith Below took the initiative to make the remaining vehicles and horse teams functional. He was ably assisted by the drivers, Corporals Arndt, Herbold, Meier and Schwerin. When the first shells landed, Arndt stayed at his position, holding the horses, exactly according to regulation, even when both horses were severely wounded and fell to their knees. They succeeded in moving the vehicles to safety in the woods east of Monchy.

The bombardment continued on 11 October, at times with heavy artillery. The MG Company could only crew two guns. Reserve Lt Seldte, now the company commander, and his NCOs hastily trained infantrymen in the cellars of the village and were able to crew the four functional MG. When additional MG were received in the coming days, it was possible to crew them, too.

The day passed like the others. The battalion commanders reported that their troops were completely exhausted and asked that they be relieved. Over the telephone, the brigade headquarters told us to be patient, and acknowledged unreservedly the offensive combat power that the regiment had once again displayed. That evening, III/ 66, which had only four officers and 200 men, was replaced by 1 and 3/ 66; Captain Niemeyer and II/ 66, with 2 and 4/ 66, went to Douchy to be division reserve.

The next day, 12 October, passed without any significant occurrences. The order that the regiment would be relieved by the Guard was received with relief; everyone was happy to leave this blood-soaked village. After the fall of darkness, the Guard Regiment 3 relieved IR 66. III/ 66 and the two companies of I/ 66 marched from Douchy to Mercatel; II/ 66, 1 and 3/ 66, the MG Company and the regimental staff took quarters in Douchy and Ayette. The completely exhausted men rested from the rigours of the preceding days.

The regiment's losses from the Battle of Arras amounted to twenty-seven officers and 1,105 men. Thirteen officers, including the regimental commander, had been killed.

13

In the Trenches at Arras,
12–28 October 1914

On 13 October, III/ 66, 2 and 4/ 66 occupied a position north-west of Mercatel, with the right flank on the road to Arras and the left on the path from the Three White Houses (*Drei weiße Häuser*) to Wailly. At the same time, II/ 66, 1 and 3/ 66 were moved to Ayette and on 14 October to Mercatel.

That was the end of the war of manoeuvre for IR 66. The regiment had once again given magnificent proof of its combat power. The troops' motto in these October days had been 'Give us this day our daily village.'

But the general situation required a new form of combat operations: trench warfare. Restricted to a narrow trench, with little ability to move, often far from the enemy, and yet in combat. Although the first weeks of the initially harmless trench warfare was considered to a certain degree comfortable, it was generally held to be a passing phase. Unfortunately, the error of our assumption soon became all too clear.

The position at Mercatel was made up of foxholes linked together to form trenches, but not large enough for a squad, and unconnected to each other. During the day, enemy fire kept the men in their holes. The troops sat there, ate and drank, smoked like chimneys and tried to sleep sitting up. After dark, it was a relief to be able to move cramped limbs, and everything became active. Troops armed with large mess cans moved to a prearranged point in the rear to meet the field kitchens. Leaders went from trench to trench, oriented themselves concerning the day's observations and discussed the duty roster and security outposts. Digging at night, by stages the individual trenches were linked together, and soon a continuous trench was created. Given the very large company sectors, from 500 to 600m, and the low strength of the companies at the time, great demands were made of the troops: security and entrenching duty, and patrolling in the communication trenches between the defensive trenches. It was possible to get some rest during the day, as less security was necessary. During the day, the enemy artillery conducted harassment and interdiction fire, while at night the enemy infantry conducted sudden bursts of fire. Initially we returned fire, but later we just ignored it. It became a requirement to observe the enemy closely. The battalion sector commander reported observations four times daily. Every two days, II/ 66 and III/ 66 relieved each other in place, while two companies of I/ 66 relieved the other two. The two sector commanders were directly subordinate to the regimental staff, which was initially located in Kühnen Harras, moving in the middle of October to Mercatel. Some 580 replacements arrived, which contributed considerably to bringing the companies up to strength. We began to reinforce the position. Resting troops collected the fence wire from grazing meadows and emplaced it in front of the position as tanglefoot. Empty bottles and cans were tied to this wire, making a silent approach by the enemy impossible. On rest days, short but intense periods of drill were conducted to tighten up discipline, which had naturally loosened in the trenches. Uniforms and weapons, which had been worn down in the war of movement, were repaired and cleaned. On 17 October, Major von Backe assumed command of the regiment, and his initial order of the day filled the regiment with pride:

> When I reported to the division headquarters today, the division commander expressed his respect for the performance of the regiment during the campaign in the highest possible terms. As I assume command it is a particular pleasure to communicate this to every member of the regiment.

Major Schmidt reassumed command of I/ 66, Capt. Trenk command of III/ 66. In general, this first period of trench warfare passed quietly. At night, increased security was necessary, and the regiment was often put on alert, as the French seemed to be very nervous. While the Battle on the Yser raged, the German forces conducted limited attacks along the entire front in order to improve their positions. The regiment would participate in these operations.

14

THE FIGHTS AT ARRAS, 29 OCTOBER TO 5 NOVEMBER 1914

The regiment was suddenly relieved on 29 October, with its positions being occupied by the neighbouring IR 26 and IR 77, and rested during the night at Mercatel. Early on 30 October, I and II/ 66 marched to quarters at Fontaine, the staff, III/ 66 and MG Company to Vis-en-Artois. We hoped for a well-earned rest and began to set up housekeeping, and were quite disappointed to hear that we were to form Brigade Battle Group Jarotzki, along with Fusilier Regiment 36, two batteries of FAR 4, a section of FAR 74, a battery of Foot Artillery Regiment 4 and two squadrons of Hussar R 10. IR 66 was attached to 14 Brigade to support an attack on Blagny-St Sauveur brickworks [*Ziegelei*] north of Beaurains. The 14 Brigade established three sectors, and as a consequence the battalions and companies of IR 66 were split up. The most interesting sector was given to III/ 66, which was placed under the operational control of the commander of IR 165 in Blagny. The attack order said:

> III/ 66 conducts a surprise attack at 1900 in the sector from the rail line to the row of houses 400 metres north of there, limit of advance the road which leads north from the west wall of the churchyard.

During the afternoon, the battalion reached Feuchy, and resumed the march at 1800, but was soon brought back, as the entire attack was called off because the artillery preparation was far from adequate, due to poor visibility.

On 31 October, the division ordered a night attack. After a daylight reconnaissance and orders group conducted by IR 165, at 1730, 9, 11 and 12/ 66, 9 and 11/ 165, a light howitzer and four squads of engineers assembled in the park at Blagny. After dark, an assault column moved through the houses on each side of the road to Arras: left, 12/ 66 under Lt Boysen and 11/ 66 under Lt Schültz, with two squads of engineers under Lt Dittmar; right, 9/ 66 under Capt. Niemeyer and two squads of engineers under Acting Officer Eisenmenger. The enemy offered tough resistance, and progress was slow. Every fence, wall and house was fought over. The infantry and engineers used axes, explosive charges and their weapons to tunnel their way forward through the forward line at Arras. On the first night, several houses were taken, and on the next day, 1 November, they were prepared for defence. On the night of 1–2 November, 12/ 66 took two more houses and 9/ 66 stormed the forward portion of the Red House, and these too were prepared for defence. Sergeant Wadepuhl described the memorable attack of 12/ 66:

We drank the last of our cognac. The 2nd and 3rd Platoons of 12/ 66 were already moving by squads through the bushes towards the village. A field gun set up in the park in order to be able to fire down the road leading to the farm. It would fire nine shells, then we were to attack, accompanied by engineers equipped with explosive charges. The 1st Platoon, under First Sergeant Meyer, crossed a road individually under enemy fire and assembled behind the wall of a small garden. The first shell was fired, a minute later the second. Shortly thereafter there was an unexpected explosion in the wall close to our right. I fell backwards but was able to hold onto a grape vine. Stone fragments flew around our heads. When the smoke cleared, I saw a lieutenant leading away a sergeant. Later we learned that Sergeant Lippolt had an arm torn away. We assembled by squads and after the ninth shell was fired went in single file through the row of houses left of the road. If there wasn't a passageway, the engineers would create one with explosives and axes. We were always separated from the French by only a wall. As soon as there was an explosion the French would withdraw to the next room. The engineers would charge in yelling 'Hurrah!' with us close behind: 1st Squad, Sgt Schmidt; 2nd Squad, me; 3rd Squad, Sgt Beinroth. We were standing in front of a gate. Our company commander, Lt Boysen, went up to Sgt B. and told him to take a patrol to the left to make contact with 2nd Platoon, from which direction bullets were landing against the house like hail. The engineers now had to blast a hole in the wall, after which we had to cross a garden five metres wide to the wall of the next house. We would then cover the engineers as they worked and then advance again. When the French saw us enter the garden, they opened rapid fire from the opposite wall, but nevertheless we only had one man lightly wounded. Moving as individuals, we reached the wall, with the French on the other side; we could grab the barrels of the French rifles, and so doing one of our men was shot in the hand. The engineers tried to blow a hole in the side of the house to the right of the wall. Pieces of wall fell down on us, but instead of the wall being broken open, the chicken coop next to it was destroyed. Suddenly the command was given for the infantry to go back, in order not to be injured by the next explosion, so we went across the garden, through the previous hole in the wall and back to the house we had just left. The next explosion was successful, and we went once again through the hole, across the garden and through the new hole into what looked like kind of a stall. We were now in the first building of a large farm: Sgt Schmidt and I with six or seven men. A gate led to the farmyard. The door to the next room on the left was a metre to the left of the gate. The engineer sergeant leading us said that he would throw a hand-grenade through the door into the room on the left and we were to immediately run one step through the gate into the farmyard and then back through the second door to the room on the left. The hand-grenade was to kill any French in the room. After he threw the grenade, he immediately grabbed Corporal Kurt, who was standing next to him, and pushed him out the gate. He turned left, entered the left-hand room from the farmyard door, and we all followed. The French fired salvoes at us from the other side of the farmyard but didn't hit anyone. The French in the room had fled through a hole in the wall. We searched the room and found several military and hunting rifles and a large quantity of ammunition. While we were doing this a face appeared in the doorway: a Frenchman and all his equipment. I was the closest to him and grabbed his weapon and yelled at him so loudly that the poor fellow stuck his arms out and was completely speechless. Now we ran in one bound over the farmyard and into the cowshed on the other side. Here we occupied the wall of the house to the rear and used every available opening as a firing port. With three men, I held the front right corner of the farm. The French had withdrawn to a factory building. From my position I could see them come out by squads and move towards us. One salvo from four rifles and the French disappeared.

Sergeant Stackmann described the 12/ 66 attack at another location:

The left-hand platoon, led by Landwehr Officer Candidate Pitschke, moved into a park and encountered the enemy, who was behind a two-metre high park wall. Since the underbrush was thick, we were able to approach quite closely: we could not see the French and they couldn't see us. In order to minimise casualties, we first sent out reconnaissance patrols, which established that the French had bored firing ports in the wall, while some were standing on ladders or such in order to be able to fire over the top of it. Reinforced patrols were sent forward with the mission of carefully using the available cover and concealment to approach the wall as closely as possible and drive the French away from it. They succeeded in coming right up to the wall:

the leader of the left-hand patrol, Reserve Sgt Kraftscheck, took a grazing wound, and the French rifles were either pushed back into the firing ports or pulled out of them, and the French withdrew. The other two platoons of the company had a harder time. The middle platoon was faced with an extension of the wall, but there were no trees or bushes for cover, and it was forced to assault the wall, and at this close range there were both killed and wounded. Here too, the French quickly withdrew, and some prisoners were taken. In the continued close-quarters fighting, in which Sgt Wesemann distinguished himself by his energetic actions and tactical skill at the most difficult and dangerous places, the platoon took serious casualties, especially among the recently arrived replacements, who had not learned to exercise the necessary caution.

War Volunteer Mertens described the 9/ 66 attack:

The 2nd and 3rd Platoons occupied the brewery, from which we could see a garden, with a wall on the left along the village street, a steep slope on the right and straight ahead a wall topped by the gable of a house, behind that a factory, into which the French had fled.

Our 1st Platoon was in a shed in the farmyard, waiting for the order to attack into the factory. I can't remember seeing such a clear moonlight night. The order to advance came as a relief. We jumped forward individually through the window of a wagon shed and crawled up to the wall. Our coats at that time were light grey and provided wonderful camouflage in the bright moonlight. Once at the wall, our platoon leader, Lt Kreider, assigned the squads missions. We were put on the right flank, where there was a small opening between the wall and the steep slope. The French held the wall and the engineers were supposed to blow a hole in it for the squads to our left. We held our breath in anticipation and could hear the engineers chiselling against the wall. Couldn't the French hear? But over there everything was quiet. Now it was time. We slid one after another around the wall into the factory courtyard and stood, still hidden by bushes, ready to move forward. Suddenly there were shots from the factory windows, all aimed at Lt Kreider and the squad that were just now moving through a hole in the wall. I heard a short shout and stood completely dazed as the factory began to burn brightly. It was not clear to me what and where it was burning, but the courtyard was brightly lit as far as our hiding place and we decided to crawl back to the wall. Lt Kreider and seven men jumped back through the hole in the wall. Only one man, War Volunteer Nilius, had been killed: they brought him back, and he was buried that same night in the garden. Advancing under these circumstances was out of the question. However, some of our men had climbed into the house through the gable window and the house was now occupied by three squads of 1st Platoon. The other squads, including ours, stayed in the garden, occupied the wall and dug a trench. Later we went back to the brewery, and I stood guard at a window facing the garden. It was difficult to stay awake. Even the people not on guard were told not to sleep. But no matter how desperately Sgt Daul tried to keep the men awake, and threatened those that had fallen asleep, every so often snoring could be heard here and there. Finally dawn began to break, we were relieved and allowed to sleep in horse stalls. It was alive with mice and the French tried to shoot into the ventilator holes in the wall. Virtually at regular intervals, rifle bullets smacked against the outside of the wall. He was a poor shot, for there were practically no direct hits. I soon took no notice of either mice or rifle fire and was fast asleep.

Schiepack, a comrade from our squad, woke me up: he had found some champagne and gave me a drinking cup full. Even though the cup was aluminium, the champagne tasted good. The day passed slowly, the hours seemed to be endless. There wasn't much to be seen outside, and from time to time bullets smacked against the outside of the walls.

That night we stood guard again at the window of the wagon shed: I had the first watch. Later I lay with Reservist Kleinau at a hole in the garden wall on the road. A squad from our 3rd Platoon went across the road to enter the house on the opposite side. They broke in the locked door and window shutters with their rifle butts. The French soon manned the barricade up the street and began a heavy rifle fire. Nevertheless, all of our people made it back to the farmyard unhit and soon it was quiet again.

The engineers had torn down the garden fence between the wagon shed and the brewery and built a sandbag wall as a firing position for a field gun, which was very carefully brought forward, laying straw and sandbags in front of the wheels to muffle the noise. The idea was to smoke the French out of the factory. But at this short range, the shells went right through the walls and apparently exploded far behind the village, with no obvious effect. The French saw the muzzle flashes and conducted heavy return rifle fire, hitting an artillery officer in the hand. Later there was still heavy fire when I was standing watch, long after the gun had been withdrawn.

On the evening of 2 November, Capt. Scheller assumed command of III/ 66. After a quiet night, our artillery shelled the malt factory. The 1st Platoon, 9/66, occupied the mill; everyone else remained in position. To this point the enemy artillery could not fire because the front lines were too close to each other. On the evening of 4 November, it began to shell Blagny with heavy guns, apparently 22cm naval guns, which made our stay, especially in the mill and the three castles, quite uncomfortable. A cellar in the western castle was caved in, burying several civilians. During the day on 5 November, there was little enemy activity, but that evening there was again unpleasant artillery fire on the park, accompanied between 2000 and 2100 by very heavy rifle fire. The planned relief of III/ 66 was delayed by half an hour. During the day, 10/ 66 was attached to I/ 165. Reserve Lt Mende wrote in the after-action report:

> Towards 1800, the company reached the Blagny–Tilloy road, and was instructed to make contact with I/ 165 on the right, as it advanced in the direction of the cemetery, which it did. The company took two enemy trenches, but soon learned that it had lost contact with the companies of IR 165 on the right, which had swung to the right against a strongly held rail embankment. The companies of IR 165 to the left of 10/ 66 had been stopped by enemy fire, so the left flank was uncovered, too. The situation was made worse when the battalion commander was incapacitated almost at once by severe wounds and then his deputy, a lieutenant, was also wounded. When I assumed command of the battalion, it was not possible to hold its companies together, and in any case I was far forward and my company was already surrounded. The bright moonlight made a withdrawal impossible. Near dawn, the moonlight abated and I was able to withdraw my troops individually to the main position on the Blagny–Tilloy road. This could not be accomplished without casualties, and the men later listed as missing had for the most part probably been killed in the withdrawal.

In the night of 5–6 November, III/ 66 was relieved by III/ 165 and fed in Feuchy. It returned to 13 Brigade and marched at 0300 through Neuville and Mercatel to Boisleux-au-Mont, where it rested on 7 November. It had lost fourteen dead, thirty-nine wounded and eleven missing.

I/ 66, which was quartered in Fontaine, moved at 1430 to Chapelle de Feuchy in order to attack Faubourg-St Sauveur with IR 27 and IR 165. Here, too, the attack was delayed until 31 October and it quartered in Wancourt. At 1600 on 31 October, the order arrived for the battalion to move to Tilloy, where it arrived at 1800. For the attack on Tilloy, 3/ 66 deployed east of the road to Arras, with IR 165, and 4/ 66 left of the road, with IR 27, while 1 and 2/ 66 remained in reserve near the white houses. 3/ 66 committed two platoons to the IR 165 attack, while the last platoon was in reserve. 4/ 66 remained to support 3/ 27 in the area of the castle park at Tilloy. When the IR 27 attack against the park wall in Faubourg was stopped by heavy casualties, two platoons of 4/ 66 were committed. It came only to within 60m of the wall, where it was forced to dig-in. Early on 1 November, a gap between IR 27 and IR 165 on the road was filled by two platoons of I/ 66. Since the attack to the east of the road had also been stopped, during the afternoon the order was given to cease further attacks and withdraw in the dark to the previous day's positions, which succeeded, in spite of the bright moonlight. That 4/ 66 was able to break contact so easily was due principally to the planning of Lt Wagner. IR 27 and IR 165 were then relieved by Fusilier Regiment 36, 5/ 66 and two platoons of 2/ 66. The rest of 1/ 66 bivouacked on the road as the reserve a kilometre south of Tilloy, where it remained until 0700. During the day on 2 November, they quartered in Wancourt. At 1900, it reoccupied the reserve position it had held on the night of 1–2 November, and moved at 0300 back to Wancourt. At 1700, it was ordered to move back to Mercatel, which it reached that evening, and was rejoined by the two platoons of 2/ 66. On 4 November, 1/ 66 was ordered to march to Boisleux-au-Mont, the regimental and battalion commanders to report to division HQ at Chérisy. Soon after arriving at Boisleux, a counter-order arrived from 7 ID, directing 1/ 66 to relieve 1/ 27 at Mercatel, with the right flank between Point 107 and the rail line to Arras, the left at the fork of the farm roads a kilometre north of Ficheux. The companies lined up in numerical order from east to west, with the HQ in Kühnen Harras. It had lost six killed, eight wounded and eleven missing.

At 1500 on 30 October, II/ 66 was alerted and moved at 1600 to Chérisy and Guemappe. From here, 5 and 6/ 66 and the battalion staff moved to Chapelle de Feuchy, 7 and 8/ 66 under Capt. Schroeder to Neuville, to support IR 27. The attack scheduled for 1900 was cancelled due to insufficient artillery preparation. That night, 6/ 66 remained in Chapelle de Feuchy, 5/ 66 in a large farm a kilometre to the rear on the Cambrai–Arras road, 7 and 8/ 66 in Neuville. For the night attack scheduled for 31 October, 5 and 6/ 66 moved to Chapelle de Feuchy and were attached to 14 Brigade, 7 and 8/ 66 were attached to IR 27. The 1st Platoon 8/ 66 moved at 1700 to the IR 27 position, where it became battalion reserve behind hay ricks. The 2nd Platoon deployed skirmishers between 10/ 27 and 12/ 27. At exactly 1800, the first line advanced, and the first French trench was literally overrun, with 100 prisoners taken. The 3rd Platoon 8/ 66 moved forward to the IR 27 trenches in support. At 2000, 1st Platoon, in reserve, was ordered forward, bringing with it all the troops it encountered on the way. A further order, to fill a gap in the IR 27 line, could not be executed because the gap was too large: the platoon had both flanks unsupported. This resulted in the 1st Platoon 8/ 66 taking very heavy casualties, with the company commander and thirty-four men missing in action. Only one platoon of 7/ 66 was committed, the other two remaining in reserve under Capt. Schroeder. The attack progressed well, the brickworks between Baurains and Arras was taken, and our troops advanced as far as the first houses of the suburbs. There they encountered murderous French rifle fire and ran the risk of taking friendly artillery fire, so they were pulled back from the suburbs and dug in 150m from them, while some troops prepared the brickworks for defence. At 0400 on 1 November, 6/ 66 and the battalion staff was ordered by 14 Brigade to move to Neuville for attachment to IR 27. 5/ 66 marched to Tilloy as regimental reserve and artillery protection; 7 and 8/ 66 reoccupied the old IR 27 positions in front of Beaurains and at dawn on 2 November moved back to Neuville. At 0615, 6/ 66 moved to occupy the brickworks, which were under heavy French artillery fire. On 3 November, 7 and 8/ 66 were formed into a single company with 200 men, which moved at dark to reinforce the IR 27 position. 5/ 66 was again withdrawn to the large farm on the main road. November 4 brought II/ 66 deliverance from the operation at Arras, which was poorly regarded by the entire regiment. At dawn, 6/ 66 returned from the front line. At 1400, the battalion was ordered to march through Mercatel to Boisleux-au-Mont: 6/ 66 and the remaining elements of 7 and 8/ 66 marched in pouring rain. Capt. Schroeder and Res. Lt Zippel were ordered to ride ahead to Ficheux and report to the commander of III/ 93. In Boisleux-au-Mont, II/ 66 received a counter-order from division HQ to march back to Mercatel and quarter there. The 5/ 66 and the elements of 7 and 8/ 66 that had remained in the trenches arrived in Mercatel during the night and reoccupied their old quarters. II/ 66 had lost eight dead, thirty-eight wounded and thirty-five missing. One officer had been killed and one wounded. In the regiment as a whole, 180 men were killed or wounded.

15
Trench Warfare at Arras, 4 November 1914 to 8 March 1915

After returning from Arras, the regiment reoccupied part of the position it had previously held on the rail embankment north-west of Ficheux. We were now stationary and transformed ourselves gradually into moles. General amazement prevailed concerning some of the already-built dugouts in the position. The great majority, however, lived in 'rabbit-holes' (recesses under the parapet), protected from wind and weather with sandbags or ponchos. If these caved in due to wet weather, they were reinforced with wooden boards, generally doors or window shutters, taken from the abandoned villages behind the front, especially Ficheux. When a company moved into the trenches, it resembled a house removal without the moving vans. On top of the full rucksack were sandbags packed with odds and ends: doors, shutters, window frames with and without glass. Everything that could be moved from the villages was taken along: the cave-dwellers could use it all. If a march column was taken under artillery fire and had to drop its valuable material, even for a short time, this often changed owners, or became the property of those who did not have such useful items at all, and rightful ownership was only re-established in the trenches on the basis of the testimony of witnesses.

The main objective in the construction of the trench system was to keep everything as invisible as possible, in order to avoid unnecessary casualties. The engineers constructed wooden firing ports and observation mirrors. To keep the trenches dry in the wet climate, gravel was laid, which was broken up by troops resting in the rear area. Since the rabbit-holes collapsed during shellings, which caused casualties, the principal work during the night was the construction of dugouts, with roofs reinforced with tree trunks, railroad ties or iron rails, covered by a metre of earth. These were considered to be bomb-proof, for at this time the enemy had no heavy shells ('coal buck-ets') equipped with delayed-action fuses. Several especially capable moles burrowed tunnels to construct secure dens covered by a roof 1m or 1.5m thick. These were by no means too cramped; even the tallest could enter these labyrinths without difficulty. Furnishing these rooms was important: many a long, dangerous trip was made at night to bring back an important item. There was a certain amount of competition to construct the homeli-est dugouts. The latest embellishment, with details of its construction, was announced with pride.

All this made life in the trenches tolerable. When not on duty, more or less intelligent conversations were held (including serious debates concerning the general military situation), letters written (for many of the troops, their principal occupation) and the like. Soon *Skat* and *Doppelkopf* [German card games] clubs were formed, and everyone could remember endless, indeed probably world-record, games of *Skat*. Welcome gifts from the home front brought many into the possession of harmonicas, and beautiful songs of love and longing for home were played, although no one expected to be home for Christmas. Service in the trenches was continually improved and better organised. The work never stopped, indeed became normal. Since the trenches were continually deepened, to 2m and more, the construction of firing steps became necessary, which caused the platoon leaders some difficulty. In case of a daylight attack, the troops fired through firing ports; in a night attack, they rested the rifle on a forked support on top of the lip of the trench, which ensured accurate aimed fire against an invisible enemy. The platoon leader was in for a severe chewing-out if the battalion commander determined that the elbow supports were not properly done.

At the beginning of January, the regiment suffered severely due to frost fol-lowed by rain. The revetting in the sides of the trenches fell in, even the roofs of some of the dugouts sagged. The entire available workforce was needed to repair the position, even the companies that were resting. A seventy-man engineer platoon was formed, principally from construction workers, under Lt Plathe, with responsibility for building dugouts. In some places, the walls of the trenches were reinforced with fascines or boards, a procedure that was not successful in later phases of trench warfare. Latrines and sanitation dugouts were constructed. The troops' health was good, in spite of continual wet weather. A recurrence of typhus, which had appeared at the beginning of trench warfare, broke out, but its spread was halted by immunising all the troops twice. The troops became infested with lice in their clothing after staying in abandoned French trenches, most of which were eliminated by steaming the clothes or cooking them in boiling water.

By the middle of February, the position had been perfected to such a degree that work on a second line was begun, 50–100m to the rear, initially as a narrow but deep trench, with numerous connecting trenches between the two as well as sortie stairs and positions for flanking fire.

Observation of the enemy could not be neglected. This included lookouts during the day and above all patrols at night, which had the mission of determining location, condition and troop strength of the enemy position and the obstacles in front of it. Prisoners were of especial importance for higher headquarters, to identify the enemy units. I/ 66 enjoyed particular success. In the middle of January, I/ 66 brought back a dead and a living Frenchman, while in the middle of February, 4/ 66 shot a French corporal. Enemy patrols were ineffective against us.

Rations were brought forward after dark. The field kitchens would normally move up to Ficheux and the food would be brought to the position in mess kits, later in kettles. A two- or three-day rotation to the trenches was followed by a similar period of rest in Ficheux, Boisleux-au-Mont or Mercatel. Here, too, great care had been taken in the construction of quarters, in order to make the rest as comfortable as possible. Short training marches and active games kept the troops fresh and limber. Inspections were held to ensure the good condition of clothing and equipment. The regimental band played daily during free time. When enemy aircraft forced good old Bothfeldt, the bandmaster, to order the band to take cover, the band was soon again at work, and he compensated for the forced interruption by giving encores. There were also black days in the villages, which from time to time came under enemy artillery fire, occasionally causing casualties: the reliable Corporal Thormann from 6/ 66 was killed. In general, troop morale was good; above all, humourous incidents were not lacking, as Medical Sergeant Freyburg illustrated in this spy story:

> Christmas Day 1914, we were in position in front of Ficheux; that night we were relieved. Shortly beforehand I went with stretcher bearer Schröder from the position to our rest area, Boisleux le Mont. A few days before the companies had been notified that the inhabitants were presumably sending light signals to the French lines. And there it was! On the road from Ficheux to Boisleux we observed such signals: during the entire hike back the light blinked on, then off. We thought it had to come from the church tower, and we ran quickly to report this to the watch. A sergeant and two soldiers from the watch came with us, and we could now see clearly that the signals were coming from the church tower. The staff of 8 ID was quartered in a castle across from the church, where the sergeant at once made his report. Several officers from 8 ID arrived and confirmed it. The watch entered the church and called out several times to see if anyone was there. At first it was dead quiet, but then we heard heavy footsteps coming down from the tower, and to general laughter our mess sergeant, 'Black' Pönitzsch, appeared with two men.

Asked by the officers what he was doing here, he answered that he wanted to serve his captain roasted pigeon on the Second Holiday [26 December] and the church tower was full of them. The three cooks were hunting pigeons with an electric lamp and cutting off their heads in the dark, which explained the blinking light.

Sergeant Freyberg also reported:

In 9/ 66, Franz Dill was well-known for his inability to hold his liquor. This time he disturbed the entire village, and First Sergeant Nebel had him locked up in a pigsty and put him under the guard of two corporals (medics) armed with pistols. An hour later Nebel walked down the street with Capt. Niemeyer, and was shocked to see Dill stumbling towards him, and, true to his character, the First Sergeant grabbed Dill. The captain had no idea what was going on. Dill was again thrown into the sty to sleep it off. As was also his way, the First Sergeant began to chew out the two guards, who were still at their posts in front of the sty. It was then discovered that Dill had escaped by digging a hole in the mud wall of the back of the sty.

During this period, on 12 February 1915, Major von Stoeklern zu Grüholzeck temporarily assumed command from Major Balcke, who had fallen ill, and was named permanent commander on 25 February. At the end of February, the Spanish Military Attache, Major de Valdivia, visited the regiment in the name of the chief of the regiment, the King of Spain.

During this initial period of trench warfare, excepting the attack at Arras, the regiment lost forty-one dead, eighty-one wounded and four missing. It received 1,268 replacements and sent eight NCOs and 246 men to form new units. Also, 293 Iron Cross II Class were awarded. The regiment had done its duty and, for the standards of this period of the war, had constructed a well-prepared position.

16

LEAVING IV AK

In the first days of March we received word that the regiment was going to be pulled out of the line. On the night of 6–7 March, it was relieved in place by IR 27 and Fusilier Regiment 36. All of its Model 1898 rifles were turned over to the 8 ID and the Recruit Depot Vis-en-Artois. The personnel detached as trainers returned to the regiment, which also received replacements from Germany. That evening, the battalions marched to the new quarters in the area of Wancourt–Guemappe–Riencourt–Hendécourt–Cagnicourt–Bullécourt–Fontaine–St Rotart. On 7 March, a rest day, all remaining weapons, flare pistols, etc. were turned in: as combat troops, it was a strange feeling to be unarmed. On 8 March, we marched in wonderful spring weather further into the rear area. Morale was outstanding, and most of us believed we were being sent to the east. Here and there the civilians would laugh at the troops, thinking that they had been forcibly disarmed for disciplinary reasons. Quite the contrary: deep in the rear area, far from all the sounds of combat, the regiment was to be re-equipped with the most modern weapons, reinforced in body and spirit and prepared for new challenges. We quartered on 8 March in the area of Ecoust–St Quentin–Saudemont–Arleux–Hamel–Palluel. It had been planned to form up the regiment for an inspection by the corps commander, but that was cancelled due to an air-raid alert. On 9 March, the regiment continued the march to Roeulx–Lourches–Neuville–Mastaing–Bouchain, and on 10 March reached the barracks.

Trench warfare
By Sergeant Felgentreff, 11 / 66

It trickles down white from Heaven.
The air is cold, but we sweat.
We stamp across the shroud covering the earth.
Cursing softly.
Our mood is sombre,
The Heavens are grey.
We're hauling posts for a barbed-wire fence.

Snow covers the shell holes.
With a soft cry someone falls in.
The snowstorm sweeps over the field.
Another falls over a dead horse.
Prudently, no one says a thing.
We're hauling posts for a barbed-wire fence.

The trench promises rest,
So why such a grim angry face?
I think about Germany, about Berlin,
Where others go to the theatre,
Where my wife laughs at a comedy.
We're hauling posts for a barbed-wire fence.

Think about this, comrade.
The wire hinders the enemy's approach
When he appears, we shoot him down,
Even if he tries to be ever so quiet.
He's smart, but we're clever.
So we're hauling posts for a barbed-wire fence.

When the Frenchman attacks,
Our rifles will fire.
Bloody war will demand its due.
Then there'll be a wonderful victory,
Followed by peace,
I know it for sure.
So let's haul these posts for a barbed-wire fence.

17

THE YEAR OF DIGGING TRENCHES

Transfer to 52 ID, March 1915

For the old men of IR 66, who were with the regiment from 1914 to 1918, 1915 will be remembered as the year of 'quiet trench warfare': aside from the bloody days at Serre in May, in general there were no big battles. In the later, harder, years we would look back longingly to the 'wonderful days at Bucqoy and Ablaincevelle' and perhaps, too, those at Puisieux and Achiet. But in this sector there was also hard military work, loyalty, courage, self-sacrifice and unforgettable deeds.

This year was used to transform the regiment's sector into an exemplary fortified position, as well as to conduct training down to the smallest military details, both in the position and directly behind it, and to uphold discipline. As a result, in the costly and difficult battles of the next years, the regiment's performance was what one can expect only from an infantry unit of the highest quality.

The first day in the new phase of the regiment's war was 10 March, as it entered the assembly area of the newly formed 52 ID, to which it now belonged, and whose commander was Major General von Borries.

The regiment occupied rest quarters south-east of Valenciennes, staff in Jenlain, I/ 66 in Curgies and Eth, II/ 66 in Wargnies-le-Petit and le Grand, III/ 66 in Villers-Pol and 12/ 66 in Orsinval. The inhabitants of these idyllic farm villages – of which several, such as Villers-Pol, had not seen German troops quarter since September 1914 – were in general polite and co-operative. The village government provided the rations, which were acceptable. The division, which included the Baden Regiments 169 and 170, was to be equipped with captured Russian weapons, and from 11 to 20 March thorough training was conducted using them. Our good old Model 98 was a superior weapon, both in terms of accuracy and handling, and fortunately we were soon able to trade-in the Russian rifles for German ones, first the Model 88, then the 98.

Training marches were conducted through the charming countryside, as well as combat training, first in smaller, then in larger units, to improve combat skills dulled by the long periods digging in the trenches. In between there was time for personal hygiene, and repair and cleaning of clothing and equipment. In the last days here we conducted live-fire marksmanship training. Replacements from Germany brought the regiment up to full strength, 250 men per company. These ten days did the troops a world of good.

The troops had no idea where they were to be sent, but many thought it would be east, and some even dreamed of the Dutch or Danish border. But on 21 March, the division marched west, and for the rest of the war we would not leave France. Each company was permitted to requisition a wagon and two horses that would join the supply trains. The regiment took quarters that night in the area west of Denain: I/ 66 in Bouchain and Mastaing, II/ 66 in Roeulx and Neuville, III/ 66 in Lourches. This was not the idyllic agricultural land that we had previously been in; these were the coal fields of the northern French industrial area, with slag heaps, chimneys, coal dust and smoky air. On 22 March, we passed through Cambrai and bivouacked in the towns of Hermies, Boursies and Moeuvres, on both sides of the Cambrai–Bapaume road. These marches were somewhat strenuous, particularly for the reservist replacements and recruits, the more so because they were usually on cobblestone roads, with frequent halts caused by other units marching on the same road. It was now generally understood that the division would defend a position west of Bapaume, only a few kilometres south of our previous location.

After dark on 23 March, in order to conceal our movement from enemy air reconnaissance, the regiment moved to an area north of Bapaume, to quarter in the villages of Behagnies, Sapignies and Mory. Previously, the civilian population had remained in the villages; these showed only limited outward signs of war, but were empty. We met Fusilier Regiment 36, which had relieved us in place a few weeks ago, and was marching, like we had, without weapons to a rest area. The men from Halle were anticipating a good rest period and were in high spirits; there were loud and hearty greetings.

The Position at Bucquoy

The regimental commander briefed the battalion and company commanders on the afternoon of 24 March. The mission was to relieve in place Guard

Grenadier Regiment 5, Queen Elizabeth, north-west of Bucquoy. The particulars of the position and the conduct of the relief were discussed. The battalion and company commanders reconnoitred the route of march and the Elizabeth's position on the afternoon of 25 March, and the relief was conducted uneventfully during that night. The regiment held the northern part of the division sector. The right flank of the front line was on the road from Monchy-au-Bois to Hannescamps, immediately in front of what used to be the edge of Monchy, but was now a pile of rubble cut up by trenches, with IR 72 to its right. The left flank was west of Brayelle Farm, with IR 169 on the left. II/ 66 (Paulus) was on the right, in sectors A 1 and A 2, III/ 66 (Trenk) in the middle in sectors A 3 and B 1, I/ 66 (Schmidt) on the left in B 2 and B 3. Each battalion had two companies on the front, one in reserve and one at rest, and conducted their own relief rotations. One battalion commander was in charge of sector A, one B, while the third rested. The regimental staff, II/ 66 and the MG Company rested in Ablainceville [Ablainzevelle], I and III/ 66 in Bucquoy. During the first night, the companies were briefed on the position by stay-behind parties from Elizabeth. In general we were pleasantly surprised. The front-line trench was, according to the standards of the time, generally well constructed, but there was not much to see of a second trench. There were a good number of solid-looking bomb-proofs, built by digging a hole and then adding on overhead cover, which is to say not so well-built as they would be later that year. The distance from the enemy – the French again – varied; on the right at Monchy, 200m, in the centre, opposite Hannescamps, 1,600m (separated by a broad hollow, with part of our position in a sunken road), on the left closer again.

The sector was considered to be quiet. Only on the right, where the distance from the French was less, was a higher state of readiness necessary (and both sides posted snipers in saps (a siege warfare term, the forward part of an approach trench)). Otherwise, the enemy infantry was not very active. His artillery showed it was still there by shelling the same locations behind our position: our artillery positions in or on the edge of Douchy Wood (*Walde von Douchy*), the high ground south-west of the Gde Fme (*Grande Ferme* – large farm), the ruins of the former village of Essarts, as well as other points that seemed to be exposed to enemy observation. These areas were soon well-known, and since the shellings were conducted at the same time each day, their effect was minimal and our losses in the initial months were very light.

During the beginning of our stay in this sector, our rest areas at Ablainceville (which was as good as undamaged) and Bucquoy (which had considerable battle damage) were seldom shelled by the enemy artillery. The enemy was denied direct observation of them by intervening high ground, although enemy aircraft overflew both, especially Bucquoy, often in large numbers and at low altitude. Since at first they seldom dropped bombs, the troops' reactions regarding their frequent presence became careless, and the orders regarding conduct at the approach of enemy aircraft were often simply disregarded. Our aircraft appeared only sporadically.

The quarters for officers and men, given the situation, were good. Horses were also not a problem: in the daytime they grazed in the meadows enclosed by hedges, which were behind the farms. These areas also provided excellent concealment for troops conducting training or in formation. On the rest days, the quarters were improved. The residents, especially the women, were for the most part still there, and a tolerable relationship formed between our involuntary hosts and the troops of IR 66; in many ways we could help each other.

In spite of the quiet situation on our front, all of the troop leaders at all levels, but especially our energetic division commander, Major General von Borries, laid great emphasis on increasing the strength of the trench systems and improving the training of the troops in trench warfare. Numerous orders were issued in this regard by all levels from corps down, and these leaders did not neglect to check and make sure these orders and measures were being carried out. It is obvious that many of these corresponded only to the present situation, and were made superfluous by events and rescinded: during the entire war, the tactics of trench warfare were being altered due to the continual increase in firepower.

18

LIFE IN THE TRENCHES, MARCH–MAY 1915

During the initial period in our new position, in the last days of March, nothing in particular happened. We learned with sadness that our former comrade, Reserve Lt Krösch, who had been with the regiment during the entire march through France, and then in December had been transferred to another regiment, had been killed by an enemy trench mortar attack while in the Champagne. In the night of 30–31 March, we lost our first killed in action, two members of 7/ 66 shot by enemy snipers. The body of one of the men, Reservist Fromm, was found months later (10 June 1915) by a patrol led by Sergeant Fickenday, in front of the enemy wire obstacle.

In the following weeks, the trenches were improved energetically, particularly because the division commander frequently appeared early in the morning in the forward positions or in the artillery forward observer posts, which led to corrective actions. In places the trenches were deepened, made wider and provided with firing steps, and traverses built to the sides of the fighting positions to prevent enfilade fire. Observation posts were constructed. Particular emphasis was laid on digging really bomb-proof positions in each company area by tunnelling down into the ground. A particular hobby-horse of our division commander was putting duckboards at the bottom of all the trenches. On the one hand, this was exceptionally practical in wet weather. On the other hand, as the enemy artillery became stronger, more active and more destructive, the duckboards were thrown about, buried and pieces of wood laying across the trench easily became obstacles. The planned construction of communications trenches connecting the front lines to the rear, and approach trenches, would later prove to be of exceptional value.

In April, the enemy artillery fire at times became a little stronger. Perhaps the French had gotten wind of the fact that a relief in place had been conducted and had become nervous? Or it could have been that in the first days our men were not careful enough and had been observed? All levels of command emphasised how important it was that during the day there be no signs of life in the position. The mass of the garrison would remain in the bomb-proofs or some other cover, and in all cases not expose themselves to enemy observation.

At night, the position sprang to life: work done on the trenches, patrols quietly went out towards the enemy, like ghosts in the night. In each company in daylight, there were one or two lookouts per platoon; at night, each squad had two to four lookouts, with the rifle lying alert on the berm of the trench. Behind the front line, rations were brought forward; in some sectors the field kitchens could move up to the forward trench. Material for construction of the position and obstacles was brought up, unloaded and distributed.

Now and again there would be sudden flashes of light in the enemy direction and a few seconds later a salvo of shells, nicknamed Krakauer (Cracow sausages) would land somewhere in our area, usually just behind the forward position, sometimes, unfortunately, directly in it. On 2 April 1915, the left foot of Reservist Strauch (10/ 66) was torn off; had the capable battalion surgeon, Müller, not been quickly on the spot, he might have bled to death. He was evacuated that night, and in a few years he was employed at the Magdeburg rail station, with a prosthetic foot to remind him of that night.

The enemy artillery fire became more frequent, above all at Essarts and the 'Shell Hedge'. Losses increased. In addition to several wounded, on 13 April, 5/ 66 lost one man killed. On 14 April, Officer Candidate Baumann of 3/ 66 was mortally wounded and buried a few days later in Ablainceville. On 16 April, the very capable Senior Sergeant Pathe lost an arm. On 19 April, 1/ 66 lost another man killed.

Our quarters, above all Bucquoy, were now being shelled. On 19 April, one landed unexpectedly in the area of the III/ 66 canteen, killed the orderly of the Purser Ramme and wounded an old woman, who was carried by our men to the hospital. For the remaining civilian population, these shellings were understandably far less pleasant than our presence, as they saw their houses and belongings slowly being destroyed and pushing them towards complete ruin. The enemy began to use heavier calibre guns. On 18 April, an 18.5cm shell landed in Section N 2, which was being held by 2/ 66.

From the very beginning, the Division and Regimental HQs laid particular emphasis on determining enemy intentions as early as possible, both in order to avoid being surprised, by taking prompt countermeasures, as well as taking the opportunity to inflict casualties and damage on the enemy, which above all would give the troops a feeling of superiority. Therefore, in all sectors patrols with specific missions were sent out frequently. So-called security patrols, actually night listening posts, were used to prevent the enemy from approaching while work was done on the wire obstacles. On the night of 22–23 April, a small four-man patrol from 10/ 66 was ambushed west of the French Bottom, and took heavy rifle fire; two men were wounded and the patrol forced to withdraw. It was soon noticed that one of the men was missing, and a stronger patrol was sent out, which succeeded in finding the severely wounded man, who could not move under his own power, and bringing him back. A 3/ 66 patrol, led by the bold Sergeant Leue, succeeded on the night of 27–28 April in shooting four French and identifying their unit, the 155th Infantry Regiment, whose presence in the division sector was heretofore unknown. Leue was promoted to Senior Sergeant and six of his men received the Iron Cross II Class. The division commander, Major-Gereral von Borries, ordered the men to come to the headquarters, where he personally praised them.

In the last days of April, there were several cases of meningitis in 1/ 66. They, and men who might have been exposed, were quarantined in the forest ranger's house in the Bois de Logeast which, in addition to the care provided by the regimental surgeon Dr Sage, prevented an epidemic.

For the next few weeks, the 52 ID sector remained quiet. However, to the north of Arras, long, dull rumblings were frequently heard, especially at night, which gave us notice of the heavy and bloody fighting going on, especially at the Loretto high ground.

We feverishly worked to improve the position, especially in the construction of a communication trench to Essarts, which would allow the covered forward movement of reserves. In Essarts itself, the reserve company dug bomb-proofs. The forward companies dug an advanced outpost at the 'Shell Hedge' on the left side of the position. This hedge deserved its title; there were continual casualties here. On 3 May, three men from 3/ 66 were killed by shell splinters.

In front of Post N 2, a six-man patrol from 6/ 66 ran into a stronger French detachment in the area of the French Hedge and lost three wounded and a man missing. The French also appear to have taken casualties.

On the basis of several reports, particularly air reconnaissance, that enemy columns were approaching Sailly from the south, the regiment was alerted on 12 May at 0900. The reserve companies were moved forward, along with some of the resting companies. The alert was lifted at 0900 the next day.

On 15 May, each company was ordered to detach a number of NCOs and men to form 13/ 66. They were brought together at the forest ranger's house in the Longeast Wood, where the company was formed on 21 May, and then transferred to IR 185. The company commander was Res. Lt Kreidner, who would soon be able to return to IR 66, where he subsequently performed several acts of bravery. Res. Lts Claus and Schulze also left IR 66 with the company.

On 17 May, the resting companies of the regiment celebrated the name day of its chief, King Alfonso XIII of Spain.

In the following days, the regiment received German Model 88 rifles and turned in the Russian rifles it had been using.

The Italian declaration of war on 24 May was met with outrage at the disloyal behaviour of our erstwhile ally, without, however, disturbing the troops very much. It encouraged the French to fight on and gave them renewed hope. French leaflets in German landed on our trenches on 27 May announcing this, and the French in the closest trenches often called out 'À revoir à Bucquoy!' (See you in Bucquoy!). Some French would soon be able to make good on their promise – as prisoners.

Aside from moderate artillery fire, that was answered by the artillery attached to the regiment (located on both sides of Gde Fme), and frequent aerial bombings of Bucquoy, causing no great damage, the sector was very quiet, which seemed suspicious.

To the north of Arras, that is, not so far from us, there was still heavy fighting, as we could hear, and at night we saw the artillery muzzle flashes and sometimes the light from the path of the shells. The increased activity by French air reconnaissance, as well as the appearance of several of their observation balloons behind their front, did not bode well.

On 28 May, Sergeant Sievert and another man were on patrol near the French barbed-wire obstacle when they were hit by rifle fire and either killed or wounded so badly that they could not return to our lines.

On 31 May, 1/ 66 ordered 2/ 66 to conduct an operation against enemy Post N 6, which was somewhat advanced, on the road to Focquévillers, in order to determine the identity of the French unit opposite us. It was conducted by a thirty-man patrol under Lt Lorleberg, and a second twenty-one-man patrol under Senior Sergeant Ehlert. It was completely successful, bringing back a dead Frenchman from the French Light Infantry Regiment 66. The French also lost several other wounded, who were able to escape.

Aside from French harassing artillery fire, the last days of May passed relatively quietly. On 25 May, Machine Gun Platoon 202, with fifty men and three MG, was attached from 52 ID to IR 66, which was responsible for its training, rations, etc. On 30 May, the regiment received its first relatively primitive chemical protection equipment and gas masks.

19

The Fight at Serre, June 1915

It was conspicuous that, when 52 ID, over a period of several days, pushed forward positions at several points, which the French had to have observed, there was little French reaction. Their artillery fire was directed at our artillery positions and forward observers, and prominent points on the approaches to the front line. The artillery fire on our trenches was weak, while the aerial reconnaissance increased. We had the feeling that sooner or later the enemy, somewhere on our section of the front, was going to become more active; we had to ask ourselves why everything was so quiet here while to the north of Arras, only a few kilometres away, the enemy was continually committing more resources to renew the attack to break through the German front.

At the beginning of June, the storm broke over the left-hand sector (Sector S) of the 52 ID front, held by IR 170, while the centre (Sector M), held by IR 169, and the right (Sector N), with IR 66, were not attacked at all; IR 66 was not even subjected to heavy artillery fire.

On the night of 3–4 June, the enemy began a heavy artillery bombardment, most of all against the rear area, especially the village of Puisieux, the Bois de Biez, as well as the approach routes to Sector M and especially Sector S. At 0030, the division alerted all the resting companies, but for the meantime left them in their quarters. Towards morning the artillery fire died down, nothing particular had happened, and the resting companies stood down from alert.

On the afternoon of 4 June, we saw a German observation balloon rise between Bucquoy and Achiet-le-Grand, which at that time was a rarity. The day passed without particular incident. On 5 June, two enemy aircraft were shot down by MG fire; one went down in no-man's-land in front of Sector N 2.

On the night of 5–6 June, there was again heavy enemy artillery fire, this time on Sectors S 3 to S 6, that during the course of 6 June (a Sunday) sometimes reached drumfire intensity. At 1130, the entire 52 ID was again alerted. The resting companies of IR 66, 5/ 66 in Ablainceville and 10/ 66 in Bucquoy, moved to their assembly areas in Sector N, and were returned to their quarters towards evening. 2/ 66 and 9/ 66 were ordered during the afternoon to move to Puisieux to reinforce Sector S, under the command of First Lt Kleinert, using as much concealment as possible and avoiding the enemy artillery fire on the

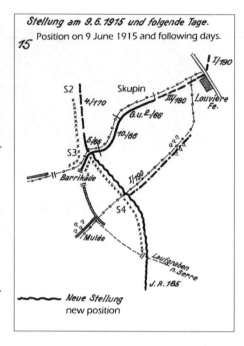

Stellung am 9.6.1915 und folgende Tage.
Position on 9 June 1915 and following days.

—— *Neue Stellung*
new position

road from Bucquoy to Puisieux, which they reached at 2100 and occupied alarm quarters. In case of enemy attack, their mission was to hold Puisieux.

During the entire day of 6 June, there was heavy enemy artillery fire on IR 170 and sometimes on IR 169, while Sector N, occupied by IR 66, was relatively quiet, so much so that during the night the troops could work on the front-line position without interruption. This state of affairs continued in our sector on the next day, aside from occasional periods of artillery bombardment.

However, the French succeeded, after a day-long artillery bombardment, which damaged or even destroyed the IR 170 trenches, in quickly taking parts of Sectors S 3 and S 4 in the area of Toutvent Fme, with a number of prisoners. At 0430, 9/ 66, under Res. Lt Borchert, was attached by 52 ID order to II/ 170 (Capt. Engel) and moved by squads to Louvière Farm. The battalion commander ordered it to occupy the second line, making contact with 8/ 170 on the right and 5/ 170 on the left. When the enemy attacked at 0700, the company immediately opened fire on enemy troops digging in 800m to its rear: to the left, the enemy had already broken through at Sector S 4–5. During the afternoon, the company occupied the part of S 3 still in German hands and began to repair the trenches, which had been badly damaged. At 1630, the company, under its energetic commander, and mixed with elements of 5 and 8/ 170, retook the rest of S 3 in a hand-grenade attack, and began restoring the shot-up trenches. This was hindered by renewed artillery fire, but the company had relatively few casualties.

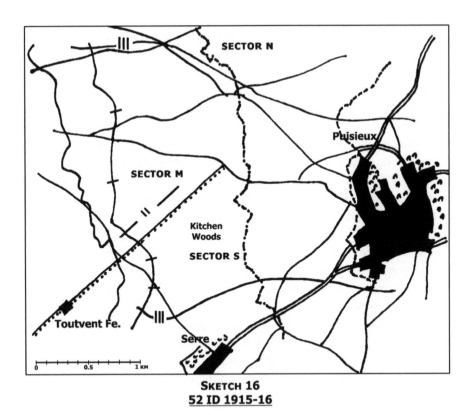

SKETCH 16
52 ID 1915-16

At 0715, 2/ 66 (Kleinert) was also ordered to Louvière Farm and attached to II/ 170. This company also moved in open order under heavy shrapnel and shell fire and arrived there without loss. It was given the mission to defend the communications trench (*Skupinweg* – named for the commander of IR 180, Major Skupin) from the farm to S 3, and at 1830 was moved forward to the junction of this communications trench with S 3. At 2030, it occupied part of S 3. Reconnaissance between 2100 and 2200 towards Serre found the communications trench between S 3 and Serre and the counter-attack (second) trench of S 3 were not occupied by the enemy. Left of 2/ 66 was 9/ 66, and there was contact to the right of it with elements of IR 180. From S 4, further to the left, the company took occasional rifle fire. The company dug out the filled-in trenches and, given the unclear situation, built firing steps both to the front and rear. At 2245, and also at midnight, there was heavy artillery fire over the entire position, and at 0130 drumfire.

On the morning of 7 June, at about 1100, the two remaining rear-area companies, 5/ 66 – which had already moved that morning from its rest area at Ablaineville to Bucquoy and occupied the quarters of 2/ 66 – and 10/ 66, were alerted. The 10/ 66 was first sent to the Gde Fme, and soon thereafter ordered to return to its quarters but remain ready to be alerted. Major Paulus, the commander of the reserve, moved from Ablaineville to Bucquoy. During the morning and afternoon, the enemy drumfire, a greyish-yellow wall of smoke and dust, could be seen in the direction of Puisieux–Serre.

On 8 June, the drumfire commenced again in the 2 and 9/ 66 sectors at 0130 and lasted until 0400. Heavy fog restricted visibility and by dawn it became clear that enemy forces in company strength, moving from S 4, had reached the second (counter-attack) trench in S 3 and were now in the rear of 2 and 9/ 66. The 9/ 66, furthest to the left, under their brave commander, Res. Lt Borchert, along with elements of 2/ 66 under Senior Sergeants Ehlert and Honrod, and of IR 180, assaulted through the hedge to the trench occupied by the enemy and took the entire garrison, seventy men, prisoner. Enemy reinforcements, and continual MG fire from S 4 into the flank, forced them to withdraw to their former position at S 3. 2 and 9/ 66, now both under the command of Lt Borchert, were withdrawn at 1700 to the intersection of S 3, the connecting trench, and S 2; S 3 was occupied by elements of IR 180. First Lt Kleinert was sent as liaison officer to the artillery, to orient them on the quite obscure situation. Due to artillery fire and close combat, both companies had taken considerable losses; 2/ 66 had ten killed, forty-one wounded and three missing, 9/ 66 eleven killed, thirty-eight wounded and four missing. Sergeant Daul was killed after the fight was over, when the firing cord of a grenade became caught on the corner of the trench and detonated, an accident caused by the narrowness of the trench.

On 8 June, 5 and 10/ 66 remained ready to be alerted in Bucquoy. Near noon they moved to the side of the village facing Puisieux, and remained there until 1600. The long wait was pleasantly interrupted when the French who had been captured that morning were marched past, in their light blue uniform coats, many with long black beards. The residents of Bucquoy, who firmly believed that their countrymen were arriving as victors, were visibly disappointed as they saw it was a prisoner column. The prisoners looked fresh and clean, and it was clear that they had come from a newly arrived regiment. At this time an orderly arrived from 52 ID with orders to move to support Sector S. During the entire day, heavy artillery fire had been landing on Sector S and part of M, the Puisieux village and the ruins of Serre. In our direction of march we saw an impenetrable curtain of smoke columns, but we got lucky; the fire died down near dark. The 5/ 66 (First Lt Rochlitz) marched first, followed by 10/ 66 (First Lt Hermens) in half platoons with large intervals between them, initially a short stretch on the road from Puisieux, then a right turn over open country in the direction of the Bucquoy–Hébuterne road, past the rear trenches of IR 169 (Sector M) and then through seemingly endless, mostly shot-up, reserve and communications trenches made muddy by the previous rainfall. The trench garrison lay or stood around, tired out by days of watching and dirty from the mud and wet. In some places the muddy water came up to the knee. They kept going on, in a long single file through Bois du Biez, Point 125, past II/ 170, recently pulled out of the line and severely shaken by the recent combat, until they finally reached Louvière Farm, already a ruin. It was 2130 and now dark. There it was joined by the combined 2 and 9/ 66, and continued, under the command of Major Paulus, through the narrow 'Skupin' communication trench in single file across Sector S in the direction of Toutvent Farm.

It was unclear how much of the trench was in our hands, how much in those of the enemy, only that there was apparently a hole that had to be stopped up as soon as possible; the next morning, the French could attack with fresh forces and push as far as Puisieux. 5/ 66 slowly felt its way forwards, followed closely by 10/ 66. Hand-grenades could be heard exploding nearby and rifle fire came from various directions. First Lt Rochlitz sent forward a strong reconnaissance patrol under Res. Lt Bötticher; Rochlitz sent a report passing back from man to man that it was impossible to advance further without knowing where they were in the dark, and that he could tell from patrol reports and his own observations that there were already French on three sides. While moving carefully forwards, Bötticher's patrol had hand-grenades thrown at it and took heavy rifle fire into the left flank. Nevertheless, at a traverse in the trench it was able to build a barricade and block the trench off, although there was sporadic firing the entire night, mixed in with hand-grenades. The enemy attacked twice, but was driven back by the alert garrison. The trenches provided practically no cover, and the companies, with 5/ 66 in front, 10 close behind, then 9 and 12, attempted to dig into the walls of the trenches, in hard, sometimes stony ground. There was a tunnelled-out bomb-proof, very modest by later standards, in which Major Paulus and half of the regimental staff took cover, while the regimental surgeon, Dr Müller, and his medics established themselves in another dugout. Fire steps had to be cut both to the front and rear, for there was no way to determine from which direction the enemy would come. It was difficult to work effectively in total darkness, as well as keep the exhausted troops awake, but it was a question of keeping everyone alive, as events a few hours later would demonstrate.

At 0900, it became lighter and the enemy cannonade began, to which the German artillery replied with a defensive curtain barrage: shells whizzed immediately over the trench from both sides. At the head of our position, the sap, held by the forward platoon of 5/ 66, grenades were thrown. As it became lighter, we could orient ourselves, and we could finally determine how our trench looked. The foremost piece, the barricade, was located a bit to the side of the place where S 2 and S 3 on the right met the Skupin communications trench on the left. The trench in the 5/ 66 area was hardly knee-deep and moving upright was nearly impossible. It was gruesome. The dead of the previous days had fallen to the bottom of the trench and been covered with dirt from the impacts of artillery and mortar rounds, with legs and other body parts still exposed. There was an awful stench from decomposing bodies and high explosives.

It was evident that the French had, apparently near dawn, approached 5/ 66 using hedges, small depressions, shell holes, etc., and were continuing to do so. They had probably been prevented from attacking by the prompt curtain barrage. There was now more than ever a danger that they would break through at the still-open hole in our line, and it was our mission to prevent this. There was light rifle fire on both sides. Our men stood on the firing steps and fired whenever they could find a target; the French fire came from the front and both flanks. This had already caused casualties; 10/ 66 had lost a man (Musketeer Metz II) shot in the back the previous evening, while the company was occupying the trench. On the morning of 9 June, Reservist Ksiozek was killed by a MG bullet in the neck and another man received a light shoulder wound.

Initially it was relatively quiet, but at 0930, a well-aimed and hours-long drumfire with shrapnel and delayed-action fuses landed on our trenches. In the early morning half-light, a MG from MG Platoon 202 had been brought forward; it was immediately buried, and as it was being dug out two men were killed and two wounded. A replacement gun was also destroyed. The companies, in the poorly dug trenches, were more or less exposed to the hail of shells. If our men had not dug small holes into the sides of the trenches, which gave them some protection against shell splinters, then they would have been helpless against the shells that were being fired straight down the length of the trench. Nevertheless, there were still heavy casualties. By evening, 10/ 66 had four dead and about a dozen mostly seriously wounded. Sergeant-Major Preuss' batman cold-bloodedly came out of the protection of his little hole, in spite of Preuss' warning, to carry a badly wounded man to the aid station; on the way, a shell took his head off. Some of the little foxholes were partly demolished and their 'inhabitants', if they were still able, ran up and down the trench like ants, seeking any kind of cover. The hole of the company commander's batman was collapsed by a shell, and he ran towards the aid station dugout; when he came back to the company, he was missing a finger. The aid station dugout was filled with the wounded and many other 'homeless', which resulted in a serious overcrowding, and it required the authority of the battalion commander, Major Paulus, to keep the entrance open. The IR 180 men in S 2 also had to use the communications trench, which resulted in continual traffic. In the immediate vicinity of the dugout was a bend in the trench where, with great regularity, about every minute, a shell landed. In spite of all the warnings of the leaders in the trench not to stop here at this time, two men were killed. In this heavy fire it was not possible to evacuate the numerous wounded, who were literally pinned into the narrow trench. The trench remained under shell and shrapnel fire for the entire day, although there was some reduction noticed during the afternoon.

All day there was also a firefight going on, with frequent use of hand-grenades. The situation became critical several times, as the ammunition and hand-grenades ran out. In addition, most of the ammunition was caked with mud. Remarkably, reports continued to reach the rear and the ammunition resupply was brought through the trenches to the front. Mortar shells land-ing 30–50m behind the front levelled out the trench and nearly cut off the forward position; anyone moving through this sector was risking his life. 5/ 66 suffered heavy casualties from mortar fire, including several killed. The fighting would fall off, then increase to intense close-quarter fighting, until towards evening it died down. None of those present will ever forget Sergeant Koop, from 5/ 66, as he threw hand-grenades over the barricade at the French, then, seeing an opportunity to make a bold stroke, sprang up over the barricade to throw another grenade, when he was hit and killed by a bullet and fell backwards.

Higher headquarters decided to close the gap in the line to our left by quickly digging a stop line, with work beginning that night. Major Skupin, of IR 180, determined from Major Paulus the location of the IR 66 troops and instructed that our sap, which hung completely in the air, and had no support on either side, be given up and pulled back to the new line, where we would dig-in. The work was done feverishly but quietly, secured by listening posts from 10/ 66. The forward end of the communication trench, 50–100m in length, was quickly filled in and a new barricade built, undisturbed by the French, who noticed nothing until the next morning. Engineers constructed a barbed-wire entanglement. Given the shortness of the night, it had not been possible to evacuate the bodies of all of the dead. Our losses had been consid-erable. It was a great misfortune that the communications trench was so full of troops.

At the same time, several companies of IR 190 were able to dig a new trench to our left, that ran parallel to the trench lost by IR 170, and perpendicular to the Skupin communications trench that we held, and extended all the way to Serre, where it linked up our lines. The route to Puisieux had been closed! With the exception of frequent enemy artillery harassment fire, 10 June passed quietly. Near dark, four men from various units were killed at the bend in the trench that was under regular artillery fire, due solely to the heavy traffic in the trench. The new 10/ 66 CP was located nearby in a poorly built dugout, and during the night was apparently hit by a dud shell, which smashed in the entire roof, leaving iron girders and split wooden beams hanging in the air, but everyone inside instinctively got quickly outside, uninjured.

On the night of 10–11 June, the French tried with full force to storm the new barricade, which led to renewed bitter fighting with rifles and hand-grenades. The living wall of men from 5 and 10/ 66 stood fast and threw them back. A MG which had been set up here the previous evening did good service. The French artillery fired at our rear lines of communication, probably to hinder the arrival of reserves from Louvière Farm. Fighting died down towards morning. 10/ 66 had about ten wounded, mostly head wounds from rifle fire in the flank.

The day of 11 June was quiet. Late in the day, the enemy artillery fire became stronger, which caused further casualties. A direct hit in a squad from 2nd Platoon killed one man and severely wounded four others. Landwehr Lt Pitschke and some squads from 10/ 66 had been sent to Louvière Farm, where there were casualties in 1st Platoon. On 12 June, a musketeer was killed while getting water. Reserve Senior Sergeant Müller of 10/ 66 (a teacher), who would be killed the next year, wrote a short description of events:

> The French did not renew their attacks on the night of 11–12 June. Rather, occasional bursts of rifle and artillery fire showed that they feared we would counter-attack more than they wanted to attack. IR 190 dug their trench to Serre, so that the left flank of 5 and 10/ 66 is covered. There was heavy artillery fire on both sides on the night of 12–13 June, but otherwise not much happened. A French deserter, who jumped over the barricade on 12 June, mentioned the effectiveness of our artillery fire. The last days that we held this position were also uneventful: the French will to attack had been broken. From the observation posts we could clearly see them digging-in to get more protection from our artillery or defend against a possible counter-attack. They were no longer interested in gaining terrain. Their attempt to break through could be considered a complete failure. All of the important points in the German position had been held in spite of the heaviest enemy fire. Since the threat was over, the four companies of IR 66 were finally relieved on 14 June.

On 13 June, 9/ 66 was sent to the position linking S 2 and S 3, while 2/ 66 remained in the rear section of the communications trench. On 14 June, they switched positions. In addition to the losses in these companies, which have already been given, 5/ 66 lost eighteen killed and thirty-three wounded, 10/ 66 seven or eight killed and thirty-six wounded, half of them seriously. They were relieved on the evening of 14 June by IR 186. They moved through seemingly endless trenches through Bucquoy to Ablainceville, which after the days at Serre semed like a spa. For a few days they enjoyed a well-earned rest, before returning to their old positions in Sector N.

The chaplain of the 52 ID, Pastor Kortheuer, summed up the results of the fighting at Serre (or south-east of Hébuterne) in his book, which had already appeared in 1916:

These were hard days, but great days. Granted, we let a section of trench fall into enemy hands. We had heavy casualties, the simple crosses at the Louvière Farm, behind the front, and in the cemeteries of the towns where we bivouacked are witness to that. But what had the immense efforts of the enemy achieved? Previously, he was on the high ground at Hébuterne, we were in the valley. Now the French trench is in the valley. We were able to build a new and better position on the high ground of Serre undisturbed; 150,000 shells had been fired at our position to no result. We fired a third of that and inflicted bloody losses on the enemy.

On the morning of 9 June, the inhabitants of Bucquoy stood in their Sunday best, waiting for their countrymen to return. And so they did – about 200 prisoners, who had fallen into our hands in spite of the enemy's great superiority. No, the fighting at Serre, as hard as it was, proves once more that the German guard in France is firm and true.

20

THE LAST WEEKS IN THE POSITION AT BUCQUOY, MID-JUNE-AUGUST 1915

In the last days of June, two groups of replacements arrived for the regiment, about 400 men in total, to fill in the gaps caused by the recent fighting. About 150 came from our replacement battalion in Magdeburg, 250 from Replacement Battalions 166 and 137, so we gained a considerable number of men from the Rhineland, for the most part *Landsturm* recruits.

The front-line position and the communications trenches from the rear were improved at full speed, in particular tunnelling to construct deep bomb-proofs in every company area; the lack of such had undoubtedly led to heavy casualties from artillery fire during the fighting at Serre. Captain Niemeyer went on leave and was replaced by Res. Capt. Schröder, the 'old man of the mountain', as the commander of the left, B Sector. In order to provide a more secure connection at the boundary between the two regiments, Capt. Trenk took over N 6 (left wing of our regiment) and M 1 (right wing of the M Sector under IR 169) on 29 June. This was also necessitated by the fact that the enemy had dug trenches west of Foncquevillers to protect his assault troops, opposite our left wing, which indicated further enemy attacks.

MG Platoon 202, attached to the regiment, had taken part in the fighting at Hébuterne, lost heavily and had all three MG destroyed. It received personnel replacements from home, as did the IR 66 MG Company, and three new MG. At the direction of xiv Reserve Corps, Res. Lt Kluge took over leadership of the platoon.

The regiment had another serious loss this month. On 16 June, the 1/66 surgeon, Dr Kross, was badly wounded by an artillery shell while in the rest area at Bucquoy and died a few days later in the field hospital at Achiet-le-Grand.

A son of Schleswig-Holstein, he was highly regarded both as a man and doctor and well-liked by all. By a miracle, the 1/66 commander, Major Schmidt, was unhurt.

On the night of 16 June, a patrol led by Leue encountered a French patrol, resulting in losses on both sides. On ours, a war volunteer was badly wounded, while the patrol leader was lightly wounded in the hand by a grenade. Otherwise, the second half of June passed without significant events. The usual bombardments caused minor casualties.

July was also extraordinarily quiet, punctuated by generally harmless artillery duels. Fire was adjusted onto targets with observers in aircraft or balloons: forward trenches, especially when new ones were observed; trench junctions; MG positions; prominent positions; communications trenches; villages used as bivouacs; artillery battery and forward observer positions. Our artillery concentrated on the new enemy sap trenches at Foncquevillers.

Our position was continually and energetically being improved. Our division commander, Major-General von Borries, often inspected the regimental sector and knew every corner of our trench system. Even higher-level commanders conducted inspections of the position and trenches, which, because of the inconvenience it caused, was not always considered an honour by the occupants of the trench. An advanced position was begun in and in front of Sectors N 1 to N 3, at the level of the sap post.

On 25 July, the much liked commander of 1/66, Major Schmidt, was transferred, and Capt. Niemeyer assumed command, a position he was to hold for the next three years. The corps headquarters also transferred Res. Lt Fahrenholz (FAR 4), who since August 1914 had served superbly as adjutant of II/66. First Lt Kleinert, commander of 2/66, left to be the head of a XIV Reserve Corps training course at Bapaume.

On 26 July, a recruit depot, commanded by First Lt Rieger (commander 11/66), was formed at Frémicourt, about 20km behind the front. Three officers or acting officers were assigned as instructors, plus a non-commissioned officer and a corporal from each company; 1/66 provided the First Sergeant. Four hundred recruits were trained here.

The commander of 12/66, Lt Rudi Schulz, was killed on 26 July by a shell fragment hitting the right side of his neck. His friendly, sunny personality had made him a well-liked comrade and commander. He was in a normally quiet position, Sector N 4, sitting in his 'summer house', and was killed by an unlucky chance hit, after having survived the battles of the advance across France and the bloody fights at Arras from August to October 1914 with only a light wound. He was buried in Ablainceville in the presence of the division and brigade commanders as well as all off-duty officers of the regiment. Res. Lt Knickmeyer took over command of the company.

Losses in July amounted to an officer and two enlisted men killed, with twenty men wounded.

August was also relatively quiet. The system for manning the trenches was changed, so that one entire battalion rested, one was in reserve and one on line, which offered advantages in terms of unity of command and training.

At the end of the month, it rained heavily, a harbinger that the wet autumn season was coming, and in order to be able to go about with dry feet, it required a great deal of work to get the water out of the trenches.

Every week a report had to be submitted listing the work that had been accomplished on the trenches, giving higher headquarters an exact picture of their strength and condition.

The recruit depot was assigned to work on the fortifications in the rear area, with reliefs of the work parties every few days, which were billeted in Ablainceville. The resting battalion was also called on to dig, mostly at night. Otherwise, it conducted training, particularly range-firing and road marches, during which the regimental band would play. There were also formations, weapons maintenance and the like. The troops could clean up and get de-loused. As relief from the boredom of the trenches, and for a change of pace, 'company parties' would be held in a meadow or garden, concealed as much as possible from enemy observation and air reconnaissance. They included sports, singing contests and other kinds of games and diversions. As a rule, they were accompanied by the regimental band and a keg of beer, with the battalion staff as guests.

In the last days of August, the British extended their front to the south, north of Arras, in order to free-up French troops, and therefore came into our sector. The troops received their first training in chemical protective equipment in August 1915, for most of us our first contact with gas warfare, which would become more and more important in later years. The training was conducted for the resting battalion by Res. Lt Gette and Assistant Surgeon Dr Purpus, who themselves had participated in the first training courses. Later, each rest camp would include a so-called 'gas chamber' for practical instruction. At the same time, immunisation against typhus was conducted.

21

In the Trenches at Puisieux, August–October 1915

At the end of August, IR 66 was transferred from northern 52 ID sector to its southern sector, where IR 170 had been. This brought a far too early end to the relatively quiet and even cosy time that we enjoyed in Sector N and its hinterland, Bucquoy and Ablainceville. The new position was far from being an improvement, which several companies already knew quite well from the fight at Serre in June. The sectors from S 1 to S 3 on the right were tolerable, but S 4 to S 6 on the left gave the impression of being inadequate and unbuilt. In particular, the shot-up and torn-up position at S 4 at the end of the communications trench left much to be desired. Many of the trenches had to be redug after the fighting in June and were still incomplete. The state of the dugouts was not so well advanced as in our old position, probably because the work had been disturbed more by enemy artillery fire. The companies were divided into four platoons. The trench system conformed to the system that had been universally implemented; the front (first) position, intermediate (second) position and reserve (third) position, each consisting of several trench lines one behind the other, connected by approach trenches, which sometimes could be used as stop-lines.

The regimental rest area and regimental HQ were at Puisieux, which was already badly damaged but nevertheless still occupied by some of the inhabitants. Achiet-le-Petit, which was somewhat farther to the rear, was also used as a rest area, as well as being the location of the regimental administrative area (rations, purser, railhead) and was therefore the target of frequent air attacks.

On 28 August, there was a fight between a numerically superior enemy patrol and one of ours, made up of men from 1 and 9/ 66, during which we took weapons and equipment.

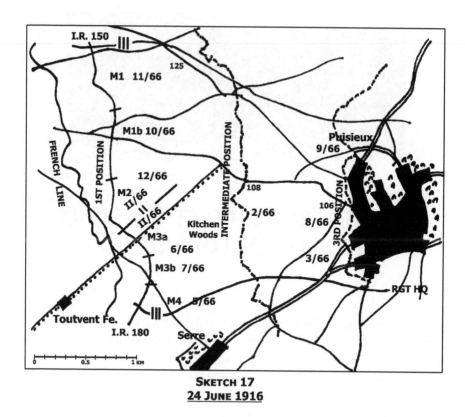

SKETCH 17
24 JUNE 1916

Two battalions were on the front line, with three companies forward, one in reserve. There was an artillery forward observer in every battalion sector, with an artillery battery in direct support. A MG was employed in each company sector. The enemy used MG to fire at our approach routes in particular and rear area in general, which both continually disturbed our operations and caused casualties. We therefore employed so-called 'wandering MG', one in each battalion area, that conducted indirect fire from positions behind the front lines against the enemy rear area. The reserve company in the right-hand battalion was in the so-called Guard trench, where the sector battalion commander and the battalion kitchens were located. The commander of the left-hand battalion was in the Kitchen Wood (*Küchenwaldchen*) trench, because in this small copse, which was a somewhat concealed location, was the battalion kitchen and the well. In the late summer and fall of 1915, this was bisected by a deep communications trench. It was an idyllic place to be; in the course of time, it became less so, and in a year there was hardly anything left. It had been replaced by a field of shell craters, a swamp and chewed-up tree trunks.

The battalions now spent ten days on the front line, then five days resting, with two companies in Puisieux, and two in Achiet-le-Petit. Even the rest area had to be dug-in somewhat. The larger quarters received names from home: a large barn became Magdeburg Kaserne. Higher headquarters ordered that 'hero cellars' be built as protection against aerial bombs, and later against artillery fire, with their entrances signposted in a manner that anyone passing by would understand their function. The commandant in Puisieux, who later died as the rector of the Magdeburg School, Landwehr Lt Schmidt, established a reading room in his headquarters.

Training courses were conducted in the corps 'capital', Bapaume, for officer candidates (squad and platoon leaders) and company commanders. The use of gas increased continually, and personnel were sent to chemical warfare classes in Berlin and Cologne-Leverkusen. In order to determine if wind conditions favoured the enemy use of gas, or not, weather stations were set up in each regimental sector.

As early as September, it rained a great deal, doubling the workload on the troops: in order to keep the muddy trenches trafficable, they had to be cleaned out and maintained, while the construction of new trenches, dugouts and wire obstacles continued.

In September, there were a series of skirmishes between patrols that demonstrated the superiority of our troops. On 4 September, a patrol from 4/ 66 brought back a wounded British soldier, which allowed us to positively identify the enemy unit in our sector. Unfortunately, one of our men was severely wounded and fell into British hands. On 13 September, another 4/ 66 patrol, under Sergeants May and Collet, engaged a superior British force, about thirty men, and shot an officer. May was promoted to Senior Sergeant, Collet received the Iron Cross 1 Class. We lost one man killed and two lightly wounded. The corps order of the day recognised the patrol led by Staff Sergeant Wehle, 8/ 66, on 19 September, who distinguished himself during contact with a strong British patrol, as did Corporal Hermann Soehler and Musketeers Kuske and Eifrig (who were wounded), and Schmidt and Handtke.

During the great British autumn offensive, a twelve-man patrol from 5/ 66, under Corporal Overbeck, encountered a British patrol. The British patrol leader, an officer, was shot, along with a corporal. The British patrol was dispersed and one man was captured by a listening post manned by two musketeers with the help of two others. We did not take any casualties. On the next day, this same patrol recovered the two British bodies, covered by blankets, which bold action allowed us to identify the enemy unit as the 5th Gloucester Territorial Infantry Regiment (145th Infantry Brigade, 48th Division).

On 19 September, Lt Tschmarke, 10/ 66, was hit by shrapnel in the head as he was moving forward from S 2 to S 4 in order to reach the sap head. Although still a young man, his friendly, tactful manner and enthusiasm made him well–liked by his superiors, comrades and subordinates. He died that evening in Field Hospital 4 in Achiet-le-Grand, without recovering consciousness. On 21 September, he was buried in the presence of his father, who was serving in the field as a doctor, at the cemetery in Achiet-le-Petit. He had been the leader of 3rd Platoon, 10/ 66, which formed the firing party. Musketeer Riedel was buried at the same time: on 20 September, S 6 had come under heavy MG fire, wounding several men; Riedel died of his wounds.

On 20 September, there was a heavy artillery bombardment on our position; 885 shells were counted, including many of a quite respectable calibre. This was unusual, for our sector had been very quiet to this time. But in the second half of September, the enemy artillery fire increased and there were short but heavy bombardments. We expected enemy attacks, which did not occur, hitting instead the III ID, which was to the north of us (south of Arras).

On 27 September, the commander of our replacement battalion in Magdeburg, Lt Col. Neuling, arrived with fourteen of his officers to get a short practical overview of our position.

Patrol Engagements

The regiment was well-known in the entire XIV Reserve Corps area for its bold patrolling. One of the best leaders in this elite group was the then Sergeant Collet, 4/ 66. The men in his patrols were awarded sixty Iron Cross II Class and three of his men became senior sergeants, along with many sergeants and corporals, promoted for their performance in the face of the enemy. He was awarded the Iron Cross I Class and promoted to acting officer. Collet described some of his patrols in September 1915:

In the course of a few days we lost our third man. In order to get better cover for our operation in this flat terrain, on the night of 12 September, I decided to take steel shields with us. With eight men I moved out shortly before 2000. It was still light, and we low-crawled, with the shields on our backs. At 2030 we were ready. I anticipated surprises, so I placed three men at the level of the paddock and facing half-left of it, three men further to the right facing it, while I was in the middle facing front. It began to get dark and I quickly crawled from man to man and said: 'Complete silence.' Then we heard a noise by the British wire. I lifted my head above the grass: it's certain, they're coming. I carefully raise my head. There they stand, three men, next to each other, upright. I signal my men to be quiet. They must be able to see us, but these fellows are blind. Others are coming behind them, I can't wait any longer. I stand upright and yell 'Hände hoch!' [hands up!] at the top of my voice, throwing my grenade at them. My men to the left and right do the same. But in the same moment that I jumped up, the British, twelve men in single file moving in my direction, fall to the ground. At the same time I see a long single-file line of British approaching in the paddock. I jumped to my left flank and threw my grenade into the paddock, and yelled to the men on the right flank 'British moving up!'. Now it starts from all sides, hand-grenades are flying back and forth and the rifles are firing as fast as they can. The British in front of us hardly defend themselves: all I can hear is loud howling and cries of pain. I worked my way to the right flank and encouraged my men. On the left one was wounded, on the right two who were next to each other had their rifles shot in pieces by a ricochet. We were now weaker by three men and the British on our flanks were beginning to assert pressure. Hand-grenades flashed and cracked, rifle fire and shouts back and forth made a wild din. We ran out of grenades and were seriously threatened with being overrun by superior enemy numbers. To fall back was certain death. In greatest danger, I resorted to a little trick. I ordered all my men to repeat my commands, and yelled 'Fix bayonets!'. My men yelled the same thing. Then 'Charge! Go! Go! Hurrah! Hurrah! Hurrah!'. In desperation we actually sprang up and charged the British with the bayonet. The effect was completely astounding. Their fire stopped as though a switch had been thrown, they ran back to their next position while we shot at them. We quickly gathered up what they had left behind: weapons, small sacks with hand-grenades, leather web gear, bayonets and caps. We went back to our position as fast as we could, before they could get their MG ready, and we were received by our company commander as victors of a great battle. The entire company is on its feet and cheering, our trophies were laid out in front of my dugout, where for days they were an object of attraction for the entire regiment, and everyone wanted to hear about the course of our little battle.

The following afternoon I readied another patrol. I assembled twenty men, thoroughly prepared the equipment and the procedures, in order that every man knew what he was to do, since we operated solely by hand signals. As it began to grow dark, I moved my twenty men to the famous paddock: this time I was strong enough, if only the British would show up. We waited the entire night, but the British had apparently had a snoot full and didn't come. As we came up to the paddock, I thought I heard a rustling in front of me, but I couldn't make anything out. Then I thought that the British wanted to figure out where and when I would come up to them, in order to take me.

Then the fateful though fortunate 14 September dawned. I was exhausted by the previous several days' exertion, and I had rubbed the skin off my knee with all the crawling, so I wanted to call off patrolling for a while. But

Sergeant May asked me to take him out on patrol, and since we would be relieved tomorrow evening, the only opportunity was to go out again tonight. Finally I gave in to him and arranged for him and his men to meet me at the exit from the position at 1900. I then slept for about an hour in order to be alert. At 1915, I and my men met Sgt May and his men – we were eighteen in total – well-armed with grenades and ammunition. The new men were given their instructions and we crawled out. We halted and assembled at a promi-nent tree in front of our position. Since it was still broad daylight, I could not go farther forward with such a large group. With Sgt May and my man Steinicke, we made our way to the paddock. May and I crawled forwards at the same level and ten metres apart, with Steinicke about ten metres behind us. We wanted to take our posts so that at dark the patrol could easily and quickly come up to us.

Crawling forward with the heavy steel shield on the back, and with a raw knee in addition, was a difficult and laborious process. I pulled myself forwards with great difficulty, until only a few metres separated us from the paddock. After a short rest I slowly and carefully pushed myself to the pad-dock, with no thoughts of meeting the big bad enemy, as it was still light, 1945 at the most. With my nose to the ground, I crawled the last few metres, when suddenly I heard a sharp order 'Stehen Sie auf, ik bin zwanzik!' [Bad German. What he wanted to say was: 'Stand up! I have twenty men with me!' What he said was: 'Stand up! I'm 20 years old!'] which hit me like an electric shock. A British officer was standing five metres in front of me, pointing a heavy revolver. Immobile, I stared at him, my heart standing still. He gave the same order a second time, and his voice struck me as sharply as a knife. I lay there as though I were lame. Then he discovered Sgt May to my right, turned in that direction and made a threatening motion with the revolver. I pulled my rifle up, fired and yelled 'Ich bin 25!' ['I am 25!'] and he fell to the ground like a tree. I grabbed my steel shield with my left hand and placed it in front of me as a terrific impact clanged over my head. Stars danced in front of my eyes. I remained motionless, covered by my shield. There was a fiery flash and a terrible bang and my shield fell on my head, blood ran over my face and a sharp pain in the head woke me up. I grabbed the shield with both hands and set it upright. I heard foreign voices to my front, then it was quiet for a minute. Are they coming to get me? I took one of my hand-grenades and threw it directly in front of my shield. The firing against my shield began again. Behind me I could hear Steinicke calling to our patrol. Then he yelled for me to get down and threw a hand-grenade in front of me. The British threw grenades far behind me, while their bullets bounced off my shield. My patrol approached slowly, yelling 'Hurrah!'. A tremendous battle developed, going back and forth; today the British were not going to quit. At our calls for help, the company was alerted and little by little we were reinforced, led forward by Steinicke, who today had the courage of a lion, until thirty or forty men were engaged. Steinicke called for the men to assault and, yelling 'Hurrah!', ran past me. I tried to warn him, but he spun around with a cry and fell. I jumped up like one possessed, to cover him with my shield. I urged my patrol to advance, and since we were getting stronger by the minute, the enemy withdrew back to his trench. I got Steinicke brought quickly back to our trench and then broke contact. I gave the order 'Rear, march!' and the seventy or eighty men of our company left the battlefield. Leaning on the arm of one of our men, I staggered dead tired to our position. Steinicke, the hero, died during the night. Two men, in addition to myself, were wounded. I went to a hospital in St Quentin, instead of a British POW camp. Here I received written and telephonic recognition for my actions from the officers of our regiment. The division commander, Major-General von Borries, and the corps commander, Lieutenant-General von Stein, did not stint in their praise.

Even before this, the chief surgeon visited our hospital and informed me that, in the name of the Kaiser, the corps commander had awarded me the Iron Cross I Class in recognition of my patrols, and that about twenty members of my patrol teams had received the Iron Cross II Class. To this time, few had been awarded the Iron Cross I Class, and I was more than a little proud. In addition, the corps commander personally presented myself and seventeen others with an attractive certificate. Such recognition for a company was unheard-of, and was the occasion for a celebration. Capt. Trenk congratulated me telephonically, and told me how immensely proud he was that his old 4/ 66 should be so highly honoured. In addition, the following night our company recovered the bodies of a British officer and a sergeant: the officer was carrying a diary that contained valuable information. My patrol was lauded in the corps order of the day and my report was distributed throughout XIV Reserve Corps.

22

OCTOBER 1915

Little of interest occurred in October, aside from increased artillery fire and air operations. It rained more frequently, especially in the second half of the month, which resulted in a Sisyphean task: everyone worked feverishly merely to keep the trenches passable and the water out of the dugouts, only to have the next rainstorm make everything for naught, and often caused more destruction than artillery fire. Many dugouts, if the water had not gotten into them, were islands in the water-filled trenches. Since the trenches were impassable, the dugouts could only be reached by moving in the open, which is to say, only at night or in fog. Everybody breathed easier when the ten-day rotation in the trench was over and the word went out: 'X-company is moving up to relieve us and the advance party is already here.' During the five-day rest period, it was still possible that the troops would be assigned to dig in the trenches at night, but there was always some variety, perhaps even a march to the corps 'capital city', Bapaume, with a visit to the 'Bali' (Bapaume cinema). There were also combined arms exercises (artillery, MG, cavalry, bicycle companies), preferably in the terrain at Courcelles, Sapagnies or Behagnies. As in peacetime, during the march back the regimental band would play – from a protected position. The brigade commander, Brigadier General Schüsler, inspected the weapons and clothing, which were found to be satisfactory.

On 12 October, there was another air attack against Achiet-le-Grand by fifteen aircraft, which were energetically engaged by our artillery. Six turned back. Three bombs were dropped on Puisieux, which caused no damage, and thirty bombs were dropped on Achiet-le-Grand, killing one musketeer with a bomb fragment and wounding another, both from 11/ 66, and setting the 12/ 66 stall on fire.

There was active patrolling which led to more-or-less bloody engagements. On the night of 15–16 October, a listening post from 7/ 66, supported by the patrol of Sgt Fickenday and Corporal Ernst, captured a lightly wounded British soldier, with Musketeer Czeripau demonstrating courage and decisiveness. The prisoner belonged to the 8th Battalion, Royal Irish Rifles. On 22 October, a patrol from 2/ 66 was detected and fired upon while directly in front of the British wire, with one man severely wounded in the head and leg by a rifle grenade. On the following day, a patrol from 1/ 66 lost a man killed by rifle fire and four wounded.

It was suspected that the enemy was making preparations for a gas attack, so on 18 October the entire division artillery and a 21cm mortar battery fired for effect on enemy positions with about 1,000 shells, to which the enemy artillery replied energetically. The regimental and battalion commanders conducted frequent gas attack drills: we were now equipped with breathing apparatus in carriers.

On the night of 18–19 October, a medium trench mortar was set up in Sector S, which later fired frequently at the British.

A number of officers from the replacement battalion arrived on 20 October to receive training in trench warfare, and were attached to II/ 66 under Major Paulus. One of the replacement battalion officers, Reserve Capt. Rothe, who was older, and probably no longer equal to the stress and physical demands involved, suffered a fatal heart attack. His body was returned home.

A fire in the forest ranger's house in the Bois de Logeast was extinguished by the troops, but not before a shed was burned down.

On 30 October, 200 recruits arrived from the replacement detachment in Frémicourt.

In the last days of October, 12/ 66 in the Sap Position (S 4) took casualties. This was the most advanced part of our position and, given the short distance from the enemy, had recently been the frequent target of heavy trench mortar fire. Two direct hits in the first trench destroyed the entrance to a dugout, killing one man inside it and wounding two more.

Over time, our regiment worked well with our supporting artillery, and we cannot neglect to mention our capable and energetic artillery forward observer, Reserve Lt Jähnert from Field Artillery Regiment 103 (previously FAR 75). He continually crawled to the forward position to conduct his observations, knew both the enemy position and ours intimately, and it was thanks to him that the infantry received fast and effective fire support. The troops trusted him implicitly. He was later killed as an aviator.

23

THE WAR AGAINST THE MUD, NOVEMBER 1915 TO MARCH 1916

November and December 1915 saw the highpoint of the 'war against the mud': dugouts collapsed or were filled with water, trenches were impassable, in many places men stood in water to the knees, sometimes to the hips, and in this sticky clay ground movement was almost impossible. Rumour had it that during one of his beloved morning walks through the position, the division commander, while moving, or rather sliding, through a communications trench, lost a boot in the muck. The troops showed real toughness and dedication to duty in these conditions, and not only held their heads up, but maintained a sense of humour.

It was worst in the Sap Position, S 4, where the ground crumbled easily and could only be maintained with sandbags. Higher HQ declared on 5 November that the most advanced portion could no longer be held and was given up, which from a tactical point of view could only be an advantage. Since the trenches were impassable, men frequently had to move in the open, which led to unfortunate casualties. On 3 November, a man from 9/ 66 was killed by a bullet in the stomach while bailing water out of the trench. A man from 11/ 66 was killed on 7 November while working on the revetment. Enemy patrolling died down, but enemy shellfire on our trenches increased, which led to the conclusion that he was conducting a relief in place.

On 2 November, the regiment, which had lost personnel to casualties, sickness and transfers, received 200 recruits and returned to full strength. From 13 to 17 November, the regiment turned in the Model 88 rifles and was again equipped with Model 98. The breathing apparatus were replaced by real gas masks on 8 November. The dugouts were provided with 'fire pots': if gas entered the dugout, they would be lit on fire and the resulting heat would drive out the gas.

S 4 was frequently shelled, which made trench maintenance particularly difficult, and casualties due to artillery fire increased in the other company sectors. 52 ID was reinforced with heavy artillery, a sign the relatively quiet period was gradually coming to an end.

Brigade Replacement Battalion 55 was brought forward to help with trench maintenance, which was not an easy task. They had to move forward at night through an unfamiliar position, sometimes under artillery fire, and then work in the dark in rain and snow, in the mud and dirt. As of the end of November, a labour battalion worked on the intermediate position.

As in the past, we patrolled energetically. On 14 November, 10/ 66 lost one of its most ardent patrol leaders, Corporal Rost. After the men in his patrol had thrown several hand-grenades into the enemy trenches, he was hit in the head while in the British wire. In spite of enemy small-arms and artillery fire, the patrol succeeded in bringing back his body.

Enemy air activity increased continually. On 10 November, a British aircraft was forced to land between Gomiecourt and Courcelles and the crew, two officers, taken prisoner. On the next day, another British aircraft was forced to land near Grévillers and two more officers were taken prisoner. There were numerous air raids by squadrons of enemy aircraft against our rest areas and towns further to the rear, with varying success. On 24 November, fifteen British aircraft dropped thirty to forty bombs on Achiet-le-Grand, with one man from 3/ 66 seriously wounded. On 30 September, the orderly rooms of 5 and 9/ 66 in Achiet-le-Petit were destroyed by bombs, but fortunately only a few men from 9/ 66 were lightly wounded by shards of glass and stone.

Artillery fire on our rest areas became heavier. In Puisieux, the regimental staff was often forced to take cover in the Hero's Cellar, since the above-ground buildings were targets for the enemy artillery; a telephonist was wounded. Nevertheless, both then and later, combined-arms officers' training was conducted in the officer's club in Puisieux.

Our artillery was also active. A particularly heavy fire mission was conducted on the night of 27–28 November against the enemy trenches opposite Sectors M and S. Casualties were due entirely to artillery fire – there was little direct infantry contact: in November, the regiment lost eight killed and thirty-three wounded. In general, the health of the troops was satisfactory, in spite of the damp and cold French autumn and winter weather and the exertions caused by work in and on the trenches. In the rest areas, the troops' physical condition was regularly inspected, and the medical personnel were exceptionally competent. The resting troops were provided the necessary relaxation and recreation, including marksmanship contests, as in peacetime.

Once again a training course of nine officers and twenty-five NCOs from 1/ Replacement Battalion IR 66, under the leadership of Reserve

Capt. Hagedorn, came from Magdeburg on 20 November for several days to familiarise themselves with the regiment's sector.

Continual rain meant that the 'war against the mud' continued in December, so that it had become a normal condition, which did not make it any more pleasant. At that time, our regimental commander, Lt-Col von Stoeklern, wrote a graphic description of the conditions in the trenches:

> The renewed and practically continual rain is awful. The positions are floating away. Mud like chocolate pudding, at least knee-deep, sometimes up to the hip. What had been successfully built up in the night has slid into the trench by noon: it is like the Danaides filling the vat. The division commander was in our trenches today. The muck was up to chest-high. He telephoned me to say it was worse than he had expected. He is requesting workers and 1,500 buckets for each regiment.

Alternating frost, thaw and rain broke down the best trench walls. The importance of trench maintenance, if only to maintain some kind of trafficability in the sector, led to the appointment of a communications trench officer, Reserve Lt Draheim, who was responsible for those trenches and would keep the regiment continually informed of the condition of the complete trench system.

As of 6 December, the recruit depot was tasked with working on the trenches: two platoons were housed in relatively secure dugouts in Puisieux, one in the forest ranger's house in Bois de Logeast. The regimental engineer park in Achiet-le-Grand, with a distribution point at Puisieux, under Sergeant-Major Preuss (later Lappins), was responsible for maintaining a continual resupply of material for the construction of obstacles, trenches and dugouts. During wet periods, masses of duckboards were fabricated here.

From the beginning of December, and then again at the end of the month, our positions and rest areas were frequently shelled, sometimes heavily; on 3 December, 3,000 shells landed in our sector. The enemy did not enjoy much success: one dead and two wounded. On the whole, casualties increased: in December, eighteen dead, thirty-four wounded and one missing. Ten of the wounded were due to rifle and MG fire. Two men were killed while on patrol, five wounded and one missing. In Puisieux, there were two dead and four wounded, as well as two wounded civilians. Puisieux came under increasing artillery fire. The village church was too exposed and completely shot-up, so the altar was moved to a barn, which was renamed St Paul's Church, but even here, as also in Bucquoy, the artillery fire became so strong that services could no longer be held, and had to be relocated to the church in Achiet-le-Petit.

In December, the regimental HQ was also moved to Achiet-le-Petit, shortly after the messenger from the MG Company, Corporal Villaret, was mortally wounded in the upper leg by a shell fragment, while standing in the courtyard of the regimental administrative office. There were still a large number of civilians, about 200, in Puisieux, naturally in the cellars. During December, several babies were born, who had to quickly become accustomed to bursting shells. The British bombarded Puisieux with 12.7cm shells, with a bursting radius of about 40m. They also employed 18cm howitzers, particularly against the Kitchen Woods. On the front line, S 1 to 3 were particularly hard-hit.

On 1 December, the 10/ 66 listening post in the sap in front of S 2 pushed back a British patrol, which left behind several pieces of equipment. Our patrols continued to reconnoitre and inflict casualties on the enemy, moving as far forward as the enemy wire. On 15 December, 7/ 66 unfortunately lost a man who was severely wounded or killed by rifle and MG fire while trying to penetrate the enemy wire. That fire also prevented the patrol from advancing further, and in spite of repeated attempts to recover him, he could not be found. During the same night, an eight-man patrol from 6/ 66 under Musketeer Becker made contact with a British force two or three times stronger, immediately in front of the British position. In a heavy exchange of hand-grenades and rifle fire, the British were thrown back with loss, but our patrol leader was killed by a hand-grenade, while another musketeer was severely wounded and three more musketeers lightly wounded. All of the wounded could be brought back, while a later patrol recovered Becker's body. In general, our patrol activity continued unchanged throughout December, without concrete results, because the British patrols would avoid all contact. The 10/ 66 suffered a painful loss. Corporal Liermann, who may not have been a good peacetime soldier, but in the field was tough, brave and dedicated, was wounded on 20 December and died on 23 December.

On 24 December, the commander of 1/ 66, Reserve Capt. Laue, who was known throughout the entire regiment for his earthy Magdeburg sense of humour, was transferred to the Prussian Guard to take command of a company.

On our second Christmas in the field, the battalions relieved each other in sequence, so that each battalion could conduct a moving Christmas service in the church at Achiet-le-Petit, the Protestant service held by the tireless and universally loved Pastor Kortheuer. Reserve Lt Schültz brightened the service with song. The companies then arranged the exchange of Christmas presents. The people at home demonstrated their love and concern for those of us at the front by sending us all kinds of mostly practical gifts. The Chief of the Regiment, King Alfonso XIII of Spain, sent his Christmas message to us on 26 December.

On Christmas Day, 100 men from the Magdeburg Replacement Detachment arrived, and in order to give the combat troops some rest, took over the guard duties in the rest areas. Two engineers and two infantry engineers were attached to each company to do the more technical parts of trench construction and maintenance. Four engineers worked on each of the fortified positions.

The second year of war, 1915, closed with no prospect of an end to the titanic fight in sight. Capt. Trenk's final entry in the III/ 66 war diary for 1915 said: 'Due to the continual rain, the week-long work on the trenches had little success, and once again they are impassable.'

The Spanish military attaché, Major de Valdivia, arrived at the regiment on 9 January and remained with us for nine days, taking an active part in everything. He reviewed the companies at rest. He conveyed to us the close ties of the King of Spain to the regiment, and his own personal friendship and regard.

Better (colder) weather improved conditions in the trenches and allowed productive work. Now and again at the beginning of January, the artillery fire grew livelier, with the British using a larger quantity of heavier guns. After 9 January, the British artillery fire dropped off noticeably, while ours was quite active. Two 21cm mortars, emplaced behind the 'public bath' at Puisieux, frequently sounded off in a deep bass voice. On the other hand, enemy patrol activity increased. On the night of 12–13 January, a member of 5th Royal Dublin Fusiliers was shot in the wire in front of S 6 by 9/ 66, his excellent rubber boots attracting particular attention. A day previously, 8 January, a patrol from 3/ 66 under Senior Sergeant Leue reported that the British seemed to be emplacing gas canisters in their position, which caused a gas alert, though no gas attack took place.

A very unfortunate accident took place on 20 January during hand-grenade training: the premature explosion of a grenade fatally injured Reserve Lt Genzel, who died the next day in hospital at Bapaume. Senior Sergeant Kröplin and another man from 6/ 66 were wounded.

The Tommies often sent their tender greetings towards our mortar in S 4, and a direct hit by British artillery damaged it, putting it out of operation for a time; there were no casualties. During the day on 22 January, II/ 66 was inspected in the rest areas by the division commander, 6 and 7/ 66 in Puisieux, 5 and 8/ 66 in Achiet-le-Petit. That night there was a surprise bombardment in the S Sector which was so heavy that it prevented II/ 66 from conducting the relief in place until morning.

The artillery in the regimental sector was reinforced. On 17 January, five Russian 15cm cannons were emplaced close behind the engineer equipment park at Puisieux. There was quite a bit of air activity, and several enemy aircraft were shot down; for example, on 11 January, one was brought down by the immortal Immelmann, who shot down a second on the same day near Cambrai.

On 26 January, the number of men on home leave was restricted, demonstrating that higher headquarters still saw the situation in our sector as tense. Perhaps it also expected an enemy surprise on the Kaiser's birthday. As in peacetime, in the field this was a festive event, with a tattoo held on the evening of 26 January in front of the regimental headquarters at Achiet-le-Petit, and a field church service on 27 January; held for the Catholics by the old, noble Father Eisele, who was later killed, for the Protestants by Pastor Kortheuer. The division commander, Major-General von Borries, gave a short, appropriate, speech to the troops, who then passed in review in squad column. The small but attractive officers' club was dedicated at Achiet-le-Petit, a simple one-storey brick building, whose solid but tasteful furniture was mostly the work of Landwehr Lt Pitschke, who had served for a considerable time as a Landwehr officer cadet and later commanded 12/ 66.

The German headquarters was preparing the great attack on Verdun. In order to keep the enemy guessing as to its intentions and to confuse him, other sectors of the front were to be more active, principally by conducting more patrols and artillery bombardments. Our patrol activity increased significantly at the end of January. The well-tested patrol leaders Leue, Collet, Frickenday and others conducted valuable reconnaissance patrols. On the morning of 30 January, the British attempted to conduct a reconnaissance-in-force. The Division Order of the Day reported:

> This morning between 0500 and 0530 the British attempted to break into Sectors M and S under cover of a heavy bombardment. S-Sector alone took about 525 heavy and light high-explosive and shrapnel shells from guns of between 7.5 and 24cm. His intention was made clear by the storm ladders, hand-grenades and torches left behind. The attempt failed due to the alert security outposts and trench garrison, and to the intervention of our artillery. I want to convey my recognition of the troop's success and my expectation that the alertness of the infantry and artillery will cause any future enemy attempts to fail in the same manner.

The 12/ 66 listening posts in particular contributed to the failure of the enemy operation.

A courageous patrol, though not a particularly lucky one, also deserves mention. Under Sergeant Müller, it attempted on the night of 22 January to take out an enemy listening post opposite S 5. It advanced as far as the enemy wire, but was soon noticed and came under small-arms fire. Several men were wounded, and as the patrol was in the open and offered a good target, had to withdraw, during which Musketeer Jaskula went missing. Corporal Müller, War Volunteer Hüselitz and Musketeer Schulz went back to look for him, and Hüselitz was wounded severely, shot in the stomach. Nevertheless, Jaskula was found, and Hüselitz and all the weapons of the wounded men were brought back, with Jaskula covering the movement. Hüselitz unfortunately later died from his wound.

To further disguise the preparations for the Verdun operation, the division commander ordered troop movements behind the front to draw the enemy's attention, in particular that of his air reconnaissance. For the same reason, our artillery significantly increased its activity, changing firing position frequently and engaging a wide variety of targets. Light, heavy and super-heavy mortars emplaced in our position conducted frequent fire missions, in order to make the British suspicious. The British return fire was not particularly strong, which, however, did not exclude occasional bombardments.

The troop rotation was changed: only six companies were now on line, which allowed ten days on line, followed by ten days' rest and training. In order to make the front-line companies as strong as possible, the infantry engineer platoon and telephone-wire-laying detachment were dissolved.

During a heavy British bombardment on 4 February, a tunnelled dugout with 4m of overhead cover in S 2 took a direct hit and one of the support beams collapsed, burying an entire squad from 10/66. After five hours of desperate digging, the company succeeded in rescuing three men, who had been trapped in a hollow cavity. After more hours of work, lasting until the next morning, the bodies of the rest of the squad were recovered: Sergeant Maass, the squad leader, his brother-in-law, Musketeer Levin, and three other men. It was later established that the dugout had been hit by a 23.5cm shell, that produced a crater 1.9m deep and 6m across.

In general, at this time our attached regimental artillery showed itself to be superior to the British and undoubtedly inflicted heavy casualties on them. It also conducted fire support for the Württemberger (IR 180) of the division to our left and for IR 170 in Sector N.

Because of the damage caused to the trenches by frost alternating with thaw, the companies continually had work to do. Duckboards were essential, and unbelievable quantities of them were used. The trench officer, Reserve Lt Draheim, became the commander of 5/66 and was replaced by Acting Officer Conrad.

Our patrols were, as usual, active. Since the British didn't leave their trenches, but restricted themselves to local security, our patrol mission became the disruption of enemy work. A patrol led by Sergeant Collet succeeded in tearing up 75m of enemy wire obstacles and bringing back the barbed wire and pickets. A patrol led by Staff Sergeant Hädrich attempted to penetrate the British trench opposite S 5 but was detected by an alert enemy. Several members of the patrol were wounded and managed to return, but the body of one man who was killed could not be recovered.

During the second half of February, the regimental commander was on home leave and Major Paulus temporarily assumed command, with Capt. Rochlitz commanding II/ 66. Capt. Trenk, the commander of III/ 66, was also on home leave, with Reserve Capt. Schröder replacing him for a few days until Capt. Freybe was transferred to the regiment. The corps headquarters transferred Reserve Lt Klaer, who had served in the regiment since the start of the war, to the replacement detachment.

On 26 February, the regiment was informed that a former IR 66 man, Capt. Hermann Bötticher, well-known to the older members of the regiment and the brother of Reserve Lt Bötticher, had been killed in action at Dünaberg [on the Eastern Front]. The Bötticher family sent five sons to serve the Fatherland at the front, and almost all of them died in combat.

The regiment sent one officer (Res. Lt Gette) and twenty-four men to the newly formed MG Sniper Squad 74. MG Platoon 208 was attached to the regiment and quartered in Achiet-le-Grand.

March brought more heavy rain, mud and hard work on the trenches. There was no more combat activity than usual. A significant amount of training in the rear area took place: rifle and MG firing ranges and, for patrols, pistol ranges and exercises with hand-grenades, with and without gas masks. Training was conducted with rifle grenades, which had been introduced in the first and second positions and were used against the enemy trenches and particularly security outposts. Field training exercises in manoeuvre warfare were held to ensure that the troops did not become dulled by trench warfare. In between, there was time for the maintenance of uniforms and equipment and relaxation, though frequently not much of the latter. We received a wonderful and elevating change of pace on 5 March when our singer, Reserve Lt Schütz, accompanied on the piano by Assistant Surgeon Dr Apitz (II/ 66), held a concert in the church at Achiet-le-Petit.

During the night of 5–6 March, the first enemy patrol in the regimental sector in four weeks was reported in front of S 5. At 2245 on 7 March, a four-man security patrol from 12/ 66 was attacked by a British patrol about twenty-five men strong. In spite of the fact that all four were wounded by hand-grenade fragments, they succeeded in breaking through and returning to our lines. Our patrols were, as usual, out every night, keeping the regiment relatively well informed of enemy activities.

For several days, the regiment had been preparing a trench raid to take prisoners and gain detailed information concerning enemy intentions and in general to cause casualties. The operation was to be conducted against the British position opposite S 5, at the Bismarck Trees and north of the Copse on the Slope, where we had observed frequent nightly activity and where the trench was apparently strongly held at night. 8/ 66 (Res. Lt Mende) was to execute the raid, directed by Capt. Rochlitz. It would be supported by the entire division artillery, numerous mortars and 200 gas shells. The division on the left would conduct fire missions on other locations to confuse the enemy artillery. The artillery would be registered beforehand against targets behind the enemy front. The operation was planned down to the smallest details. The officers, NCOs and men chosen to conduct the raid (everyone in 8/ 66 had volunteered) prepared thoroughly using a practice position in the rear at Achiet-le-Petit. The point where the penetration into the enemy position would take place was reconnoitred in detail by patrols from 1/ 66 and 8/ 66. Exact times for opening and shifting fires, etc., were co-ordinated with the artillery. The operation was conducted during the night of 18–19 March. Watches were synchronised for the last time, by telephone, at 0245 hours. At that time, two patrols under Lt Schönain and Res. Lt Menkel occupied attack positions. Each was thirty men strong, including several combat engineers from 1/ Bavarian RK Engineer Regt, and a security detachment of an NCO and twelve men. Uniform: bareheaded, with no unit shoulder straps, white armbands. Equipment: each man carried two hand-grenades, a knife and sharpened entrenching tools; half were armed with pistols, half with rifles and fixed bayonets. The leaders had whistles. Due to our own gas attack, the straps of the gas mask carrier was worn over the shoulders and the mask under the coats.

At exactly 0300, the artillery and mortars opened fire, the artillery expending 3,657 shells in a half-hour, including 560 against the enemy artillery. The heavy, medium and light mortars fired 197 shells. The artillery gas shells (so-called K-shells) and mortar gas shells laid a thick cloud over the entire point of attack. The force of the detonations was so powerful that several times the lanterns in the front line of S 5 were extinguished. At exactly 0310, the artillery fire was lifted from the point of attack and a barrage laid behind the enemy position. At the same time, the patrols ran forward to the enemy wire obstacle, which had mostly been destroyed. As Schönain's patrol left the attack position, it took shrapnel fire, but was able to run through it. It met no opposition in either the first or the second enemy trench, which had been levelled, the dugouts destroyed or their entrances blocked with earth. There were moans and groans coming out of the few clear dugout entrances, and hand-grenades were thrown down them. There were weapons covered in blood in front of some dugouts, which the troops took with them. The patrol swept through the objective area without meeting any enemy opposition, with the exception of a MG firing from the direction of Hébuterne, and then returned to the attack position in perfect order, carrying the captured enemy equipment. Menkel's patrol took heavy fire from the first enemy trench: about fifteen British, wearing gas masks, who were eliminated with pistols and entrenching tools. As the patrol swept through the objective, a group of four more enemy troops resisted and were shot or stabbed. Part of the patrol, moving along the Kaiser Wilhelm Hedge, met a group of about fifteen British who were leaving a communications trench to counter-attack. Lt Menkel shot the first man with his pistol, three men surrendered and hand-grenades had a terrible effect on the rest. The British artillery then fired shrapnel on their own position. The patrol took five prisoners, two of whom tried to resist as the patrol returned and were shot. The patrol was back in our position as planned at 0335, and a minute later our artillery ceased fire.

Our losses were light: only one man was missing (presumably killed), whose absence was only detected later. The 8/ 66 lost one man killed, one lightly wounded. One man from 4/ 66, who had been attached to the mortars, was killed. According to the patrol leader's reports, British casualties must have been heavy. Lt Menkel's patrol alone found thirty British already dead in the position and another thirty-five were killed by the patrol in the course of the fight. Including the dead and wounded in the destroyed dugouts, total enemy casualties must have been around 100. We took two unwounded and one wounded prisoner from the 6th Battalion Gloucestershire Regiment, as well as a quantity of weapons and equipment. The operation was a complete success, thanks to thorough preparation, good leadership, exemplary co-operation between infantry and artillery, and above all the courage of the aggressive members of the patrol, especially Corporal Handke of 8/ 66, who performed in an exceptional manner. Several days later, Res. Lt Menkel and Corporal Handke were awarded the Iron Cross I Class, and twenty men of 8/ 66 received the Iron Cross II Class.

The enemy had been completely surprised, as shown by the fact that his artillery took six minutes to react to the artillery bombardment, and when they switched to rather heavy protective fires, they were unable to determine the point of the assault.

The British now became nervous, and tried to push their patrols once again into no-man's-land and against our forward trenches. During the night of 24–25 March, a British patrol was turned back by an alert security post in front of S 3, leaving various pieces of equipment behind. They had laid 251m of field telephone cable, which our patrol followed back to the British trench, cut and then brought back. It appears that an enemy operation against us had been nipped in the bud. On the night of 22–23 March, a British patrol tried and failed to penetrate Sap 1 in S 3, which was held by 7/ 66, and again at S 5 on 30 March. British artillery fire remained weak and was only occasionally stronger, as on the night of 22–23 March in the section from S 1 to S 3. Previously, Puisieux suffered severely under British artillery fire, but as of the middle of March it was untouched. Our patrolling remained very active, particularly 6/ 66 patrols in the last days of March, leaving from S 4, sometimes led by the company commander, Lt Plathe, pushing as far as the first British trench, and bringing back intelligence concerning the British position, OPs, dugouts and the condition of the British wire obstacles.

There was a great deal of air activity during the last days of March. In three days, five British aircraft were shot down in the area of Arras–Bapaume: Immelmann scored his 13th victory. On 20 March, Lt Hesse departed from our regiment to begin flight training with Flight School 8.

On 25 March, from 1800 to 2200, there was a practice alert in the 52 ID sector. The second position was manned and the resting companies moved forward to Puisieux. On 31 March, Puisieux was heavily shelled, for the first time in several days. Corporal Mandla, one of the best patrol leaders in 7/ 66, was killed while trying to rescue a comrade from a burning building. Four other members of 7/ 66 were killed or wounded.

During the first half of April 1916, there was no significant change in enemy activities from the previous months. Artillery fire was the same and the conduct of his infantry gave no reason to suspect any special preparations. From the middle of April on, the enemy artillery fire rose significantly. In particular, there was an apparent increase in the number of medium-calibre batteries. As of the night of 9–10 April, the British were observed digging a new trench 200m in advance of their front line, opposite the regimental right flank (S 1, S 2). Frequent barrages by our artillery disturbed their work significantly, and it progressed slowly, and sometimes stopped altogether. Every man felt the tension in the air increase, and that sooner or later the storm would break: the harbingers of the Battle of the Somme.

The rotation for the occupation of the position was changed in April, so that once again two battalions were forward while one rested – fourteen days in the trenches and seven days in the rear area. In place of 1/ Bavarian RK Engineer Rgt, Engineer Company 104 was attached to the regiment, minus its 1st Platoon, which was replaced with a platoon of infantry engineers under Sergeant-Major Preuss.

In mid-April, the regiment received 250 recruits from home, who were formed into the 2nd Recruit Company under Lt Raddatz in Achiet-le-Grand. On 26 April, all the recruit companies in 52 ID were consolidated into a recruit depot in Frémicourt under the command of Capt. von Herzberg. His adjutant was Res. Lt Schütz from our regiment, Dr Apitz acting as medical officer. A number of officers from our regiment were transferred to other units in April: Res. Lt Neuling and Landwehr Lt Trautmann to 22 RD at Dun on the Meuse, shortly thereafter Res. Lt Buschbeck and Res. Lt Menke to 19 RD at Longuyon.

We worked energetically on both entrenching our position in depth and constructing communications trenches. The experience of trench warfare on other fronts had demonstrated often enough that only a trench system several kilometres deep was capable of resisting a full-scale enemy attack over time.

Our patrols continued to dominate no-man's-land. On 28 April, a patrol under the proven leadership of Senior Sergeant Leue, 3/66, was able to surprise a British party working on the barbed-wire obstacles, inflicting heavy casualties, capturing equipment and bringing back two badly wounded prisoners, who soon died. We were able to establish that we were still opposed by the 6th Battalion Gloucestershire Regiment.

The regiment did everything it could to determine the purpose behind the new British trench that was being constructed to our front. It was about 500-800m long and already partially protected by a barbed-wire obstacle. Progress on its construction continued slowly but steadily, in spite of harassment and interdiction fire from artillery, mortars and MG. Our reconnaissance patrols went in that direction every night. During the night of 1–2 April, a patrol from 10/66 under Sergeants Mosch and Nonnemann engaged a strong British patrol, inflicting casualties and capturing equipment (rifles, etc.). On the night of 13 April, a patrol from 5/66 under Lt Hebeler was detected early while attempting to break into the British trench and took heavy fire. Lt Hebeler was badly wounded, four other men were also wounded and Sergeant Jänicke went missing and was almost certainly killed.

The indicators that the enemy was up to something multiplied. British air activity increased, enemy observation balloons were omnipresent, our air reconnaissance found new artillery batteries, especially heavy batteries, in concrete emplacements, and enemy artillery fire increased. The fact that our higher headquarters anticipated an enemy attack was shown by the arrival of reinforcements in our sector and the thickening of the front line. On 16 April, the divisional and regimental boundaries shifted. Our right flank position, S 1, was handed over to the newly arrived Guard Reserve Regiment 2, which was inserted between us and IR 169, while the left-flank positions of both our regiment and 52 ID, S 5 and 6, were handed over to IR 180 of 26 RD. IR 66 and Guard Res. Rgt 2 were formed into the newly established Res. Infantry Bde 56. Field MG Platoons 202 and 208 formed the new MG Company 2 under Capt. Rochlitz, with six German MG, while MG Company 1 under Res. Lt Seldte had seven German and two Russian MG. The artillery in the divisional sector was also reinforced. The regiment, including the staff, now received Puisieux as the sole billeting area, with Res. Guard Regiment 2 in Achiet-le-Grand. The reconnaissance officer for our sector, S 2 to S 4, remained Res. Lt Heine.

Our losses in April were six killed, thirty-seven wounded and one missing. One of the killed was Corporal Pfeiffer, who was in an OP in S 4 along with an artillery FO when it took a direct hit. The artillery FO was not injured.

With the passage of time, the weather became milder and drier and we could re-establish the trench system. We constructed more dugouts and the barbed wire obstacle in front of our position was outstanding. The troops were well equipped with close-combat weapons, MG, mortars and grenade launchers, had good communications with the artillery, were confident of their own strength and could look forward to the coming events with calm confidence.

24

BEFORE THE SOMME

Sergeant Felgentreff 11/ 66

The happy lark sings joyfully
Green adorns Mother Earth
We must praise God's grace
The blood-soaked ground is green
In spite of much pain and sorrow
Germany's sons stand guard

We overlook the hills and valleys
Strangers in France's meadows
The plough stands peaceful and still
Soon enough come grief and misery
Meadows and fields lie fallow
Germany's sons stand guard

This misery is the enemy's doing
Who could not tolerate peace
Heaping scorn and derision on Germany
Together we stood, sooner than he realised
Regret comes next
Germany's sons stand guard

We have gone from victory to victory
Rings out joyfully, as from the mouths of angels

Only the Good will prosper
Justice will prevail
Duty is like iron, night and day
Germany's sons stand guard

We do our duty cheerfully
The enemy will never tread German soil
Loved ones, we will guard you
Awaken merry every morning
The good fight goes well
Germany's sons stand guard

25

THE BATTLE OF THE SOMME

Prelude, May–June 1916

In May, the indicators of an enemy attack multiplied. Our batteries had to repeatedly engage enemy movements. Hardly a night went by when it was not necessary to shell enemy work on trenches and wire obstacles. Above all, the British dug new trenches in front of our right flank, which required continual observation. On the night of 7–8 May, a 12/ 66 patrol under Res. Senior Sergeant Lauber observed about two squads of British troops erecting a barbed-wire obstacle in front of a newly dug trench. Without being observed by the enemy, Lauber and his men were able to enter the trench. They found the trench only half dug and returned with a steel helmet, hand-grenades and an ammunition bandoleer with blood on it. Another 12/ 66 patrol, under the aggressive Corporal Tassler, succeeded during the night of 8–9 May in entering the trench and surprising the security detachment. It returned with a wounded British soldier and several pieces of equipment. The patrol was given a cash reward of 100 marks by the division commander. In addition to Tassler, two other 12/ 66 patrol leaders deserve mention, Corporals Quast and Gladowski. Their patrols gained them a reputation in the entire regiment. All three earned the Iron Cross 1 Class and promotion to sergeant. Gladowski was decorated with the Military Merit Medal, which was seldom awarded. 12/ 66 could be proud of the fact that at the same time the Military Merit Medal was awarded to another member of the company, Acting Officer Stackmann. Sergeant Reddiga and Corporal Schoida were also successful patrol leaders who received the Iron Cross 1 Class. The well-tested patrol leaders, above all Senior Sergeants Collet, 4/ 66, and Leue and Riess, 3/ 66, were tireless, the latter receiving the

Iron Cross 1 Class on 4 May. During this period of heightened readiness, the Barbed Wire Squad and its leader, Sergeant Kühle, worked night after night in difficult conditions to ensure that there were at least several wire obstacles in front of our trenches. Many other comrades deserved to be mentioned, but their names have been lost in the passage of time.

The enemy artillery fire increased from day to day. Puisieux, Louvière Ferme, the Kitchen Woods, Serre and the engineer park at Miraumont were repeatedly shelled with shrapnel and heavy artillery (23cm). In Puisieux, four men were severely wounded, and the 7/ 66 kitchen was hit and burned down. In spite of cold and rainy weather, enemy air activity continually increased. They conducted low-level flights over our first trench line: for example, on 27 May at 0500, our MG fired 3,000 rounds at them. All of these were unmistakeable signs of an enemy attack; it became increasingly evident that we would have to prepare to defend ourselves against a major enemy offensive. From time to time our artillery would practice massing fires against changing targets, and opening fire at the most effective time. Our mortars in S 5 and the grenade launchers in S 4 participated actively in these bombardments. In order to establish if the enemy planned a gas attack, on 13 May a part of the enemy position was bombarded with 300 heavy howitzer and 100 mortar shells.

On the night of 15–16 May, at about 0230, 1/ 66 conducted a large-scale trench raid against a British sap head. The intent was to destroy the position, inflict casualties and capture as many prisoners and as much equipment as possible. The operation was commanded by Capt. Freybe. The northern patrol was led by Lt Lorleberg, the centre patrol Lt Elsmann and southern patrol Lt Henze, along with the proven patrol leaders of their companies, Senior Sergeants Leue 3/ 66 and Collet 4/ 66, and 160 men. After a heavy artillery preparation – about 3,600 shells were fired – the enemy position was penetrated at the Skupin Hedge (*Skupinhecke*), Bismarck Trees (*Bismarckbäumen*) and the Kaiser Wilhelm Hedge (*Kaiser-Wilhelm-Hecke* – not on map). We took twenty-nine prisoners (seven of them wounded) and brought back two British dead, captured nineteen rifles, two carbines with bayonets, thirty-four gas masks, thirty-one sets of personal web gear, ten hand-grenades, twelve picks and four coats. We had two men wounded. During the operation, enemy artillery fire was very weak, began firing about ten minutes after the start of the operation and was spread pretty evenly along the trench in the section to our left. Weak fire also landed in our rear area: during and after the operation, one heavy and one light shell landed every minute in S 2a and S 2b. Tear gas was detected in the first trench of S 2a. Senior Sergeant Collet described the raid:

In the trench we excitedly awaited the order to attack. Finally, the clock showed that it was time. To our front, an unforgettably beautiful fireworks, flashing and shaking. The ascending mortar bombs big and little looked like comets trailing fiery tails. From the rear came blazing 'champagne bottles', the heavy shells. The smaller shells sped past them like shooting stars, a colourful mixture. The earth in front of us shook with massive flaming explosions, thousands of smaller artillery and mortar shells cracking between them, as though fired from a huge machine gun, a regular thunderstorm of iron flew over our heads. We pressed ourselves against the wall of the trench and held fast to our heads, which were in severe pain from the force of the explosions. The ten minutes of artillery preparation never seemed to end. With a pistol in the coat pocket and a bandoleer of hand-grenades over the shoulder, we had hands and feet free to run over trenches and shell holes and wire obstacles. Nine minutes. I yelled 'Get ready!'. Ten minutes, and the unbelievable artillery fire stopped like a deep intake of breath. 'Go! Go!', I shout to my left and right, and like cats we climb up the assault ladders and out of the trench. The artillery fired, half so strong as before. Now the enemy artillery answered, and far to the rear the tapping of an MG could be heard. S-s-s-s humming, like a swarm of bees, the MG rounds fly past our ears. The men in front throw themselves flat on the ground, the men behind them fall on their backs in a pile. The MG ceases fire and we're back on our feet again. It's somewhat uphill to the British position, and the MG opens fire again, the rounds going over our heads. We quickly close on the enemy, any second we will reach the wire obstacle.

Then, as though by a giant hand, I am seized, thrown into the air and carried away: I see a tall column of fire, because it's dark. I wake up in a large shell hole, with several of my men around me. Shells land left and right, but I don't think that I have been wounded. We are lying nearly in the middle of our own barrage. It's practically impossible to get through it, but that's what we have to do. I call out to my men, who are in the surrounding shell holes, 'We go back and link up with Patrol Lorleberg!', whom we were attached to for this operation. Then we return nearly as far as our position, then parallel to it past the remains of the Skupin Hedge, and soon we catch up with Patrol Lorleberg, scattered about in the terrain. We still can't get into the enemy position, blocked once again by our own barrage. What now? Capt. Trenk is the sector commander, and I send a runner back to him, requesting that he get our thrice-cursed artillery to cease fire. After about ten minutes they actually do so. We encourage one another and soon we rush forwards, when the damn artillery again begins landing near us. Everybody yells 'Go back! Go back!'. We take cover in our old sap head trench, in the middle of no-man's-land. Now I send a second runner to Capt. Trenk. The first runner reports back that the barrage has already been shifted forward twice: we haven't noticed a thing. He also brings us the report that the other patrols have already taken prisoners. We are quite aggravated with our artillery, as they have really spoiled our fun. The withdrawal signal is sounded. Lt Lorleberg collected his men, the operation was called off. Lying next to me are Krieger V [there are five men in the regiment named Krieger], Schmuhl and Breckau, and two men from 2/ 66. Krieger V is really gung-ho, and says to me: 'Sergeant, I'm not going back without a Brit, even if it kills me.' Schmuhl agrees: 'We're going to stay here until the shelling stops, then we're going over there and get us a Tommy.' Somebody calls from our position, 'Collet, move back!'. Lt Lorleberg's whistle sounds, while our artillery continues to fire merrily. Our damn artillery doesn't cease fire until 0400. As one man, we yell 'Let's go!' and with a few steps we're in a jungle of shot-up wire obstacles and trenches, and we see our first British, running away. I encounter a collapsed dugout and shine my flashlight into it: a heap of men lying this way and that, among wooden boards and debris. We move further down wrecked trenches, over an indescribable confusion of boards and beams and dead bodies.

Suddenly we confront five British: there's yelling and hollering and the first hand-grenades fly back and forth. We split up to get behind the British and cut off their retreat. I call out to them to surrender and 'Hände hoch!' [Hands up!]. They reply with fire. No more mercy. We have surrounded them in a half-circle and they are trapped. We throw hand-grenades and then charge, firing our pistols. Two of them run directly into me. I yell 'Hände hoch!' and fire. The first one sinks to his knees in my arms, the second falls on his back. I grab the nearest one by the shoulders and haul him upright. He raises his hands, staggers and falls back. Krieger V yells victoriously, 'I have one, I have one!'. I don't let mine loose again. He hangs limp and I grab him by an arm and leg and drag him back. He's like lead. Finally, each of us is carrying a dead Brit and heads for home. It's a heavy burden, and no one has the strength to haul his trophy out of the trench. We all yell for help, but no one wants to abandon his prize. There is nothing for it but to help each other haul the bodies over the lip of the trench. In groups of two or three, we get to the British wire obstacle. Dawn begins to break, and completely exhausted by the torn-up terrain, we lay down to rest between the bodies. We call over to our position for help. Then we load a dead Brit on Krieger V's shoulders and he carries it to our position. Soon Lt Lorleberg appears with an entire group to help out. 'What are we going to do with dead bodies?' he says. 'Leave them and bring back live ones.' But the entire area near the British position is empty: there are no more to be had.

We look through the British position, searching for booty. We're supposed to collect rifles, helmets, web gear, shelter halves, tinned meat. Slowly the British begin to fire on us from their rearward positions. It's time to go home. It's daylight by the time we all assemble, with no casualties, at our position with our meagre trophies. Although our patrol failed to reach its objectives because of our artillery's mistakes, nevertheless we were somewhat satisfied.

Our regimental commander was in a fury, not because of the artillery screw-up, but because he thought I was a casualty. When I and five men did not return, in spite of repeated signals to do so, he ordered the artillery to continue the barrage on the British position, to prevent them from carrying us off. So while the artillery fired for an hour in revenge for me, I was sitting in a shell hole with a few men and cursing. When the regimental commander found out what had actually happened, he ordered me to report to him and thoroughly chewed me out. I really had not expected this kind of a reward, but inwardly I was gratified to see that my commander valued me so highly that he had the entire division artillery fire for an hour to either rescue me or exact revenge. A few days later our commander gave me compensation and promoted me to Senior Sergeant, probably on the recommendation of my company commander and Capt. Niemeyer.

A few days after this operation, a patrol from 7/ 66 under Corporal Ernst penetrated into the enemy position, shot the sentry and brought back his rifle. Unfortunately, two days later he was killed attempting to break into the position at the same place, and two men in his patrol were wounded.

The threat of an enemy offensive made it necessary to reinforce the front line. New units were brought in and the unit sectors reorganised. In the night of 20–21 May, IR 170 of 2 Guard Reserve Division took over the northern part of S 2. Our regiment occupied the newly established Middle sector, consisting of the southern part of S 2, S 3, S 4 and S 5 and the north part of S 6, which we took over from IR 180. Lt Heine assumed command of 3/ 66 and Res. Lt Taube became reconnaissance officer. The so-called Sap Head Position was reinforced with a new system of trenches, as was the Paulus Position [named for the ii/ 66 commander], which overlooked the surrounding terrain, especially to the south, and provided good fields of fire and observation.

On the morning of 1 June, we discovered that the British had dug a new trench in front of our position, this time in front of our left flank. Our artillery ensured that he could not work on it at night undisturbed. The enemy artillery conducted lively registration fire. Mortar fire on both sides became more intense. Enemy air activity increased from day to day. At 0300 on 4 June, after an hour-long bombardment of S 5 and S 6, the enemy attempted to break into our position at S 4 but was foiled by the alert garrison. Only one British soldier succeeded in reaching the German trench, and he did not come out alive. More dead British were found in the wire. We lost five men and the 11/ 66 laundry and battalion headquarters took direct hits.

There were very frequent enemy attempts to break into our position or destroy our wire. The German musketeer did his duty and in many cases they failed. During the night of 15–16 June, Corporal Garlipp, from 10/ 66, the leader of a sap head post, drove off a British patrol that apparently had a mission to blow lanes through our wire obstacles. The British had thin tubes 4m long, filled with explosives and equipped with cord to ignite the fuse [Bangelore Torpedoes]. When a patrol under Sergeant Mosch engaged the British, one of these charges exploded in our wire, inflicting casualties on the British and forcing them to withdraw. The patrol found two more tubes, two rifles with fixed bayonets and a steel helmet. One of the tubes exploded in our trench, damaging it severely but causing no casualties. The other was blown up at the engineer depot at Puisieux. All involved were recognised by the division commander in the Division Order of the Day on 12 June.

The indicators that the enemy intended to conduct an offensive became continually clearer, leading to increased patrolling by us. On the night of 16–17 June, a patrol from 6/ 66 under Sergeant Naumann encountered an enemy patrol, which withdrew after a hot firefight. A seriously wounded British soldier was brought back to our position. A patrol from 4/ 66 under Senior Sergeant Collet inflicted severe casualties on a British patrol in a bitter hand-grenade fight. One of our men was killed, three wounded; all were brought back, along with a British prisoner.

The enemy artillery often conducted sudden, short bombardments of our position, the communication trenches, the Kitchen Woods and Puisieux. Enemy air activity reached a previously unknown intensity. It was becoming increasingly difficult for German aviation to fly over the enemy positions: we could observe enemy aircraft relieving one another. Our artillery shot down a British aircraft east of Puisieux, killing the crew. Once the enemy artillery had registered on our forward position, the intermediate position and the edge of Puisieux, new batteries of all calibres appeared continually. There could no longer be any doubt that a major enemy attack was about to take place.

The entire regiment waited tensely for the day of battle. It was confident in the strength of the position, which had been constructed with so much hard work, and in its own unshakeable prowess in combat, and was certain that it would defeat the enemy. Neither the troops nor the commanders suspected that the coming battle would be one of the most difficult of the entire war.

26

DRUMFIRE

On 24 June, a tremendous bombardment began on a 40km front from Gomiécourt to far south of the Somme. The British and French employed thousands of guns and an immeasurable quantity of munitions, of which the Germans had not the sixth part to oppose it. Thirty-seven assault divisions were arrayed against eleven German. The battle began with an unheard-of seven-day drumfire preparatory bombardment. At 0645, the entire regimental sector, above all the communications trenches, were shelled by light and heavy batteries. The regiment was deployed:

Right-hand battalion: III/ 66
1st and 2nd trenches M 1 – 11/ 66
1st and 2nd trenches M 1b – 10/ 66
M 2 – 12/ 66
3rd and Guard trenches   9/ 66

Left-hand battalion: II/ 66
1st and 2nd trenches M 3a – 6/ 66
M 3b – 7/ 66
M 4 – 5/ 66
3rd trench, south half 8/ 66
north half 3/ 66
Intermediate position (Regimental reserve) 2/ 66

Brigade reserve 1/ 66 and 4/ 66 with two MG

52 ID ordered the regimental HQ to move to the Command Post (CP). Regiment ordered the battalion HQ to occupy their CPs. During the afternoon, the fire grew weaker, then increased in intensity towards evening. The fire was concentrated on M 1b, M 2, M 3b and M 4. The brigade reserve, 1/ 6 and 4/ 66, were returned to regiment control at 2045. The regiment issued the following order:

Regimental operations order   2130 24 June 1916

1/ 66 and 4/ 66 move after dark. Each man will draw three hand-grenades from the engineer park and three days' rations from the ration dump at Puisieux. 4/ 66 is attached to III/ 66 and occupies the Paulus trench. 2/ 66 occupies the Krüger Path (*Krügerweg*) and the 3rd trench south of Scupin Hedge (*Scupinhecke*). 9/ 66 moves into the 3rd trench north of the Scupin Hedge. 1/ 66 occupies the intermediate position right of the Forest Path (*Waldweg*) exclusive, 2/ 66 the intermediate position on the left. Both companies remain regimental reserve. The two MG from the former brigade reserve are in regimental reserve at Puisieux. The two MG Company commanders occupy their posts in the position. Staff 1/ 66 in the regimental CP.   Signed von Stoeklern

The intensity of the enemy artillery fire increased on 25 June: numerous new heavy batteries began firing. Many of the observation posts (OPs) were destroyed. At many places the communications trenches were levelled by 12cm shells. Our nightly repair work was often disturbed for a time by sudden enemy bombardments and fire from individual guns. Twelve men from the medical company and twenty-four regimental musicians were kept in the aid station dugout to serve as stretcher bearers.

From 0600 to 0620 on 26 June, Puisieux was subjected to an intense bombardment: 1,000 shells from five or six heavy batteries destroyed what was left of the village. Heavy mortar shells landed on M 1b, M 2, M 3b and M 4, initially without apparent damage. Nevertheless, our casualties mounted from day to day. At 1430, a gas cloud rose above M 1b, M 2, M 3 and M 4 in the area of the Bush Tree (*Buschbaum* – not on map), the Scupin Hedge and the Bismarck Tree. A south-west wind (strength 4 to 7km/h) drove the cloud over M 1a and the right side of M 1b. The gas remained rather thickly in the trenches, condensed on the weapons and then burned the grass. 10/ 66 was in M 1b, the duty NCO was Corporal Kelling. In order to quickly warn the company, he did not mask and became a gas casualty, but thanks to him only one other man was gassed.

Our dugouts suffered severely under the force of the enemy bombardment. Our men were at work everywhere reinforcing the weakened areas with trusses and props. These were days of the greatest stress. The men in the OPs were true heroes. As Major Paulus, unflinching as ever, was walking the forward trench in his battalion sector in heavy artillery fire, he was severely wounded by a shell splinter, as was his runner. Capt. Rochlitz took over command of II/ 66. The enemy artillery fire fell continually on the entire regimental position, day and night. At 0230 on 27 June, heavy shrapnel fire began on the forward positions of M 1a and M 1b. When the fire was shifted to the rear at 1230, strong British detachments appeared to the front. Sergeant Mosch, 10/ 66, was on security patrol with Corporal Rümpel, Musketeer Hoffmann and five others, observed the British and informed the company commander, who requested a defensive artillery barrage.

At 0230, the three men from II/ 66 in the OP in M 1a heard two heavy explosions in the sap to the right, followed immediately by shouts for hand-grenade and signal flares. The squad on alert, eight men led by Res. Lt Kretchmann, stormed forward and discovered a group of fifty to sixty British in front of the sap, leading to a viscious hand-grenade fight: in spite of outnumbering the Germans by several orders of magnitude, the British were put to flight, leaving behind a large quantity of equipment.

The British began using a new, previously unknown, type of Torpedo mortar against M 3 and M 4, five shells against each position, and a dugout in M 3 collapsed. A stretcher bearer from 7/ 66 was thrown by a Torpedo blast from the forward trench 30m to the other side of the wire obstacle. These mortars gave us a shock, as they could destroy previously invulnerable dugouts. The Cannonball mortar shells were terribly effective, causing great destruction in the trenches and wire obstacles, and the detonation was a torture on the nerves and the eardrums.

At 0245 on 28 June, another British patrol tried to penetrate M 1 but was detected soon enough by a security patrol led by Sergeant Grott and Corporal Sachse. Sergeant Grott's squad immediately engaged with rifle fire, and Lt Heberer moved forward with two squads to reinforce. After an intense hand-grenade fight the enemy withdrew, leaving two dead and many pieces of equipment. It was not possible to pursue, because First Sergeant Pfeffer, II/ 66, in a correct appreciation of the situation, had called for a defensive artillery barrage and the British ran into it. It could safely be assumed that not much was left of the British patrol. During the next night, five British dead were found.

The artillery and mortar fire increased. Our counter-battery fire against the enemy mortars had some success. At 0945, the British released gas, which drifted harmlessly by. The situation made further reinforcement of the front necessary. The battalion on the left received another MG, and the two MG in the regimental reserve were emplaced in the intermediate position. Landwehr Lt Pitschke was wounded. Prisoners had said that the attack was to take place at 0500 on 29 June, but nothing happened. As a precaution, our artillery had fired a slow barrage on the enemy front line and communication trenches at 0430. During the day, the enemy artillery fire was somewhat less. The enemy mortars did not fire until late afternoon, but when they did, were energetically engaged with artillery counter-battery fire, directed by infantry FOs, with visible success. Another dugout was destroyed by mortar fire.

There was no enemy attack on 30 June, although deserters south of the Somme had said that it was to begin at 0800. At 0740, our artillery again conducted a surprise shelling of the enemy front line and communication trenches, to which the enemy artillery responded energetically. From 0930 to 1030, enemy artillery drumfire seemed to indicate preparation for an infantry assault. M 4 in particular took heavy artillery and mortar fire. Our artillery replied quickly with a defensive barrage and silenced the mortars. When the enemy mortars opened fire again at 1800, they were engaged by our artillery of all calibres, after which they ceased firing. Another dugout was destroyed.

27

THE FIRST ASSAULT, JULY–AUGUST 1916

No particular indicators of an enemy attack were observed during the night of 30 June–1 July. But on 1 July, the long-awaited assault by British infantry began. As of 0715, there was drumfire on the entire regimental sector. At 0800, the British began releasing clouds of gas and smoke, which restricted visibility. The regimental CP was bombarded with gas shells. Before the infantry attack, the commander of 5/66, Res. Lt Draheim, was killed by a direct hit while observing from beside his dugout at the second trench at M 4. In spite of the heavy artillery fire, the left-hand battalion awaited the enemy attack on the breastwork. The OP at the Scupin Path reported that enemy reserves were assembling at the Three Gable House (*Dreigiebelhaus* – not on map), Toutvent-Fme (Toutvent Farm) and Signy-Fme (not on map).

At 0830, the enemy artillery fire was shifted to the south half of M 4, while further north it continued as before, and the enemy infantry began its assault. The commander of MG Company 1, Res. Lt Seldte, was severely wounded while bringing the MG forward from the battalion CP to engage these troops; the same shell wounded Res. Lt Mende, commander of 8/66, who was alerting his company in the third trench. While observing the enemy, Res. Lt Ebers was wounded in the stomach and soon died; Res. Lt Rappold was wounded in the same way. All the MG engaged the enemy assembly areas: some guns were able to directly observe their targets, others fired from Sector South into their flank. Sergeant Ackermann in particular conducted effective MG fire. Enemy troops advancing between M 4 and S 2 (IR 169 sector) were engaged with flanking fire and shot to pieces; only a few made it as far as the wire obstacle. The enemy attempted to conceal the movement of his infantry with smoke shells. The following waves were stopped by defensive artillery barrages. Clouds of gas and smoke were released towards the battalion on the right. The attack waves opposite M 1a, M 1b and M 2 were prevented by our artillery fire from even deploying. Our trenches were under heavy enemy artillery fire until 1600. All of 5/ 66 was deployed on the firing line at M 4, so that the battalion HQ moved two platoons of 8/ 66 forward to occupy the second trench. The situation made a second reinforcement necessary, and one platoon of 8/ 66 reinforced the first trench, two the second, while 2/ 66 and 3/ 66 held the third. When an enemy concentration was detected in the late afternoon, it was engaged with heavy artillery fire. There was no second enemy infantry attack.

While the attack on our sector was completely thrown back, the British were able to make some penetrations in Sector North (IR 170) and Sector South (IR 169). At the request of the IR 170 commander, at 1745, 1/ 1/ 66 was placed under IR 170 operational control. It was not committed, as the enemy had already been thrown out of the IR 170 trench by two companies of IR 15. At the end of the day on 1 July, there were no enemy penetrations of the division sector. Our losses on 1 July were two officers and thirty-four enlisted men killed, three officers and eighty-nine enlisted men wounded.

On 2 July, the enemy artillery was active, alternating breaks in the fire with surprise bombardments: the enemy heavy artillery was silent. Our troops worked with the highest intensity to repair the trenches and the wire obstacles. Ammunition, hand-grenades and rations were resupplied. There was intense night patrolling. A badly wounded British soldier and large quantities of equipment were brought into M 4. One hundred and fifty British dead were found in front of M 4 and S 2. A patrol from 8/ 66 under the two Lts Kühne brought back a Lewis gun, a large number of rifles and pieces of equipment and a sack with letters, from which it was determined that the attacking troops belonged to 12th and 14th Battalions, York and Lancaster Regiment.

On the morning of 4 July, there was a light rain and humid weather, which turned into a torrential downpour in the afternoon, bringing masses of water into the trenches, filling some of them hip-deep and flooding numerous dugouts. The trenches were damaged to such a degree that they became impassable and all movement had to be delayed until after dark. The infantry worked energetically to clear the water out of the trenches and dugouts. Re-establishment of the trenches, which had first been damaged by shelling and then filled with mud, required drawing on all available manpower. Three hundred recruits were brought forward from the training units. The enemy disrupted the work and the forward movement of materials with artillery fire, and occasionally sent up smoke clouds [which could not be distinguished from gas clouds]. A patrol from 12/ 66 under Sergeant Tassler brought back a quantity of equipment from the forward enemy trench, including the smoke candles used to create clouds of smoke. A patrol from III/ 66 reported enemy digging a large position in front of the regimental right flank, which was disrupted by MG, mortar and artillery fire. On the morning of 12 July, it was reported that the enemy had pushed forward a new trench, and during the following nights we conducted active patrolling in that direction. We repeatedly detected work parties and disrupted them with fire. A patrol from 1/ 66 made contact with a British patrol in front of M 3b and drove them back in a hand-grenade fight, bringing back a lightly wounded prisoner and the body of a British soldier. On 19 June, Tassler's patrol was once again able to enter the enemy's forward trench, drive off the security post and bring back steel helmets, weapons, hand-grenades and small-arms ammunition.

In August, the enemy artillery and mortars were again quite active. Their principal intent was probably to disturb the re-establishment of our defensive positions. Parts of the Sap Head Position were repeatedly levelled, as were other parts of the regimental trench system. Enemy air activity continued unabated; squadrons of thirty aircraft flew over our lines. Nevertheless, higher HQ did not anticipate a renewed enemy attack, and division HQ ordered regimental HQ to move back to Achiet-le-Petit. Three squads were withdrawn from each company for a three-day rest period: above all the men needed an opportunity to conduct personal hygiene. On 16 August, 1/ 1/ 66 and 9/ 66 were inspected by the brigade commander, Colonel von Thiedemann. On the night of 22–23 August, the regiment was relieved for several days by Reserve Infantry Regiment (RIR) 107. The regimental staff and III/ 66 quartered in Vaulx-Vraucourt, II/ 66 in Langnicourt, I/ 66 in Noreuil. The rest period was used for equipment maintenance and training. On 28 August, the regiment was inspected by the corps commander, General von Stein. The division commander, General von Borries, and the brigade commander observed our tactical training. The inspection went well. In the afternoon, the officers assembled at the regimental quarters in Vaulx. Brigadier General von Dresler-Scharfenstein, the last peacetime commander of the regiment, was a guest. During the night of 28–29 August, the regiment returned to its old position and relieved RIR 107.

28

THE SECOND ASSAULT, BETWEEN ST PIERRE–DIVION AND THIEPVAL, SEPTEMBER 1916

To the south, the great battle had continued unabated. At those places where the British and French had made gains on 1 July, they continued their attacks with new units and succeeded in gradually widening their penetrations. The enemy could employ several times more material and men. By the end of August, the Württemberg 26 Reserve Division (RD) was seriously threatened by advances in the neighbouring sector to its left. IR 180, which was on this flank, moved left to concentrate on Thiepval, while IR 66 extended left to fill in the resulting gap.

Our stay in Position Middle was short: on 1 September, the regiment was relieved by RIR 99. IR 66 and IR 180, forming Res. Brigade 52, attached to 26 RD, took over Sector Grandcourt. 1/ 66 quartered in Irles, with 4/ 66 in Miraumont. III/ 66 rested in Achiet-le-Petit and moved on the night of 2–3 September to St Pierre-Divion and occupied C 1 and C 2, attached to IR 180. In spite of heavy enemy artillery fire, and gas shellfire on Grandcourt, the battalion occupied its positions without casualties. The trenches had been completely levelled, some of the dugouts wrecked. In places the wire obstacle had vanished, especially in front of C 2. The communication wire had been shot to pieces and a makeshift overhead wire had to be put up.

The companies had hardly moved into position when artillery drumfire landed at 0515 on 3 September, particularly on the first and second trenches of C 2. After half an hour, the first assault columns appeared. They were thrown back by 11/ 66 and 10/ 66 in bitter close-quarter fighting. The enemy was able to penetrate to the first trench of 9/ 66, since the company had already taken considerable casualties and there was no wire obstacle whatsoever. With iron determination, the unwounded men of 9/ 66 attacked the British, who had

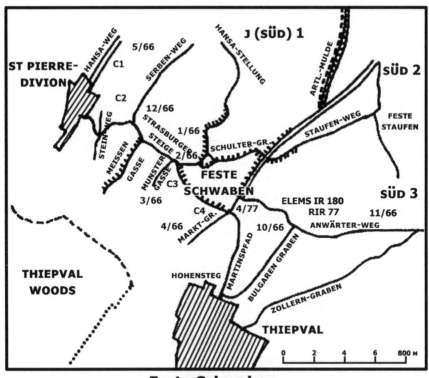

Feste Schwaben
26 JULY
SKETCH 18

already begun to build barricades. A terrific hand-to-hand battle ensued. First Lt Hermens, the commander of 10/ 66, collected all the men he could and moved quickly to assist 9/ 66. This counter-attack in the dark, over unfamiliar terrain, was a complete success. The British who did not flee were cut down. This was only possible because Res. Lt Mewes, the platoon leader in 10/ 66, immediately recognised that the enemy had lifted his artillery fire and shifted it to the rear, which allowed his platoon to quickly occupy the first trench. Sergeant Nonnemann also distinguished himself in close combat. After he had assisted 9/ 66, he moved with his squad to assist 4/ 180, where the British had also established themselves. Lt Bötticher, commander of 9/ 66, was the true hero of the day. When the enemy broke into the first trench, he attacked them with the men from the second trench. He was killed by a hand-grenade fragment, along with many of his brave troops. Res. Lt Kröplin was wounded: his leadership deserved the highest praise. At 0830, the battalion HQ was informed that the position was free of enemy troops. This success would not have been possible had not the troops once again demonstrated exemplary fearlessness in battle. They threw themselves on the British without any concern for their own safety. The casualties were heavy: two officers and thirty-seven enlisted men killed, one officer and 133 enlisted men wounded. Lt Meyer, a platoon leader in MG Company 3, described the fight:

> When I reached the dugout in the first trench, I heard someone say: 'They're coming! They're already here.' The British were already hammering on the gate to our fortress with hand-grenades and bayonets. A MG of MG Company 2, which I was supposed to relieve, was already firing: it had been brought into position while the enemy artillery preparation was still falling, but after 100 rounds it jammed, so our MG under Sergeant Horn and Corporal Müller had arrived just in time. We recognised that the enemy attacked immediately after the last shrapnels of his bombardment had landed. We found British orders to the effect that casualties could be kept to a minimum if the troops stayed as close as possible to their barrage. Their dead, only fifteen paces in front of the trench, showed how close they had pushed forward: a dead British officer lay immediately in front of my position. My gun team leader, my gunner and two other men were wounded. While on the defensive in a great battle, your entire focus is on holding your position. Your first priority is the enemy, to the degree that you cannot even help a wounded comrade. Our Corporal Müller had a leg blown off by a shell. He would have been saved were a doctor there, but he died in a dugout. My MG generally fired half-left, where the enemy had broken into the first trench, and prevented the enemy from pressing forward in masses. In the trench 50 metres to my left, 9/ 66 was involved in a ghastly close-quarter grenade fight, losing ⅔ of its men, a number of whom I knew. Several NCOs lay there, in pieces and with a smashed skull. There were many bodies, including British, that could not be moved away because the rear area was under heavy fire. Even the wounded could not be moved for a long time, and a doctor had to come forward. Their crying and groaning did not reinforce our morale. About thirty British broke into the 9/ 66 position and threw hand-grenades into the dugouts we still held. Lt Kusel barricaded himself in the rear half of a dugout and was freed by a counter-attack from the second trench, during which Res. Lt Bötticher and Lt Hädrich were killed. The trenches were completely levelled and only the entrances to the dugouts were clear: everything else was shell craters.

During this fight, 1/ 66 in Irles was alerted and moved to the *Hansastellung* (Hansa Position), 1/ 66 in Süd (South) 1 and Süd 2. 2/ 66, 3/ 66 and 4/ 66 moved into *Feste Staufen* (Fortress Staufen). II/ 66 in Sector Middle was relieved by III/ RIR 99 and moved to Ires and Miraumont, a difficult manoeuvre in daylight while the Miraumont-Grandcourt road was continually under heavy artillery fire. On 4 September, the regimental staff was relieved in Sector Middle and the commander of IR 66 took over Sector Grandcourt. 1/ 66 relieved IR 180 in C 3 and C 4 and *Feste Schwaben* (Fortress Schwaben – the usual translation, Schwaben Redoubt, is wrong). C 1 and C 2 were under heavy artillery fire as III/ 66 moved into position.

IR 66 completed its redeployment. C 1 and C 2 were occupied by 11/ 66, 9/ 66, 12/ 66 and 10/ 66, *Strasburger Steige* (Strasburg Steps) by 3/ 66 and MG Company 2, *Feste Schwaben* and the *Schwabenriegel* (Schwaben Barrier) by 4/ 66. 11/ 66 was in reserve with 8/ 66 at the *Hansastellung*, with 5 and 7/ 66 at Süd 1.

It was not possible to evacuate all of the wounded from the previous days' horrific fighting, which could only be accomplished the next day. No one concerned themselves with the dead. Since 9/ 66 had taken such heavy casualties, it was consolidated with 12/ 66 to form Company Pitschke. The trenches could be repaired only with the greatest difficulty. The men worked feverishly to re-establish the wire obstacle and deepen the trenches, which did not even provide concealment, much less cover against shells and shrapnel. The collapsed entrances to the dugouts had to be quickly cleared. Day after day, enemy artillery, up to 28cm calibre, fired on the forward trench line and Fortress Schwaben, which destroyed a great number of dugouts. The regiment requested engineer support from 52 Res. Brigade to repair the dugouts, but none were available. Bringing forward rations and engineer material required considerable manpower. It was more or less accomplished, with great difficulty and the loss of many horses, although the enemy tried to prevent it with heavy artillery fire all night. It was relatively quiet in the morning, which was used to transport the wounded. Once the wire obstacle in the regimental sector had been somewhat re-established, enemy mortars destroyed it again. Company Pitschke, and 10/ 66 in particular, suffered from cannonball mortar shells. These were days that ground down the nerves of the entire regiment. Senior Sergeant Collet described the fight at Fortress Schwaben:

4/ 66 arrived at Fortress Schwaben in heavy fog, moving down a newly dug trench, a hasty night's work, in places knee-deep, in others chest-deep. We lay down in a simple, zigzag communications trench, without any dugouts or overhead cover, no wire obstacles to the front, completely defenceless in an open trench, and they called this Fortress Schwaben. We were all of the opinion that we could not remain here, for to do so was certain death by artillery fire. Our battalion commander, Capt. Niemeyer, arrived and ordered us to dig-in as quickly as possible, because when the fog lifted the enemy artillery would open fire. We had no choice but to dig and see what happened, come what may. Everyone set to work, as fast as they could, if possible two by two. The fog slowly lifted and the sun broke through, and suddenly a veritable thunderstorm of shells and shrapnel fell. We ducked into our holes, literally level with the ground. One man after another ran to the rear, and soon the miserable trench had been completely abandoned: to remain in it was certain death. When the insane shelling ceased, the leaders rounded up their men and reoccupied the worthless trench. We deepened and widened our holes as much as possible, but the British were watching us closely and resumed their hail of fire and iron. Everyone disappeared immediately, either in their holes or somewhere else, until the barrage stopped. We were subjected to these surprise shellings for the entire day, but nevertheless had practically no casualties. Finally it was dark and the enemy silent, but for us it meant furious activity. We brought wood beams to the position and step by step deepened our dugouts, without pause, until daylight; with pickaxe and shovel, the company commander relieved the musketeer and the musketeer relieved his platoon leader. During the entire war we never worked harder than we did from 5 to 13 September 1916 in the hell called Fortress Schwaben, which actually consisted of nothing more than thousands of shell craters, in which we dug from dark to dawn like men possessed, while from morning until night shells rained down so that we could be driven nearly to despair. The worst days were 7 and 9 September.

In spite of all of our attempts to remain hidden, the British observed our work on the position. The British dropped shells on our heads at a slow tempo, to bury us or squeeze us out of our holes. Shells with delayed-action fuses dug 2 to 3 metres into the earth and then exploded and squashed everything around them. I lay with twenty men on the steps of an incomplete dugout, packed like herrings. We had about 6 metres of earth above us. Light artillery and shrapnel raged and yapped on the top of the dugout like angry dogs which could not reach us. Then we would hear in the distance a heavy gun-fire, then a dangerous roar in the air, which as it grew closer was transformed into a gurgle. Each of us knew from this noise that a monster was headed directly towards us and listened tensely, then a heavy impact, we wince, the earth shakes, the wooden beams creak at all their joints, we give out a moan and then it's quiet, except for the barking dogs upstairs. Everyone lets out his breath, then in the distance another heavy gun fires, anxious seconds, our nerves completely on edge, a roar followed by a gurgle, a terrific impact, the stairway sways as though it will collapse. Every available wood beam is used to prop up the sides and roof, so that they can withstand the terrible force of the explosions. One of these monsters follows another in an endless chain, hour after hour until it is dark. Then even the raging dogs up above are silent. The soldiers crawl on all fours to the surface, stiff to the point of paralysis, exhausted, nearly unconscious from the ordeal they had been through. The cool night air revived them, and once again it was back to work, deeper into the earth. It went on so: horror and anguish by day, hard work at night. Fortress Schwaben was a veritable Hell.

How did 4/66 manage to hold out here from 5 to 14 September? The old motto proved once again to be true: 'Words can teach, but you lead by example.' Our battalion commander gave an example of loyalty to his men like no other. He was in our midst day and night in the holes of *Feste Schwaben*, surrounded by fire and iron, where the fire was hottest, as everything else went to Hell. Fortress Schwaben stayed in our hands because of Capt. Niemeyer's leadership. I remember well even today how more than once he remained with a small group in his hole, when all around him had fled. When the fire slackened we would quietly slip out, so that he would not notice, to bring the men back: his example truly shamed us. Our trust in our commander was limitless.

The leader of 3/66, Res. Lt Heine, described the effect of the enemy bombardment on the Strasbourg Steps:

I reported to the commander of a Guard regiment at *Feste Staufen*. At about midday the next day, I received the order to move down the *Lachweg* communications trench to Fortress Schwaben and relieve IR 180 there. Since parts of the *Lachweg* had been levelled out by shellfire, we had to move in the open, something we would never forget. The enemy literally rained shells on us and the 270-man company scattered, and like a herd of cattle tried to move forward on its own. The approach of the British heavy 38cm shells was particularly awful. That the troops assembled at the Fortress Schwaben is proof of the highest levels of discipline. We lost two men, who were found that evening when we checked the shell holes. They appeared uninjured, but one side of their bodies was blue. The men believed that this was due to the incredible shock wave of the 38cm shells throwing their bodies into the air.

The company occupied three dugouts. I was in one, 10 metres deep, with 130 men. We were on the highest point of Fortress Schwaben, in the third trench behind C 4, and had the mission of supporting the first line in case of a British attack. Continual hand-grenade fights forward required we maintain the highest degree of readiness. The enemy artillery held our dugouts under systematic fire. The trenches were so shot up that it was difficult to keep the dugout entrance clear. Numerous enemy aircraft observed the effect of their artillery on our dugout. Their location was probably well known to them, as they had occupied Fortress Schwaben for a short time on 1 July. During the day we hung a poncho over the entrance. At night we dared to come outside.

Then the trenches were to some degree made passable again and the entrance to the dugout cleared. The British shells were not entirely without effect. Some of the wooden beams and props began to break, and it was necessary to reinforce them. These were bitter times, day in, day out, packed together in a dugout, with the earth shaking continually from the impact of super-heavy shells. Then the worst happened: a direct hit from a 38cm shell on the dugout 10 metres right of us, which totally destroyed the entrance. Now it was a question of digging out the thirty-eight men inside. Above all, Res. Lt Mau risked his life attempting to dig through to the trapped men, but he and his brave men were prevented from doing so by the continually collapsing walls.

In spite of the exertions and strain caused by massive enemy artillery fire, our night patrols were quite active. The enemy also sent patrols into no-man's-land. A patrol from 2/ 66 captured a signal lamp, which we proceeded to use. During the night of 12–13 September, attacks by enemy patrols on C 1 and C 3, preceded by an artillery bombardment, were thrown back. A completely drunk and wounded British soldier was brought in. At 0035, 10/ 66 reported that the enemy was closely packed in front of the first trench and sap head, prepared to attack, which our artillery then shelled. At 0730, the British began an artillery preparation on the entire right-hand battalion position. The trenches and a dugout in the 10/ 66 sector were heavily damaged. Since there were indicators of an enemy attack, the company requested a defensive barrage, which was so effective that no attack took place. At the same time, the enemy north of the Ancre River conducted a strong surprise artillery bombardment, released smoke and fired from his trenches, but once again there was no infantry attack. Enemy air activity increased from day to day. We were heavily shelled at 0800 on 14 September, in conjunction with limited enemy attacks south of Thiepval.

On 15 September, heavy preparatory fire south of Thiepval was followed by a large-scale enemy attack, which by afternoon had taken Courcelette. During this time our regiment was under heavy fire, particularly *Feste Schwaben*. The mission for the brigade order on 19 September was, 'IR 66 and IR 180 take all steps necessary to clarify the situation. If necessary both regiments are author-ised to independently commit their reserves' and, 'The regiments will use all means to hold their current positions. The enemy has pushed into Courcelette' (3.5km due east of Thiepval), which indicates how serious the situation had become. The regimental sector became involved in this attack, especially C 3 and C 4, held by 2/ 66 and 4/ 66. Senior Sergeant Collet described the fight:

By 15 September, we were well-established in our position and ready for the British. And they came. At 0730 a rain of fire and iron fell on us. 'Alarm!'. Everyone was at their posts with rifle and hand-grenades. Our artillery was still silent. There was the sound of firing and exploding hand-grenades in the first trench. The enemy artillery fire stopped or went over us. We sent up red star clusters and our artillery fired a defensive barrage. To our left, where Thiepval once was, we could see the British in the first trenches of IR 180, and opened a heavy fire at 500 metres range. To the right, the British approached up to the shell holes of 2/ 66, where the British were attacked on all sides and ground down in close combat: the British took quite a bloody nose. In the 4/ 66 sector, September 16 passed uneventfully.

On 16 September, there was heavy fighting on the right flank of III/ 66, which was on the Ancre River. At 0010, Company Pitschke detected work in the enemy first trench and the smell of gas in front of C 3. At 0100, enemy drumfire artillery landed in the RIR 55 sector north of Pierre-Divion. In conjunction with this fire, a British fifteen-man patrol moved along the north bank of the Ancre to lay a plank over the stream, where the two-man OP (observation post) of Musketeers Kohlrausch and Einbrodt was located. They, along with the two-man patrol of Herbert Schmidt and Hasenkrug, immediately alerted the garrison of the trench. A heavy rifle and hand-grenade firefight ensued. A squad was sent from the dugout in reinforcement. The British took casualties and were forced to withdraw. At 0230, supported by MG fire, they attempted to recover their wounded, but were prevented from doing so by the OP. At dawn, Musketeer Pitschinetz swam the Ancre and brought back the British footbridge, 8m long, 0.5m wide, with wooded cases nailed to the bottom. A wounded first lieutenant, who already lay on a stretcher, was brought back, along with a dead captain and a private. Unfortunately, Musketeer Hasenkrug (11/ 66) was also killed.

On 17 September, Major Paulus returned from hospital and resumed command of II/ 66. That night another enemy patrol approached the 10/ 66 position, covered by artillery fire, and attempted to break into the left sap head, but was driven back by the garrison with hand-grenades and rifle fire. A British officer and two soldiers were shot and brought in. At 1945, an enemy attack towards Thiepval was thrown back by our MG in C 4. Collet described the fight:

17 September brought an immense spectacle. Near dark the British attacked from their position on a hilltop down to Thiepval. Next to my position was an artillery FO (forward observer). A wire team had just re-established communications, which had not worked for days. He stood in his concrete bunker and directed the defensive barrage against the British. We took practically no fire and were standing in the trench. The British attacked from their trench in large groups on a front of 200–300 metres downhill towards Thiepval, followed by more masses, a stream of men from the British to the German

trenches. We fired as fast as we could, but could not see any effect. Then our artillery put a barrage in front of our position, which laid a wall of fire in front of us. The British stopped short, turned around and fled back. Then our artillery put a barrage in front of the British trenches, a second wall of fire, and dropped 15 and 21cm shells between the two. The attackers now ran in all directions, were thrown in the air by the heavy shells, blocked everywhere by barrages. We were so overjoyed we forgot to fire. Next to us a MG fired until the barrel glowed: it had never had such a worthwhile target in the entire war. The attackers were literally ground up.

On the night of 19–20 September, 4/ 66 threw back an enemy patrol attacking C 4 in a hand-grenade battle and brought back one enemy dead. Enemy attacks on Courcelette, Combles and Raucourt resumed on 22 September, and it was to be expected that he would attack at other places. Heavy enemy artillery fire with all calibres of guns against the entire regimental front made further attacks likely. Numerous dugouts collapsed, bringing heavy casualties. The enemy was observed constructing footbridges across the Ancre. Enemy attacks to our left resulted in the loss of Hamel and the Thiepval Wood, which meant that the relief of III/ 66 by II/ 66 could not take place. British attacks on Courcelette and Thiepval led to further gains.

II/ 66 had been working vigorously on the fortification of S (*Süd* – South) 1 and the *Hansastellung* (Hansa Position). When it arrived, thirty dugouts had been completed and provided with recesses in the walls. Seven hundred rolls of wire were added to the obstacle field. A new, 500m-long trench, the *Hansariegel* (Hansa Barrier), was constructed and made defensible, work that later brought considerable advantage. After the loss of Pierre-Divion on 13 November, S 1 was on the front line and withstood repeated attacks. III/ 66 relieved II/ 66 on the night of 23–24 September.

On 24 September, the entire regimental sector was under fire from heavy artillery. After an intensive artillery preparation, at 1330 on 26 September, the enemy launched strong attacks on Thiepval and the positions to the east. The companies of IR 180, that had heroically defended Thiepval for months, had to withdraw after a brave defence in the face of superior enemy forces and the employment of numerous tanks. Their defeat was an honourable one, and was considered such by the British, who took their IR 180 prisoners to be Prussian Guard. Thiepval, the 'hinge of the German West Front', was thus in enemy hands. Our regimental sector was now threatened with being flanked. The enemy undoubtedly intended to roll-up our front from the south. In taking Courcelette, the enemy came into the possession of the dominating ridge, and it would be easy for him to take *Feste Schwaben* from the south. He succeeded on 26 September in driving 4/ RIR 77 back to the *Hohen Steg* (High Steps), to push into the *Martinspfad* (Martin's Trail) and *Bulgarengraben* (Bulgarian Trench), so that Lt Armbrüster and 9/ 180 had to defend the junction of the *Bulgarengraben* and *Anwärterweg* (Candidate's Trail). The enemy also succeeded in entering the *Zollerngraben* (Zollern Trench) and the *Gassenweg* (Narrow Path – not on map). The regiment's position was now very exposed, especially 3/ 66 and 4/ 66 in C 3 and C 4 and 1/ 66 and 2/ 66 in *Feste Schwaben*. Further enemy penetration into our rear had to be prevented at all costs. The south-facing front, composed of elements of IR 180 and RIR 77, had to be reinforced. 1/ RIR 77 was sent a platoon of 1/ 1/ 66 to hold the *Anwärterweg* left to the *Lachweg* (not on map), and two platoons to clean out the *Martinspfad*, where the British had established themselves. 2/ 66 occupied the *Schwabenriegel* (Swabian Barrier) in Fortress Schwaben. Reinforcements were also absolutely necessary in order to hold *Feste Schwaben*. At 1945, 12/ 66 moved there with a MG. Brigade ordered 10/ 66 to occupy the *Bulgarengraben*, 11/ 66 the *Anwärterweg* and part of the *Martinspfad*. 12/ 66 reinforced 1/ 66 and, together with 2/ 66, occupied the *Strassburger Steige*. 6/ RIR 15 and 5/ RIR 91 replaced the IR 66 units pulled out of S 1. We tried to clear the enemy out of the area from the *Martinspfad* to the *Hohen Steg* without success.

Until the evening of 26 September, our front faced south from the *Hohen Steg* to the *Bulgarengraben*, *Zollerngraben* and *Hessenweg* (not on map). For all of the next day there was a tenacious hand-grenade fight on the *Martinspfad* and the *Bulgarengraben*. Repeated British attempts to storm the *Bulgarengraben* and the *Anwärterweg* met fierce resistance from 10/ 66, 11/ 66 and the remnants of 9 and 10/ 180, and were thrown back. Everywhere casualties were heavy. After initial success, the attack on Fortress Staufen was brought to a standstill. Two platoons of musketeers reinforced Fortress Schwaben and S 1. By the evening of the second day of fighting, the enemy occupied the *Hohen Steg* and *Hessenweg*. The eastern part of Fortress Staufen was still in our hands, but by late afternoon we had lost the southern part.

On 28 September, the enemy attacked all along the regimental front. Following a short drumfire bombardment, at 0900 the enemy attacked the completely exhausted remnants of 10 and 11/ 66 and 9 and 10/ 180, together about 200 men, in the *Bulgarengraben* and *Anwärterweg*. After fierce hand-to-hand fighting, during which all of the officers were wounded, at 1100 the British took *Bulgarengraben* and the *Anwärterweg*. The surgeon, Dr Sage, stopped retreating troops. Early on 28 September, the regimental HQ ordered 1/ 66 out of the *Schwabenriegel* and back to the north side of the *Hansastellung*. At about 1200, there was renewed artillery drumfire from all calibres of guns on the entire regimental sector, followed at 1330 by a strong infantry attack from the west against C 3 and C 4, against the *Marktgraben*, Fortress Schwaben and the *Anwärterweg* from the south, and against the *Lachweg* and *Schwabenriegel* from the east. The frontal attack against C 3 and C 4 was thrown back. The enemy succeeded, however, in entering the *Lachweg*, *Anwärterweg* and *Marktgraben*. He was thrown out of the *Lachweg* and *Anwärterweg* by a counter-attack with 2/ 66 under Lt Lorleberg and 1/ 66 under Lt Henze. The fight around the barricades in the first and second trenches in C 4, where 3/ 66 was located, was especially hard-fought. Res. Lt Man, who had already been badly wounded that morning, was killed by an enemy hand-grenade while at the barricade in the first trench. Res. Lt Höger was wounded at the barricade in the second trench, as was the brave Sergeant Heine. Senior Sergeant Kremkau fought energetically. While 3/ 66 was stopping the attack on the front and flank, the British broke through the weakened 4/ RIR 77 in the *Marktgraben* and attacked 3/ 66 from the rear. Assaulted on three sides, and taking heavy casualties, 3/ 66 was forced to leave the position to the British. Res. Lt Heine described the last phase of his company's fight:

> On 24 September, we relieved 2/ 66 in C 4. Lt Elsmann's platoon was in the left half of the first trench, that of Res. Lt Man the right half. Lt Höger's platoon was in the left part of the second trench. 4/ 66 was in C 3 to the right of 3/ 66, 4/ RIR 77, to the left at Thiepval. On 26 September, the keystone of the German front, Fortress Thiepval, fell, in spite of heroic resistance by IR 180. A squad retreated with an MG past C 4 and was stopped: our company had been reduced by serious losses in the last week from 270 men to 110 and needed all the reinforcements it could get. The enemy entered the 4/ 77 trench which occupied the *Hohen Steg* and blocked the first and second trenches with barricades. But the enemy pushed through the *Martinspfad* past the *Hohen Steg*, so that 4/ 77 took fire from the rear that caused heavy casualties. The commander of 4/ 77, Res. First Lt Sauerbrei, came over to me, and we agreed that 4/ 77 would pull back to the *Markt Graben*. 3/ 66 occupied the defensive trench between the first and second trenches with Höger's platoon, while at the same time blocking off the first and second trenches with barricades. That was the situation on the evening of 27 September. It was clear to me that the enemy would try to attack through the barricades and into the

first and second trenches. The defensive position from the *Markt Graben* to the first trench did not have any dugouts, so that the troops there suffered serious casualties when under the heavy enemy artillery fire. The enemy would soon attack us from the high ground in the rear, but if the troops in the Fortress Schwaben held out, we would be secure. This was my thought at the beginning of 28 September. Then Lt Elsmann reported himself sick: this young, capable officer had suffered a severe nervous collapse. Lt Mau replaced him at Barricade 1. He was soon severely wounded in the jaw by a shell fragment. The first trench now did not have an officer. I was in the process of moving to Barricade 1 when Lt Mau reported with blood-soaked bandages and said resolutely, 'It's important at this critical time that I remain with my men.' At noon there was a fearful cannonade. Our men fought heroically on the barricade. Res. Lt Höger was wounded in the arm, had to leave his platoon and was replaced by Senior Sergeant Kremkau. Lt Mau received the British while standing on the edge of the trench, with a sack of hand-grenades next to him, his brave men beside him. They all died heroically. The barricade held. Then the enemy came from the high ground in our rear. He had broken through the left wing of 4/ 77 in the *Markt Graben*, pushed back 11 and 12/ 66 in the *Martinspfad* and destroyed 1/ 1/ 66 by attacking it from both the front and rear. 3/ 66 had too few men with which to stop this attack, as most of the company was fighting on the barricades. With a few men, including my brave messengers, we attempted to hold the British off. Direct hits with hand-grenades took out most of these men. My orderly was severely wounded with four bullets into a lung, and as I moved to help him I was wounded in the side with hand-grenade fragments. We both were taken prisoner, in the middle of a confused knot of bodies rolling on the ground.

In spite of the determined defence by 4/ 66, the enemy penetrated into C 3, supported by low-flying ground-attack aircraft guided by horn signals. While 1/ 1/ 66 was defending against attacks from the south, the enemy penetrated from the west and destroyed the company. Lt Henze was severely wounded and taken prisoner. Collet described the 4/ 66 fight:

Suddenly, around noon, a very heavy drumfire began, which became weaker around 1300. Several wounded men from 3/ 66 arrived in our position and reported the approach of the British, which we had not been able to observe. Our company commander, Res. Lt Kühne, ordered us to occupy the shell holes, although shells and shrapnel were still falling. Then the rest of 3/ 66 pulled back to our position. The first British appeared half-left behind us on Fortress Schwaben and we took them under fire. We easily threw back a frontal attack against our first trench. A low-flying ground-attack aircraft strafed us with MG fire, while sounding the charge on its horn, and we took it under fire. The aircraft directed artillery fire on us, and slowly one shell after another landed on our position, causing severe casualties. Our company commander was hit and I took over command, waiting for the British attack, holding a pistol and hand-grenade. It wasn't long before the first British appeared, moving through the communications trench. I yelled out 'Halt! Hände hoch!', then opened fire and the British pulled back. There was a furious exchange of hand-grenades. The British tried unsuccessfully to pin us down with MG fire and their attack stalled. The ground-attack aircraft came down and strafed us with MG fire again, its horn continually blowing the charge. We took it under fire. The British attacked repeatedly and we stopped them with hand-grenades. The fight went on for two hours, the gaps in our ranks grew while hand-grenades flew back and forth. I sent the walking wounded back with instructions to get reinforcements and ammunition. We were using up our hand-grenades, and I told the men not to throw any more in order to save them. I left two men as security, and ordered the rest under cover. I took off my field service jacket and slowly and carefully threw a hand-grenade everywhere that an enemy showed himself. The men under cover fired at the aircraft. One hour followed another in hopes that at any moment help must come. As the hand-grenades ran out, I set everyone to searching for more, and found ten. The situation was becoming serious. I said to everyone, 'whoever is wounded and still able to get away should leave now'. Two medics stayed with the badly wounded. I remained alone on the hastily constructed barricade with my two observers somewhat behind me in the nearest dugout. I had only five hand-grenades, then four: I considered carefully before I threw it. The medics set out their flag in front of the dugout, which now contained only the badly wounded. I put my field service jacket back on, threw one of my last three hand-grenades, went unobserved to the dugout and talked to my badly wounded men, then went slowly to the rear with Schulze and my two observers.

Further British advance was stopped at the *Strasburger Steige* by the heroic resistance of 2 and 12/ 66 under the leadership of Lt Lorleberg and the MG Company under Lt Caesar and Senior Sergeant Kienader. At about 1700, the British attempted to break into C 2, attacking the flank of the first and second trenches, while attacking frontally at the same time on a signal from an aircraft. The frontal attack was mown down immediately by the infantry in the first trench and MG Company 1 under Sergeant Jütte in the second trench. At the same time, the leader of the left flank platoon in the first trench, Lt Krause, was killed and his deputy, Senior Sergeant Voigt, severely wounded. Therefore the enemy pushed back this platoon and entered the first trench, but got no further, stopped by Lt Seyffert's platoon behind a hastily erected barricade. In the second trench, at the junction with V 7 (not on map), Senior Sergeant Fickenday and a few men stopped the enemy in a hand-grenade fight. The enemy also attempted to break into the first trench at V 7, but was stopped by the company commander and six men. After a short hand-grenade fight, the enemy called off his attack and built a barricade at the junction of the first trench and V 7. Reinforcements from 8/ 66 under Lt Eifrig attempted unsuccessfully towards evening and again at 2200 to take the enemy barricade. The regiment had halted the attack coming from the south, delaying the loss of St Pierre-Divion and the south bank of the Ancre by six weeks. Lt Seyffert was killed on 30 September while attempting to take the barricade. The British attack on 28 August had been conducted by two brigades (8,000 men): British casualties must have been very high.

In order to prevent a further enemy penetration to the north, 5/ RIR 91 was sent to reinforce Fortress Schwaben. The brigade order attached II/ IR 180 and I/ RIR 119 with instructions to retake the lost terrain. To support the counter-attack, heavy artillery fired for effect into Thiepval Wood for the entire night, as well as firing barrages all night on the approaches to C 3, C 4, Thiepval, the *Zollerngraben* and Fortress Schwaben. At 0350 on 29 September, the regimental order reached the commander of I/ 66, Capt. Niemeyer: 'Capt. Niemeyer will reinforce the *Strassburger Steige* with 8/ 180. All of Fortress Schwaben will be retaken by 5/ 180 and 7/ 180, along with 9/ RIR 119 and two MG, which will arrive in the *Hansastellung* at 0500. The attack will be conducted at 0600 from the *Meisengasse* and *Schwabenriegel*.' The attack was conducted during the morning: the British offered determined resistance and fell back slowly, step by step. By noon we had occupied the north part of Fortress Schwaben and the west part of the *Schwabenriegel*. During the night of 29–30 September, a brigade order withdrew I/ RIR 77 and I/ 180, and I/ 66 was relieved by II/ 180, and protected by elements of RIR 119 on 30 September. During the night of 30 September–1 October, the garrison of Fortress Schwaben was relieved by I/ 170 and III/ 170 without any difficulty, except for I/ 170, moving through the *Artilleriemulde* and *Lachweg* (not on map), which encountered British resistance at the *Schwabenriegel*. 9/ RIR 119 and 5/ RIR 91 had been pushed back to the *Schwabenriegel*, without reporting this to regimental HQ. I/ 170 scattered and assembled in the *Artilleriemulde* and II/ 66 remained in its position.

A renewed enemy attack forced us out of Fortress Schwaben and the trenches to the left and right. The brigade commander ordered an immediate counter-attack to retake the lost ground and prevent a British penetration to the *Artilleriemulde*. It never took place, as division HQ had requested and received from Army Group the storm troops of XIV RK to conduct this difficult mission. An officer and 100 men from II/ 66 were attached to the assault troops.

Our artillery was directed to conduct a slow barrage to cut off the trenches in question. The gains would be held by infantry companies with MG (6,000 rounds per gun). The II/ 66 assault column had the mission of clearing out the second trench in C 3 as far as the juncture with the *Münstergasse*. At the same time, 3/ 170 would advance from the *Strasburger Steige* to the *Münstergasse* and link-up with II/ 66. The attached artillery close-support battery would soften up the second trench of C 3 and the *Münstergasse*. The II/ 66 assault column was commanded by Lt Kühne and composed of fifty men each from 5/ 66 and 8/ 66 and a MG. The co-ordinated attack was to begin at 0600. The planned artillery preparation was not conducted, and soon after he jumped over the barricade Lt Kühne was severely wounded, along with a number of his men. Senior Sergeant Schütte from 5/ 66 took over command. In the meantime, the enemy had received reinforcements and there developed a hand-grenade fight at the barricade. A patrol established contact with 6/ 170, which had also made little progress in the *Münstergasse*. Senior Sergeant Fickenday had attacked with two squads, immediately took the first barricade and then two other enemy barricades, constructing a new barricade at the junction with V 7. The enemy was quiet during the day, but after a preparation with mortar fire attacked at 1700 to recover the lost terrain. Lt Peyer, who had assumed command at the new barricade, held it against repeated enemy attacks. The other assault columns had little success, and in general the attempt to retake Fortress Schwaben failed.

At 2130, II/ 66 was relieved by II/ 170 and moved to a rest area at Bois de Logeast. The recruit companies were instructed to send replacements to the regiment. That afternoon the division commander inspected I/ 66. In the order detaching the regiment from 26 RD, the division commander said: 'I have followed the deeds of the regiment with admiration and have been proud to have commanded such determined and heroic troops.' This praise had been well earned in the most difficult days for the regiment in the entire war. The IR 66 defence of the trenches between St Pierre-Divion and Thiepval was an unparalleled heroic epic.

The days of intense combat and dedication under the most difficult circum-stances on the Somme were now behind us. The men of IR 66 could look back on this time with pride. The regiment's deeds are immortal. It had lost 1,716 men and thirty-five officers. I/ 66 had a combat strength of 349 men, II/ 66 666 and III/ 66 335. All of the officers of the recruit depots were transferred to fill the company commander positions.

29

THE THIRD ASSAULT, OCTOBER–NOVEMBER 1916 AT HÉBUTERNE

In spite of its enormous losses, the regiment could not be given a long rest. The addition of 1,000 replacements and recruits brought the companies to a middling combat strength, although there were far too few officers. But the situation on the front was so serious that we could take no account of our exhaustion. Both the corps and division acknowledged in their operations orders that bitter necessity forced them to commit the regiment to combat again.

The regiment celebrated a church service on 5 October, then that evening II/ 66 moved into Sector North and relieved the companies of RIR 15 in N 1 and N 2, with the regiment returning to 52 RD control. Res. Lt Kreidner rejoined the regiment and took command of 4/ 66. On 7 October, 2 and 4/ 66 with the MG Company relieved IV/ RIR 99 in Copse 125.

That morning a patrol from 7/ 66 under the leadership of Corporal Näter returned. It had maintained itself from the evening of 28 September to 7 October in a dugout on the north side of C 3 near Thiepval, with a British barricade on one side and a German barricade on the other, both being under enemy fire. Under the determined leadership of Corporal Näter, these eight men dug an underground tunnel back to our trenches. They lived off iron rations, rations they discovered, water from acetylene lamps and finally by boiling their own urine. The two corporals were promoted to sergeant, four of the musketeers to corporal. All received fourteen days' leave to recuperate.

On 8 October, IR 66 assumed responsibility for Sector North, and occupied it as follows:

Right: II/ 66   N 1 first trench 6/ 66, second and third trench 5/ 66
          N 2 first trench 8/ 66, second and third trench 7/ 66

Left: III/ 66   N 3 first trench 9/ 66, second and third trench 2/ 66
                      N 4 first trench 12/ 66, second and third trench 10/ 66

Intermediate position: right 4/ 66, left 2/ 66

The regimental sector took lively enemy artillery fire on 8 and 9 September, and 1 and 3/ 66 moved forward as division reserve to the Bois de Logeast. Artillery and mortar fire increased from day to day. Operation *Veilchenduft* (scent of violets – heavy-handed irony, since this involved a gas attack on enemy artillery batteries) was conducted at 0200 on 10 October. Nevertheless, on the next day the enemy artillery was extraordinarily active and shelled every sector from Gommecourt to Serre. We had to maintain the highest levels of alertness. The indicators of an enemy attack multiplied: the enemy used heavy artillery, principally against installations to the rear, and employed numerous aircraft.

Enemy patrols operated against our position, one about 100 men strong towards N 1 on the night of 11–12 October. A patrol from 6/ 66 under Sergeant Bünte warned the position, which drove the enemy away with MG and small-arms fire with a loss of about thirty men. We brought back two British dead. At the same time a security patrol in front of N 2 from 8/ 66 under Sergeant Feigenspan engaged in a hand-grenade fight with a British patrol, which was thrown back leaving a wounded man behind. A patrol from 9/ 66 succeeded in bringing back a dead British sergeant and a wounded corporal.

On 20 October, His Majesty the Kaiser arrived in St Leger: the regimental commander, Major Paulus, and a delegation from the regiment were presented to him, and the Kaiser decorated Lt Riep with the Iron Cross 1 Class.

On 21 October, 1/ 66 was relieved by IR 170 and occupied Sector Middle Left: M 3a 2/ 66; M 3b 1/ 66; M 4 3/ 66; third trench 4/ 66. III/ 66 occupied Sector Middle Right: M 1a 11/ 66; M 1b 10/ 66; M 2 9/ 66; third trench 12/ 66. II/ 66 occupied the Intermediate Position M Right with 5/ 66, M Left with 7/ 66. On account of the heavy enemy artillery and mortar fire, Sector Middle was in very poor condition, especially the *Kopfstellung* (Sap Position) and Fortress Paulus, and during the day artillery fire continued to land on our position. The much-feared Torpedo mortar shells reappeared and caused considerable damage, caving in numerous dugouts and burying several men alive. M 2 especially suffered from the terrible effect of these awful weapons. On 24 October alone, three dugouts were caved in and 9/ 66 took many casualties. Acting Officer Hagen was killed. The Sap Position and Fortress Paulus were slowly turned into a pile of rubble. We were treated to a daily routine of heavy shellings, gas attacks and nightly harassment fire. Puisieux and the communications trenches were from time to time taken under exceptionally heavy fire, and as a consequence the regiment had great difficulties bringing forward rations and water. The enemy was also patrolling very actively. A strong enemy patrol was pushed back at M 3b and enemy equipment captured. An enemy raid patrol was detected by security patrol Riedel from 10/ 66, which alerted the garrison, and a combat patrol under Corporal Lange made contact and inflicted casualties on the enemy, who was able to bring back his wounded, but left one man dead, whom we recovered.

On 1 November, Major von Stoeklern returned from leave and resumed command of the regiment. The next day brought a terrific rainstorm, which turned the trenches into a morass. Due to the enemy shelling, the Sap Position was nothing more than a field of shell craters without almost any dugouts, which had collapsed: now it became completely untrafficable. Fortress Paulus, the *Krügerweg* (Krüger Path) *Seupinweg* and the left part of M 1b were not in much better condition: all were flattened. The *Großherzogweg* (Grand Duke Path) was a flat, water-filled trough. The Sap Position M 2 could only be held by night security detachments and the *Paulusgraben* (Paulus Trench) 1 and *Borchertgraben* (Borchert Trench) became the main defensive line. As of midnight on the night of 6–7 November, there were numerous surprise shellings on the entire regimental sector. From 0200–0300, there was a heavy drumfire. During this time the enemy pushed into the first trench on the left side of M 1b, which was held by 7/ 66. The security patrol in this area had probably detected the enemy, but had not been able to report. The sentries, believing themselves to be secured by the patrol, were completely surprised, so that the enemy succeeded in occupying a small section of trench for a short time, throwing hand-grenades into the nearest dugout. On 12 November, the regimental sector lay under heavy fire, particularly the left-hand battalion and Sector South, so that the brigade ordered a higher alert level.

On 13 November, there was heavy drumfire on the entire regimental sector and Serre. There was a thick fog and the resting companies were alerted. The enemy attacked the left-hand battalion and the area to the south between 0700 and 0800, probably twice, and was thrown back with heavy losses. South of the Kaiser Wilhelm Hedge, the enemy was able to use the cover of the fog to penetrate as far as the second trench of M 3b, where M 3b and M 4 joined. The first trench of M 4 held, in spite of the fact that this enemy was in their rear. After a determined defence, 1/ 66 and part of 2/ 66 were overrun, Lt Schönain, the commander of 1/ 66, was killed, Lt Lorleberg severely wounded and captured, Acting Officer Pescht killed manning his MG. 3/ 66, under Res. Lt Zander were able to throw back the enemy attack and seal off the penetration, but Res. Lt Zander was killed. Res. Lt Werner deployed 2/ 66 in the shell craters immediately to the north of Kaiser Wilhelm Hedge and ambushed the pursuing British. The continual fire from the MG of Sergeant Küger, MG Company 3, brought the British advance to a halt and prevented them from taking the Kitchen Woods. Captain Niemeyer was informed of the situation by Res. Lt Köhne: only 4/ 66 was available to counter-attack. Niemeyer wrote:

> The situation was painful for me; I hadn't expected it. I have to admit openly, my first thought was 'what is the regimental commander going to say about this fine turn of affairs?'. I thought for a bit: these were uncomfortable minutes. Then I called the artillery section located behind me, west of Puisieux. During the entire Somme Battle, I never lost telephonic communication with the artillery. I ordered him to fire for effect on my two forward trenches south of the *Kaiser Wilhelm Weg* (Kaiser Wilhelm Path – not on map) at a specific time for ten minutes. I ordered Kreidner, the 4/ 66 commander, to attack over the top of the trench immediately after the last shell had landed and throw the British out of the battalion sector. It was awful watching our own shells land on our own trenches. We then saw 4/ 66 climb up out of their third trench, get organised, with the unforgettable small, thin figure of Kreidner in front, spurring his troops on. The company attacked, leaders in front.

Collet, then an acting officer, described the energetic counter-attack that followed:

> I lay with my platoon, left and right of the *Krosigweg* (Krosig Path – not on map), with 2nd Platoon and the company commander right and left of the *Borries-Graben* (Borries Trench – not on map) and our 3rd platoon on the left, in the third trench on the *Schüsslerweg* (Schüssler path – not on map). The 3rd Platoon had already conducted a heroic attack in the first hours of the afternoon, across open ground to both sides of the *Schüsslerweg*, into the raging battle to the front, taking a large number of prisoners. Sergeant Krüger [Krieger?] V from Magdeburg and Sergeant Schmuhl from Halle accomplished great things in the trench fight here. About the same time our 2nd Platoon counter-attacked along the *Borries-Graben*. Our new company

commander, Lt Kreider, gave his men an unparalleled example of courage and cold-blooded composure in counter-attack and close-quarters fighting. It came as no surprise when the British surrendered to him.

Our position on the *Krosigweg* lay under heavy artillery fire for the entire day, without a break. It took a lot of work for me to move my people out of the third trench and 50 metres forward, where we could lay down and escape the shelling completely. I brought Senior Sergeant Grund and two squads along the *Kaiser Wilhelm Hecke* up to near the second trench, without the British noticing a thing. I told them to lie down here, until they heard men yelling 'Hurrah!' at the *Krosigweg*. Then they were to do the same and charge the British. With the rest of my platoon, I crawled carefully through the low ground at the thoroughly shot-up *Krosigweg* until we were within one good bound from the second trench. We assembled for our surprise attack in a huge shell hole. I told my men that we had to yell so loudly that the British would think we were a large number of attackers – the whole platoon did not amount to forty men. We rushed the second trench with a bloodcurdling howling: its effect on the enemy was catastrophic. The British retreated so fast that they ran into each other: they didn't fire a shot. I quickly spread my men out in the trench as far as the Kaiser Wilhelm hedge and pulled the surprised British out of their dugouts. I found one of the first dugouts I climbed down to be completely full with twenty men. They looked at me as though I was a ghost. I laughed, bid them good evening, and asked what they thought they were doing in our position. One of them spoke good German, and soon we were in agreement. I was then shocked when two men from IR 170 happily crawled out of a corner. They had left that morning to carry coffee forward and were surprised by the British attack and captured. We then extended our position to the left to try to meet our troops and soon the company commander came towards us, and we greeted him enthusiastically. Then we all together moved loudly towards the first trench. The British heard all the racket we made (I told every man to yell out commands and the entire platoon was howling and screaming), they probably thought we were really numerous, and offered little resistance. It wasn't quite dark as my platoon retook the entire sector. We hadn't lost a single man, while our quick and complete victory filled my young troops with a powerful confidence in their superiority over the British. After this success I had once again an unbeatable unit, with which I felt myself to be in full control of the situation.

The 4/ 66 had counter-attacked from the third trench over open ground and thrown the British back. The last pocket of British on the Kaiser Wilhelm Hedge between the first and second trenches was cleaned out by evening, principally by Acting Officer Collet. We took about 200 prisoners; most of the British were killed, with only a few able to return to their original attack position. Capt. Niemeyer, who once again fought superbly, said:

> Less than an hour had gone by, and the first British prisoners passed my headquarters, and by early afternoon I could report to regiment that there had been British practically everywhere in my entire sector, but they weren't there any longer. The attack had to be conducted over the top of the trench, because there was no time to be lost and the avenues of approach, with the exception of the Kaiser Wilhelm Trench, were completely filled with mud and untrafficable. If one considers that, according to my map, the third trench lay 300 metres behind the second, and that the attacking company had to cross a wide, if badly damaged, wire obstacle, this accomplishment deserves even greater praise. The attack order came to the company as a complete surprise, and there was very little time to prepare. All of these difficulties were overcome by the high skill and morale of 4/ 66 and the outstanding military ability of its brave commander. Everyone who knew Lt Kreider would agree with me that he was one of the best soldiers that ever wore the number 66. He demonstrated that even in the gigantic scope of the World War, it was still possible for such a small unit to decisively affect great battles.

By evening, the entire regimental sector was firmly in our possession. Innumerable British bodies and pieces of equipment lay in the completely shot-up trenches. The position could hardly be recognised as such. There were no longer any wire obstacles. There was evidence of hand-to-hand fighting in front of Lt Lorleberg's dugout. Res. Lt Kluge had been mortally wounded. The highest headquarters fully recognised the regiment's accomplishments. The regiment was praised in the Army Official Report:

> Army Group Crown Prince Rupprecht:
> The battle north of the Somme continues. 14 November was another day of heavy combat continuing from morning until dark. Hoping to exploit early success, the British attacked north of the Ancre with large masses of troops … everywhere else on the broad attack sector the British attack collapsed in front of our position with serious losses. The defeat of the British attack was due in particular to the efforts of Magdeburg IR 66.

The following days were horrible. The trenches were flooded with rainwater and thick mud filled the shell craters. The battlefield, which had been pounded for five months, was transformed into a thick morass. During the night we could hear the British wounded, who were still lying outside our position, call out for help. Our medics proved themselves to be unselfish humanitarians.

As late as 16 November, the medics from 1/ 66 recovered ten badly wounded British, who were lying in a deep shell hole in water to the waist. But enemy activity continued unabated. On the afternoon of 14 November, strong troop movements in the enemy trenches and heavy enemy artillery fire on the entire sector indicated a renewed attack. Our artillery and MG fired a defensive barrage and probably for that reason the attack never materialised. Enemy patrols were repeatedly attacked and thrown back. A patrol from 6/ 66 led by Musketeer Wetzel attacked an enemy patrol and captured a badly wounded British soldier. There were numerous enemy aircraft over our position. One day two collided and fell behind our position: both pilots were dead.

On 18 November, all of our sector, as well as Sector South, to our left, and the sector south of it, lay under extremely heavy shellfire. The enemy attacked Sector South and succeeded in breaking into S 3 and S 4 and penetrating as far as the position on the edge of the village of Serre. Our regiment sent 9 and 10/ 66 in support; 9/ 66 was ordered to retake Serre. The approach march from the intermediate position was made difficult by lively enemy MG fire from the edge of Serre, and because the trenches were impassable. The company moved carefully through a shallow depression towards the *Obstgarten* (fruit orchard) and rolled up the enemy position on the edge of the village, which consisted mostly of MG nests, which were captured, with a few British able to flee back to the old position. Res. Lts Borchert and Kröplin and Senior Sergeant Schmidt particularly distinguished themselves. 10/ 66 under Lt Hermens also fought exceptionally well.

Once again, both companies had conducted a brilliant counter-attack, protecting the weak regimental flank. A counter-attack by IR 169 completely re-established the situation. The companies remained in the first line at Serre and helped materially by bringing forward entrenching material and rations. Our regimental commander and Lt Lorleberg were awarded the Knight's Cross of the Order of the House of Hohenzollern with Swords. The regiment held its sector for another week. On 26 November, it was relieved in place by the Bavarian IR 8. The regimental staff and III/ 66 marched to Croisilles, from there moving by rail to Autigny. I and II/ 66 marched to Gomiécourt, where it also railmarched to Autigny.

Thus ended a glorious and bloody episode in our regiment's history. IR 66 had to drink the Battle of the Somme to the dregs, with only a few days of rest. Nevertheless, the sons of Magdeburg and the Altmark found the strength for stiff-necked defence and vigorous counter-attack, in spite of fatigue and unprecedented enemy shelling, during weeks of iron and morass, gas and fog, mud and collapsed dugouts. There were great heroic deeds, but they cost heavily: from 1 May to 26 November 1916, 442 dead, 1,794 wounded and 473 missing, including twenty-three officers killed and forty-eight wounded.

30

AFTER THE BATTLE

It was blue summer when the battle began
Now grey winter clouds let down their veils
Twenty-two hard weeks of bloodletting
Dark night covers our silent march away

Put aside the hand-grenades
Put aside the steel helmet that has protected you
Dream not of drumfire, storm and strife
Prop your rifle up against the wall

Let us finally sleep soundly
No tension, no fear, no shellings
As do our many dead, true comrades
There at Serre and in the clay of Thiepval

Dear Lord God, let the Tommies make peace
Look, we stand brave and grim
If it must be, so take our lives
But do not allow the dead to have died in vain!

31

The Upper Alsace

Rest at Valenciennes

The troop train brought the regiment to the area of Valenciennes. After a three-hour foot march, it arrived in the rest area. The staff and III/ 66 went to Roeulx, II/ 66 to Neuville sur l'Escaut and I/ 66 to Mastaing, 4/ 66 to Émerchicourt. Tired, with unshaven and gaunt faces, and hollow eyes that still saw the horrors of combat, uniforms muddy and torn, front-line soldiers who were equal to every combat situation, who had learned to fear not even death, entered the peaceful, pretty villages. Everyone had only one thought, to really rest, and one need: to hear no drumbeat of mortar and artillery shells, no cracking of hand-grenades or rattling of rifle fire.

Our recovery came quicker that we anticipated. One short day of rest showed in our happy faces. Our quarters were relatively good. Everybody worked energetically to put himself back in order, inside and out. Since the division was now OHL (*Oberste Heeresleitung* – the senior German HQ) reserve, it appeared that our rest would last a good long time. Due to the damp of the last few weeks, many men had intestinal problems, which the doctors worked to heal: many men healed by themselves. The then Musketeer Tschichholz from 12/ 66 wrote:

> When we were in the defensive position we no longer wore our suspenders, even less so in the days of the march to the rest area. Everybody was happy to think about curing his horrible diarrhoea, one way or another. But whatever we tried didn't work. The aid stations were filled with the very worst cases: nothing was able to effectively put an end to this debilitating sickness. We were

at our wits' end. Christmas was getting nearer, and we said to each other: this will be quite a Christmas Day! Then at the last minute came salvation in the form of the owner of the house that 3rd Squad 12/ 66 was quartered in, who had a motherly heart for us. After we had continually disturbed her sleep with our constant 'down the ladder, up the ladder' occasioned by our diarrhoea, one night she said at the dinner table: 'Kamerad. La diarrhée? La canelle!'. Dear God! What did she mean by that? None of us knew what 'canelle' meant. So we hauled out our pocket French dictionaries. It didn't take long before we figured out it meant cinnamon. We were going to do everything necessary to get some. It would have been quicker if dear Madame had some in the house. The cure came with our evening meal: we ate our bread and a thin layer of butter, then Madame made a sprinkling motion with her fingers over the bread and said 'du beurre, du pain, jeter' (some butter, some bread, throw). We understood that we should sprinkle cinnamon over the bread. Madame said 'kurrier' (perhaps *courir* – run?). The entire 3rd Squad got together under the joint chair of our short Sergeant Meyer and Madame, who understood each other well. Everyone donated a few *Pfennig* to buy cinnamon, and soon two of our comrades were off to procure this manna from heaven. It wasn't very long and we had a beautiful bag full of cinnamon. Then we smeared our bread and sprinkled the cinnamon. Madame supervised: to whomever was too stingy, she made it clear that it would only work when the layer of cinnamon was thick. Once we had all been outside, we went hopefully to bed, that is, we lay down in our underwear on our shelter halves filled with straw and hay and covered ourselves with our coat and blanket. One after another everyone went to sleep, and with a couple of exceptions the night was the first quiet one in a long, long time. The next morning saw us much happier and more alert on guard duty. One more dose of cinnamon and we'd done it. Naturally we shared our cure with our comrades, and after a regular hunt for 'la canelle', the garrison of Roeulx was healthy.

Rest quickly improved the troops' health. Drill could begin in a few days, followed by tactical exercises, foot marches and training in trench warfare. Our combat strength was increased by replacements and a draft of 150 north German men from IR 169. On 8 December, Crown Prince Rupprecht of Bavaria inspected the regiment in parade formation and thanked us in the highest terms for our outstanding performance in the battle.

Christmas. The battalions held Christmas services and each squad held a Christmas celebration. Musketeer Tschicholz described that of 3rd Squad, 12/ 66:

It was time for the holy festival of love, Christmas. We naturally wanted to celebrate it, too, as well as we could, so we made our preparations. We said to ourselves, 'Who knows, this might be our last.' And for too many, it was. The main thing was – a Christmas tree! Where to get it? There was a big one in the church yard. Then we had an attack of conscience. So what – we were warriors, our souls had been toughened. Why should we be soft, sentimental, like women? The dead would happily grant us the tree; so must the living. It rained on Christmas Eve as we sawed off several metres from the top of the tree. It was so dark that no one could see us. So, we had our tree, and we soon had candles, and hanging them on the tree wasn't much of a problem. For tree ornaments we used cigarettes, Zwieback and such. Our Madame gave us twine. We managed to scrounge some cotton balls from the aid station. Our tree looked very nice. Our field kitchen made a special effort, and we had wurst and salad and an aromatic punch. Each man received a Christmas gift of five Marks from 52 ID. We had just received our pay, and there were presents from our families or donors. The canteen had been able to stock supplies, and the letters that arrived from home were the crowning touch. What more could we want? We had all washed and shaven, our hair was cut and combed, moustaches trimmed. We thought we were 'living like God in France' [a common German expression]. There was even a little rich food and tobacco. If we had been lacking anything, I think our Papa Pitschke (the First Sergeant) would have gotten it for his children of 12/ 66, who were close to his heart. Christmas Eve! In front of our glittering, beautiful Christmas tree, Sergeant Meyer gave a fine sermon to the assembled squad and our Madame, after which, according to old German custom, we exchanged gifts. Madame and her children were also provided for. I know for a fact that we had comrades that had not received a single letter from home, no loving words, no package or any thoughtfulness at all. So, at the beginning of Christmas Eve the mood was quiet, heavy and anxious. But we made sure that everyone received something. There was in 3rd Squad our comrade Reinhold Moritz. He was killed while bringing water at Colligis in the summer of 1917. This poor devil apparently did not have any parents or siblings. He was hard of hearing and made fun of, unjustifiably so. Moritz was a willing comrade, and strong, but kept to himself, probably because of his poor hearing. Everybody in the squad gave him a gift. Then we mixed the punch with a few drops of something stronger from the canteen, and ate our wurst and salad, and joked, and smoked, and sang wonderful German Christmas carols; we almost forgot the hard life of the soldier, the horrors of war, the bitter days behind us. With thoughts of home, where a Christmas tree also shone, we went to sleep. On Christmas Day there was a particularly good afternoon meal, with sweetened stewed fruit for dessert. That afternoon and evening we visited with other comrades in the company, and word got around that 3rd Squad has a wonderful Christmas tree. Everyone wanted to once again see a good

German Christmas tree, and all came to our quarters to admire it. That was Christmas in 3rd Squad.

On 26 December, the regimental band held a concert at Neuville, with which the bandmaster and his musicians warmed everyone's hearts. On 27 and 28 December, the brigade commander, Colonel von Westerhagen, inspected the regiment and expressed his deepest satisfaction with our outstanding spirit. In this manner we passed the last days of the year, and on New Year's we were still in the rest area. New Year's Eve was celebrated properly, as related by Musketeer Tschicholz from 12/66:

New Year's Eve! We had a wonderful evening. Once again the field kitchen provided plenty to drink, and since a number of men had home leave, there was more food for the rest of us. Everyone had something interesting to say, or sing, about home. We all sang songs together, played New Year's jokes on each other, and such like. At midnight we wished each other a Happy New Year. Now and again someone would say, 'Hopefully there will be peace soon.' Suddenly there were several shots, then more and more, and finally a fusillade. What was happening? Had the enemy entered the town? Then as suddenly as it began, the firing stopped. It turned out that several of our comrades came from towns where it was the custom to welcome the New Year with a *feu de joie*: we were all happy to hear that it was harmless. So we drained many a glass, until the last drop was gone. A number of our comrades had a thick head the next day, but aside from that everyone had a good time.

The third year of war was over!

32

Movement to the Upper Alsace, 1–11 January 1917

We began New Year's Day with a church service, and thereafter we had the opportunity to recover from the exertions of the previous night's celebration. It was also the last actual day of rest at Valenciennes. On 2 January, 52 ID received its marching orders. The regiment received rations for five days, and on 3 January it boarded troop trains at the rail stations at Bouchain and Jury, at which time it was released from the operational control of XIV RK. Acting Officer Voigt of 10/ 66 described the rail march:

That afternoon, III/ 66 was the last unit loaded. The companies marched singing to the rail station. We boarded the train without difficulty. We succeeded in smuggling our cow aboard, the pride and joy of the company, which I could have sold the previous day for 1,500 francs. By 1700 everyone was aboard. All the troops were in goods wagons that were provided with stoves and plenty of fuel. The officers and the four first sergeants were lucky enough to get a second class passenger wagon, where we made ourselves comfortable. However, this wagon had the disadvantage that it could not be heated: we were lucky that it wasn't very cold. Punctually at 1730, the locomotive got steam up and left the Bouchain rail yard, but no one knew where we were headed. The wildest rumours immediately began to fly. Some maintained we were going to Verdun, others Romania and others Russia or even Italy. The trip went first to Valenciennes, then Mons, Charleroi, Namur, Huy, Liège and, without quite realising it, at Herbestal we re-entered Germany. From here on we constantly checked our compasses, to see which cardinal direction we were moving in. The trip went south: Trier, Strasbourg, Schlettstadt and Mühlhausen to arrive at Sierenz [Sierentz, between Mühlhausen and Basel] at 1900 on 4 January. We were well-fed at Mons, Trier and Schlettstadt. The trip wasn't boring: we spent the time playing *Skat* [a German card game] or sleeping. As far as I was concerned, I could have kept going on that train until peace was declared.

At 1000 on 5 January, the companies had reached their quarters: regimental staff at Blotzheim, 1/ 66 staff and 1/ 66 at Niedermichelbach, 2/ 66 in Niederranspach, 3/ 66 Attenschweiler, 4/ 66 Obermichelbach, staff II/ 66, MG Company 2, 5 and 6/ 66 Häsingen, 7/ 66 Buschweiler, 8/ 66 Wenzweiler, MG Company 3, staff III, 9, 11 and 12/ 66 Blotzheim and 10/ 66 Haberhäuser.

The next day the Kaiser issued an Order of the Day:

To My Army and Navy

In conjunction with my allied rulers, I have offered to enter into peace negotiations with our enemies.

Our enemies have refused to do so. In their thirst for power, they desire to destroy Germany. The war will continue.

Before God and humanity, the heavy responsibility rests on the enemy governments for the further terrible sacrifices, which I had wanted to spare you.

In our just cause we are outraged at the enemy's arrogant and monstrous crime. With the determination to defend our holiest of values and to secure for the Fatherland a happy future, you will be victorious.

Our enemies have rejected our offer to come to an understanding. By the Grace of God our weapons will force them to do so.

Great Headquarters, 5 January 1917
(signed) Wilhelm

It would turn out otherwise, but we could not know that.

We enjoyed several more rest days among the friendly Alsatian population. Some companies changed their bivouac areas on 7 January: 1/ 66 went from Niedermichelbach to Oberanspach, 3/ 66 from Attenschweiler to Völkensberg, 10/ 66 from Haberhäuser to Niedermichelbach, 12/ 66 from Blotzheim to Attenschweiler. On 11 January we learned that we would defend a sector at Altkirch.

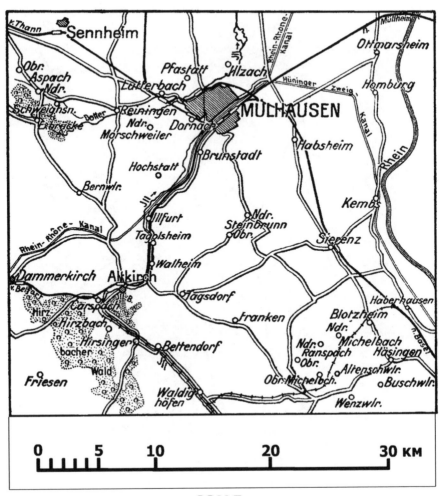

SCALE

Trench warfare at Carspach and Hirzbach, 12 January to 31 March 1917

During the night of 11–12 January, we conducted a foot march to new quarters: regimental headquarters in Hirsingen; staff I/ 66 and 3/ 66, Franken; 1/ 66, Wahlbach; 2/ 66, Zäsingen; 4/ 66, staff II/ 66, 5 and 6/ 66, MG Company 2, Hirsingen; MG Company 1, Hundsbach; staff III/ 66 and 9/ 66, Tagsdorf; 10/ 66, Emlingen; 11/ 66, Heidweiler; 12/ 66 and MG Company 3, Wittersdorf. Acting Officer Voigt was quartered with a farmer who had fought against us in 1870 and had served in a light infantry unit in North Africa. That evening, II/ 66 relieved II/ *Landwehr* IR 110 in the Hirschbach sector, with all four companies in the first line and the battalion HQ in the castle at Hirschbach.

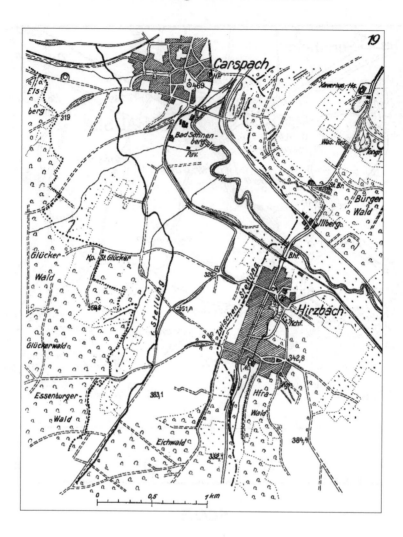

On 13 January, III/ 66 relieved I/ *Landwehr* IR 110 in the Carspach sector, with the HQ in Carspach.

The new regimental position consisted of two trenches connected by numerous communication trenches. The dugouts, with only 3m of earth as overhead cover, were not capable of resisting heavy artillery fire. Digging them deeper was difficult, and in some places impossible, due to the high water table. The trenches were constructed with loving care, but given the regiment's previous experience did not appear able to resist artillery drumfire. The enemy position was 600 to 1,000m away in the *Glückerwalde* (Glücker Woods). It had not been possible to determine his location and strength. It was only known that the French were there, probably Territorial troops, but the last time a determination had been made was half a year ago. We began actively patrolling. The enemy artillery was silent; ours began registering.

The regimental position was designated Sector *Süd* (South). Temporarily, the regimental HQ was in the county courthouse in Hirsingen; 1/ 66 foot-marched on 15 January and quartered there, with 1/ 1/ 66 in Hirzbach. Given a report that the enemy intended to conduct a night attack, the troops were on alert. The combat and field trains quartered in Bettendorf. A platoon of Engineer Company 104 under Reserve Lt Feilhauer (later Res. Lt Proelss) was attached to the regiment.

In a few days it was obvious to everyone: during the entire war the regiment had not seen such a beautiful position. The regiment of *Landwehr* from Baden which we had relieved had been here since the autumn of 1914, where it had hoped to wait out the war. We could understand why: a beautiful countryside lay under a thick blanket of snow, in the distance to the north the High Vosges, to the south Swiss mountains. There were women and girls in all the villages, even in Hirschbach, immediately behind the first trench. That was only possible because the area was completely at peace, at least as our men understood peace. When our regiment arrived, with its experience of high-intensity warfare, this would soon change, beginning with the construction of the trench system.

Capt. Niemeyer was tasked with constructing a new, third trench system, using 1, 3 and 4/ 66. 2/ 66 was constructing a telephone cable net under Acting Officer Seemann. The battalions occupying the positions worked principally on digging additional dugouts and deepening the existing ones, reinforcing the barbed-wire obstacles and reducing the excessive trench revetments. Patrolling was difficult due to the snow, but could be conducted if white camouflage shirts were used.

An infantry engineer platoon with forty-two men was formed under Acting Officer Conrad and attached to Engineer Company 104. The construction of a regimental HQ dugout was begun in the *Bürgerwald* (Citizen's Wood). Sergeant Major Schneider was named commandant of Bettendorf, Res. Lt Hartmann in Hirsingen and Res. Lt Nessau in Hirzbach.

Part of the right wing of the regimental position, including the village of Carspach, was given to IR 69, part of the left wing to IR 151 (37 ID). The battalion HQ Right was moved from Carspach to the rectory at Hirzbach.

On 19 January, the enemy shelled the regimental sector for the first time, with light artillery. Thereafter the enemy artillery fired almost daily, but only with a few light artillery shells and without doing any particular damage. Very active nightly patrolling soon made the regiment complete masters of no-man's-land. In front of each company sector, lanes were cut in the enemy wire obstacles and patrols penetrated into the first enemy trench to establish the locations of security posts, blockhouses and fortifications. If there was contact, the enemy security fled immediately. There were no enemy patrols in no-man's-land, until the night of 19–20 January, when one tried to approach the obstacles in Sector 6.

It was detected by the Sector 6 security and driven off with hand-grenades and rifle fire, following which the enemy shelled the position for half an hour with light artillery and mortars. A patrol from 10/ 66 detected an enemy patrol in its sector on 21 January, attacked it and drove it off. The next night, a patrol from 9/ 66 attacked an enemy listening post with hand-grenades.

On 24 January, a patrol from 12/ 66 under Sergeant Schwenke entered an enemy trench but found it unoccupied. A patrol from 10/ 66 cut a lane in the enemy wire on 26 January, but was detected and had to withdraw. Sergeant Limik and a five-man patrol from 6/ 66, which had entered the enemy position during the night of 30–31 January, making valuable observations, remained hidden in an OP during the day. It succeeded in shooting a French sergeant and taking a prisoner, without loss. This established that for months the enemy position had been held by Territorial Regiment 250 of the 134 Territorial Division. The patrol leader was decorated with the Iron Cross I Class, the other members of the patrol with the Iron Cross II Class. Any who already had this decoration were promoted to corporal. In addition they received cash awards from battalion, division and army totalling 400 Marks.

The companies also did excellent work in improving the positions. The freezing weather made work difficult, but the new third trench line was so far advanced that work could begin on constructing the dugouts. The defensive positions in Hirzbach were also improved. Work here was actually pleasant, because by our standards the enemy artillery was very quiet. Since the work proceeded so well, the rest periods were longer. On 27 January, the Kaiser's birthday was celebrated by 1/ 66 with a church service, inspection and company parties. On 29 January, a German aircraft was hit by enemy anti-aircraft fire and the pilot was forced to land behind our first trench at Carspach.

February also began with freezing weather, and it became steadily colder. The IR 66 men rode bobsleds from the high ground into Hirzbach. According to the locals, the Hirz stream, which flowed through Hirzbach town, had not frozen over since 1836, but it did so now. The enemy artillery was more active, but with a few exceptions still moderate. Between 1215 and 1430 on 8 February, there was an unusually heavy bombardment of the Ill valley at the Hirzbach rail station with 156 medium-calibre artillery shells. At 1130 on 16 February, the enemy conducted a surprise shelling on Carspach and Bad Sonnenberg with approximately sixty light-calibre shells. The shellings of Carspach, Hirzbach and Hirsingen increased, without doing significant damage. The war diary of 10/ 66 said: 'Apparently the war has begun here, too.' Aircraft were active on both sides. In good weather there was even an enemy observation balloon visible on the western horizon.

We continued to patrol. The French occasionally risked moving out of their position, and began to use snow camouflage shirts, as a patrol from 10/ 66 observed on 7 February. On 14 February, a patrol from 11/ 66 thoroughly reconnoitred the enemy obstacles between *Nordeck* (north corner) and *Südeck* (south corner – neither on map). A patrol from 12/ 66 found three dugouts west of the *Glückerkapelle* (Kp. St Glücker – Glücker chapel). Frequently patrols spent the day in the enemy trenches or in front of the enemy wire obstacles, for example, the patrol of Senior Sergeant Fickendey and Sergeant Sauer from 7/ 66, as well as that of Corporal Wiegräfe from 8/ 66. On 26 February, a day-time patrol from 8/ 66 under Sergeant Schwarz and Musketeer Zäge, Schwarz succeeded in entering the enemy trench at Kapelle St Glücker and overpowering an enemy security post. The resulting enemy alarm forced the patrol to withdraw. After Schwarz had disposed of another enemy soldier with hand-grenades, at dawn he reached the left-hand battalion position under cover of an artillery barrage, while Zäge, apparently badly wounded, was captured. The patrol established that the enemy trench was strongly held by units consisting of young, fit men.

On 20 February, there was a sudden thaw. On 23 February, a serious accident occurred in 12/ 66: a platoon was resting in a dugout near Carspach, that also contained a hand-grenade depot, which for unexplained reasons exploded, killing seven men, severely wounding seven more and lightly wounding thirteen. First Sergeant Mönkeimer and both company clerks were also wounded: Mönkeimer remained with the company.

On 23 February, 9 and 12/ 66 were withdrawn and assigned to fortify the *Illberg* (Ill Mountain, east of Carspach). The Carspach position was going to be abandoned, but until the *Illberg* position (not on map) was completed, would be held by 10 and 11/ 66. The first trench would then be located on the west slope of the *Illberg* to the inn, then over the Ill and along the road to the Hirzbach rail station [Bhf – *Bahnhof*] and from there to trig point 320 and position *Süd* 5.

Each battalion formed a mortar platoon with six light mortars.

During March, there were no unusual incidents: the position was extensively improved, while the enemy artillery became more active. Construction of the *Illberg* position met with the approval of all the higher headquarters. During the first half of the month it snowed heavily. Landwehr Lt Pirschke, the commander of 12/ 66, built a wooden house in the woods complete with a cabinet with mirror, marble-topped wash table, writing desk and a real bed from the village, which was exceptionally comfortable, the envy of the entire division, and led to the regulation concerning 'Waste of Materials and Misuse of Manpower'.

There was heavy snow during the first half of March. At 1700 on 10 March, there was an air battle over the position. A French aircraft was shot down behind French lines and an enemy observation balloon was shot down by German aircraft.

A strong patrol from 8/ 66, with three elements, attempted on 15 March to draw the enemy out of his trenches. It was unsuccessful, as the enemy fired gas mortar shells. A patrol from 5/ 66 led by Corporal Oberbeck on 16 March against an enemy blockhouse was unsuccessful. The previous night, lanes had been cut through the thick enemy wire obstacle, and engineers blew up the blockhouse, but the assault team found the blockhouse to be empty. The advance on the main enemy position through a communications trench was stopped because it was blocked with Spanish Riders.

On 18 March, I/ 66 relieved II/ 66 in place and continued digging in. It was decided that if the enemy attacked, Carspach would be abandoned, but until then retained as a dummy position. 5 and 7/ 66 worked on the new *Hirschberg–Illberg* position. A patrol from IR 170 took twenty prisoners from the French Reserve Infantry Regiment 300 and determined that for the last ten days the division had been facing a newly formed French division. On 25 March, it was announced that IR 66 and Infantry Brigade 104 would be transferred from 52 ID to 113 ID. IR 66 would relieve IR 48 in place between Niederaspach and Schweighausen:

Division Order of the Day

On 1 April 1917 Infantry Brigade 104 and the 3rd Magdeburg Infantry Regiment 66 will be transferred from 52 ID.

Both the brigade and regiment were elements of the 52nd Division in peacetime and fought as part of it from the beginning of the war, and for more than two years added to their military reputation. They performed superbly as part of 52 ID in two areas of operations, both in the hard work of constructing defensive positions and in combat. As true comrades they shared with us success and sorrows.

In the Battle of Serre, conducted by Infantry Brigade 104 in June 1915, four companies of 3rd Magdeburg Infantry Regiment 66 rushed to help their hard-pressed comrades from Baden and provided effective support.

In the Battle of the Somme, on 1 July 1916, IR 66 defeated all the British attacks, and in September fought heroically in the neighbouring division sector on the blood-soaked fields of St Pierre Divion and Thiepval. In spite of heavy losses they prevented the enemy from gaining a foot of ground. The regiment also defended its position at Puisieux in November with bravery and determination. Numerous patrol battles on the Somme proved the regiment's continual offensive spirit, initiative and boldness, paired with flexibility and stability under pressure.

I release the brigade and the regiment from the 52 ID with my best wishes for the future and with my recognition of its deeds on the battlefield and its outstanding service. Infantry Brigade 104 and the 3rd Magdeburg Infantry Regiment 66 are assured of a place of honour for all time in the history of the 52nd Infantry Division.

Signed von Borries

Patrols from 1 and 4/ 66 pushed into the enemy position at 0500 on 27 March, and stayed there for fourteen and a half hours, bringing back valuable intelligence information. The patrol leader, Acting Officer Collet, was hit by three rifle bullets and severely wounded. The blockhouse, which had been in enemy hands, was occupied by our patrol, equipped with a telephone. On the same day there were several other IR 66 patrols, some with, some without artillery preparation. A patrol from 7/ 66 under Sergeant Sauerbier was praised in the regimental order of the day.

A severe blow struck the regiment on 30 March: the best patrol leader in the regiment, Acting Officer Leue, from 3/ 66, was fatally wounded by a rifle bullet while conducting a daylight patrol. The battalion commander, Capt. Niemeyer, informed the regiment in the following report:

> I refer to the patrol report submitted by 3/ 66 this morning.
>
> After the return of Patrol Fuhrmann, Acting Officer Leue asked to go back out with a patrol three squads strong with the intent of capturing men from enemy work parties. The company commander gave his permission. The patrol left our trenches at 0900 towards Blockhouse 3 and found it unoccupied, as was Blockhouse 4, which the patrol had approached carefully. Leue decided to inspect Blockhouse 5. As he approached with eight men to within 20 metres of the wire obstacle there was a rifle shot and Leue collapsed immediately. According to the statement by Sergeant Fuhrmann, Leue was killed instantly. Fuhrmann and several men sprang up at once and carried Leue's body away, while under heavy fire, through the wood and the abatis, to our trenches. In spite of the enemy fire, the patrol took no further casualties. No enemy workers were encountered. This report is based on the statement of Sergeant Fuhrmann.
>
> The death of Acting Officer Leue was an unfortunate accident, which is made even more regrettable because he always led his patrols with great care and circumspection. His considerable successes were due to the calm and well-considered manner in which he acted, which made him well known and valued in the regiment, the division and even beyond.

Signed Niemeyer

Regimental Order of the Day

Early this morning, Acting Officer Leue died heroically on the field of battle.

I, and all the officers and men of the regiment, are deeply shaken by the loss of the boldest of all patrol leaders in the regiment. What Leue meant for the regiment, what his fearlessness in the face of mortal danger added to its reputation and history, what his untiring reconnaissance accomplished for the leaders and the Fatherland, is acknowledged by every member of the regiment.

His brave shining example should be emulated by every officer and soldier. His name will always be a monument in the regimental history:

Signed von Stoeklern

Division Order of the Day

On the morning of 30 March a patrol from IR 66 pushed into the enemy position, gathered valuable information and thereby came under heavy small-arms and hand-grenade fire, during which the brave and accomplished leader of the patrol, Acting Officer Leue, died heroically on the field of battle. In the face of great difficulties and heavy enemy fire, the patrol succeeded in bringing their mortally wounded leader back to our lines, for which I expressed my unreserved admiration.

Signed von Borries

Corps Headquarters
To the 3rd Magdeburg Infantry Regiment 66

It was reported to me that, shortly before the regiment was to leave the corps area, Acting Officer Leue, while conducting a difficult and audacious patrol, was lost to enemy fire.

The regiment will deeply mourn the loss on the field of battle of a man who provided outstanding leadership on so many successful patrols.

I extend to the regiment my most sincere sympathies.

Signed Freiherr von Lüttwitz
Major General
Commander III Corps

Everyone from the corps commander down mourned the loss of the boldest of all patrol leaders. He heroically died on the field of battle, his home leave pass in his pocket. The deeds of this brave man will be remembered forever by every IR 66 man.

On 31 March I/ 66 was relieved and marched to Pfastatt. On 1 April at 1000 IR 471 took responsibility for the IR 66 sector. IR 66 was assigned to 113 ID, which greeted it with the following order:

> I extend a warm welcome as IR 66 joins the 113 ID. I am certain that it will continue to maintain its outstanding reputation.
>
> Signed Von Bergmann

The last elements of the regiment were relieved that evening. III/ 66 quartered on 31 March at Lutterbach, and was joined there on 1 April by the regimental staff and on 2 April by MG Companies 1, 2 and 3. On 1 April, I/ 66 quartered at Pfstatt, on 2 April II/ 66 at Brunnstadt.

In the Niederaspach Position, April 1917

From 1 to 20 April the regiment took part in trench warfare at Niederaspach and Schweighausen, in the middle of the Burgundian Gate. The trenches were filled with mud, the wooden revetting had mostly fallen in, but on the other hand parts of the wire obstacle were in quite good shape. Nevertheless, the position was difficult to defend. The weakest point was the so-called *Pfropfenstellung* (Cork-stopper position) and the area north of it. The position had been destroyed by mortar fire, there were no trenches worth mentioning and the wire obstacle weak and full of holes. The dugouts were tunnelled very deeply and had withstood the shelling. The position was 150m from the enemy. Three hundred metres north of the *Propfenstellung*, the first trench was set back 200m to the rear. Here the trenches had been badly damaged by heavy rain, but were still defensible, and the wire obstacle was 15m deep and barely serviceable.

The *Dollerstellung* (Doller position – the Doller is a small river, a tributary of the Ill) began south of the *Pfropfenstellung*. It consisted of only one trench, which however was secured by an extraordinarily strong wire obstacle 40 to 50m deep. It was also protected by flanking fire from both sides, so an enemy penetration here was unlikely.

South of this was the village of Exbrücke (Aspacherbrücke), which had numerous concrete bunkers, a good wire obstacle and was easily defended. Strongpoints in depth were the village of Schweighausen, the *Mühlwaldstellung* (Mill-wood position – this and the following two not on map), the *Kohlberg* (Charcoal Hill) and the *Hirtenmühlstellung* (Herdsman's mill position).

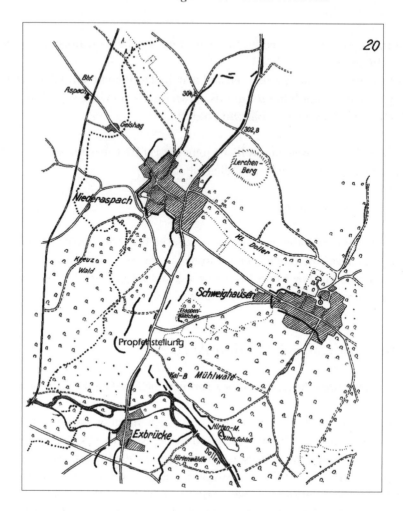

On the night of 1–2 April, III/ 66 occupied its position, on the night of 2–3 April, I/ 66, including its light mortar platoon, and on the night of 3–4 April, MG Companies 1 and 3. II/ 66 was the resting battalion at Brunnstadt. During the day, heavy artillery and mortar fire seemed to indicate an enemy attack was being prepared, and the march orders were often changed. The regimental staff set up in Reinigen and, at 1000 on 3 April, assumed responsibility for the sector. Enemy aircraft and artillery were very active and mortar shells with fins were frequently employed.

Capt. Trenk was concerned that the enemy might attack the *Pfropfenstellung* on the night of 3–4 April, and all the necessary defensive precautions were taken. At 2300, after about eight enemy batteries conducted a drumfire bombardment, the enemy attacked, but it broke down in the German defensive fire, and the enemy was not able to even get close to the position. There were many indicators that this was a serious attack and not a feint. The enemy had cut lanes in his own wire obstacles. Our patrols pursued the retreating enemy and found engineer tape in no-man's-land, which presumably served to show the assault troops the route back. Shortly after the enemy bombardment ceased, frightful yelling was heard in no-man's-land: apparently the French had gotten involved in a blue-on-blue hand-grenade fight. By midnight it was completely quiet. The enemy operation had failed. The newly introduced light mortars under Res. Lt Vogt had demonstrated their value for the first time.

Regimental order of the Day

I want to recognise 9 and 12/ 66, MG Companies 1 and 2 and the light mortar platoon of III/ 66 for successfully throwing back an enemy attack, and thank the artillery group for their effective support.

Signed von Stoeklern

Telephonic Message from Corps HQ to IR 66

A French attack on the night of 4 April, south of Niederaspach, collapsed in front of our wire. IR 66, already known to me as a combat-hardened unit from its energetic patrolling in the *Hiszbacher Walde*, proved itself once again under difficult conditions. I extend my highest praise to the regiment. This same recognition applies to the mortars and artillery batteries of Section South and *Landwehr* Division 26, whose barrages effectively supported the infantry.

Signed Schmidt von Knobelsdorf

There were numerous aerial battles over the regimental sector on 5 April. At 1845, a French aircraft crash-landed in the French wire. Our artillery, the highly capable FAR 225, immediately fired on it, as did one of our MG. Both occupants of the aircraft sprang out of it as soon as it landed and disappeared into the first French trench. At 1935, the French aircraft itself suddenly vanished, presumably destroyed by an artillery direct hit, but exact observation was difficult due to the smoke and the gathering dark. At 2000, Lt Elsmann from 4/ 66 went forward with a patrol and found the wreckage of the aircraft in the French wire.

The regiment worked on digging in the first position and the trenches behind it. Enemy artillery fire increased from day to day. A patrol from 9/ 66 under Corporal Kunze on 10 April attacked a French communications wire-laying party, put them to flight and captured a briefcase, which revealed that we were opposed by the French Infantry Regiment 256, which made another operation to determine this information unnecessary.

From 11–15 April, the enemy artillery continually conducted surprise bombardments. It did not appear, however, that the enemy artillery had been reinforced. There was also extraordinary enemy air activity. That indicated the enemy did not intend to conduct a large-scale attack, but rather a local one. Our position had suffered severely in the last few days from the enemy artillery fire. The trenches had been partially levelled, the wire obstacle destroyed and many dugouts had collapsed, usually the ones that had not been dug deeply.

Artillery fire increased even more on 16 April. In particular, the first position, Niederaspach, the communications trenches and the battery positions lay under heavy fire. Our artillery replied with surprise bombardments. Towards evening, the enemy fire died down. At 0320, after another fire preparation, a French patrol pushed through the destroyed wire obstacle on the regimental left flank and into the shot-up first trench. The security alerted the garrison, who threw the French back out. A patrol led by Sergeant Schwarz pursued the retreating French and caught up with them just outside the French wire obstacle. Musketeer Schaue then went missing. In their retreat, the French threw away numerous hand-grenades, wire cutters and web gear. Musketeer Schaue's cut-up web gear and gas mask were also found, and it was determined that the French had been carrying him, which meant he had been wounded. Schwarz's patrol made two prisoners, who confirmed that Schaue had been badly wounded and carried off by the French. On the next night, patrols pushed far forward, right up to the enemy position. A patrol from 8/ 66 found the missing Schaue alive in a shell crater and brought him back. The enemy had indeed carried him with them, but had been pressed so hard by Schwarz's patrol that they had to leave him behind.

Regimental Order of the Day

Having read yesterday's reports, I want to recognise 8/ 66 for its prudent conduct. This applies principally to the security outposts, who promptly gave the alarm, and the patrol of Sergeant Schwarz, which, correctly evaluating the situation, pursued the enemy patrol and put it to flight, leading to Musketeer Schaue being freed from enemy captivity.

Signed von Stoeklern

The French artillery even got on the horses' nerves, as is illustrated by an incident described by Sergeant Schroeder in the 5/ 66 field kitchen:

The field kitchen stopped on the evening of 16 April in front of the company orderly room in Schweighausen. The driver of the 'goulash cannon', August Weise, and the cook, Otto Schinke, had also brought the mail, which they took into the orderly room, and which we immediately began to sort out, so that it could go forward with the field kitchen and be distributed. We were just about finished when there was a crack and shell fragments flew through the windows. At the same moment August Weise sprang up, yelling 'The horses!' and was soon outside. 'The stallion has run off,' he said. He was right: only the chestnut was still standing in front of the field kitchen. The shell-crater was about 5 metres in front of the shaft. The chestnut was not injured, but the black stallion had disappeared. The traces had been torn. We searched down the village street, but there was not a sign in the entire village. It was a riddle. It was not possible that a horse this size could have gone to 'the big army in the sky' and we would not see the body. 'Well, chestnut, there's nothing for it, we are going to have to get along without the stallion,' August Weise said (in a broad Lower Saxon dialect) and he drove off with his load of dried vegetables. At the same time the next evening, August Weise was back, and he had the stallion with him. When we asked, he told us that that morning the men in the combat trains had searched the area, and the runaway was found in a shell hole about 5km away from Schweighausen, sleeping, and lightly wounded in the chest. But nothing more could be done with him. With the explosion of every shell he would rear up frantically: he was shell-shocked and we had to send him back to the rear area.

On 19 April, II and III/ 66 were relieved by Bavarian IR 3 and quartered in buildings between Lutterbach and Schweighausen, and in Lutterbach and Pfastatt. I/ 66 was relieved on 20 April and quartered in Lutterbach and Cloister Oelenberg. With heavy hearts, the regiment left beautiful Alsace. No one was under any illusions that the quiet time was over, and while our longing was directed to the south, the wagons rolled once again to the north, where the regiment felt at home. Except for a quarter-year in Alsace, it knew nothing else.

33

In the Shadow of the Chemin des Dames

Double Battle on the Aisne and in the Champagne, 24 April to 16 May 1917

III/ 66 boarded the troop train at Mülhausen (Mulhouse) on 20 April, the next day II and I/ 66, and the regimental staff and the three MG Companies on 22 April, rolling through Lorraine, Luxembourg and Belgium. 113 ID was brought to the front at Laon, where the French had launched their great offensive at the Chemin des Dames several days ago, seeking to produce a breakthrough and bring an end to the war. It involved a tremendous concentration of troops and an unheard-of mass of artillery and shells. But the German situation was more favourable than it had been a year previously, on the Somme. The German 7th Army had seen completely through the French plan, and had massed just as much artillery as the French had. When the French began their days-long preparatory bombardment, the German artillery replied in equal strength, so that the French task was not an easy one. In the face of such strong German resistance, the French attack immediately lost its force. Nevertheless, the French were able to take the completely destroyed front-line trenches on the south slope of the Chemin des Dames.

The regiment unloaded from the troop trains at La Ferté, west of Marle, on 22, 23 and 24 April, and conducted an unforgettable 20km foot march to Laon, along a ruler-straight road, with the city and its beautiful cathedral on the horizon to the south, like a fortress. It bivouacked, on alert, south of Laon, at Chivy, moving to the woods at Vorges, Bruyères and Montberault on 26 and 27 April. The villages showed the effects of the enemy long-range artillery, and were avoided as far as possible in favour of the woods. On 26 April, the division

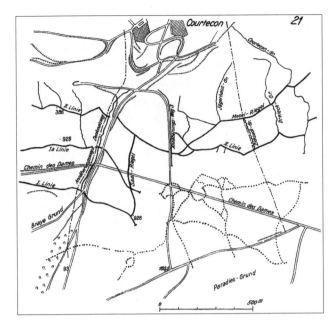

received its operations order: it was to be inserted between 45 RD and 20 ID, as the front here was weak. IR 66 was to relieve IR 79 at Courtecon. The new regimental position lay on the Chemin des Dames, a 25km-long and rather narrow east–west ridge, which fell off steeply to the north and south. It took its name from the high road from Soissons that had been constructed for the French princesses and ran along its entire length. To the south was the valley of the Aisne, to the north the 1–2km-wide Ailette valley separated it from the high ground further north.

The objective of the French offensive had been to seize this important high ground, which blocked the route north to Laon. It was to be expected that the French would renew their offensive, the strongest indicator of this being the continued intense air activity and artillery fire. The regiment therefore had to reorganise for intense trench warfare. The French had already taken the first trench of the position that the regiment was to occupy. What was left had not been well-constructed. The new front-line trench had numerous dugouts and corrugated-metal shelters, but the trenches to the rear had virtually none at all, nor wire obstacles. This was not a good omen for a successful defence. The left part of the position was on the reverse slope, thus nearly invisible to the French artillery. On the right side, a salient extended at an angle forward of the position and was flanked by French fire, and the French artillery could observe it well. The so-called *Saarriegel* (Saar barrier) located here would later be the scene of heavy fighting. The communications trenches were almost completely shot to pieces and filled-in, and forward movement had to be made across open ground from shell-crater to shell-crater. The plateau first descended gently to the north, then down a steep slope, to the village of Courtecon. The reserve units were located on the steep slope, but unfortunately without dugouts, so the troops had to dig foxholes as protection against the frequent enemy artillery and mortar fire. The resting battalion was located 2km away, on the north side of the Ailette valley, on the *Colligieshöhle* (Colligies Caverns). If it was to be committed to combat, it had to cross this swampy valley on duckboards, small bridges and foot bridges under gas and high-explosive shellfire.

On 28 and 29 April, IR 66 organised for combat. 1/ 66 under Capt. Niemeyer occupied the forward position; 4/ 66 (Res. Lt Kreidner) was in the *Saarriegel* salient on the right side, at the bend to the left was 2/ 66 (Res. Lt Werner), left of that 3/ 66 (Res. Lt Bierbach) and on the far left 1/ 66 (Res. Lt Kühne). II/ 66 under Major Paulus was behind 1/ 66, with 6/ 66 (Lt Martin Plathe) on the steep slope behind 2 and 4/ 66, 5/ 66 (Lt Steiger) in the second trench and on the steep slope behind 3 and 1/ 66, 7/ 66 (Res. Lt Nessau) and 8/ 66 (Res. Lt Thurm) in readiness in the sunken roads on the steep slope. III/ 66 was in the *Colligieshöhle*. MG Company 1 (Lt Riep) and 2 (Lt Meyer) were spread out along the entire position. The light mortars of all three battalions took up positions on the steep slope, along with several medium mortars, which did good service. The regiment was confident it could face whatever would come.

And it was not long in coming. All the next day, every calibre of artillery fired, mortars fired unceasingly: the Chemin des Dames was covered in smoke. The Ailette valley was frequently under fire from gas shells. The *Saarriegel*, occupied by 4 and 2/ 66, took especially heavy fire, as did the steep slope to the rear. Now and again very heavy artillery fired on the *Colligieshöhle*, so that large blocks of stone were broken off and crashed to the floor of the caverns. Gas shells were also fired at the caverns. The regiment's casualties increased. Several times it appeared that the enemy intended to advance, but the fire from our artillery and mortars pinned him in his trenches. Res. Lt Ladicke, a platoon leader in 7/ 66, wrote:

My company moved up during the night. It had hardly spread out in the reserve position, when it had to reassemble, to be ready to move forward again. Increased combat readiness had been ordered, so III/ 66 also moved onto the steep slope. I had to occupy part of a sunken road with my platoon. To my right front was a company of III/ 66. I had no idea where the other two platoons of my company were located. We had to dig in into the sunken road, which was not easy work, as the ground was rather hard. We could not work continually: I had assigned the squad leaders to be air guards, and from time to time the warning whistle would sound. Then everyone had to hunker down motionless on the small slope that formed the sunken road. Although the work was frequently interrupted, it progressed so far that by afternoon everyone had some cover. We were as careful as we could have been, but nevertheless the aircraft must have observed us. The white chalk spoil stood out so strongly against the dark brown surface of the sunken road, that the aircraft crew must have been blind as camels had they not observed the change in the terrain. With very mixed feelings we sat in our foxholes, which provided relatively little cover, and waited for what must come. It was clear to all of us that, if the enemy shelled our sunken road, few were going to survive until evening. And that's what he did. At noon an insane shelling began. The entire slope of the Chemin des Dames was torn up by shells. To top it all off, there were mortars behind us, and their ammunition caught fire and one mortar after the other was blown into the air. The French continued to fire like crazy on the mortar positions, and we sat right in front of them in our sunken road and had to take it, without being able to defend ourselves: an awful situation! The fire became worse towards evening. The casualties were heavy. Wounded crawled away or were carried, medics ran back and forth. Then I received an order to move my platoon to safety somewhere else.

In spite of these difficulties, everything took place normally. The reporting system functioned perfectly. The wire teams of Master Sergeant Seemann continually repaired breaks in the telephone cable; the runners did a superb job carrying their messages. The signal lamp stations, established with energy and skill by Sergeant Kuhnert, proved their usefulness. Ammunition, material and ration resupply functioned well: the company first sergeants ensured that every night every man received a warm meal.

It went like this until 4 May, when it was clear that the enemy intended to attack soon. The gas attacks on the Ailette valley were unceasing, thick clouds of gas hid everything, heavy artillery fire landed on our battery positions, assembly areas, caverns and communications trenches. There was activity in the enemy trenches, and that afternoon they were packed with assault troops. 4 and 1/66 reported an impending attack. Our artillery counter-preparation began and hailed down on the French. Towards evening the artillery fired another counter-preparation. Enemy losses must have been heavy: we could see them evacuating masses of wounded.

Even at night the artillery on both sides would not sleep. The darkness was continually lit up by their muzzle flashes and the light of flares. There were continual gas alarms in the Ailette valley. Nobody got any real rest, but waited for the coming day. There was only two hours' quiet just before dawn. Whoever was able to get to sleep was soon awake. At 0745 on 5 May, the entire enemy artillery on the whole front, thousands of guns, opened fire. Immediately, the Chemin des Dames was covered in smoke, mist and rubble. Drumfire! An impenetrable, thick wall of soot and steam rose, out of which explosions blazed and towers of earth as tall as trees appeared, a thundering and roaring, howling and cracking that drowned out human voices. The Ailette valley was a sea of fog, white with gas. The *Colligieshöhle* shook under the impact of heavy howitzers. Our artillery fired slowly, saving munitions for the time when the enemy infantry would conduct its assault.

The fire continued for hours in undiminished intensity. The forward companies remained ready, taking cover as best they could. The security looked carefully to the front, hunched over the lip of the shell holes. Hardest-hit were 4 and 2/ 66. Explosion after explosion, whistling shell fragments, falling rocks. These were terrible hours. Especially in the *Saarriegel*, the dead lay next to the dead, wounded next to wounded. Whoever still lived held rifle and hand-grenades ready.

Suddenly the artillery fire lifted and shifted to the rear. Figures appeared in the smoke and mist, first individuals, then more and more, followed by thick waves. One could see that the entire enemy position was swarming with bayonets and blue helmets, they flowed forward from the trenches, like a boiling kettle that was running over. It was 0945.

The cry went up in the entire German position: 'They're coming!' First individual shots rang out, then a wave of rifle and MG fire that made the French tremble. Everyone was on the lip of the trench, the edge of the shell holes, the top of the furrows. First 1/ 66, then 3/ 66, fired kneeling, then stood up and fired standing off-hand into the advancing mass. 5/ 66 raced forward from its position in the rear to reinforce 1 and 3/ 66, shouting 'Hurrah!' as though it were attacking. Sergeant Schroedter from 5/ 66 wrote:

> We fired as though it was a peacetime gunnery exercise. The effect was colossal. French fell down and didn't move, others crawled into shell holes. Most of them ran back towards the protection of their trenches, jumping up and down, bent over, throwing away their weapons and packs, straight into our artillery and mortar barrage, which now flung the carefully saved-up munitions into the running masses.

Res. Lt Kramer described the 1/ 66 defence:

> I had trench watch that morning, when a heavy drumfire began. There was a MG next to our dugout that was completely buried by a shell. The MG crew and I dug it out. It was clear that they were coming, and we moved the MG to the edge of the trench. I slid into the dugout to wake Lt Sommer. Before I could do so the MG crew gave the alarm. The French soldiers must have sweated heavily in their coats and the heat. They got a proper reception from us. The MG next to us swept them away. Sergeant Voigt jumped out of the trench and fired kneeling, then fell back into the trench, dead from a bullet in the throat. I was hit in the head. Corporal Föhre defended our sap,

but was also badly wounded. I held under fire an enemy sap that extended to 8 metres from our trench. When the French packed into their trench that was 40 metres away from ours, our medium mortars opened fire and that was all for the French attack. We shot down the ones that tried to run back: I can only compare it to shooting game being driven by beaters at a hunt. After an hour it was quiet again, and I went back to the aid station to get my wound dressed. When I returned to the front, a massive drumfire began. After a short time I walked down the trench and could find only dead security men, most of them so torn up they were unrecognisable. We lost many more men to this surprise artillery bombardment than we had during the actual attack. I found one man on security in the 1st Platoon sap quietly smoking a cigarette, and his calmness had a good effect on me. I lit one up, too, and as we could observe the entire front, we felt more secure than in the dugout. His name was Springstüber, or maybe the opera singer Hans Springer. We naturally expected another attack. Sergeant Bellentin was killed that evening, as he foolishly walked around in front of our trench. Fritz Gädicke was brilliant during the attack: he was one of the bravest.

Res. Lt Kühne, the commander of 1/66, described the defence on 5 May:

It was lucky that our first trench was within hand-grenade range of the French position: the French preparatory bombardment could not fire on us and most of it landed instead on the second trench. I had observed this several days ago, and since the second trench did not have adequate dugouts, we suffered heavy casualties there, so, in spite of express orders to the contrary, I had moved the entire company into the first trench. It was completely clear to me that, since the enemy trench was so close there was a real danger that we could be surprised and overrun, so that we had to be continually alert and ready. The French opposite us had obviously been told that we were completely demoralised and were just waiting to be able to give up. For several days before the attack they had been showing us bread, wurst, schnapps and tobacco to make us 'long for the fleshpots of Egypt', which was naturally answered appropriately from our side. A very friendly atmosphere developed. The attack took place, if I remember correctly, at 1000, after a heavy preparatory bombardment, during which the Ailette valley behind us was completely filled with gas. Out of concern that we could be overrun, the attached MG officer and I walked once again through the trench shortly before 1000, encouraging the men and ensuring that the MG that were partially buried in dirt were dug out and put in firing order. We had hardly returned to our dugout when the attack began. We were completely ready, so much so that the French in their first trench could hardly get up out of it. They were able to try to break in at the sap, which was only protected by a Spanish Rider, but were thrown back by the energetic defence put up by Corporal Föhre (who was unfortunately badly wounded) and his squad. We were very liberally provided with MG, which massacred the thick French masses coming out of their rear trenches. Our position was especially favourable, in that it formed a salient, and we were able to put flanking fire down the rest of the regimental position. Due to the gas in the rear area, initially we could not request artillery and mortar support. When it began we were standing on the breastwork of the trench, and we could see how this fire, especially that of the mortars, landed in the tightly packed French trenches and set off a literal panic. Nothing could stop the French: they streamed to the rear in thick masses and we shot them down as though it were target practise.

One of the first to fall during the attack was Sergeant Voigt, who from the beginning was firing kneeling on the breastwork. Res. Lt Kramer took a serious grazing wound to the head, but did not go to the aid station until the attack was over, and then returned immediately. Our satisfaction at our victory was considerably dampened by a terrible drumfire on our first trench, whose effectiveness during the attack had apparently been noticed by the French, and we took very heavy losses. But the expected attack did not materialise this day.

The battle in 4/ 66's salient had been similar. No Frenchman made it as far as our trench. Only at the juncture of the 4/ 66 position with 2/ 66 at the *Saarriegel* was there a grenade fight, as the remainder of the garrison defended itself against French troops assaulting from all sides. It was an unequal battle: the last hand-grenades were thrown and the remaining five men pulled back to a neighbouring platoon. The French were stopped here by 4 and 2/ 66. Barricades were quickly thrown up and determined riflemen and grenade men denied the French further progress.

Major Paulus, on the steep slope, received a report of the enemy penetration. He placed Lt Rothe and Senior Sergeants Frenzel and Reinemund and their three platoons from 6 and 8/ 66 at the disposal of 1/ 66. The storm troops moved out to counter-attack, liberally supplied with hand-grenades. The platoon from 6/ 66 quickly arrived at the barricade, oriented themselves on the situation, and then began throwing hand-grenade after hand-grenade, and as they were exploding the entire platoon charged the surprised French with the bayonet, Lt Rothe in the lead. The fight only lasted minutes, whoever did not flee was killed; one prisoner was taken. The counter-attack began at 1145: at 1245 the regiment reported to brigade that the entire position was in our hands.

In addition to the brave infantry, the machine gunners played a great part in our success. One of the first among them to fall was the leader of

MG Company 1, Lt Riep. Senior Sergeant Velten of MG Company 2 reported on the actions of the MG:

> 1st Platoon of MG Company 2 consisted of four weapons, positioned at the second trench somewhat closely pressed together in foxholes. The first trench was about 70 metres in front of us, hidden behind a low rise, while the main position was about 150 metres behind us down the steep slope. From 30 April to 2 May, the enemy artillery had been very active, but there was never an outright drumfire. I discussed the situation thoroughly with my four gun commanders, Sergeants Siudzinski, Scholler, Müller and Schönemann. We were very concerned that from our positions we could not engage the enemy in no-man's-land. Our field of fire extended only 40 metres to the flat high ground to our front. It seemed questionable to me and my gun commanders that we could stop the attackers. As of 3 May, the French began a passable artillery drumfire. As we had experienced on the Somme, heavy and light mortar shells threw up so much smoke that our observation was severely limited. We became even more alarmed when we visited the first trench and saw how weak the infantry garrison was. At this time the Army order was that heavy MG only be employed in the second trench. But after two guns were buried by shells, on my own initiative I ordered the guns to be moved one at a time to the first trench. After the buried guns had been dug out and brought forward, we occupied a dugout with two exits, determined our fields of fire, and waited for what was to happen. It came in the form of the company commander, Lt Meyer, who chewed me out severely for bringing my guns to the first trench. But in spite of all that we remained, and we did not regret it. The drumfire lasted for all of 4 May and increased on the morning of 5 May to its greatest intensity. We had not taken any losses and with the highest confidence I ordered my platoon to be alert and ready to move to firing positions. Our company problem child, who stuck out in any situation, Wilhelm Kaltenborn, was on watch and closely and cold-bloodedly observed no-man's-land, in spite of heavy enemy fire. At 0900, the bombardment suddenly lifted and shifted to the rear. Now we knew for sure and the order 'Everybody out! They're coming!' found us ready. Six or seven waves deep, the French advanced in brand-new blue uniforms towards our position. We let them approach to 150 metres, then threw the MG onto the lip of the trench and received them with continual final protective fire from four MG, which was so effective that the entire area was soon strewn with dead enemy troops. To our right they had gotten closer to our position, and we had the opportunity to deliver effective flanking fire. Actually, measured against the Somme, the day was rather tame. We had one man wounded, gunner Schubert, who

unfortunately later died. It is an open question what would have happened had we remained in the rear. Our actions were justified by the fine success we enjoyed during this attack.

The light mortars also proved themselves brilliantly. They opened fire upon seeing the first signal flare and in quick succession put barrages on the enemy trenches and in no-man's-land. All of the companies recognised the value of the rapid intervention of these new weapons in the fight, and quickly became highly prized. In the afternoon, their fire brought down an enemy aircraft, a singular accomplishment. Lt Meyer, the commander of MG Company 2, reported his impressions from 5 May:

> The route to my MG led me through the 7/ 66 sector, which had really been torn up by the artillery. The dugouts, many of them deeply dug galleries with corrugated-metal roofs, had frequently collapsed, killing the occupants. The one MG was intact and ready to fire, the crew alert. The MG on the left flank of the trench came to a tragic end. The crew never had a chance to fire the weapon. Due to the shelling, carbon dioxide penetrated into the dugout. Death's scythe, through asphyxiation, had a rich harvest. Everyone else was ready to fire when a French assault column was discovered at the *Saarriegel*. It appeared to us that the French were given a bloody lesson, and they won't try this again. The garrison of the trench and the MG crew were in good spirits. Throwing back an enemy attack always raises morale and gives enormous confidence in one's weapons.

At 1400, the French renewed their attempt to penetrate into the *Saarriegel*, which quickly collapsed under the fire of 6/ 66 garrisoned there. Our neighbour to the right, RIR 32, enjoyed equal success. The enemy was able to make a deep penetration into the IR 36 position, but here, too, was thrown out by a counter-attack, led by Capt. Hermens from IR 66, who was given control of the 113 ID Storm Troop under Lt Eisenbeck.

The enemy artillery fire continued the entire afternoon. 10 and 11/ 66 had to move under this fire through the Ailette valley to the steep slope. Fortunately, there were very few casualties, although there were flocks of aircraft overhead. A German fighter plane brought one of them down, another took a direct hit from French artillery, so that there were a total of three downed enemy aircraft in the division sector.

By evening, the entire division felt that it had won a complete victory. The French attempt to break through, conducted by the French XX Corps, the elite corps of the French Army, had been bloodily repulsed. That evening the division commander radioed the regiment: 'Brave 66: you have done well!'

In spite of their failure, the French continued the attack. On the afternoon of 5 May, strong enemy troop concentrations had to be taken under fire, and the French artillery continued to fire that night and the following day. At 1700 on 6 May, the French artillery fire increased to a renewed drumfire, and after a quarter of an hour the French infantry rose up to assault again. The events of the preceding day were repeated. Immediate artillery fire and defensive rifle and MG fire quickly broke the enemy's will. Corporal Bosse, one of the gunners in MG Company 2, distinguished himself. Once again, the enemy fled in the face of close defensive fire. Some threw off their packs in order to be able to run faster – straight into the German artillery barrage. They were only able once again to enter the *Saarriegel*, where 6/ 66 had been inserted between 2 and 4/ 66. But Lts Plathe and Rothe were ready for them, and immediately attacked the French from two sides, inflicting such heavy casualties that few were able to return to the French trenches. Unfortunately, both officers and Acting Officer Bernau were badly wounded leading the attack. In the bloody fighting on this day, 6/ 66 lost forty-five men, and on the preceding day twenty-eight men, so that it was now reduced to sixty-eight riflemen. Musketeer Költzsch from 6/ 66 distinguished himself by his determination and aggressiveness while fighting in the sap and contributed significantly to the company's success, for which he was afforded the Iron Cross 1 Class. 11/ 66 had already been moving forward to assist 6/ 66 and relieved it in place. The enemy attack had been conducted by a fresh regiment from XX Corps.

On 7 May, the French artillery continued to be very active. At 0915, the French infantry again massed, but an immediate German barrage nipped this attack in the bud. The same procedure was repeated that evening. The mortar and artillery fire shook the French infantry to such a degree that none of them came out of the trenches. That evening, 1 and 3/ 66 were relieved by 5 and 7/ 66.

The day of 8 May was, finally, quieter. The French seemed to have given up their attacks for now. 1/ 66, which had been doing most of the fighting, could be relieved. At the same time, the front line was occupied by two battalions, III/ 66 in the two company sectors on the right, II/ 66 the two on the left. 1 and 3/ 66 remained on the steep slope, while 2 and 4, the battalion staff and two recruit companies under Capt. Rochlitz bivouacked on the *Colligieshöhle* as division reserve. Major Paulus, a tested veteran of many battles as commander of II/ 66, left the regiment and was replaced by Capt. Rieger. First Lt Lademann, the commander of MG Company 3, became the regimental MG officer.

The next few days consisted of active trench warfare. The enemy artillery fired heavily and caused numerous casualties, but the battle had clearly died down. Our patrols once again pushed forward as far as the enemy position and showed the French that the regiment was still aggressive. A Bavarian division occupied the sector to our left, and conducted an attack to improve its position, which brought the regimental sector under increased artillery fire. Otherwise, nothing of significance occurred.

On the evening of 14 May, the regiment was relieved in place by IR 150 of 37 ID, and quartered in the town of Vorges. When it was light, everyone was astonished to see that spring had arrived, green and blossoming. In the torn-up front lines we had seen nothing of the sort. From 23 April until 14 May, we had taken the following casualties: Lt Riep, the commander of MG Company 1, and another lieutenant had been killed, a lieutenant, six reserve lieutenants (including a relative of the author) and an acting officer wounded, eighty-six enlisted men killed, 450 wounded, thirty-one missing, most of whom had probably been killed.

The regiment had shown 113 ID in four weeks of combat that it was just as effective as the regiment it had replaced: the brigade and division commanders gave official recognition of its accomplishments. The regiment could look back with pride at its weeks of combat at the Chemin des Dames: it had not lost a single foot of ground.

In the Forests of St Gobain, 17 May to 11 August 1917

After a day of rest, the regiment marched on 17 May to the peaceful area near Crépy en Laonnais, where II and I/ 66 and the regimental staff were quartered, with III/ 66 in Couvron and Chéry-lès-Pouilly. On 18 May, the regiment stood in parade formation and passed in review before the division commander, General von Bergmann, who praised the regiment for its bravery and performance of duty during the last weeks. The next day we celebrated the birthday of the Chief of the Regiment, King Alfonso XIII of Spain, with the division commander and the brigade commander, Freiherr Prince von Buchau, participating. There followed several rest days, which were used to maintain equipment and conduct inspections.

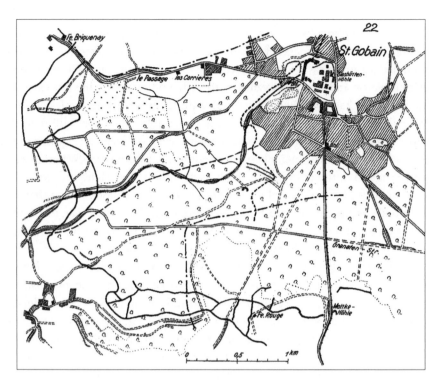

On 22 May, the division occupied a very quiet sector of front. IR 66 relieved RIR 215 in the middle of the division sector. It formed part of the *Siegfriedstellung* (Siegfried Line), which our troops had just withdrawn to. The construction of the position was not complete. According to current standards, only the first position was fully defensible as work on all of the rearward trenches and positions had just begun. In many ways, the position was very favourable. The thick woods made defence easier, the position was provided with electric lighting and piped-in water, a long light rail line provided resupply, and large caves could shelter a great many troops. III/ 66 occupied Sector Hagen on the right, II/ 66 Sector Isolde on the left; I/ 66 rested in the Baden and Mecklenberg forest bivouacs. I/ 66 was honoured to take part in a parade in the presence of His Majesty the Kaiser and the Crown Prince at Erlon west of Marle. Sergeant Zimmerer (MG Company 1) was awarded the Iron Cross i Class and Musketeer Stichnoth (4/ 66) the Iron Cross ii Class by the Kaiser himself.

The regimental sector was covered by a tall birch forest, which extended far behind the front, so that all lines of communication to the rear were concealed from enemy observation. It was almost quieter than the position in Alsace. The enemy showed no offensive intentions, his artillery was weak and fired little. The front-line companies occupied tunneled-out bunkers, reinforced with concrete, but still had a great deal of work to do in constructing the second line of trenches, some of which had not even been started, and which had no dugouts whatsoever. The reserve company for the left-hand battalion occupied a roomy cave. The deserted city of St Gobain was behind the regimental sector, and in a deep valley at the edge of it was the biggest cave that the regiment had ever seen. You could walk for hours in the high corridors and still not come to the end. We were never able to explore and map the entire thing. Res. Lt Heidtmann was named Cave Commandant, a guard room established and the regimental engineer equipment stored here. When recruits were assigned to the regiment as work parties, they were quartered here with no difficulty. The regimental staff occupied tidy small blockhouses that had been built behind St Gobain by a preceding unit. Before the war, the woods had been a hunting preserve, principally wild boar. In places the forest floor was torn-up by rooting boars, and a few boars were shot.

During this relatively quiet period, Lt-Col von Stoeklern insisted that the position be completely dug: the regiment worked hard and accomplished a great deal. Above all, the regiment patrolled actively, and enjoyed considerable success. Given the exceptionally wide regimental front, it was possible to send out six patrols every night. On 14 June, III/ 66 sent out a daylight patrol to the position we had named *Steigbügel* (the Stirrup – not on map). Sergeant Huncke and Corporal Larm from 5/ 66 each led patrols which entered the enemy position and inflicted casualties with hand-grenades. On 12 June, Res. Lt Wadepuhl (12/ 66) encountered an enemy patrol in no-man's-land and threw it back, inflicting casualties. A man from 12/ 66 was wounded, but was brought back in exemplary fashion by Corporal Wenkebach, who was himself wounded, and by Sergeant Rümpler. On 24 July, Res. Lt Wadepuhl and Sergeant Quast, with a daylight patrol from 12/ 66, broke into the enemy position opposite the regimental right flank and captured an enemy sergeant-major, but was only able to bring back his equipment. At the beginning of August, a patrol from 9/ 66 led by Corporals Kunze and Winkler also broke into the enemy position. 1/ 66 conducted a large-scale patrol on 14 July. At 0230, our artillery and mortars began preparatory fire on the *Steigbügel*. Six minutes later, the storm troops led by Lt Kühne, Res. Lt Peters and Acting Officer Collet succeeded in breaking into the enemy position. After a short fight, they inflicted significant damage on the enemy, then returned with one wounded prisoner and a body, both from a cuirassier regiment. The attack by Res. Lt Kramer was not able to penetrate an enemy wire obstacle. Unfortunately, the storm troops lost one man dead and seven wounded. Other patrols in July that deserve to be mentioned were led by Lt von Herrmann, Res. Lt Könnecke, Senior Sergeant Felgner and Senior Sergeant Schmidt.

In June, our light mortars again performed brilliantly. On 12 July, they were deployed to the RIR 259 sector (78 RD) at Pinon, and on 20 July, contributed to the preparatory fire for an attack by storm troops. On the next day they fired barrages against several French counter-attacks, and again during four French attacks to retake the trenches on the night of 21–22 June, and against three French daylight counter-attacks conducted on 22 June. During the following days, they successfully engaged numerous targets in the enemy position. Unfortunately, there were heavy casualties. The highly experienced leader of the II/ 66 mortars, Acting Officer Kreutz, was killed along with three of his men, and an NCO and four men were wounded.

On 7 August, the advance parties of IR 15 from 13 ID arrived in the regimental area. On 9 August, II/ 66 was relieved in place at Crépy by III/ 15 and marched to Barenton-sur-Serre, where it was quartered. On 10 August, I/ 66 was relieved and transported by light rail to Crépy, foot-marching from there to Verneuil-sur-Serre. On 11 August, III/ 66 was relieved and quartered in Barenton-Bugny along with the regimental staff. On 14 August, the regiment marched to the area of Sissonne. III/ 66 went to the camp at Sissonne, II/ 66 in the forest camp *Neu-Berlin* (New Berlin) near Marchais and I/ 66 in the camp at La Paix. After a short stay at Pavillon des Eaux, the regimental staff was quartered at Sissonne.

Behind the Front near Sissonne, 14 August to 13 September 1917

As unwilling as everyone was to leave our summer vacation in the woods at St Gobain, we all recognised that, long term, the regiment had no right to such a quiet sector. But if anyone expected employment in another combat sector, he was wrong. There was a change of an entirely different kind: 113 ID began to conduct training in deliberate attacks against a prepared position, followed by manoeuvre warfare, although these were still called counter-attacks in depth. The old soldiers were thrilled, as were the young ones. Finally, positional warfare would be replaced by manoeuvre battles. The training was intense: combined-arms tactics with the the infantry and the heavy MG, whose numbers increased considerably, with light MG, which had been introduced in the past few months, and light mortars, which had proven themselves brilliantly. Artillery had once again to become accustomed to fire support in mobile operations, above all the close-support batteries that would become so important. Exercises were held at company level, then at battalion and regimental levels, and several with the entire division. The old French major training area at Sissonne was the perfect place for the large-scale exercises.

Unfortunately, training was also interrupted by other missions. From 15 to 22 August, II/ 66 had to provide security for the construction of the second trench in the sector of our old 52 ID. It therefore had to dig-in at

Arranceau-Fme (farm), Grand-St Jean-Fme and the surrounding area. From 26 August on, 9 and 10/ 66 alternated in work at Fleuricourt-Fme. The remaining companies continued to train. On 2 September, the division held a sports competition, with members of the regiment winning the most prizes. It was a proper peacetime festival, with music, clowns, a parade and garlands. That evening there was a *Zapfenstreich* (tattoo) by the combined regimental bands. Our good mood was not dampened by a French air attack on Sissonne.

On 6 September, our regiment was assigned as counter-attack unit in *Gruppe* (Group) Liesse. The regimental staff and III/ 66 was quartered in Coucy-lès-Eppes, I/ 66 in the Bièvres-*Höhlen* (caves), II/ 66 in the *Siegerhöhlen*. The last two battalions had to spend many a night carrying mortar shells to the forward position; not a pleasant task. III/ 66 went to Ployart on 7 September as the counter-attack battalion, and also improved the rear area defences there. On 12 September, the regiment was reunited, I/ 66 went into the Baganbart Lager (camp), III/ 66 again to Coucy-lès-Eppes and II/ 66 in Lager Alexander at Mauregny. The regiment would soon be committed to combat again.

In Position at Hurtebise-Fme and Bouconville, 14 September to 29 December 1917

On 13 September, 113 ID was ordered to relieve 52 ID during the following nights. IR 66 thus once again came in close contact with 52 ID, which it had been an element of for two years. IR 66 would take over Position Augusta, which was being held by IR 169. During the night of 14–15 September, I/ 66 relieved III/ 169 in the forward position, in the next night III/ 66 relieved IR 169 in the reserve position, and II/ 66 remained as the resting battalion in the camp at Mauregny. The regimental staff was in the command post on the north side of the Bover Ridge (off map, about 3km to the north).

Tactically, the new position was extraordinarily unfavourable. The first line was squeezed into the bottom of the north slope of the Chemin des Dames and the enemy could observe it from the front and both flanks. The woods had been blown down and provided little concealment. The first and only trench was poorly dug, narrow and shallow. The wire obstacle was weak. Immediately behind the position was the Ailette valley, an extensive swamp, which stretched as far as Bouconville (off map, about a kilometre and a half to the north of the position) and could be crossed only at a few footbridges. The enemy also had excellent observation over the swamp and could cover it with well-adjusted artillery, MG and rifle fire. The enemy had full observation into the area from the forward position to the Bove Ridge. Therefore no one could expose themselves during the day. The MG were scattered through the Ailette

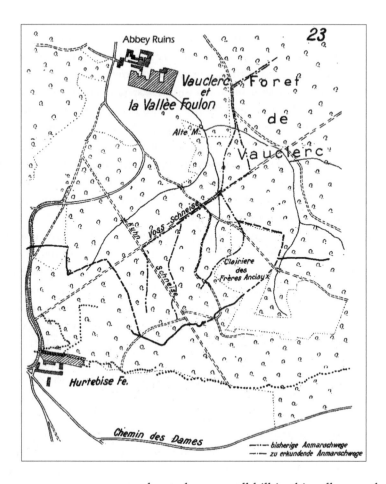

valley, a reserve company was located on a small hill in this valley, another in the ruins of Vauclerc Monastery. There were no bomb-proof dugouts in the entire position. The positions to the rear were tactically more favourable, but their construction left much to be desired. An enemy attack on this position would have been very unpleasant. Fortunately, it did not appear that the enemy intended to do so. The enemy infantry did not do anything unusual. I/ 66 in its foxholes on the slope took light mortar fire and occasional intense surprise attacks with rifle-grenades. The enemy was very alert; if his wire obstacle was disturbed only slightly, the security outposts would open fire. Château Bove, which was now a ruin, the village of Bouconville and Cloister Vauclerc were regularly shelled with light and medium artillery. An ammunition dump in Cloister Vauclerc was set on fire. Our artillery was more active than the French. Fortunately, it was relatively quiet at night, so that supplies and rations could be brought forward undisturbed.

Since duty in the front-line trench was so difficult, battalions were relieved every seven days. II/ 66 took over from I/ 66 on 22 September and was relieved in turn by III/ 66 on 29 September. I/ 66 came back to the front line on 9 October, but had to hold out there until 12 November because events elsewhere on the front occupied the other two battalions.

In spite of the fact that the enemy position was quite close, our patrols were able to establish its character exactly. But the French never entered no-man's-land, so we could not identify the units opposite us. On 6 October, 9/ 66 was suddenly attacked by a large enemy patrol, but did not stay on the defensive; Acting Officer Wasserthal, with a small group, aggressively pursued the fleeing French on his own initiative in order to take a prisoner, but came under rifle and hand-grenade fire from the French trench. Wasserthal was badly wounded and several of his men took light wounds.

As of 12 October, combat became heavier, due to a local attack conducted by RIR 32 on our left against a projecting section of French trench. During the operation, our light mortars conducted a heavy fire on the enemy position to distract the French. As a consequence of this operation, the enemy artillery became quite active to prepare a French counter-attack. On 14 October, 12/ 66 was moved to Sector Bia of RIR 32, and on 16 October 9/ 66 was, too. On 18 October at 1330, the French attacked RIR 32 and won some terrain. 12/ 66 under Landwehr Lt Pitschke counter-attacked, but met little opposition and occupied the trench. At 1900, 10/ 66 was sent to reinforce RIR 32 Sector Bia, moving under heavy artillery fire. It was ordered to relieve 12/ 66 and prepare for a renewed enemy attack. The sector was 150m long: three squads occupied the first trench and two squads were chequerboard in shellholes behind them. There was a light MG in the sap to the left, another in the middle of the first trench and a third to secure the exposed sap on the right. Both saps were within hand-grenade range of the enemy position. The position, such as it was, consisted of shell holes provided with firing steps and connected by shallow trenches. 12/ 66 remained behind 10/ 66. On 19 October at 0800, covered by thick fog, French storm troops sprang with fixed bayonets out of their trenches opposite the right sap. But our security was fully alert. Sergeant Rümpel's squad-strength patrol opened fire with rifles and hand-grenades and quickly drove the French back. Unfortunately, the next day this experienced and brave NCO was mortally wounded by an artillery shell: 10/ 66 had lost its best storm troop and patrol leader. On 20 October, 10 and 12/ 66 were relieved; they left the position proudly, having done their duty brilliantly under very difficult circumstances.

On the night of 20–21 October, the regiment took over Sector Afta, the right-hand sector of RIR 32, with three companies of II/ 66, while 7/ 66 remained in regimental reserve at Bouconville. While moving forward to the new position, MG Company 2 came under attack with gas shells and nine men were affected. During the next few days, the enemy artillery was increasingly active, which hindered the troops bringing forward supplies. The defensive position was somewhat better than that of Sector Augusta, which was still held by 1/ 66 with three companies, with one company the battalion sector reserve. III/ 66 was resting at the camp.

At the same time, there was heavy fighting on the right flank of the Chemin des Dames. The French succeeded in making the situation here so unfavourable that it would have required large-scale counter-attacks to make it at least tolerable. Committing even more troops into costly actions would have been out of proportion to the expected results. Therefore, 7th Army decided to evacuate the entire ridge at the Chemin des Dames and occupy a rearward position north of the Ailette valley.

This intent was transmitted to the officers on 26 October and was greeted with great satisfaction by the regiment. Everyone knew that the regimental position would not stop a serious French attack, while because of the terrain alone an attack against the new position on the north bank of the Ailette valley was very unlikely. Nevertheless, it was first necessary to construct the new position. Therefore, 9 and 11/ 66 under Landwehr Rittmeister (cavalry captain) Weskott, who had been assigned to the regiment a few weeks ago, began energetically constructing the new position near Bouconville. Amazingly, in a few days they produced a more-or-less serviceable position.

The forward companies prepared to leave, beginning by moving the reserve munitions and rations to the rear, aided by a recruit company. Here, too, the carrying parties worked willingly and with determination, so that it was possible to move all of these supplies in five nights. Even frequent artillery fire could not dampen the troops' energy.

The withdrawal was completed on the night of 1–2 November. In every battalion sector, a rearguard composed of two officers' patrols, each two squads strong with a light MG, had the mission of firing rifles and flares to give the impression that the position was fully manned. The dugouts had been previously destroyed or filled in and the trenches levelled out as much as possible. Many of the more inventive men left presents for the enemy: explosives and hand-grenades rigged as booby-traps. The withdrawal proceeded without any friction. At dawn, the rearguards pulled back. At 0600, the last man crossed the Ailette. The artillery registered their barrages in the Ailette valley.

III/ 66 had already occupied the position at Bouconville, with 9 and 11/ 66 in the first trench, 12/ 66 in the second trench, 10/ 66 connecting the two. Everyone was curious to see what the enemy would do. II/ 66 was in reserve, with two companies on the reverse slope of Bove Ridge, near the regimental HQ, one company at the Arranceau-Fme and one company in the *Grundhöhle* (Deep Cave) to maintain contact with the front line.

Two companies of I/ 66 occupied the second position; the other two were in Camp Alexander, resting.

On 2 November, the enemy shelled the old position as usual: apparently they hadn't noticed that anything had changed. Bouconville village was shelled heavily. Only after it had become dark could hand-grenades be heard detonating in the direction of the old position: apparently the enemy was in the process of assaulting it. But the French still were not sure, and a patrol from III/ 66 under Sergeants Quast (12/ 66) and Kunze (9/ 66) and Corporal Marx (11/ 66) moved to the south of the abbey without meeting any enemy.

On the next day, the French artillery showed their vexation at being fooled and fired actively on our positions and the rear area. From the early morning on, patrols under tested leaders were in no-man's-land all day. They found French detachments that had established themselves near the old HQ of the Battalion Sector Düppel; our patrols attacked them and drove out the bewildered French. On 4 November, a combined patrol led by Corporal Marx (11/ 66) and Corporal Gladowski (12/ 66) boldly and skilfully avoided the enemy security and even went beyond our old position, staying out for seven and a half hours. It was able to establish that the enemy was holding his old position and had only pushed security elements into the Ailette valley, which earned the praise of every command echelon up to division. A patrol from III/ 66, led by Sergeant Quast and Corporal Gladowski (12/ 66) and Sergeant Kunze (9/ 66), enjoyed even greater success, overrunning an enemy security detachment in the Ailette valley, killing three and wounding two, one of whom was brought back as a prisoner; he belonged to the Colonial Regiment 7, 3 Colonial Division. The members of the patrol were praised by the commander of Corps Group Sissonne, Major General Schmettow, in the corps order of the day. Several participants were promoted for excellent service in the face of the enemy: Corporal Scholz (9/ 66) to sergeant, Musketeers Austräger and Tempel (9/ 66) and Schoida (12/ 66) to corporal. Sergeant Kunze and Corporal Gladowski received the Iron Cross 1 Class. The French became more careful and pulled their security back. For that reason the next night's patrols, led in part by Res. Lts von Herrmann and Knies, were unable to develop any information. In any case, the area far to the south of the Ailette belonged to the regiment's patrols.

It turned out that moving the position to the rear was a complete success. Combat activity was considerably reduced at once. Only the two artilleries thundered now and again against the Chemin des Dames and the Bove Ridge. The new position could be held with far fewer troops than was previously the case. We could work on improving the new position almost unhindered. The defending battalion built new dugouts and reinforced the wire obstacles. The reserve battalion prepared the Bove Ridge for defence and built a 700m-long communications trench over the ridge, an accomplishment that astounded the entire division. Both forward MG companies built MG nests behind the first position and on Bove Ridge. Everyone worked with renewed strength, because they saw that improving the position would pay long-term rewards. The companies were very energetic in assembling used materials, the recovery of which was generously rewarded. 12/ 66 in particular had great success here, as the company commander, Landwehr Lt Pitschke, had assembled transportation resources on a large scale. II/ 66 paid 6,389.49 Marks in December alone for the recovery of used materials.

The resting battalion built up Camp Alexander to the point that each company had two large, well-lit, barracks, an orderly room, mess hall and officers' quarters. The barracks were made habitable in winter by reinforcing the walls and building stone ovens. Duckboards were laid for vehicle and foot traffic, as precipitation soon turned the forest floor into a muddy swamp. The construction of bomb-proof dugouts was begun. The camp commander, Sergeant Major Steinwehr, administered it capably and energetically.

Nothing particular occurred in the position in November. Patrols from I and II/ 66 were extraordinarily active. They often threw back enemy patrols and in long daylight patrols made important observations concerning the disposition of the enemy forces. A patrol from 2/ 66 succeeded in rescuing a German soldier from Fusilier Regiment 35 from his French pursuers and throwing the French back. This brave German soldier had been a prisoner of war since 1916 and had succeeded in making his way during several nights through enemy territory and positions, to return to his Fatherland and his unit. A second man, who had accompanied him, had apparently been shot by his pursuers. In December, further patrols destroyed the dugout at old HQ of Battalion Sector Düppel and searched through Vauclerc Abbey as far as the south wall.

On 22 December, RIR 32 was pulled out of the line and its position was taken over by Fusilier Regiment 36 and IR 66. 8/ 66 moved to the right-hand company position of Sector Alexander and 1/ 66 was moved forward to occupy the rear position.

On 26 December, 113 ID was relieved by 3 RD, IR 66 by RIR 2. Due to the hazy weather, the sector had grown extremely quiet and the relief was conducted without difficulty, was completed by 29 December and the regiment occupied its new quarters: regimental staff in Sissonne, 1/ 66 in Camp Düppel, II and III/ 66 in Camp Paderborn. Unfortunately, the barracks were not built well enough for the cold weather, and the troops immediately began winterising them.

Training at Sissonne, 29 December 1917 to 21 January 1918

Training in offensive operations, which had been interrupted when the regiment had been committed at Bouconville, was resumed with renewed energy. However, the regulation now stipulated new attack methods, which the regiment had to learn. After the preparatory bombardment had been completed, the attacking infantry had to accustom itself to follow the rolling barrage as closely as possible, and use its protection to overrun the defenders. Light MG, heavy MG, light mortars and the close-support artillery battery attached to each battalion supported the infantry attack to break the final enemy resistance. Infantry storm troops advanced with rifles and hand-grenades. Defensive strongpoints, such as woods and villages, would be kept under fire during the attack, bypassed and taken by envelopment. Each element would continue the attack without worrying about maintaining contact with the units on the flanks. If a unit met resistance to its front, it should use gaps created by other units to penetrate the enemy line, then take the enemy in its sector from the flank.

The infantry considered these new offensive techniques to be outstanding. Practising them and making them habitual required hard training. It was clear to the troops that the most proficient units would get the interesting and important missions, so every member of the regiment gave his best. The training lasted from 1 to 19 January, then to the disappointment of all it was broken off for a few weeks. We were afraid that the offensive would be called off, and returned reluctantly to the trenches. Thank God the interruption did not last too long.

Trench Warfare at Juvincourt, 21 January to 20 February 1918

On 21 January, the regiment was ordered to relieve IR 354 at Juvincourt. The position was in hilly terrain, and had well-built trenches and dugouts and a good wire obstacle. The first position was on the reverse slope and could be seen by the enemy only from the direction of the Winterberg, which rose threateningly to the west. Behind the first position lay the artillery protective line, then further north the second position was being constructed.

On the evening of 23 January, I/ 66 occupied the first position; II/ 66 had already occupied the reserve position the previous day. On 24 January, III/ 66 occupied the very comfortable Camp Friedrichshafen. On 2 February, II/ 66 occupied the first position, III became the reserve and I/ 66 went to Camp Friedrichshafen. On 12 February, III relieved II/ 66, I/ 66 became the reserve and II/ 66 moved to the camp, so that each battalion was ten days in the first position, ten in reserve and ten resting.

The companies resumed the accustomed duties of trench warfare. Given the frequently foggy weather, along with the various gas attacks, a high state of security had to be maintained. There was also the possibility of surprise tank attacks. A few months ago at Cambrai, the British had successfully conducted just such an attack, and in April 1917, in exactly the terrain that the regiment now occupied, the French had supported their attacks with tanks. They had been thrown back with counter-attacks, but wrecked tanks at Juvincourt admonished us to be cautious.

As in all previous positions, the regiment worked to improve the current one. Above all, in all three positions the number of dugouts had to be increased and the MG nests improved. Our patrolling had gradually made the regiment famous, and was renewed here with our old zeal. This time, 1/ 66 had the lion's share. Sergeant Kreuz and his patrol pushed into the enemy trench, where it encountered an enemy NCO security post with four men: after a short fight, it returned to our position with a prisoner from the French 246th Infantry Regiment of the 55th Division. A few days later, it was recognised and praised by the divisional commander, General von Bergmann. At the same time, a patrol from 4/ 66 broke into the enemy position but did not encounter any enemy troops, and brought back a large diagram of the French trench system. For the next few nights it was so dark that the patrols from II/ 66 could not obtain any notable successes. For the ten days that III/ 66 was in the first position, the nights were clearer, but all attempts to enter the enemy trenches failed due to alert enemy security.

All indicators pointed towards the possibility of an enemy attack. It was suspected that the enemy was constructing positions for mortars firing gas shells as well as other preparations for an attack, which would evidently be directed against Juvincourt. The regiment was therefore ordered to construct a stop line behind Juvincourt, with a company of the front-line battalion and 150 men of the reserve battalion. The regiment's observations did not agree with the fears of higher headquarters.

On 17 February, the division was informed that it would be relieved by 5 RD. On the same day, II/ 66 left the camp so that it could be occupied by a battalion of RIR 8, which was to relieve us, and marched to Lappion and Dizy-le-Gros. On the next day, the reserve battalion, I/ 66, was relieved by II/ RIR 8 and moved to the former quarters of II/ 66, which had marched to Dagny. III/ 66 was to move on 19 February, but was delayed by an enemy operation.

From 1500 on, the enemy conducted preparatory fire on the first position, which at times was as intense as that for a major offensive, and continued until 1900, directed principally against the right and left flanks of Position W 2 and the middle and left of W 3, causing great damage. A lane 25m across was cut in the wire obstacle, which was 50 to 70m deep, the saps and trenches were filled in and the entrances to the dugouts blocked. To the rear, the light rail line, mortar positions, mess hall and battalion sector HQ were all heavily damaged. It was clear that the enemy was serious. For that reason, III/ 66 was not released.

At 1900, the shelling rose to a drumfire of the greatest severity. Numerous enemy MG fired on the berms of the first and second trenches. The garrisons of these requested a defensive barrage, in which the light mortars manfully participated, although they were under heavy fire. At 1930, observers detected through the smoke enemy movement at some places in no-man's-land. The defensive barrage was adequate in front of W 3, but not in front of W 2. All light MG opened fire, with the exception of one in W 3, whose crew had been buried. One enemy element advanced against W 1, two against W 2 and two W 3. The enemy assault groups in front of 9 and 12/ 66 were stopped by rifle and MG fire and hand-grenades, but an assault group entered the first trench in the 11/ 66 sector, put the troops in the sap and the light MG overwatching it out of action, and advanced as far as the entrance to the dugout opposite it. The men in the dugout were in the process of coming up the stairs, when they were all made *hors de combat* by an explosive charge. The commander of 11/ 66, Res. Lt Nessau, arrived with a storm troop, and immediately on seeing them the French fled, leaving behind several pieces of equipment. The French were prevented from moving down the trench by a man on security, who, seeing the French suddenly appear directly in front of him, began beating them with his fists and put them to flight. In spite of pursuit by fire and with patrols, it was not possible to take a prisoner, in part because the French sprayed no-man's-land with MG fire. Disappointed by their failure, the French gassed the entire regimental area for two hours, without causing any casualties. 9, 11 and 12/ 66 had proven themselves in their successful defence against the enemy night attack. The corps and division HQ recognised this fully and once again praised the regiment. III/ 66 suffered one dead, twenty-one wounded and eight who were buried but were dug out and remained with the unit. Res. Lt Mönch, the mortar leader, and Acting Officer Stackmann received the Iron Cross I Class, and fourteen enlisted men received the Iron Cross II Class.

By 2300, it was completely quiet and III/ 66 could be relieved by II/ RIR 8, but remained until 21 February in reserve. It then marched to Lappion. On the same day, the regimental HQ handed over responsibility for the sector to RIR 8 and moved to Montcornet, then on 22 February to Plomion, where I/ 66 was located. III marched to Vigneux-Hocquet and the next day to Jeantes la Ville; II/ 66 remained at Dagny. For a considerable time, trench warfare was over for the regiment. New, difficult missions would bring the regiment even more honour.

34

THE GREAT BATTLE IN FRANCE

Deployment, 22 February to 20 March 1918

In bivouac in and around Plomion, the regiment prepared to move and attack. Most important, the regiment was provided with some of the horses it lacked, which had made all the marches in 1917 so difficult. At the same time it gave up any equipment that was not absolutely necessary, which the division stored in a depot at Fourmies. This included the cattle, cows, pigs, chickens and geese that each company and the staffs had collected. They were given to the commander of the supply company at Hary, Res. Lt Korfes, who had been garrison commander here since July 1917 and had hosted many a tired and hungry officer and horse and fed them well. Supernumerary weapons also went into the depot, as each MG company was permitted to attack with only six MG and each battalion only two light mortars. Through replacement of authorised vehicles and disposal of unauthorised ones (excess vehicles were left in the villages), the regiment's combat and field trains looked similar to those we had deployed with in 1914. Worn-out coats and boots were exchanged for new, in order to properly equip the men for the coming exertions. All of these actions were executed with speed and efficiency. Any material that was still lacking was supposed to be supplied in the attack assembly area.

The division began the approach march on 25 February. The marches were conducted at night in order to be concealed from enemy observation. Such marches were not pleasant, but everyone saw they were necessary and adjusted. The division mission was to reach the area of Bohain in three night marches.

The regiment marched in a closed column under the regimental commander, Lt-Col von Stoeklern, along with other elements of the division, on the evening of 25 February, and by the next morning had reached La Vallée-aux-Bleds (regimental staff and I/ 66), Vaulpaix (II/ 66), Feronval and Haution (III/ 66). During the night of 26–27 February, we reached Guise, with crowded quarters in an oven factory. On the night of 27–28 February, the regiment marched to quarters, which were good and comfortable, III/ 66 in Mennevret, the rest of the regiment in Bohain, and remained there until 14 March.

We were immediately behind the front line, opposite the section of the enemy front that we would attack. The area was packed full of troops, guns, munitions and aircraft. All movement was at night. During the day, the troops remained in villages and woods, vehicles and material carefully hidden from aerial observation. Gaining surprise was the most important precondition for the success of the attack.

The regiments of 113 ID used the few remaining days to practise the break-through tactics. Several of these exercises took place in division strength. Only once during such an exercise was II/ 66 bombed. Otherwise we did not see any aircraft, and the weather was not clear in any case. Unfortunately, some companies occasionally had to be detailed to unload munitions. The last prep-arations for equipping the troops took up the rest of the time. The horses we still lacked arrived; unnecessary equipment, the company orderly rooms, records, cooking equipment and the contents of the men's rucksacks were taken to the depot at Fourmies. A small field kitchen for the regimental staff never arrived, in spite of frequent requests. Therefore a field kitchen had to be taken by 'midnight requisition' from a Bavarian construction company during one of the last nights before the attack, which was quietly accomplished by the NCOs and men of the staff, Sergeant-Major Eckert, Sergeants Dietsche and Scheibner, so effectively that the Bavarians did not miss it until the next morning. The supply trains were divided into three echelons: 1st echelon, ammunition vehicles; 2nd echelon, field kitchen and the staff pack wagon; 3rd echelon, ration vehicles. These preparations were completed on 13 March.

Movement into the front lines began on the evening of 14 March; the bivouacs were displaced forward by echelon. First the regimental staff and II/ 66 moved to Fresnoy-le-Grand, I/ 66 to Croix Fonsomme and III/ 66 to Etaves. III/ 66 moved on the evening of 15 March to Fontaine-Uterte, with the regimental staff following on 17 March, while, that night, I/ 66 moved to Remaucourt and II/ 66 to Essigny-le-Petit. The staff and I and III/ 66 spent the night of 18–19 March in Sequehart and II/ 66 quartered at Méricourt. On the evening of 19 March, the entire regiment was in the ruins of the village of Levergies, and spent 20 March, the last day before the attack, here in impatient tension. Once again all of these movements were conducted at night.

During the day, all the officers and platoon leaders went to IR 353 to be briefed concerning the assault trenches, no-man's-land and the enemy position, as much as could be seen. Carefully prepared maps of the sector were distributed. On the way there, we were impressed by masses of munitions and the marked-out positions for artillery up to 30.5cm: we had the comfortable feeling that everything had been prepared to the smallest detail. The regiment waited for its hour, quietly, confident of victory and that it had attained the highest level of military ability possible: neither previously, nor afterwards, did a better regiment launch such a mighty attack.

35

THE ATTACK, 21–25 MARCH 1918

113 ID was a first-wave assault division on the right flank of the 18th Army (General von Hutier), 7km north of St Quentin on the road to Cambrai. To the left was 88 ID, then 28 ID, all elements of III AK under General of the Infantry von Lüttwitz. The second wave consisted of 6, 206 and 5 ID. The third wave and army reserve was the Saxon 23 ID. To the right, 208 ID attacked as the left-flank division of the 2nd Army.

The British 5th Army under General Gough held the front between the Omignon and Oise rivers. In front of 113 ID was the British 61st Division, holding a front from the Omignon to about 2km north of St Quentin. Together with the British 30th Division (right of 61) it formed XVIII Corps, which also had the 3rd Cavalry Division in reserve at St Christ, but it took little part in the battle. The British had asked the French for reinforcements: General Debeny's 1st Army moved from Reims to the line Montdidier–Moreuil, but only on 30 March, too late for the fight on 21 March.

IR 66 arrived on the night of 20 March in its attack sector on the right flank of 113 ID, opposite the village of Pontruet, relieved IR 353 at 2200, and deployed with:

III/ 66 on the right, 9 and 10/ 66 leading, opposite Pontruet, 12 and 11/ 66 following, a platoon from MG Company 3 with 9 and 12/ 66, battalion staff with the forward companies;

I/ 66 on the left, 3, 4 and 2/ 66 leading, each with a platoon of MG Company 1, 1/ 66 following, generally opposite the *Tommy-Höhe* (Tommy Hill), with the regimental staff

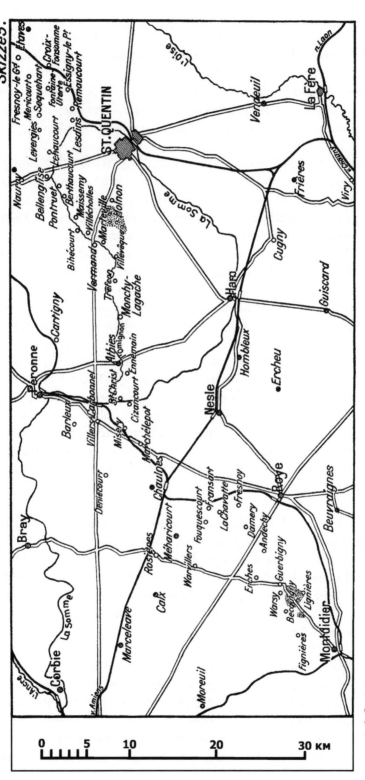

Photolith.v. Bogdan Gisevius, Berlin W Bülowstr. 66.

Inf.-Regt. 66

| 0 | 5 | 10 | 20 | 30 KM |

II/ 66 on the left, following I/ 66, with 6 and 5/ 66 leading, staff, 7 and 8/ 66 following, just in front of the St Quentin–Cambrai road. Contact with Fusilier Regiment 36 on the left.

1st echelon supply trains (ammunition) was on the St Quentin–Cambrai Canal at Lehaucourt, 2nd echelon (field kitchen and the staff pack wagon) at Sequehart, 3rd echelon (ration vehicles) at Fresnoy-le-Grand.

The night of 20–21 March was relatively quiet. Apparently the enemy did not expect an attack: if he had, he would surely have fired a counter-preparation barrage into the attack assembly area, which would have caused heavy casualties in an area packed with men and horses. Not a shell would have missed. In fact, in the nine hours we were there, we hardly had any casualties, which was a factor not to be underestimated in maintaining and even increasing the troops' aggressiveness. In general, the troops' morale was the highest possible. The preparations for the attack had built up immense confidence in the success of the attack. Artillery ammunition lay like 'heaps of manure' on the fields near the routes of the approach march and convinced the troops that there would be plenty of artillery support.

On the evening of 20 March, as the division commander, General von Bergmann, was moving with his staff to the Levergies Heights, he encountered III/ 66 moving forward, and he spoke short encouraging words to the men, whereupon someone called out to him, 'Herr General, we'll have the situation straightened away in short order!', which visibly pleased the general and showed that the troops were going to battle with the highest level of confidence.

Suddenly, at 0440, a massive preparatory fire with artillery and mortars began and lasted for five hours. Lt-Col von Stoeklern wrote in his diary:

> At 0415 I stood with my staff in the open, in order to see and hear the artillery firing at the beginning of our offensive. Three minutes, said one of the officers, now 2, now a minute 40 seconds, etc. and at exactly 0440, as ordered, all of the batteries from Arras to la Fère opened fire. There was a great roaring, the sky flared up, with the masses of shining red fires, and then darkened from smoke shells. We stood there and listened, and shouted loud into the night, 'Tommy, your hour has come!'

The bombardment began with counter-battery fire and shifted gradually to preparatory fires against the enemy infantry positions and the area in between, while still suppressing the enemy artillery. Standing both inside and outside the trenches, the troops watched the spectacle our artillery fire created. Thousands of guns let loose a massive hail of iron on the enemy. The muzzle flashes turned night into brightest day. The fire of individual guns could not be heard, but a continual thundering and howling filled the air. The earth shook and shivered under the force of the exploding shells, enemy munitions dumps burned brightly, the light mixing with thick and heavy moving clouds of gas and smoke. That was the beginning of the Great Battle in France, and this artillery fire had to fill us with confidence and optimism for the coming battle. During this entire time, the enemy return artillery fire was remarkably weak.

The thick fog that lay over the fields of Picardy at the beginning of the bombardment remained after dawn, so that the intended fire direction from aerial observers could not take place. It also meant that there would be no strafing from ground-attack aircraft to support the infantry attack. Although the fog was in many ways a hindrance to the advance, with some units becoming disoriented, going in the wrong direction and losing contact with each other, after the fact we determined that this was outweighed by the advantages the fog gave us. Above all, it was far easier for us to surprise the enemy. The capture of the very strong and well-sited *Holnon-Stellung* (Holnon Position), which in the British defence plan was their principal point of resistance, in a little more than three hours, would never have been possible without it.

Two regimental attack zones were designated, IR 66 right, Fusilier R 36 left. IR 91 followed immediately behind IR 66, all under the brigade commander, Colonel Count von Schulenberg.

The 113 ID attack operations order for 21 March was written on 18 March, Order Nr 98 since mobilisation, by the Ia (operations officer), and contained the following interesting paragraph:

> The attack will proceed without stopping through the enemy third position (east of Trefcon to the east of Beauvois) as far as possible into the enemy rear. Capture of the enemy artillery and all positions up to and including the third position is the minimum that must be achieved on the first day of the attack.

These objectives were deep in the enemy position, and could only be demanded of troops in which the leadership had the highest confidence, and would have been reached, had not the fog so strongly hindered all movement.

The assault on the first enemy position was set at 0940. The first line of infantry had a long approach march to the assault position, which the fog aided greatly. It left the German trenches at 0920. Patrols from 2/66 under Senior Sergeant Schmidt with light MG had moved in the dark to the Tommy Hill, which was found unoccupied. The last minutes before the beginning of the assault were described by First Sergeant Voigt from 10/66: 'At 0930 everyone was ready to conduct the assault. The fog was so thick, that you couldn't see ten paces.'

At 0940, when the last artillery round landed, the infantry pushed through the wire obstacle, which in spite of the artillery preparation was largely intact, and into the first enemy trench. 1/ 66 under Capt. Niemeyer advanced south of Pontruet and Berthaucourt. Pontruet was to be taken by 9 and 10/ 66 under Capt. Trenk, Berthaucourt from the south by 11 and 12/ 66. Res. Lt Wadepuhl described the advance on Pontruet:

> During the advance we had to rely more on instinct than our eyes. We could not hear a thing at all. We hurried forwards, restricted by the gas masks we were wearing, with their well-known horrible smell and taste. We fell into shell craters, got hung up on barbed wire, collapsed exhausted due to a lack of air, overran enemy security foxholes, were shot at from the front, back and all sides, and continually gathered together in small groups, glad not to be alone. That was the story of our assault on Pontruet, which all at once, before we were even quite aware of it, was behind us.

Lt-Col von Stoeklern described the first minutes of the attack:

> I advanced with the staff from the left flank of the forward trench to the right at Pontruet. I had no idea where I was, and could only navigate by the compass. By a lucky chance we encountered a British officer, took his map away from him, oriented myself on the ground and everything was good. The names of all the fighting and communications trenches were entered on the map, as the British identified them with signs in the trench system. So we advanced, British map in hand.

The first British trenches were smoothly overrun by 1/ 6 and 11/ 66: the British did not offer determined resistance until the third trench. The advance of 5/ 66 on the morning of 21 March was described by the then Sergeant Schroeder:

> Holding our rifles ready to fire, we went forward in skirmisher line. After twenty paces we lost contact both left and right. I was a runner for the company commander, Lt Steiger. Our first objective was the so-called Tommy Hill, which lay directly to the west. We could only follow the compass bearing, which turned out fine. After about ten minutes we reached the first enemy trench, and men of our company and other companies joined us. Lt Steiger told us to pass the word: everybody here obeys my commands and is a member of Company Steiger. The air was so pestilential from gunpowder smoke, gas and fog that we had to advance with a handkerchief over our mouths. We came like this to the second British position, the Holnon Position, where we suddenly took MG fire, and everyone took cover. Men from Fusilier 36 lay down next to us. In the thick fog we could see nothing of the enemy. I lay in a shell crater with Lt Steiner, some men from 5/ 66 and a

captain from Fusilier 36, and we fired in the direction of the enemy MG. The MG was hammering away directly in front of us, I quickly pulled my head under cover, and at the same time I heard Lt Steiner call my name, and then 'Jennrich!'. I looked up and saw white froth coming out of his mouth, he fell backwards, hand on his heart, his face white as snow. I tore open his uniform coat and saw a small red spot near his heart. One of our best had just died! The other four in the shell crater with us were dead, including the captain from Fusilier 36. I left my dead lieutenant to his batman, Corporal Hobohm, and in a blind rage charged the enemy MG, along with Lt Peters. In a couple of bounds I reached it, and, swinging my rifle butt, I broke a British soldier's skull, while Lt Peters shot another with a pistol. My lieutenant was revenged! Three other British already lay dead near the MG.

After 1/ 66 had taken the third trench, it continued the attack to the *Lansing-Höhe* (Lansing Heights). The *Indianer-Weg* (Indian's Trail), strongly held with British MG, had to be rolled up: the commander of 3/ 66, Res. Lt Bierbach, was killed.

Our advance was unstoppable. The northern part of the *Lansing-Höhe* was taken by Battalion Niemeyer, which ended the heavy fire from there into the flank of Fusilier 36. We continued the attack against the Lloyd George *Stellung* (Position), which was taken by 1100. The British had emplaced MG in the area between the trenches and in this position itself and conducted a determined defence: the fighting here was particularly bitter.

By this time, Capt. Trenk and the elements with him on the right flank had advanced so quickly that on the path to Maissemy, at the same level as the Lloyd George Position, they came under friendly artillery fire. They had to cower for ten anxious minutes in shell holes until the rolling barrage shifted forwards. Lts Pütter and Poppenhausen were then ordered to storm Maissemy. The fog was lifting and at 1135, the staff of III/ 66 suddenly found itself surrounded by the enemy. They held out by forming a 'hedgehog' (all-around defence). East of Maissemy, Res. Lt Wadepuhl, together with Sergeant Quast and men from 12/ 66, boldly overran and captured two British officers and thirty-four men. At 1245, the west side of Maissemy was reached. 12/ 66 under Landwehr Lt Pirschke continued on the road to Villecholles, but were brought to a halt by flanking fire from Hill 119.6 and enemy MG on the opposite side of the Omignon. The remaining elements of III/ 66, which had been held up by fog and combat, arrived. 9/ 66 in particular had encountered heavy enemy resistance on the ridge south of Maissemy, which it overcame with the help of Staff Sergeant Ackermann's MG platoon. Res. Lt Bochert described the 9/ 66 fight:

At 0900 exactly 9/ 66 moved out, with Schmidt's platoon next to the Omignon and the other two platoons attacking Pontruet frontally. We were initially somewhat disappointed, because gas drifted towards us from the British position, but it soon proved to be harmless. We hardly met any resistance in the ruins of Pontruet, and ran into the first British on the path to Berthaucourt. The fog caused the units to become intermixed and move out of their assigned sectors. We overcame stronger resistance on the *irischer Weg* (Irish path) that ran parallel to the edge of Berthaucourt. Res. Lt Bolle and his platoon quickly eliminated the British garrison there, but the lieutenant was killed in this bold attack. By that time I and the rest of the company, accompanied by the reliable Senior Sergeant Ackermann (MG platoon), my true comrade in all three offensives, had drifted somewhat to the left, moving parallel to the Berthaucourt–Maissemy road. Suddenly the fog lifted and the Indian path appeared, and we attacked with wild enthusiasm. Some of our men even fired standing. In spite of being almost completely hoarse, Lt Meyer gave out a wild war cry and, shouting a thunderous 'Hurrah!', our men took the position. It was the most glorious fight of the day. The British who were not killed fled to Maissemy. We now rolled up any resistance to the right of the road. For a short time we were treated to very uncomfortable MG fire from the north side of the Omignon, but there was no stopping us. Maissemy was right in front of us. More and more, the fight became manoeuvre warfare. Our close-support battery came racing forward at a dashing gallop and reached Maissemy at about the same time we did, at 1300. Schmidt's platoon and elements of the other two platoons under Capt. Trenk had, together with 10 and 12/ 66, reached the far side of the village. We occupied a flat sunken path that led south from Maissemy.

The then Senior Sergeant Ackermann described what he and his platoon experienced on 21 March:

A quarter-hour before the start of the attack I already lay with my guns in front of the first British trench, to avoid the British fire, which was becoming stronger, and to be able to keep up with the infantry. As soon as the rolling barrage moved we ran forward and in no time we were past the first British trench without meeting any resistance. When we reached the wire obstacle in front of the second trench we were met with rifle fire and hand-grenades. A MG went into position and fired a belt at the trench and the enemy fell silent. At another area, that appeared less dangerous, we cut a lane through the wire obstacle, which to our amazement was man-high and undamaged, and swept through the trenches to the left and right, taking three Scots prisoner, and continued the advance without stopping. Several infantrymen, who had lost contact with their companies, provided welcome protection for our guns, since we were now operating independently. We reached the third trench, which we swept with MG fire, covering the infantry as it cut a lane through the wire. We went at full speed towards the trench and in short order occupied it. Once again we cleared out the trench for a distance to the left and right, but found only wounded. Since we couldn't see any of our own people, and some of our own artillery was landing in the area, and we could hear heavy MG fire to the rear, I decided to wait here for a while, either to be reinforced or to greet retreating British. In the meantime, I oriented myself in the terrain, the MG were set up for defence, and we tried out some Lewis guns we had captured. Suddenly a column appeared in our rear, whether friend or foe, given the poor visibility, we could not easily tell. When it turned out to be Lt Borchert and an assault column from 9/ 66, our joy knew no end. Everyone was amazed that MG, which were not supposed to be able to assault, were on the objective and in front of the infantry. I had acted far outside of my mission parameters, but I could now go on with reinforced confidence.

Elements of 12/ 66 under Res. Lt Wadephul cleaned out the enemy MG nests still holding out in Maissemy. 11/ 66 under Lt Schültz swung south and, together with 8/ 66 led by Lt Eisenbeck, occupied the west and south sides of Maissemy. In the meantime, strong enemy attacks from Villecholles had pushed back 10/ 66 to within 200m west of Maissemy, where it remained for the rest of the day. It was not possible to move off the numerous captured enemy guns, but it was possible to make enemy attempts to recover them very difficult.

Between the Lloyd George Position and the Holnon Position, the other two battalions had stormed many artillery batteries and MG nests. The Indian Path had been cleared, principally by 7/ 66 under the command of Res. Lt Lentze. At 1145, 4 and 6/ 66 under Capt. Rochlitz reached the Holnon Position on Hill 119.6, soon followed by the remaining companies of 1/ 66 and 11/ 66 under Capt. Niemeyer. Immediately after this position had been taken, Res. Lt Kreidner and 4/ 66 attempted to take Hill 119.6. The attack broke down under enemy MG fire with heavy casualties. Res. Lt Schröter, of 2/ 66, described the fight:

Lt Kreidner and I lay in the sunken road from Maissemy to Holnon Wood east of Hill 119.6 to get oriented. I warned Kreidner not to be hasty, but I couldn't stop him once we had established where Hill 119.6 was located. He called out to me, 'We have to advance. The artillery barrage is already far ahead of us', and we moved out, charging forwards along with the right wing. Suddenly the heavy fog lifted and we stood immediately in front of a large group of enemy troops, which opened up immediately with heavy MG and rifle fire, with massive effect, especially on 4/ 66, since we all were on flat open ground devoid of cover. With my few men I jumped into a trench to the right and was immediately involved in a tough defensive battle. The British mercilessly mowed down everyone who was not under cover. I heard Kreidner call out, and cry for help, but I could no longer do so.

One of our bravest officers had died on the field of battle, after he had proven himself for nearly four years of combat. So long as we, the survivors, remember our dead, Kreidner's name must be among those who were the very best.

Further attempts by I/ 66 to bypass Hill 119.6 failed, so that even though the Holnon Position had been completely cleaned out, the attack stalled. In and around this position was, from right to left, Battalion Trenk (III/ 66 and 8/ 66), Battalion Rochlitz (4, 6 and 7/ 66) and Battalion Niemeyer (1, 2, 3 and 5/ 66), sometimes dug-in in the open terrain, everywhere thoroughly intermixed with elements of Fusilier 36.

By 1330, the entire Holnon Position was in the hands of the two assault regiments and all of the artillery batteries were slowly displacing forward to the Lansing Heights, in thick fog and over shot-up, muddy terrain criss-crossed with trenches. Some of the guns had to be pulled by ten or twelve horses.

IR 91 had followed IR 66, and its lead elements were close to the east edge of Maissemy. It was now clear that the entire attack had stalled. At noon, the fog lifted, and air reconnaissance from both sides were active. Unfortunately, the enemy had superior numbers of aircraft and the forward infantry in particular came under very uncomfortable bombing and strafing attacks. The enemy aircraft also directed their artillery fire very effectively, which became heavier and was directed particularly at the Holnon Position and the area directly to the east; several times heavy artillery fire was seen.

Mortars and mountain artillery was employed against the MG nests on Hill 119.6, as were the batteries of FAR 225 that had reached the Lansing Heights. I/ RIR 32 was attached to IR 66 in order to get the attack moving again, and it moved directly east of Maissemy. By 1800, there was so much artillery in position that it was possible to renew the attack against Hill 119.6, the possession of which was essential for the advance. The regimental commander ordered: 'From 1900–1915 preparatory fires against Hill 119.6. I/ 66 storms the hill at 1915.' This attack succeeded: by 1915, Hill 119.6 was in the possession of elements of I/ 66, but due to very heavy fire the front line was pulled back to the start line. That evening, two companies of I/ RIR 32 were inserted in the gap between III and II/ 66.

At 2130, an enemy attack against Hill 119.6 failed, principally due to fire from light mortars and the close-support batteries. Around midnight, the enemy artillery fire died down and it conducted only harassing fire. Lt Walther Schmidt described the night of 21–22 March:

It was the evening of 21 March in the Holnon Position, after the failed attack on Hill 119.6. Night had already fallen on the British position, which had been torn up by our artillery. The fighting had been unusually bloody. The heavy artillery fire had ceased, except for a few shells. After the failure of our assault, 1/ 66 had left the sunken Maissemy–Holnon Wood road and lay in shell craters in the open field [Schmidt obviously does not agree with Korfes that Hill 119.6 had been taken]. In front of us was the intact British wire obstacle of Hill 119.6, behind us the dead of Companies Kreidner and Menkel. We lay on the right flank of 1/ 66, stared into the night, and thought about the harvest Death had taken in today, especially in our battalion. Every so often these thoughts were disturbed by the dull thud of a British gun firing, followed quickly by the howl of the approaching shell, which continually fell to our right, not far away. The British gun fired again, and soon from the right we heard the command 'Stand at attention!' shouted out. The shell howled towards us, exploded with a crack and immediately thereafter the command was given, 'At ease!'. We listened, and in spite of fatigue and nervousness, we felt strangely calm. Each time a British gun was heard firing, this same clear boyish voice shouted out in the dark night. We moved back and dug in, when Lt Schmittsdorf from II/ 66 came over to us to establish contact. He told us, laughing, that the British had it in for him and the twenty men, from various companies, that were with him in a large shell crater, because the shells that came to us so regularly, always exploded at the same place, that is, near them. The men were becoming unsteady, and in order to hold them, every time a shell was fired and exploded, he gave those commands clearly and firmly. He kept twenty men, who were completely unknown to him, under control and secured the gap between 1/ 66 and II/ 66.

During the night the units were reorganised as much as possible, ammunition resupplied, wounded evacuated and the number of casualties determined. In spite of the enormous exertions and serious casualties, morale was good and the troops were confident. The large quantities of food found in the enemy positions and the villages was quite welcome.

At 0230 on 22 March, on the Tommy Heights, 113 ID gave the operations order. IR 24 from 6 ID had been attached to the division. I and II/ 24 would become division reserve, moving behind the right flank, following IR 66. It was clear that bringing up the additional artillery that had also been attached to the division would take all night, so the artillery preparation was to begin at 0900, the attack at 1000. A slower tempo was set for the rolling barrage, since the previous day's experience had shown that, with the single exception of III/ 66, the infantry had not been able to keep up with it. The brigade order established the organisation for combat:

IR 66 under the command of Lt-Colonel von Stoeklern, in the right-hand sector, with 1/ RIR 32, as well as a company from MG Section 34 (from division), attached.

II and III/ 32, II/ 36 and III/ 24 in the left-hand sector, under the commander of RIR 32.

Behind IR 66 was the divisional reserve, I and II/ IR 24, with the close-support artillery batteries, and two companies of MG Section 34.

I and III/ Fusilier 36, which had taken heavy casualties the day before, was behind the 113 ID left flank.

On the morning of 22 March, Lt-Col von Stoeklern went to Maissemy and greeted his men with the words: 'Men, today is the birthday of the old Kaiser Wilhelm I and mine as well. Don't let me down. Go get them!' Lt-Col von Stoeklern wrote it differently in his diary: 'Just get them! The Tommies (and other less complimentary descriptions) need to get to know us!'

The preparatory bombardment, including Mortar Company 113 firing from their 21 March positions, began at 0900. As on the preceding day, there was a heavy fog so the bombardment was not as effective as intended. This was clear when the infantry attack began, which encountered a large number of MG nests. Battalion Trenk (III/ 66, 8/ 66 and 2/ RIR 32) on the right, so successful on the first day, pushed into the hollow south-east of Bibécourt. Capt. Trenk's order was laconic: 'After the artillery preparation, the battalion will attack in the usual manner. The high ground (probably west of Hill119.6) has to be taken. There will also be attacks to the left and right.' The attack quickly stalled due to resistance in front and on the flanks, from the north bank of the Omigon as well as from MG west of Hill 119.6. Elements of II/ 66 and I/ RIR 32 attacked to the south and broke through the artillery battery positions south-east of Bibécourt, and at 1115 continued the attack against the ridge east of Villecholles. Heavy British barrages were not able to stop the brave attackers. At the same time, the attack on the regimental left – II/ 66, I/ RIR 32 and I/ 66 – very quickly was brought to a halt west of Hill 119.6, taking very heavy casualties. In 8/ 66, all the officers were killed, and 5/ 66 took severe casualties. Both of these companies were pulled back, along with elements of I/ 66, and assembled on the Maissemy–Holnon Wood road. The staff of II/ 66, with 6 and 7/ 66, succeeded in bypassing MG nests to the north and continuing the attack south of Maissemy.

This was the situation when Lt-Col Stoeklern made the bold decision to stop the attack west of Hill 119.6. Weak elements of I and part of II/ 66 would remain here, while all other available units would be committed in the centre to the attack on Villecholles and Marteville. At 1230, he ordered a frontal attack and double envelopment of Villecholles. This had already partially been overtaken by events, as elements of II/ 66 under Lt Menkel had reached and held the ruined mill south-east of Villecholles, while weak elements of III/ 66, moving through the Omigon valley, had entered Villecholles from the north and were holding demolished houses. Elements of III/ 66 and I/ 32 attacked Villecholles frontally, and the British committed strong forces against them, some moving in lorries, which were engaged by our MG and destroyed.

At 1400, the enveloping attack conducted by Capt. Trenk against the south side of Villecholles began to make itself felt. At 1215, Res. Lt Borchert, with his 9/ 66 and 10/ 66, assaulted the village and by 1430 it had been taken. Capt. Trenk immediately ordered Lt Borchert to bypass Marteville and advance on Villévèque; 6 and 7/ 66 went with Borchert on their own initiative. Lt Wadepuhl and a mixed group from III/ 66 took Marteville with the assistance of a gun from 6/ FAR 225. III/ 66 captured numerous enemy guns at Villecholles, but it had no time to stop, and pursued the fleeing British as quickly as possible. Lt Borchert described the 9/ 66 attack:

At 1000, after an hour-long artillery fire preparation, a thick skirmisher line attacked from Maissemy. After the success of the previous day, morale was outstanding, and everyone remembered Le Cateau. 9/ 66, on the left flank of the battalion and in contact with II/ 66, moved forward smoothly, initially meeting no enemy resistance, but the thick fog was a problem. After a while MG fire went over our heads. We soon reached the Artillery Hollow south of Bihécourt, climbed up the opposite slope and continued in the direction of the ridge east of Villecholles. We used the terrain and the fog to get close to the British position, which we could not see. Suddenly we received heavy MG fire from point-blank range. I ordered everyone to lie on the ground. My runner, Corporal Hertel, and I, along with a man from IR 24, jumped into a shell hole to our left, which was barely big enough for us. The seriousness of our position became clear to me when, after a while, the fog began to lift. In front of us was an intact wire obstacle, 20–30 metres wide, and behind it a knee-deep British trench filled with Lewis guns. The bravest of our men were stuck to the wire. The British, dressed as usual, pipes in their mouths, walked upright back and forth in the trench, while their MG took anyone who showed themselves under well-aimed fire, while shells from a medium-calibre artillery piece began to land. Truly hellish! Several men lost their nerve and tried to run back to the hollow behind us, paying with their lives. Old experienced combat soldiers lost their heads, such as Acting Officer Schmidt, a brave man from the Saarland, who yelled over to me, 'We can't lie here!'. I replied, 'Going back is impossible.' A few seconds later I looked carefully to the side and saw Schmidt jump towards the rear and then fall down, dead. This happened to many. The man to my left was hit in the upper thigh, and it was only with difficulty that I prevented him from trying to crawl to the rear, for which he later heartily thanked me. Using field expedient shovels, we dug the shell hole deeper, convincing ourselves that we now had cover against head shots. With my field glasses on the lip of the hole, I watched every move the British made. This hell lasted more than an hour, with every minute an eternity.

Then suddenly – probably thinking we were all dead – Tommy turned around in his trench and went to the rear. Using this opportunity, our line jumped up, got through the wire and reached the British trench. A few hand-grenades followed the British as they withdrew in the direction of Holnon Wood. Our small group of survivors shook each other's hand, everyone agreeing that that was the worst hour of the war so far. We shuddered to look back at all those who had not been able to make that last dash forwards. We were shaken to hear of the death of First Sergeant Nebel. I had five bullet-holes in my rolled-up coat, evidence of our recent ordeal.

We now had to exploit the new situation. I gathered up my small band, which included altogether about twenty men including a Scot prisoner, and went down the trench to the west to get back in our assigned zone of action. We soon left the trench and moved over open ground which fell gently towards the Villecholes–Marteville road. On the way we were joined by another man. Nothing hindered our movement, and when we reached the rail embankment in front of Marteville we were overjoyed to find an equal-sized detachment under Lt Wadepuhl. With no concern for the situation left or right, we pressed on. A man on a bicycle he had taken from the British, who had become detached from his unit, joined us and did outstanding service. We reached the Marteville–Villévèque road, looking like a small group, out for a walk in the countryside. No British to be seen far and wide. Halfway to Villévèque there was a short stop in a roadside ditch to avoid detection by a squadron of British aircraft circling over us. Our trusty bicyclist rode ahead and with great daring stopped an auto towing a heavy artillery piece, just as it was leaving Villévèque. Rations found in a tool case were most welcome. We reached Villévèque and moved through it without encountering any resistance. When we reached the other side of the village we took small-arms fire, took cover behind a garden wall, and then moved individually to a sunken path on the edge of the village. Our advance had temporarily come to a stop: the strongly held British third position, the so-called Vaux Position, was a few hundred metres to our front. We were somewhat isolated, but in what I judged to be a secure position, so I put security out, and told the men to take off their packs and rest on the slope of the sunken path. The British were digging in, as their trench was only knee-deep, but provided with a good wire obstacle. I had taken off my pack and was walking up and down the sunken path, making for the fork in the road which led to the British position, when two Tommies with drawn revolvers suddenly stood in front of me: a very painful situation. They seemed to be as surprised as I was and stood as though nailed to the ground. I did not let them out of my sight and yelled, 'Give me a rifle!'. At that moment our excellent bicyclist shot the first Tommy, while the other tried to run and was shot in the back.

The high ground west of Villévèque was strongly held by the enemy, and such heavy MG fire was directed at the advancing elements of Lts Menkel and Borchert that they had to take cover in a sunken road east of Villévèque and wait for reinforcements. So as not to be flanked by the enemy, who was in Vermand, in the sector to the north, Capt. Trenk attacked it with 3/ RIR 32, numerous heavy MG, snipers and two guns from 6/ FAR 225, and took the town.

The British were still holding the area west of Hill 119.6. At 1330, they even conducted a strong attack against the hill, which was thrown back by a counter-attack conducted by elements of the regiment and RIR 32 to our left. Battalion Niemeyer was then ordered to leave only weak elements opposite this enemy, and follow the regimental right flank through Villecholles. Only late that afternoon did Lt Kühne, with elements of 3 and 4/ 66, succeed in enveloping the defenders of Hill 119.6 and take numerous MG and 250 prisoners.

At 1600, there was only weak resistance by retreating enemy forces in the regiment's right-hand zone. His artillery was no longer firing, in good part because most of his batteries had been captured. Weak elements of II and III/ 66 under Capt. Rochlitz were pursuing the enemy, followed by II/ 24, under Major Winter, which had been attached by division to IR 66, and which at 1530 arrived at Marteville, where the regimental staff was located. Elements of Battalions Trenk and Niemeyer assembled and followed it. The pursuit was conducted on a broad front to Villévèque, but soon it became clear that there was no enemy resistance and for the first time in four years a march column was formed on the battlefield:

II/ 24
I/ 32
IR 66
II/ 36

II/ 36 had gotten separated from its parent unit to the left and placed itself under Lt-Col von Stoeklern, who used it as his reserve in the march to Villévèque. At 1615, the column was in front and to the left and right of Villévèque.

At 1630, Capt. Rochlitz cleared Villévèque after a short fight. A 30.5cm gun and its prime mover were captured while attempting to drive away. The enemy left the village in panic flight and occupied his third position (Vaux Position). An attempt to take this position immediately did not succeed, as the enemy infantry and MG were too strong. Lt-Col von Stoeklern decided to conduct an artillery preparation.

By 1830, the 113 ID situation was as follows: both march columns had deployed in the Villévèque area to attack the Vaux Position. In spite of great difficulties during the approach march, almost all the artillery of 113 ID and 6 ID, including the heavy artillery, had arrived and set up south of Villévèque. The 113 ID mortar company went into position on the east side of Villévèque. Two companies of MG Section 34 were on the ridge east of Villévèque, from where they could support the attack with overhead fire.

The artillery commander ordered preparatory artillery and mortar fires from 1900 to 1945, at which time both columns attacked. In the Column von Stoeklern sector, the first two lines in the Vaux Position were overrun by 1/ 32 under Capt. Rieger. The attack stalled in front of the third line, due to the fact that the wire obstacle was strong and undamaged, and the position was provided with numerous MG. Since the necessary reconnaissance could not be conducted in the dark, the continuation of the attack was deferred to 23 March. Both columns would maintain their task organisation on the next day. During the night, they remained close to the enemy position. The units reorganised, although most of the troops were so exhausted that few went to the field kitchens when these arrived at 0200.

All the 113 ID artillery and mortars began the preparatory fire at 0730 on 23 March against the enemy third position, and the attack started at 0800. At 0845, the division commander at the south-west entrance to Marteville received the report that the Vaux Position had been taken after a short fight and both columns were continuing the advance. The right-hand column, under Lt-Col von Stoeklern, organised march column as follows:

Advance Guard: 1/ RIR 32
                5/ FAR 225
Main Body: II/ IR 24
                II/ Fusilier 36
                IR 66
                113 ID Mortar Company
                1/ FAR 225 (-)
                MG Section 34
                Foot Artillery Battalion 407

The march continued without interruption towards the Somme. Weak resistance at the Haig Trench and, later in the pursuit, from cavalry, was brushed aside after short fights. Column von Stoeklern was ordered to march through Trefcon, Monchy-Lagache, Devise and Ennemain to St Christ, and cross the Somme there (Trefcon–St Christ, 10km). IR 24 (minus II/ 24) followed.

Near noon, two aerial reconnaissance reports to division stated that the enemy was in retreat and that the Somme and canal bridges at St Christ were intact. Division HQ ordered both columns to exploit the enemy flight and use all means available to cross the Somme that day.

Column von Stoeklern was forced to deploy the advance guard west of Monchy-Lagache. The close-support battery forced the enemy to withdraw. At 1500, the column reached the west side of Ennemain. Lt-Col von Stoeklern gave his attack order at the crossroads there. Reconnaissance would first be conducted to determine the crossing points and possible enemy opposition, and then the crossing made to the west side. Column von Stoeklern would occupy an assembly area in a depression west of Ennemain on both sides of the road to St Christ, with the artillery occupying positions near Ennemain. Officers' patrols, including both infantry and engineers (with Res. Lt Peters especially distinguishing himself), determined that the bridges and footbridges could be crossed with difficulty by individuals. The other side of the Somme was strongly held by infantry with large numbers of MG. Nevertheless, Lt-Col von Stoeklern ordered II/ 24 to force a crossing and establish a bridge-head on the west side. The attack failed with heavy losses; the battalion left security on the east bank, at the bridge site. I/ 66 and II/ 66 were behind a wood, north of the Ennemain–St Christ road, and III/ 66 was south of the road on the west side of Ennemain.

Late that afternoon the division commander, General von Bergmann, and officers of his staff, arrived by automobile at Ennemain to personally evaluate the situation. At the south-west entrance of the village the general met members of the regiment, whom he thanked and praised in the highest terms for the regiment's outstanding performance of duty, that of Battalion Trenk in particular. In spite of the enormous exertions of the previous days, the general found the troops' morale to be very high and they were eager to continue the attack.

The situation on the evening of 23 March was as follows: 19 ID was north of the Omignon, and had tried without success to cross the Somme at Brie. 113 and 52 ID were on the east bank of the Somme, with the west bank being strongly held by the enemy. In the 113 ID sector, elements of RIR 32 had succeeded in crossing the Somme and the canal at Pargny, but had suffered such heavy casualties that during the night they had to cross back over to the east bank. South of us, 5 ID had succeeded in crossing the Somme.

III AK (Lt-General Lüttwitz) ordered a general assault across the Somme at 0800 on 24 March, followed by a pursuit to the west. The attack did not take place on time, because the infantry and artillery did not have enough time to find the enemy positions, particularly MG nests, which was necessary in order to be able to engage them: the artillery would have been degraded, from conducting an effective fire preparation to harassing fire. Interrogation of prisoners taken the previous night revealed that fresh forces had been brought in on lorries, and that the enemy had reinforced his artillery. The regiment therefore remained in the previous day's positions and conducted reconnaissance. II/ 24 was relieved by elements of I/ 32 and I/ 36 and moved to the rear.

That evening, Column von Stoeklern attempted another crossing at St Christ. Elements of I/ 32 and II/ 36 succeeded in crossing the Somme and the canal, but suffered severely under the fire of the reinforced MG nests, which had not been located and were completely undamaged. In addition, enemy artillery had been brought up, which was able to fire accurately and at close range into the crossing points. 2/ RIR 32 penetrated the farthest, was attacked by strong enemy forces and cut off from the crossing point. When Column von Stoeklern reached their position the next day, they found most of the company dead from bayonet wounds to the chest. A few men, including the wounded company commander, Res. Lt Ebert, were able to swim over the canal and infiltrate upstream along the west side of the Somme, to make contact with German forces at Pargny. Given the difficult situation, Lt-Col von Stoeklern brought the mass of the two battalions back across the river, leaving security forces on the west bank.

On the evening of 24 March, the situation was as follows: 19 ID in the north reported that only weak elements had been able to cross the Somme, and that the enemy defence had inflicted heavy casualties. To the left of 113 ID, at noon, 5 ID had been able to exploit the previous evening's success, and the left-hand column of 113 ID was able to cross the Somme behind it. After a serious artillery duel, it advanced through Epénaucourt to Licourt, slowly gaining ground to the north. During the afternoon, the crossing at Faloy ordered by III AK was proceeding at full speed. II/ IR 24 returned to its division. The regiment took casualties from aerial bombs and strafing. It spent a second night in a very poor bivouac around Ennemain; the artillery fire on both sides continued all night and inflicted casualties.

On the morning of 25 March, a large number of aircraft bombed the assembly areas, causing casualties. 113 ID ordered that the costly attempts to cross the river at St Christ be stopped until pressure from the division's left-hand column could pry the defenders away from the crossing points. By afternoon, the effect of the left-hand column was noticeable in front of Column von Stoeklern, as the British abandoned their position on the west bank at St Christ. Covered by the fire of MG Section 34, which was on the west bank, as well as the 113 ID artillery, Column von Stoeklern crossed in order II/ 36, I/ 32, IR 66. II/ 36 and I/ 36 linked up halfway between St Christ and Misery, surrounding and capturing 140 British and four guns. I/ 32 cleaned out St Christ and Cizancourt and took more prisoners. At about midnight, the regiment crossed the Somme and the canal: I/ 66 quartered in Broist, II/ 66 in St Christ, III/ 66 bivouacked in a sunken road south-east of Cizancourt, with the regimental staff at first in Cizancourt. The next day, III/ 66 and the staff also moved to St Christ. In his diary, Lt-Col von Stoeklern mentioned the capture of two British officers and twenty men west of St Christ:

> I was moving forward with another officer when the two of us encountered a troop of about twenty unarmed British, in formation and commanded by an officer, who ordered them to halt and reported to me with the words *sur Stell*, by which he meant *zur Stelle* (present, awaiting orders). He and his men apparently had enough of our artillery fire. I sent them without guard to the rear: none of them had any intent of escaping.

On the evening of 25 March, 19 ID, attacking to the north, had its left flank at Villers-Cotterêts. The 6 ID had been inserted in front of 113 ID and had reached the line Maisseny–Marchélepot. The 113 ID was no longer engaged. From 21 to 25 March, the regiment's casualties were:

	Dead	Wounded	Missing
Officers	22	23	1
NCO and EM	160	531	94
Total	182	554	95

It had captured thirty-five officers, 700 men, fifty guns, 200 MG and a great mass of material, supplies and equipment.

36

BETWEEN THE BATTLES, 26 MARCH TO 24 MAY 1918

After a rest day on 27 March, the regiment moved south-west on 28 March, through the Somme battlefield of 1916 and the area of [the scorched-earth] Operation Alberich (prior to the withdrawal to the Siegfried Line in 1917), to reach Marchelopot. The entire area had a desolate appearance, particularly in the damp, rainy weather. Every village through which we passed had been thoroughly levelled. The first few signs of the recently begun reconstruction were everywhere: small huts for the civilian population, and tables, chairs and chests with the inscription 'For the devastated Somme'. They had been collected for this region from all over France, and now most of them had been destroyed, too. The British had constructed large barracks areas in the ruins of the destroyed villages, and the regiment used those that had not been burned down as quarters. On Good Friday, 29 March, at 1800, in Fresnoy-les-Royes, with the artillery salute of the nearby front in the background, the division passed in review before the commander, General von Bergmann. The general extended his greetings and best wishes to the regiment. On this day, 113 ID passed under the command of XXV Reserve Corps (RK) and on 30 March became the corps reserve, quartered in Guerbigny, until 8 April. On 9 April, the regiment was attached to 6 Bavarian RD as the counter-attack force. It quartered in an extremely unsuitable location south and south-west of Guerbigny, exposed to French artillery fire, with the regimental staff and 1/ 66 in Fignières, II in Forestel-Fme, III in Lignières. Fignières in particular took French artillery fire. On 10 April, 6 Bavarian RD alerted the regiment, but it was quickly cancelled. Lt-Col von Stoeklern described our unpleasant stay in Fignières in his diary:

At 1800 a heavy shelling of Fignières began: the crossroads and entrances to the village in particular. Since the staff quarters was near a small intersection of three paths on the side of the village facing the enemy, we took 12 to 15cm shell fire from three directions. No one could leave the cellar. The shelling lasted the entire night. We expected that at any moment the brick cellar would cave in. Several shells went through the house above us, and the flames from the exploding shells shone in the cellar windows.

This shelling led the 6 Bavarian RD to move the regimental staff and III/ 66 to bivouac in a gully between Guerbigny and Lignières, and I/ 66 to a wood south of Becquigny. On 13 April, II/ 66 was moved to a wood south-west of Becquigny. On 16 April, First Lt Siegener, the second aide-de-camp to the 113 ID commander, wrote in his daily notes:

At 1100 march battalion Magdeburg under First Lieutenant Burgund, with about 750 men, arrived directly from home at the division HQ at Erches. These replacements were not so good as the ones we had received on 8 April from Recruit Depot 113 ID. For the first time we heard that men had left the column while it was under way.

New Missions

On 24 April, 113 ID was relieved by the 6 Bavarian RD and bivouacked near Erches in old enemy positions. On 28 April, the regimental staff and III/ 66 was in Fransart, I/ 66 in Fouquescourt, II/ 66 in La Chavatte. The ruins of the houses in these towns offered scanty billets. On 29 April, 113 ID marched for five days far to the rear area near Guise le Nouvion. We had to cross the combat zone of the last weeks and years yet again. Therefore the quarters north-east of St Quentin were very poor, but the prospect of several weeks' rest allowed us to bear these last exertions easily. On 5 May, the regiment reached the area west of Le Nouvion. The staff and II/ 66 quartered in Boué, III/ 66 in Buergues and I/ 66 in Barzy and La Louzy. We now began a period of rest and recovery. In a scenic area with good quarters, away from the enemy artillery fire and the threat of nightly air attacks, the strains of the last weeks were quickly forgotten. More replacements from home arrived under Capt. Fischer. The men helped the local civilian inhabitants with their farming. There were also sporting events, games and films at the theatre. Firing ranges were built. The terrain was cut up by hedges, which made larger exercises quite difficult, so company-sized training was held. In this idyllic area we celebrated the birthday of our regimental chief, King Alfonso XIII of Spain, as well as Pentecost. Large-scale division-level exercises prepared the regiment for the next operations.

On the evening of 22 May, we began to march to the south-west, to the south of Laon. The marches were always conducted at night, for three nights, with the division organised in four march columns. By day, all the routes of march were to be kept free of troops. The bivouac areas were also to be camouflaged against enemy air observation. All of these preparations pointed to another offensive operation, this time over the Chemin des Dames. The regiment reached its bivouac in the woods at Laval, south of Laon, at 0400 on 25 May. Laon was under long-range French artillery fire, and parts of the town, especially the area of the rail station, had been completely destroyed.

37

THE CHEMIN DES DAMES OFFENSIVE

The Assault, 26–27 May 1918

On the morning of 26 May, the second aide-de-camp of 113 ID, First Lt Siegener, brought the divisional attack order, which was to start at 0200 on 27 May. The first paragraph of the order said: 'The enemy forces opposite us are significantly weaker. The attack will be conducted after a two-hour preparatory bombardment.' 113 ID would attack as the centre division of Attack Group A (HQ VIII RK) between Monampteuil and Chevregny, south of the Ailette, against the enemy position east of Royère-Fme. On the right of 113 ID was 14 RD, whose left-hand unit was the attached Württemberg Mountain Regiment (Rommel's unit), and 37 ID attacked to the left. The first 113 ID objective was to cross the Aisne as soon as possible and take Chassemy and the hilly and wooded terrain adjacent to it.

The regiment deployed two battalions on the first line, III/ 66 right, I/ 66 left. I/ MG Section 34, 5/ FAR 225 and the staff and 20 and 21 Batteries/ Mountain Artillery Section 7 were attached to the regiment. RIR 3 attacked on the left with one battalion forward. The regiment had to occupy the attack position by 0100 on 27 May. After dark, there was considerable activity in the woods south of Laon. The regiment moved forward almost silently, III/ 66 along the path Urcel–Monampteuil, I/ 66 over the *Siegfriedrücken* (Siegfried's Ridge) and through Chevregny, both to the so-called Ailette Position. II/ 66 occupied an assembly area in a copse between the Ailette Position and the narrow-gauge field railway line, with the mission of following III/ 66. Capt. Rochlitz had become ill and was replaced as II/ 66 commander by Reserve Capt. Münnich. Elements of Engineer Company 225 were attached to all three battalions.

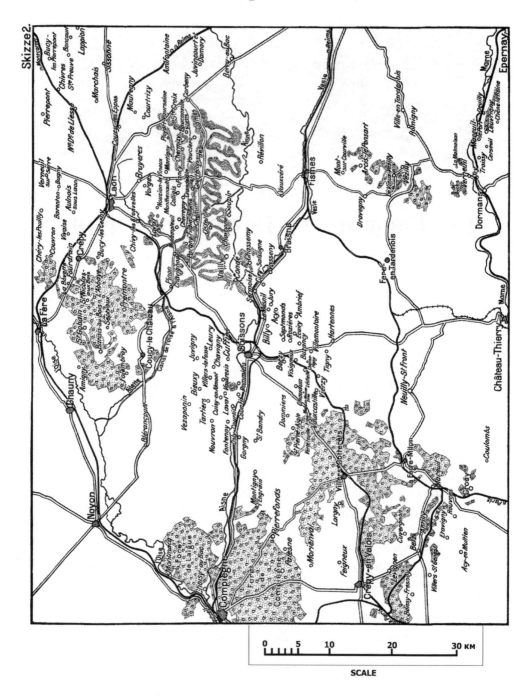

Temporary bridges, footbridges and such were carried to cross the Ailette and the canal. As of 2130, the regimental staff was located in a sunken road immediately south of Monampteuil. The first and second echelon supply units occupied assembly areas near Laval, the third echelon in a wood south of Laon.

The regiment completed its occupation of the attack position by 0040, without being disturbed by enemy artillery fire. The conduct of the infantry attack was once again in the hands of the infantry brigade commander, Colonel Count von der Schulenberg. The front-line troops in the regimental assembly area were from Landwehr IR 82 of the 13 Landwehr Division. First Lt Siegener described the artillery preparation, which he observed from a position south of Laon:

> It was 0155 27 May. The division commander and his staff were in the forward HQ, listening in the dark. It was generally quiet on the front, with only a few shots being fired. Then orders were shouted in the night. In the nearby heavy gun positions, the lamps on the aiming poles were lit. Everyone waited, tense. Then a signal light shone straight up from the HQ towards the stars, and immediately the artillery began to fire on a broad front. There was thunderous cracking as one had never heard before. The night was turned to day by the muzzle flashes of the guns, a hurricane of steel hail hammered incessantly on the enemy positions and batteries.

Opposite us, the steep slope of the Chemin des Dames ridge seemed to be spitting fire. Tall columns of flame in and behind the enemy position betrayed munitions dumps that had been hit. Thousands of signal flares lit the night, to help our advance or to call for artillery barrages. Very quickly, however, a thick haze spread over the entire area, blocking long-range visibility. The French artillery answered weakly; there was enemy fire only at the crossings of the Ailette.

During the artillery and mortar preparatory fire, at 0330, I/ 66, III/ 66 and their support troops had crossed over the Ailette and the canal, using field-expedient bridges, and moved into the front line, which was still held by elements of Landwehr IR 82. II/ 66 followed immediately behind. The only casualties were caused by a direct hit on the staff of III/ 66, which killed four men and wounded eleven. The energetic Capt. Trenk, supported by Acting Officer Rein, were quickly able to restore order.

At 0400, the German artillery preparation rose to hurricane intensity, mixed with the desperate barking of French MG. The regiment moved slowly through the thick bushes and undergrowth, in order to be as close as possible to the edge of the preparatory bombardment at 0400. Due to the limited number of paths, the companies had to move slowly, in single-file, until the terrain permitted them to spread out. During this march, the units became completely intermixed. The assault was set at 0440. III/ 66, on the division right flank, had been seriously delayed by an enemy MG on a slope called the Russian's Nose (*Russennase*). II/ 66, led by 7/ 66 and MG Company 2, crossed the heavily gassed Ailette valley and reached the Triangle Wood (*Dreieckswäldchen*), finding no enemy in the dugouts and trenches there, but were held up by French MG nests in tiers up the slope of the Russian's Nose, which defended themselves desperately, in spite of being heavily engaged by MG Company 2. While II/ 66 and III/ 66 engaged the enemy on the Russian's Nose frontally, 12/ 66, under Res. Lt Wadepuhl, attacked from the west and after a hard fight reached the top of the Russian's Nose ridge at 0715. A few minutes later, 9/ 66, under Lt Borchert, which had been stopped halfway up the slope by MG fire, joined 12/ 66. Lt Borchert described the fight:

We crossed the Ailette over the Weniger Bridge and the canal on footbridges to occupy the attack positions. Given the difficult terrain – undergrowth and fallen trees – it seemed to me best to advance with a strong point element with the company following single file. I set off with Res. Lt Reichert, Sergeants Hager and Grebin and a light MG squad. Maintaining orientation was difficult, as smoke and fog lay over the valley. Nevertheless, we reached our first checkpoint, the spot where the Bush Mill used to stand. The first MG fire came from the left flank and went over our heads. To our front we could see the Russian's Nose, and we began a difficult climb, but without any trouble from the enemy. The air was still, except for the snapping twigs. According to the map, there was supposed to be an enemy strongpoint halfway up the Russian's Nose. Before we knew it, we were standing in front of its wire obstacle. The slope here was very steep, and 10 or 15 metres above us we could see the yellow spoil of the position between the trees. The silence was absolutely uncanny. Was the strongpoint already empty? I leaned against a large tree and was just about to begin cutting the wire, when suddenly there was MG fire, which from the sound of it had to have come from a German MG, and from close range, which whistled over our heads. We yelled at the men that they were crazy, but in the next moment a salvo of hand-grenades exploded behind us. So, the enemy was there. My wire cutters flew forward, while I threw myself back, everybody went more or less head over heels several times and finally we found ourselves several metres farther downhill, by twos and threes in shell craters. Several men were lightly wounded. The French now went wild, their MG hardly stopped firing, but couldn't hit us, because we were in dead ground. We were out of range of hand-grenades, so they fired several rifle-grenades. Everyone crouched together in the craters, and my former batman, Sergeant Grebin, observed drily, 'If it goes on like this, we should look around carefully, so we can find this spot again tonight.' After we agreed on a plan, we crawled to the right and once again back uphill to the same level as the French strongpoint. By swinging far around the enemy position, we succeeded in taking it in the flank, and the garrison surrendered.

We hadn't been wrong – there was a German MG in the strongpoint. For now, the enemy resistance had been broken. Panting, we immediately continued climbing the steep slope and by 0800 we reached the top.

This put a hole in the enemy front. At practically the same time that 9/ 66 reached the top of the ridge, 7/ 66 joined them, having stormed the Russian's Nose from the east. 1/ 66 had worked its way up to the Jacobi Slope (*Jacobi-Hang*) and the Shell Hole Wood (*Trichterwäldchen*). Some daring men from 2/66 under the leadership of First Sergeant Schmidt climbed up the slope and took out the enemy MGs. At 0900, the regiment crossed the Chemin des Dames, driving the enemy in front of them in panic flight. At 1100, the view from the top of the Chemin des Dames was magnificent. For a short time, the 113 ID commander and his staff watched from just south of the crest as the division advanced. To the north was the immense field of ruins and battlefield, the Ailette valley, and behind it on a hill the double towers of the old town at Laon. Brilliant sunshine lay on the cliff-lined fields. To the south there was visibility as far as the high ground south of the Aisne and Vesle, with columns of smoke rising up from the valleys, marking the enemy's withdrawal. Heavy motorised vehicle traffic was clearly visible on the roads south of the Vesle, as the French threw reserves on lorries into the front. Our artillery had not yet come up to engage these high-value targets, but our infantry columns and all kinds of vehicles pushed south towards the Aisne, from whose valley light small-arms fire could be heard. Numerous prisoners from the French 21 ID were brought in, and large quantities of equipment of all kinds was taken, including considerable stocks of food. The then Musketeer Otto Kroll of 10/ 66 said:

> ... at around 1000 (or perhaps earlier) we reached the crest of the Chemin des Dames, where I met my platoon leader, Lt von Pöppinghausen. The assault had succeeded, and the first thing I did was stow a large piece of Swiss cheese in my rucksack, after sharing it with Lt v. P. In addition to two 21cm guns, which we captured north of Gerlaux Ferme, we also found a barrel of marmalade, as a consequence of which we had to continually relieve our bowels, which was most inconvenient in combat.

II/ 66 and III/ 66 each advanced south-west in a single-file column on the paths of the high ground south of the Chemin des Dames, through fields covered with shell craters. Enemy MG and rifle fire did not delay the regiment: the initial elements reached the road west of the Gerlaux-Fme, where the regiment first assembled and then continued the march to Vailly. The regiment captured many artillery pieces with their crews. The sections of Lts Borchert and Wadepuhl advanced boldly, but encountered strong enemy resistance on the Orme Ridge and the Red Houses. 1/ 66 and 6/ 66 advanced through Aizy and turned towards Vailly. 11/ 66 crossed the Vailly–Pargny road, and took more prisoners. 5/ 66, in the lead, moved to the Marcone Wood, taking numerous prisoners and four guns. MG Company 2 was able, from the area north of Vailly, to take under effective fire enemy elements withdrawing to the Aisne. Towards 1100, the regiment was near the north side of Vailly, and at 1115 Res. Lt Müller, leading 10/ 66 and accompanied by elements of 11 and 12/ 66, entered Vailly, while the remainder of III/ 66 under Capt. Trenk was locked in heavy combat at the Red Houses. At 1120, the regimental commander, Lt-Col von Stoeklern, and his staff entered Vailly. He noted in his diary:

> In Vailly, Landwehr Lt Preuss, Captain Korfes and First Lt Plathe and several men attacked French troops from Infantry Regiment 93, some of whom were wandering around the town, some fleeing towards the Aisne bridge, some shooting at us, who were overwhelmed, along with a French field hospital and five medical officers.

At 1130, 1/ 66, under Capt. Niemeyer, reached Vailly from the east, and shortly thereafter 11/ 66 arrived from the north-west. Both battalions had crossed the Aisne along with the fleeing French troops and held a weak bridgehead on the south bank. 1/ 66 captured a railway gun at the Vailly rail station, as it was trying to move off: for a considerable time this gun had been the terror of Laon.

At 1400, elements of III/ 66 were still in bitter combat at the Red Houses. Every attempt by Capt. Trenk to outflank the position, or take it by frontal assault, failed in the face of a very strong and well-maintained wire obstacle. Suddenly, unarmed French appeared from the direction of the high ground north of Vailly, and told us that this was held by two French companies with numerous MG. Lt-Col von Stoeklern immediately ordered two sections under Res. Lts Nessau and Gut to attack from Vailly to the Red Houses [in the flank]. At 1600, this attack was decisive. Six officers and 400 men were taken prisoner, along with numerous MG. III/ 66 was now able to continue the march and assemble at Vailly.

The III/ 66 fight at the Red Houses, south of Vailly, had stalled the regiment's attack, giving the enemy an opportunity to set up in a strong position on the treeline north of Chassemy, and with numerous MG hold under fire the bridges over the Aisne and the canal, which he had not been able to blow up. Nevertheless, elements of 1/ 66 and 11/ 66 were able to run quickly over the Aisne bridge without suffering serious losses, and then cross the canal with a rowboat, as the high walls of the canal created a dead zone for enemy fire. 11/ 66 occupied the south side of the canal embankment, with strong security to the east, as there was no contact with RIR 32. By noon, the elements of 1 and 11/ 66 that were over the Aisne advanced as forward detachments into the old trenches south of the gravel pits at Vailly, with the staffs of both battalions in the gravel pits. 5/ 66 sent a strong patrol along the south bank of the canal as far as Condé, and established that the village and in particular the bridge over the Aisne were still in enemy hands. The right flank was therefore held by a strong security detachment which was pushed 500m west of the canal sluice south-west of Vailly. The regimental staff and III/ 66 remained in Vailly. This was the situation at 1700. Further advance was not immediately possible, since the regiment had been engaged all day without artillery support. The close support batteries did not arrive until 2000, about the same time that the rest of the division artillery completed its displacement forward. The enemy artillery fire on the bridges cut communications between the north and south sides of the river. Nevertheless, II/ 66 succeeded in maintaining communications with the north side by sending messengers over the Aisne on field-expedient bridges located 800m to the west of the permanent bridge.

After an artillery and mortar fire preparation from 2100 to 2130, the elements south of the Aisne assaulted the enemy MGs to the front. Only 7/ 66 succeeded in taking a section of trench located 300m south of the gravel pits: the other companies made no progress in the face of the enemy MG fire. The captured trench was occupied by security posts; otherwise, the troops put the line they had occupied into a state of defence. The elements of I and II/ 66 that were still north of the river were able to cross during the night, so that both battalions were full-strength, and strong enemy attacks were thrown back. On the first day of the attack, the regiment had scored a signal success, and it was ready on the next day to throw back the enemy forces north of Chassemy, which were sure to be weak.

Pursuit, 28 May to 3 June 1918

Early on the morning of 28 May, the 5/ 66 security detachment on the regimental right flank sent out a patrol which found Condé free of enemy troops, and the bridge there undamaged. The regimental light mortars had set up on the north side of the Aisne and, together with an anti-aircraft gun, engaged the enemy MG nests on the south side of the river. I/ 66, under Captain Niemeyer, together with 6 and 7/ 66, moved along the south bank of the Aisne towards Condé, with the mission of driving the enemy away from the gravel pits, then continuing the attack to the bridge at Condé and then south towards Vesle. While conducting this attack, two locomotives were captured, with steam up and many wagons attached, as well as a large-calibre gun and a great quantity of engineer equipment.

Our neighbour to the left, RIR 32, had finally succeeded in moving over the high ground south-east of Vailly, which allowed II/ 66 to resume its attack at 1400. 8/ 66 sent storm troops into the canal basin and from there to the trenches in the woods north of Chassemy, as did 5/ 66 from the trenches south of the gravel pits that it had taken the previous night. They rolled up the enemy position in the direction of St Martin Wood; the fleeing enemy was very effectively engaged by heavy MG in the gravel pits. II/ 66 then moved through the wood north of Chassemy in three columns, along a narrow-gauge rail line that ran through there at the time, with 5/ 66 on the right, in the middle the battalion staff, elements of 5/ 66 and a heavy MG platoon from MG Company 2, and 8/ 66 left. 5/ 66 was able to surprise and capture an approaching French infantry company, with two officers and 130 men. Another section from 5/ 66 captured eighty French troops, twelve MG and a revolver canon. II/ 66 reached Chassemy at 1510, and occupied an assembly area in the woods north of the Chassemy–Ciry road, close by Chassemy. Patrols immediately reconnoitred the Vesle crossing points.

III/ 66 and the regimental staff moved out from Vailly at 1500 to follow II/ 66. The enemy had withdrawn quickly and blown all the bridges and foot-bridges over the Vesle, and covered these points with MG and artillery fire from the high ground on the south bank. Under covering fire from Mountain Gun Battery 21 and the regimental mortars, an attempt was made to force a crossing east of Limerie, using a portable bridge, which failed. An attempt by recently arrived elements of the regiment to cross at Limerie and La-Plaine-Fme, south of Condé, also failed. These elements therefore swung to the east and at 1900 reached the wood west of Chassemy. III/ 66 succeeded in crossing at the Chassemy–Ciry road, in spite of enemy fire. Capt. Trenk described the fight:

> By questioning wounded men, I determined that a company of IR 147 (of the division on the right) was on the far side of the river opposite Limerie, could not advance and was taking heavy losses. I conducted a personal recon-naissance, accompanied by Lt Gut, and ordered him to take a fighting patrol, including a light MG, cross the Vesle, make contact with the 147 unit, and find a point where the battalion could force a crossing. Lt Gut went upstream

along the Vesle, silenced an enemy MG nest in a sand pit that was putting fire on the road bridge, and established a bridgehead. MG Company 3 under Lt Hentschel was committed, and it provided fire support as 10/ 66 climbed over the remains of the destroyed bridge and took cover behind the road. All this time 10/ 66 was taking fire from a MG on the Gobinne Hill (Hill 62.7 west of La-Plaine-Fme). It was 1700. A report that the battalion had established a bridgehead was immediately sent to the regimental commander.

The remainder of the battalion crossed in three echelons. 11/ 66 under Lt Preuss moved to Sermoise: 12/ 66 was between 10 and 11/ 66 in the second line, 9/ 66 and MG Company 3 followed 10/ 66 in the third line. At 2000, after a tough fight, III/ 66 was on the high ground west of the line Sermoise–Ciry, and was continuing the attack to the west in the direction of Le Mesnil–Acy. Lt-Col von Stoeklern ordered I/ 66 to follow III/ 66. He held II/ 66 in reserve: the battalion was now commanded by Capt. Korfes [the editor of the IR 66 history], who had been the regimental adjutant. Landwehr Capt. Münnich, the previous commander, had contracted peritonitis and died a few days later in hospital. The battalion reached Ciry at 0230, the regimental staff St Jean-Fme at 0430.

III/ 66 learned from interrogations of French prisoners that strong enemy forces were approaching, and moved forward to a favourable position on the high ground beyond Le Mesnil–Acy. It was a clear night, as 10, 12 and 11/ 66 lay far ahead of the rest of the German units, not knowing the situation around it, or where the enemy was. Capt. Trenk had kept 9/ 66 and MG Company 3 with him north-east of Jury, halfway to St Jean-Fme. Lt Borchert, the commander of 9/ 66, wrote:

> The whole situation was uncertain. We had bypassed nests of French every-where, who became active in the dark. 9/ 66 had cleaned out several caves in the area and taken several prisoners. A ration depot near Ciry was captured and visited by several patrols: our unforgettable patrol leader, Sergeant Kunze, was shot by cowardly French stragglers. The night was unquiet: there was firing all around. In order to be ready for everything, along with the battalion staff we formed the famous Trenk hedgehog [all-round defence] in a shell crater. Patrols sent to make contact with the companies to the front did not find anything or failed to return. Capt. Trenk therefore had no information at all. He appeared to be quite annoyed, and when we wished him a happy birthday that night, he was not at all pleased and told us we had more important things to do.

Patrols from 12/ 66 that went into Le Mesnil to look for food, did not come back, with the sole exception of Sergeant Piater, who reported to the company commander, Res. Lt Wadepuhl, that Le Mesnil was occupied by the enemy. A strong patrol from 12/ 66, led by First Sergeant Gehrike, was thrown back with losses. 1/ 66 occupied the high ground north-west of Acy with security detachments, while the company remained in the town.

Early on the morning of 29 May, Lt-Col von Stoeklern and his staff moved on the road from St Jean-Fme to Jury, meeting Capt. Trenk and Lt Borchert with 9/ 66 on the way. Lt Borchert wrote:

> At 0500 we resumed the attack on Jury. Given the uncertain situation, Captain Trenk sent me forward with a point element; and he followed 100 metres behind with 9/ 66 and MG Platoon Ackermann. We soon reached the edge of the plateau, and were treated to a spectacular view: far down in the valley below, in the gardens of Jury, a French battalion was bivouacked, secured only by a MG on the Jury–Ciry road. They didn't appear to have seen us. We quickly and quietly brought the light and heavy MG into position, and at a whistle signal a literal rain of bullets descended on the unsuspecting French. They ran through the farmyards and streets in a panic, leaving everything behind. We could not hold our men back: everyone charged down the hill to Jury. We took fifteen officers and 400 bewildered men prisoners. Their stacked arms, some of them knocked over, still stood in the gardens at the edge of the town. We didn't hit much in the early morning light, but nevertheless had the desired effect. We now saw the light signal from 1/ 66 and our companies on the hill opposite us at Acy. The Mesnil–Jury–Acy valley was now clear of enemy troops and we reached Acy after a short march.

That morning, 1/ 66 sent detachments to Jury and Le Mesnil to requisition food, and these took several hundred prisoners. The regiment then marched from the start line at Mesnil–Arcy, III/ 66 on the right, order of march 9, 10, 11, 12/ 66, in the direction of Septmonts, 1/ 66 on the left on the Acy–Ecury road [on map Ecuiry]. II/ 66 and the regimental staff remained on the west side of Acy. The battalions advanced slowly in the burning heat, while French artillery put terrific fire on the high ground between Acy and the Crise stream west of Mesnil–Ecury–Septmonts. I and III/ 66 were delayed into the afternoon by small-scale contacts. Repeatedly the battalions took MG and artillery fire. Covered by several heavy MG, 2/ 66 pushed into Ecury and took some 600 prisoners, including the adjutant of the French 1 ID, who was in the process of mounting his horse. Had 1/ 66 arrived only a few minutes earlier, it would have captured the entire staff of the French 1 ID. At the same time, III/ 66 was in heavy contact south of Billy: despite their exhaustion, the troops conducted a wonderful, vigorous frontal attack which destroyed the enemy. Lt Borchert wrote in his diary:

The plateau lay under heavy enemy MG fire, and we made good use of the communications trenches left over from the trench battles of 1914, which led in the enemy's direction. Res. Lt Wadepuhl and I moved with the point elements of our companies, which followed in single file. We reached the dilapidated trench without loss. We suddenly came upon a break in the trench, which led to an unexpected short rest. Then the unbelievable happened. The exertions of the previous days, the terrific heat, a glass of champagne, and Wadepuhl and I both fell asleep. The troops saw what had happened and did likewise. Suddenly Captain Trenk appeared and said forcefully: 'Gentlemen, if you're going to act like this, what do you think your men will do?' We rubbed our eyes and, half-asleep, mumbled that the trench stopped. Trenk's answer was predictable. We ran a short stretch over open terrain and then back into the continuation of the trench. We had now approached rather close to the enemy MG, but still could not determine where they were hidden. We attempted to go over the top in skirmisher line and assault them, but that failed in the face of their heavy defensive fire. When we fell back to the trench, a young soldier could not work up the courage to move and remained lying in the open. I will never forget seeing Lt Wadepuhl very ungently pulling him back into the trench. Finally we discovered a sunken road half-left, which led away from our position at an angle. We jumped over to it, accompanied by a MG, and to our great surprise saw the annoying MG nests 15 metres further down the same sunken road. We opened rapid fire and the crews fled. We continued the advance in skirmisher line, but there was no enemy to be found. Just before Septmonts we encountered forty French, who jumped out of a wood to our left and surrendered: they appeared to have had more than enough of fighting.

The way south was now free for III/ 66 and 14 RD to its right. While III/ 66 continued the march to Septmonts, Res. Lt Wadepuhl conducted a reconnaissance ride on a bicycle towards Bersy, undisturbed by the withdrawing French. Even when two speeding French bicyclists overtook him, they did not hit on the idea of using their weapons against him. Wadepuhl returned to his battalion that evening, and could report that according to his observations the neighbouring 14 RD was hanging back. Late that afternoon, heavy French artillery fire lay on the Crise valley. I/ 66 attempted to advance through Buzancy to Visigneux and Villemontoire. Lt-Col von Stoeklern, the regimental staff and II/ 66 followed the two forward battalions through Mesmin and reached Buzancy at 1700: the movement through the enemy artillery fire in the Crise valley succeeded without casualties. The regiment reorganised: II/ 66 was committed north of I/ 66, while III/ 66 and the regimental staff remained in Buzancy. Lt-Col von Stoeklern wrote in his diary:

On 29 May in Buzancy we found quarters in a castle with a beautiful park, masterfully appointed as a 'rest centre' in the American manner. But it was also apparent that someone had been having a very good time, and that many young ladies had been active in the hospital/officers' quarters: ladies' undergarments of all kinds, shoes, pictures with very questionable subjects were pretty clear proof. In addition, there was a large depot with underwear, so that our troops got clean clothes. We also found all kinds of food.

Immediately upon leaving the wood north of Buzancy, moving towards Charantigny, the point element of 7/ 66 took casualties: the leader of the point, Lt Droege, was killed. II/ 66 crossed the Soissons–Hartennes road and reached the high ground east of Charantigny. 7/ 66 sent out patrols which established that there were no enemy troops in Charantigny, and the company immediately pushed through to the south side of the village and occupied it. The French were in a prepared delay position, dug-in and strongly wired, south-west of the village, the so-called Paris Position. 6/ 66 advanced south-west until it was level with 7/ 66 and then, in the open field, dug-in for the night. Although II/ 66 had no contact with friendly forces either to the left or right, and Charantigny was dominated by French-held high ground to the south, south-west and west, Capt. Korfes ordered the rest of the battalion forward to the village that evening, a decision that would be justified by the fact that Charantigny would serve as the basis for taking the Paris Position the next day. 8/ 66 and MG Company 2 occupied a cave on the northern entrance to Charantigny, 5/ 66 in the caves in the village. During the night, two battalions of Grenadier R 7 from the division to the right crossed the Charantigny–Visigneux road and came up level with Charantigny. 6/ 66 reached the high ground east of the village and established contact with RIR 32. An attack by 1/ 66 from Villemontoire was stopped by heavy enemy MG fire from the high ground to the south-west of the village. The battalion spent the night on the road to Hartennes. It appeared on the evening of 29 May that the regiment's attack, which until then had been advancing smoothly, had now come to a halt.

At 0830 on 30 May, several waves of French colonial troops, accompanied by cavalry, attacked the neighbouring division from the high ground west of Charantigny towards Visigneux-Aconin. This offered the heavy MG of MG Company 2 on the north entrance to Charantigny excellent targets for flanking fire, and the attack failed with severe losses.

III/ 66, at Buzancy, was alerted at 0930 and occupied the high ground north of there with two companies forward and one echeloned to left and right rear, to block the valley to Rozières. A patrol led by Lt von Herrmann went north to the west of Noyont, and discovered that, on the basis of erroneous reports, the two battalions of Grenadier R 7 (9 ID) to our right had received orders to withdraw, making these units unsteady. Vigorous action by Capt. Korfes succeeded in getting one battalion to stand fast, so that the high ground west of Charantigny remained in our hands.

At 1530, II/ 66 was ordered to attack the Paris Position after a preparatory bombardment of several hours. RIR 32 to the left would attack at the same time. 6/ 66, east of Charantigny, was relieved in place by I/ 66, whose right flank was now at the east side of Charantigny. At 2100, I/ 66 and II/ 66 began the attack on the Paris Position, which took the first enemy trench, then stalled due to fire from numerous MG, which had not suffered from the artillery preparation, but opened fire as the advance began. Strong night patrols attempted to reconnoitre the enemy position so as to renew the attack the next day. During the night, it was possible to feed the exhausted troops and replenish ammunition.

113 ID had intended to renew the attack on 31 May along the entire division front, but the French attacked 47 RD on the left first, in strength and with numerous tanks. The attack was thrown back, but 113 ID could only conduct its attack late that afternoon. After a short, sudden, but very intense preparatory bombardment by the entire division artillery, on a small section of the second trench of the Paris Position, I/ 66 succeeded in breaking into the enemy position south-east of Charantigny. A platoon of Mountain Battery 21 eliminated the principal enemy points of resistance at point-blank range. II/ 66 took 100 prisoners from the French 53 ID, and succeeded with 5, 6 and 7/ 66 in taking the entire enemy trench on the road leading south from Charantigny, and then continuing the attack in the direction of Vierzy. At the same time, 8/ 66 advanced from the wood east of Léchelle along the Soissons–Vierzy rail line to the southernmost point of the wood at the rail tunnel, where it linked up with a company of RIR 53 (14 RD). On the evening of 31 May, the French in front of 113 ID strongly held Vierzy and the Paris Position north of there in the direction of Chaudun.

The Battle of Vierzy, on 1 June, was one of the most glorious pages in the history of the regiment. As on the previous day, brilliant sunshine foretold a hot day. At 0800, the entire divisional artillery began a terrific bombardment of Vierzy and the trenches of the Paris Position to the north of it. Two hours later, Battalions Korfes and Niemeyer attacked, reinforced by 12 and 10/ 66. 5, 6 and 12/ 66 rolled up the French trenches to the west in bitter fighting, powerfully supported by the MG firing from an overwatch position: the fleeing French were caught in annihilating fire. Capt. Trenk described in his diary the fight of 12/ 66 and its commander, Res. Lt Wadepuhl:

Supported by heavy artillery fire from Mountain Battery 20, brave 12/ 66 attacked to the Charantigny–Vierzy road and threw back the French, led by First Sergeant Schröter and his platoon, along with Lt Kummer. Both leaders distinguished themselves. In spite of heavy enemy resistance, First Sergeant Schröter, Corporal Hertling and First Sergeant Jaeger, along with several men, rolled up the enemy trench far to the north-west, reaching the Vauxcastille–Léchelle road. Now the French launched a counter-attack, which, thanks to 12/ 66 under the leadership of Lts Wadepuhl and Kummer and Sergeants Möhring and Rzepka, failed, although the company had to expend all of its ammunition and took heavy losses. Lt Kummer was killed, Lt Wadepuhl badly wounded.

5 and 6/ 66 also distinguished themselves. Lt Schmidtsdorf was killed, along with many of his brave men. After we had reached the area north of Vierzy, the neighbouring division on our right was also able to advance. Several hundred prisoners were taken, along with four revolver cannons and a large number of MG. 1/ 66 attacked Vierzy from the east. 10/ 66, under Res. Lt Müller, with a platoon of MG Company 3, were, at 1500, the first German troops to break into the burning village and pushed on to 500m south of the rail station, taking 300 prisoners. 11/ 66 attacked into the village from the north, 1/ 66 from the east, and Capt. Trenk attacked with 11/ 66 and a platoon of MG Company 3. 8/ 66 moved from the rail tunnel to rejoin the battalion; 9/ 66 and a platoon of MG Company 3 were regimental reserve at Charantigny.

At 1630, III/ 66 assembled in Vierzy and Captains Trenk and Korfes immediately considered continuing the attack to Maison Neuve Fme. The neighbouring regiment to the left, IR 60, was still far to the rear, having reached only the high ground south of the Vierzy–Longpont rail line, and strong machine-gun fire was coming from Vauxcastille and the area south of Chaudun, so that a further advance that evening was not possible. The battalions put out strong night security to the north and north-west and remained for the night in the caves at Vierzy. Rich booty of all kinds fell into the hands of the troops, who were exhausted after five days of combat.

The attack resumed at 0830 on 2 June after an artillery preparation. The French employed numerous MG in a gulley that extended from Chaudun south, as well as on the plateau between Maison Neuve Fme and Beaurepaire Fme. An advance against them was not possible without prohibitive losses, so the regiment waited for II/ Fusilier R 36 to come up. At 1400, II/ 66, III/ 66 and III/ 36 launched a co-ordinated attack against the line Maison Neuve Fme–Beaurepaire Fme.

II/ 66 had reached the area west of Léchelle and attacked in conjunction with IR 16 from the division on the right, 8/ 66 in the first line, making good progress and reaching the high ground west of Maison Neuve Fme. The advance of the other companies was blocked by heavy enemy defensive barrages around Maison Neuve Fme. Capt. Korfes, who was with 8/ 66, had the feeling that something out of the ordinary was needed to move the companies forward. He told the battalion bugler, who was next to him, to sound the charge. He stood up as though he was at the local training area back home and '*Kartoffelsupp, Kartoffelsupp*' ['Potato soup, potato soup', which is what the German soldiers thought the charge sounded like] rang out over the high ground at the Maison Neuve Fme, pulling the other companies forward to join 8/ 66. Major Knauff had galvanised II/ 66 with this call on 28 August 1914 to assault Peronne, and the effect was the same here on 2 June 1918. The unit on the left, RIR 16, and on the right, III/ 66, had come up level with II/ 66. Elements of 8/ 66 pushed into the gully south of Chaudun and captured 120 French in a cave. 8/ 66 remained in that cave overnight, while 5 and 7/ 66 were relieved by 2 and 4/ 66, which were attached to II/ 66.

III/ 66 attacked the area north of Vauxcastille with 11/ 66 and a platoon of MG Company 3 in the first line, 10/ 66 in the second and 12/ 66 and a platoon of MG Company 3 in the third. When the attack stalled, Capt. Trenk moved forward quickly to 11/ 66, and committed 10/ 66 to envelop the enemy right, with 100 prisoners being taken. French troops falling back in front of II/ 66 were taken under effective flanking fire. When this resistance had been broken, Capt. Trenk advanced on the road from Maison Neuve Fme to Beaurepaire Fme with 10/ 66, 11/ 66 and the two MG platoons on line; 12/ 66, which now consisted of only two squads, followed. At 1500, the left flank of 11/ 66 reached the airfield north-east of Beaurepaire Fme, while the right flank was about 200m west of Maison Neuve Fme, with elements of 10/ 66 between them. Both companies dug-in. A small element of III/ 66, with the MG Platoon of First Sergeant Jütte, under the leadership of Lt Hentschel, advanced through Maison Neuve Fme to the main Soissons–Paris road, where they encountered great numbers of French that initially wanted to surrender, but seeing how few Germans they were faced with, took up their arms again, forcing Lt Hentschel to withdraw his isolated detachment.

The front-line battalions spent the night in the positions they had taken. The regimental staff and 1/ 66 quartered in caves at the exit from Vierzy. During the night, 9/ 66 was returned to its battalion. The three companies of III/ RIR 32 under Capt. Sunkel that were attached to IR 66 also quartered in Vierzy.

The regimental commander formed four detachments to continue the attack on 3 June:

Detachment Korfes, with elements of 1/ 66 and II/ 66, west of Maison Neuve Fme
Detachment Trenk, to its left with III/ 66, elements of 1/ 66 and II/ 66
Detachment Niemeyer, with elements of 1/ 66 and II/ 66 at Maison Neuve Fme

Detachment Sunkel with III/ RIR 32 in Vauxcastille
Regimental staff remained at Vierzy

That afternoon, the Spanish military attaché, Lt-Col De Valdivia, accompanied by First Lt Siegener from the 113 ID staff, visited the regimental staff in the tunnel at Vierzy and drank a glass of French wine to the health of the regiment. The division commander could not grant Lt-Col De Valdivia's request to visit Capt. Korfes' battalion at Maison Neuve Fme.

After a short, sudden bombardment at 0800, the almost completely exhausted battalions attacked towards the main Paris–Soissons road. Initially, the attack was smothered by heavy enemy artillery fire and desperate resistance. II/ 66 was only able to advance after RIR 212, from the fresh neighbouring division on the right, reached the Paris road. III/ 66 also made it to the road and linked up with 8/ 66, as did 9/ 66, which that morning had relieved the tired-out 10/ 66. At 1145, 11/ 66 did the same. At 1600, the remainder of 9/ 66 came forward. Since III/ 36 was hanging behind, 10/ 66 was committed echeloned left to block the hole, and was reinforced by a platoon of MG Company 3. Heavy enemy MG and rifle fire came from a wood to our front, north of Le Translon. Both battalions were also continually taking flanking fire from Le Translon. During the afternoon, 2, 4 and 6/ 66, and the light mortars of II/ 66, were brought forward to the Paris road. Although the wood north of Le Translon was engaged with heavy artillery and mortar fire, it was not possible to silence the numerous MG there and get the advance moving again. The French continually sent in reinforcements, using the cover of the enormous woodland at Villers-Cotterêts. The regiment's advance had been stopped.

Rest at Vasseny, 4 June to 9 July 1918

During the night of 3–4 June, the regiment was replaced by RIR 32 and withdrawn to the ravines west of Léchelle. A general sigh of relief went through the thin ranks of men who had held out in spite of their complete exhaustion. In eight days of intense and difficult offensive operations, in blazing heat, the regiment's accomplishments were unprecedented. Its losses were:

	Killed	Wounded	Missing	Prisoner
Officers	7	15	–	1
Enlisted and NCOs	121	518	55	9
Total	128	533	55	10

The dead officers included a captain and six lieutenants.

The regiment took fifty-six officers and 3,810 men prisoner and captured eighteen artillery pieces of all sizes, including a 30.5cm railroad gun, as well as five revolver cannons, 200 MG and numerous pieces of equipment of all kinds.

During the night of 6–7 June, the regiment moved from Léchelle through the recent battlegrounds to Vasseny in the Vesle valley, in which area 113 ID would rest for several weeks, which the regiment took full advantage of. Some attack exercises and a river crossing with pontoons provided welcome diversions. Unfortunately, the regiment was also hit with a flu epidemic that spared no one. In recognition of the regiment's accomplishments, its commander, Lt-Col von Stoeklern, was awarded the Pour le Mérite (the Blue Max).

On 9 July, the rest came to an end. The regiment conducted several night marches and bivouacs towards the Marne, which was reached on the evening of 13 July at Gèvres Wood (*Bois de Gèvres*) at Verneuil on the Marne.

38

THE MARNE OFFENSIVE

Preparations

The regiment went into the third great offensive in 1918, not fully recovered from the March and May offensives and severely weakened by the flu epidemic in the preceding rest period in Vesles. The mood in the days before the attack was influenced by the uncomfortable hot and humid weather and nights spent lying in damp forests, and gave a presentiment that the new offensive was doomed to fail. The regiment had many days of hard fighting behind it, but it never at any time during the entire war had such a stunning failure as that which these July days on the Marne would bring. What oppressed us after those black days of Chêne-la-Reine and Misy Wood, and as we turned our backs to the Marne and marched north, was not the heavy casualties that we once again suffered, nor the great exertions and privations (with which we were all too familiar), and not the bitter feeling that we had to surrender land bought with so much blood, but the dull foreboding consciousness that the German Army, in spite of its unbroken willingness to attack, was no longer able to conduct a successful large-scale offensive. And this offensive, even though most of the troops committed to it regarded it as a failure, was a strategic necessity.

Unpredictable factors led to the failure of the third link in the chain of the great German offensives in 1918. In his well-known work, General von Kuhl wrote about the offensives in 1918:

> We now know from the publications of our enemies, that the French had anticipated a German offensive in the Champagne since the beginning of July. There had been careless talk of it in Germany. At the beginning of July

reliable reports from Switzerland had reached the French intelligence service at Belfort. Statements from German prisoners made a German offensive sometime after 10 July likely. At the last minute, on the day of the attack, German prisoners revealed exact information concerning the time of the artillery preparation and infantry attack. There was no surprise, which was an essential prerequisite for the success of the attack. This made it possible for the enemy to fall back in good time in front of the attack, which is the principal reason that it failed. Foch had brought about eight French divisions from Flanders to the Champagne, so instead of striking a weak enemy, we found a fully prepared and strong one.

We were also surprised by the fact that, for the first time, the French commander, Petain, did not defend the first position in strength, but rather a well-prepared position in depth. General von Kuhl said:

> The first position was a line of security outposts, which was weakly held. The artillery was positioned behind the main defensive position and echeloned in depth. Since the enemy knew that the attack would commence early on 15 July, during the night the entire French artillery conducted a massive counter-preparation fire against the German attack positions. The German infantry assault overran the resistance of the French outposts, which sacrificed themselves, but then had to advance three kilometres to the French main position, suffering heavy casualties from French infantry. Here the attack stalled.

The reasons for the failure of the attack are clear: it was not the fault of the attacking troops, including our regiment, which had done their entire duty.

The overall concept of the operation was to attack on both sides of Reims up to or across the Marne, with the two arms of the attack meeting in the area of Épernay to encircle the wooded and hilly terrain around Reims. Fifty divisions and 2,000 batteries would be employed. The attack to the west of Reims, where our regiment was employed as a part of 7th Army, presented even these highly experienced assault troops with a challenge. First, covered by the artillery, the troops had to bring a large number of pontoons undamaged across the wide valley to the river, then put across a covering force strong enough to suppress the enemy forces defending the far bank, which were expected to be strong, while the first attack wave crossed the 70m wide river. Having succeeded at this, everything depended on the first wave forming a deep enough bridgehead to allow bridges to be built to quickly bring over more forces, especially artillery. This was a completely new and difficult mission for the leaders and troops, which required the highest levels of organisation, daring and stamina. But even after a successful crossing, the troops were faced with the difficult mission of attacking south of the Marne to the first objective, Épernay, over cut-up hilly terrain covered with vineyards and woods. In addition to that, the bend in the Marne east of Verneuil forced several regiments, ours included, to cross in the sector of a neighbouring unit and then move sideways to our own attack sector, a tactically complex operation. But it had to be risked, and tactically the leadership and troops overcame all difficulties; one could well say that the Marne crossing was the most difficult mission that the regiment had to accomplish in the entire war.

In order to make the scope of this mission clear, the regimental attack order for 15 July is presented in full:

Regimental Attack Order

1. The enemy will be attacked on a broad front on Day Y after an artillery fire preparation beginning at X-Hour.
2. The regiment is on the left flank of the division. To the right is RIR 32, on the left 10 RD. Attack zones are given on the map.
3. The mission is exceptionally demanding. The concept of the operation requires that on the first day the regiment take the wooded area west and south-west of Épernay and at the minimum take the high ground east of the line Cuis–Cuis road–Chouilly. Every man must know this, and, given such a deep objective, all other considerations, even the welfare of the troops, must be secondary.
4. Prior to the beginning of the attack, 37 ID will take the enemy-held rail line south of the Marne. Its left-flank regiment has the mission, at the beginning of the attack, of taking the houses on the Verneuil–Try road and the village of Try.
5. On the night of Day Y-1 to Day Y, II/ 66 and III/ 66 will occupy the previously reconnoitred attack position on the south edge of Verneuil, I/ 66 on the north side of Verneuil. Close-support Battery 28, 2/ MG Section 34 and first echelon combat trains remain in the assembly area as on Day Y-1 (Sèvres Wood – *Bois de Sèvres*). For their forward movement, see Paragraph 9.
6. Preparatory fires begin at X-Hour, on the entire front, against enemy infantry and artillery, and continues until X-Hour + 220.
7. Beginning at X-Hour + 220 the assault battalions (II and III/ 66) will cross the Marne behind the left flank of 37 ID. After the left flank of 37 ID has taken the village of Try, the first battalion to cross, II/ 66, will advance [east] along the rail line to the regimental area of operations, occupy the enemy positions on the rail line and Hill 94 north-east of Troissy, and attack on the left half of the regimental area of operations. It is particularly important to

quickly take Mareuil le Port and the high ground east of there, and reach this area at the same time as the enemy forces which would be withdrawing in front of the 10 ID attack across the Marne at Port à Binson. After crossing the Marne, III/ 66 will take Troissy and the high ground to the east, then turn, with its right flank passing by Cerseuil, to the right half of the regimental area of operations. The *Schwerpunkt* of the attack is along the high ground east of Leuvrigny, the west side of the Épernay Forest, the road Pierry–Épernay, the high ground south-east of Épernay, road Pierry–Chouilly to reach the high ground east of this road.

I/ 66 must occupy the II/ 66 and III/ 66 attack position no later than X-Hour + 20, in order to cross as soon as possible after the assault battalions. I/ 66 follows as regimental reserve behind III/ 66 and protects the regimental right flank. Continuation of the attack will be co-ordinated with the battalion commanders.

8. For combat in towns, a flamethrower platoon from the Flamethrower Company of Guard Reserve Engineer R 3 will be available to the regiment at the east side of Try. After it has crossed on the pontoon bridge, Close-support Battery 28 is attached to III/ 66. 5/ FAR 225 will later be attached to II/ 66.

9. At X-Hour-300, a mounted officer from Close-support Battery 28, an officer from MG Section 34 and the leader of the first echelon combat trains (Acting Officer Brandt) will report to the Bridge Control Officer, Captain Geyer. The first echelon combat trains will advance along the Try–Troissy–Mareuil road, followed by MG Section 34. Further instructions orally. The close-support batteries will report to their assigned units ASAP.

10. Regimental command post from Day Y-1 at the CP of the front-line RIR 109 on the north edge of Verneuil. Reports concerning the occupation of the attack positions and completion of the crossing by the assault battalions to be sent to this location. On completion of the crossing by the assault battalions, regimental CP will be at Try, then Troissy, Hill 112 north-east of Troissy, Lasnier Mill, Hill 239 east of Leuvrigny, Les Pâtis Fme, Les Lignons Fme, north edge of Pierry, rifle range south-east of Épernay, road one kilometre south-west of Chouilly.

Signed von Stoeklern

Crossing the Marne, 14–15 July 1918

At 0000 on 15 July, the battalions had occupied their attack position on the south edge of Verneuil-Bas Verneuil, II/ 66 in the west side, III/ 66 the east side, I/ 66 the north half. The only report to arrive, at the last minute, was from

II/ 66; the other messengers got lost in the unfamiliar village, under artillery fire, at night. The German artillery preparation began at 0110 and continued until 0450. Soon after the start of the German artillery preparation, the enemy bombarded the village with increasing quantities of medium and heavy shells. MG Company 1 was to provide covering fire for the 37 ID crossing. On the evening of 14 July, it occupied positions on the slopes of the Sèvres Wood, with orders to cover the high ground on the south side of the Marne between Try and Vassieux with heavy fire between 0300 and 0450 on 15 July.

At 0345, carrying parties from the assault battalions left the cellars of Verneuil, and went to the pontoons, which had been placed between the rows of houses at Verneuil. Even as they began to carry the pontoons, it was clear that enemy artillery fire had rendered some of them unserviceable. At 0450, after a short delay, 5, 6, 9 and 11 / 66 moved out from the south edge of Verneuil. It was 800m to the river. Pontoons were damaged by artillery and long-range MG fire, and some of the men in the carrying parties were hit. The pontoons were heavy, but the metal bottoms could be slid over the corn fields. MG Company 2 lost Acting Officer Hellrung and two MG. Finally, the river bank was reached, and there was, thank God, no fire from the opposite side. A light MG was set up to provide covering fire, the first pontoon flopped into the water and was boarded by the company commander, two engineers and a light MG. They pushed off and paddled across the river in the dim dawn light.

When 6/ 66 reached the opposite bank, the engineers secured the wire rope that would be used by the following pontoons, and the infantry tensely climbed the river bank, weapons ready to fire. At any moment it was expected that the defences on the river would open up, and that it was possible that they were being lured into a trap, but nothing happened. After a few hundred metres, a deep rail cut was encountered, which, according to our information, was always strongly held. After a moment of extreme tension, the troops jumped into it, only to find dugouts and the usual shot-up and abandoned position. Finally, something moved out of the dugout, but it was only a few sad figures, unarmed, who called out, 'Have pity! Have pity!' No dead, no wounded. It was now clear that our artillery had hammered positions that the French had already abandoned. The advance continued towards Try with the remainder of the company coming up half-left. The village should have been taken by IR 151, but French resistance here was stiff, and was broken only after a tough fight.

The course of events was similar in the III/ 66 sector, which crossed left of II/ 66. But here the regiment suffered the greatest loss, the unforgettable Capt. Trenk. He had been with the regiment from the beginning; as battalion commander he was the soul of his battalion, had become as one with his officers and men. He was killed just after he had stepped on the far bank, confident of victory. He never received the Pour le Mérite, which had been awarded to him. Lt Wadepuhl of 12/ 66 described the crossing:

> Just before we reached the far bank, we were surprised by enemy MG fire, which caused casualties. My platoon, farthest on the left, had fortunately reached the bank without loss. A sand pit very close to the rail embankment provided the initial cover. There was an enemy MG left of us, hidden by trees, which we would have to eliminate in order to avoid heavy casualties when we advanced. I moved forward with two men in order to determine exactly where this disturbance was located. In doing so, one of the men was wounded in the lower arm, but we achieved our objective. With sixteen men we made a bold jump over the rail embankment to take the MG from the rear. Thanks to a well-thrown hand-grenade by one of our sergeants, and the equally accurate rifle fire from one of our musketeers, we also took a French security outpost, and the crew of the MG surrendered, as far as I know the first prisoners the regiment took in this battle. Here we learned that our battalion commander, Captain Trenk, had been killed by MG fire. A hero's life had been ended, for us far too soon.

The initial crossing was completed by 0630. I/ 66 then crossed and by 0645 was assembled and ready on the rail embankment north of Try. II/ 66 crossed the major road west of Try, assisted IR 151 in taking the village and, as ordered, attacked along the rail line between the Try rail station and the wartime rail station, with 5, 7 and 8/ 66 in the first line, 6/ 66 following. 6/ 66 was committed when the attack was stopped at the point where the rail embankment and the Marne divided: the battalion was then able to silence the enemy MG, most of which were emplaced in MG nests on the rail embankment.

Further advance by II/ 66 became steadily more difficult, because Troissy had not been taken and, due to the strongly held edges of the village, could not be bypassed. Capt. Rochlitz then decided to attack through Troissy itself in order to reach its area of operations. 6/ 66 remained facing MG and infantry at the Troissy rail station, while Capt. Rochlitz and the other three companies attempted to envelop Troissy from the south. They were stopped on the west side of the village by heavy MG and artillery fire, south of the line Try–Troissy, and took serious casualties.

The regimental staff was moved by Pontoon Group 3 over the river, so quickly that it caught up with III/ 66 a few hundred metres east of Try. Res. Lt Borchert assumed command of III/ 66, and was briefed by the regimental commander concerning the situation and mission. 9 and 10/ 66 and 11/ 66 (minus 6/ 66) attacked through the south side of Troissy, while 10 and 11/ 66 swung around the town to the south. 6/ 66, supported by MG fire from RIR 36 (10 RD) on the left, took the Troissy rail station and worked its way up to the plateau east of Troissy, in order to catch up as closely as possible to the rolling barrage. Elements of 6/ 66 succeeded in advancing as far as a piece of the road to Mareuil-le-Port, but further advance was stopped by heavy MG fire. At 0930, Troissy was in the hands of elements of II and III/ 66, with over 100 prisoners and several MG taken. I/ 66, on the order of the regimental commander, followed along the Try–Troissy road, then through Troissy and onto the plateau east of the village. The enemy strongly held a position north-west of Mareuil, but the advance of II and III/ 66 forced them, under continual fire from heavy MG, to withdraw to the west side of Mareuil, which they prepared to defend.

The 10-Kilometre Advance, 15–16 July 1918

In spite of local successes, the regimental situation was quite difficult. Although all three battalions had succeeded in crossing the Marne, the regiment had no contact with its neighbours nor, what was worse, with the artillery. Due to enemy artillery fire, it was not possible to put a bridge in the water south of Bas Verneuil in a timely fashion, so the artillery could not follow. The close-support battery for RIR 32, 6/FAR 225, was not able to cross until 0900. On the order of the regimental commander, it had engaged the Troissy rail station and park. The IR/ 66 commander justified this measure by the fact that the leading battalion of RIR 32 had just arrived from Try, but had not advanced against the south side of Troissy as provided in the division plan, rather had swung to the high ground to the south. IR 66 was therefore alone in the division area of operations and, if it did not quickly reach the plateau east of Troissy, ran the risk of being thrown back to Try or even the Marne. Infantry Close-support Battery 28, attached to IR 66, arrived ten to fifteen minutes later and 6/ FAR 225 was released back to RIR 32. The flamethrowers that were supposed to be attached to the regiment to help take Troissy never appeared. The commander of FAR 225 arrived at the seltzer water factory halfway between Try and Troissy. Since one section had been unable to cross the river, he had put it into battery north of the Marne at Bas-Verneuil.

The plateau east of Troissy was almost completely covered in high legumes which blocked visibility, and for several hours was hit by aerial bombing, artillery fire and heavy MG fire from the hills covered with vineyards at Mareuil-Leuvrigny West. Communication with the artillery on the other side of the Marne had been lost, and the close-support artillery could not come up to the regiment due to lack of visibility. The regiment took heavy casualties, and, without artillery support, no further advance was possible. When 2/ MG Section 34 arrived, it set up in the middle of the regimental sector and engaged the enemy MG in the vineyards, as did Section Weidner when it arrived later. Between 1500 and 1600, the regimental commander, located on Hill 94, issued an oral order:

> Two sectors will be formed: Res. Lt Borchert and III/ 66 will control the area south of the Try–Troissy road and take Leuvrigny. Captain Niemeyer and I/ 66 will control the sector north of it and take Mareuil le Port. Both will take the plateau to the east of these villages and hold them under all circumstances. II/ 66 [which apparently had taken the most casualties] will follow the first line through Mareuil as my reserve.

By 1700, the advance resumed. The enemy left Mareuil and it was taken by I/ 66 without a fight. When it advanced towards the Misy Wood south of Mareuil it encountered heavy resistance and, without artillery support, could not advance further.

Capt. Korfes took command of III/ 66, which with an energetic attack took Leuvrigny at 1845. The battalion continued the attack in the direction of Clos Davaus, which it was not able to take as it met resistance from strong enemy forces, including black colonial troops. The attack by I/ 66 on the plateau south of the Misy Wood stalled. The regiment was opposed by a well dug-in enemy force, supported by artillery, in the line Clos Davaus–Deuilly. The regiment intended to continue the attack that day, but was ordered by brigade to defend in place. After dark, the regiment succeeded in making contact with both RIR 32 to the right and IR 155 to the left. Nevertheless, the situation for I/ 66 and III/ 66 in the front line was anything but rosy, since the enemy artillery fire continued for the entire night and he conducted local attacks. The regimental reserve consisted of the worn-out II/ 66 in Leuvrigny, as well as an attached battalion from Fusilier R 36 under Capt. Lademann.

The regiment's attack was the most successful one on this day. It was not only able to smoothly execute, with some loss of time, two difficult tactical manoeuvres – crossing the Marne and then moving sideways to its area of operations – but in Group Conta, to which 113 ID belonged, together with RIR 32, it gained the most ground to the south-east, carrying the load for the entire division. Heavy casualties, lack of artillery support, supply line completely cut, no rations and oppressive heat had not been able to prevent the regiment from advancing nearly 10km.

On the morning of 16 July, RIR 32 was attacked from Clos Davaus, but it counter-attacked, succeeding in turning the tables and taking Clos Davaus. This opened the way for III/ 66, which under Capt. Korfes reached Chêne-la-Reine by afternoon. Unfortunately, the neighbouring units could not keep up with III/ 66's rapid advance. Due to flanking fire from Le Mesnil Huttier, RIR 32 was not able to advance much beyond Clos Davaus. Left of III/ 66, I/ 66's attack from the Misy Wood over the bare and exposed plateau south-east of the woods gained ground slowly and bit by bit. II/ 66 was following I/ 66, and both suffered under artillery fire. The much-liked Capt. Niemeyer, who had commanded I/ 66 for more than two years, was severely wounded, as was the adjutant, Lt Hebeler. The adjutant of II/ 66, the reliable and conscientious Res. Lt Erler, was fatally wounded. Since the neighbouring regiment to our left moved during the course of the day into the left half of our sector, late in the afternoon both battalions were withdrawn from the Misy Wood, which was full of poison gas, and moved behind III/ 66, so that during the night II/ 66 was in Chêne-la-Reine and I/ 66 on the slopes between that town and Leuvrigny. All the troops in Chêne-la-Reine were subordinated to Capt. Korfes; a company of Fusilier R 36 was also attached to plug some of the gap with RIR 32 on the right.

The night of 16–17 July was anything but comfortable for IR 66, III/ 66 in particular. The general locations of the neighbouring units were known, but the regiment's flanks were nonetheless open, and might be turned during the night, all the more so because active enemy patrolling did not allow the companies in front of Chêne-la-Reine to get any rest. One of the officers wrote:

> In spite of the great physical exertions of the last days, most of the men did not get any sleep. I quite well remember the agitation that went through the entire company, when a man on security gave out two loud calls for help. When we got to him, he lay dead on the ground next to his rifle. Since no shots had been fired, we assumed that a French black colonial had sneaked up to him, been noticed at the last second, then stabbed him. We already knew that we had black colonial soldiers in front of us.

In addition to this disturbance, there was continual shelling by artillery and air activity, directed against the villages we occupied as well as the rear lines of communication. As a consequence, the field kitchens could not come forward with hot rations. The villages had nothing and the iron rations had generally already been eaten, and many men remembered fondly the masses of rations we had captured during the May offensive. It was now the third night without food. Since the vehicles could not come forward, we lacked all the supplies that a soldier needs in combat.

Defence Against Enemy Counter-attacks, 17–19 July 1918

Since it was impossible to defend Chêne-la-Reine against a strong enemy attack, on the early morning of 17 July the division ordered the regiment to pull back from it. III/ 66 took up a position north-east of Clos Davaus, making contact with RIR 32 on the right and IR 155 on the left. I/ 66 was behind it in the second position in the woodlots between Clos Davaus and Leuvrigny and II/ 66 was regimental reserve in Leuvrigny. 12/ 66 was left in Chêne-la-Reine as a screen, and elements stayed there until the enemy launched an attack. One of the men on this forlorn hope, which held out to the last, wrote:

> The village gradually collapsed. In order not to get cut off by the rubble, we moved to a cellar closer to the German lines. We ran individually to the cellar that I had picked out. I saw a cellar with a MG covering the main street. I put a man on watch over the main street, to determine when the enemy would lift and shift his fire to permit his infantry to attack, and relieved him often. At about 1400 the artillery fire decreased, and as I stepped out of the cellar with my batman, I could see the black colonial troops already in the next cellar. We had seen how these beasts would slaughter everyone. When they saw us, they gave out a wild howl and came at us swinging knives. We were a forlorn hope and didn't have any choice, so we ran away.

After a four-hour preparatory bombardment, the enemy attacked at 1400, and strong attack waves moved through Chêne-la-Reine, supported by tanks and artillery that had been brought far forward, and forced back III/ 66, which had very little artillery support. The situation was critical; Capt. Korfes gathered together all available men, and together with Major von Zepelin of RIR 32, attacked, threw the French back to Clos Davaus and retook the previous position, although the heavens aided the French with a massive thunderstorm. Casualties were heavy: Capt. Korfes was wounded, Lts Püttner and Neubauer killed, along with many NCOs and men. Had the enemy attack succeeded, the result would have been an unprecedented catastrophe for the troops of 113 ID south of the Marne. In spite of further attacks and shellings, on the evening of 17 July, the position on the plateau north of Clos Davaus was firmly in our hands. But the battalions were thoroughly intermixed, in part with elements of RIR 32. Lt-Col von Stoeklern, who had been the regimental commander for three-and-a-half years, had been very ill for several days, but remained at his post. Finally, he was no longer able to perform his duties, and was replaced by Capt. Rochlitz. The battalions had also lost their commanders; II/ 66 was now led by Lt Menkel, III/ 66 by Lt Borchert, I/ 66 by Lt Kühne. It was finally possible to bring the field kitchens forward on the night of 17–18 July.

It was again obvious very early on 18 July that the enemy wanted to destroy the German troops on the south side of the Meuse. At 0800, there was an even stronger attack against our entire front line, in the course of which a large gap appeared on the regimental right flank and contact with RIR 32 was lost. The remainder of II/ 66 (5 and 6/ 66) were committed to fill the gap and re-establish contact with RIR 32. Lt Menkel took command of the front-line elements of the regiment, whose units were still very intermixed, as it had not been possible to reorganise them during the night due to the heavy enemy harassing artillery fire. As much as possible, the units were now reorganised, and co-opeartion with the MG established. From left to right, the regimental front line was composed of 6/ 66, 5/ 66, elements of III/ 66, 7/ 66, parts of I/ 66, in addition to MG Companies 1 and 2 and the guns of MG Section 34 attached to the regiment. 8/ 66 established contact on the right behind RIR 32. The remaining elements were committed on the flanks between RIR 32 and IR 155.

The situation on the regiment's position on the plateau on 18 July was terrible. The sun blazed down on the men in the shell craters, who did not dare to move. The French artillery systematically shelled one crater after the other: obviously, their forward observers could see our position clearly. Frequently, a direct hit would kill everyone in a crater. Very low-flying ground attack aircraft would sweep the German line with MG fire. The men were dying of thirst. Nevertheless, that afternoon an attack, conducted by black colonial troops, preceded by a drumfire artillery preparation and supported by cavalry and aircraft, was quickly defeated. The defence had been given the necessary support principally by MG Companies 1 and 2 under Res. Lt Kampf and MG Section 34. There was little artillery support because, as on the previous day, it lacked effective observation of the battlefield. Some of the artillery that had crossed over to the south bank was withdrawn back to the north side. The evening of 18 July, the fourth day of continual combat and great exertions, saw the ranks of the regiment even thinner. But a relatively quiet night, hot rations and ammunition resupply, and a rumour from the rear areas that on the next day we would withdraw back over the Marne, raised everyone's spirits. During the night, the units were reorganised and the shell-crater position improved.

The next day, 19 July, initially brought no change in the situation. The forward troops once again were fully exposed to the enemy artillery fire and were strafed by aircraft. The rear area also suffered under heavy fire; in particular, the reserves in cellars in Leuvrigny several times took casualties from direct hits. Communication between the elements of the regiment was completely cut off, so that everyone felt himself to be isolated. During the afternoon, the intensity of the artillery fire increased significantly and enemy movements into attack positions were observed. The attack, again accompanied by cavalry, developed at 1700, but was stopped, principally by MG Section 34, and did not reach the plateau the regiment was occupying. The situation was most difficult on the left flank; the French were able to break into the position of the regiment on our left at the fork in the road south-west of Deuilly. The flank was blocked off by moving reserves through the Misy Wood, and by MG firing into the French flank. But since the entire front line had once again taken heavy casualties (the wounded had to remain in the shell craters), the situation that evening was not very hopeful. Everyone gave a sigh of relief when at dusk the front line received the order to fall back at 2300.

Evacuation of the South Bank of the Marne, 19–20 July 1918

The detailed withdrawal order issued by 113 ID said that by 2200 a delay line from the north side of Leuvrigny to Misy Wood would be occupied by elements of Fusilier R 36 and IR 66, and would be held until 0300. At 2300, the forward units would pass through the delay line and move on to the Marne. The time for the forward units to prepare was very short, but they succeeded in withdrawing without being detected. With a sense of relief, and hoping that there would not be another unpleasant surprise, the exhausted troops moved (naturally without being fed) through the vineyards to Leuvrigny, which was now a smoking mass of rubble, and Mareuil-le-Port to the wartime rail station at Troissy, where some elements would establish another delay position along the rail line. The night was unusually quiet, uncannily so. Even the enemy artillery fire was weak. At 0400, the men in the forward position pulled back without incident and went across the Marne on footbridges. Their numbers had been massively reduced, they were more than physically exhausted, and psychologically depressed by the failure of the offensive. The regiment reassembled 3km from the north bank of the Marne at the Malmaison-Fme, where the vehicles and, most important, the field kitchens were located. As the regiment moved away from the Marne, a veritable hurricane of artillery fire landed on the abandoned positions in front of Leuvrigny. From the high ground north of the Meuse, we observed strong waves of infantry accompanied by tanks advancing towards the terrain that we had evacuated at exactly the right moment. Thankful to have escaped the hell of the Marne, after having eaten our fill we rested at the Malmaison-Fme until the afternoon.

The regiment had participated in the front line to the end in the third offensive of 1918. It cost the regiment and 573 men and twenty-three officers, including the majority of the officers and NCOs that had been tested by years of war. They could not be replaced.

The failure of this offensive was due to factors that could not have been foreseen. Our regiment had advanced the farthest from the Marne and then held out for five difficult days of combat, cut off from any support. It can be just as proud of its accomplishments as of the laurels of victory that it won in the successful offensives of March and May 1918.

Withdrawal from the Marne Bend, 20 July to 9 August 1918

Whoever hoped that the regiment was going to receive a period of rest and recuperation was going to be disappointed. The withdrawal over the Marne was successful, but the situation had by no means been stabilised. While we were at Clos Davaus, on the south bank, attempting to take Épernay, the situation on the entire front had become serious. On the morning of 18 July, the assault divisions of General Mangin, reinforced with Americans and hundreds of tanks, had conducted a surprise attack from the great forest at Villers-Cotterêts, south of Soissons, against the flank of the hard-pressed divisions of our 7th Army in the bend of the Marne, and pushed our front back from Soissons to Château Thierry. At the same time, there was a concentric attack from the east and south against the 7th Army, in an attempt to destroy it in the bend of the Marne. These strong counter-attacks had also been directed against us in our position south of the Marne on 18 and 19 July. Even the north bank of the Marne could not be held, and OHL decided to pull back to the Vesle, about 30km north of the Marne, reducing the bowed-out position on the Marne between Soissons and Reims to a straight line. The withdrawal of the weakened German units had to be conducted slowly, by stages, from 21 July to 2 August, since an enormous amount of supplies had been assembled south of the Vesle for the unsuccessful offensive and had to be moved, as well as for tactical reasons. It did not involve us in serious combat, but, without any consideration for the exhaustion of the troops, the regiment was continually called upon to act as a counter-attack reserve and occupy delay positions. It moved back and forth, order was followed by counter-order, and on overcrowded, muddy roads, on foot or in lorries, in wet weather, in woods under enemy harassment and interdiction artillery fire, digging in for all-round defence, continually alert, the last reserves of energy were drawn out from the troops. Only the essentials of what occurred in these days will be mentioned.

On 20 July, after the regiment had assembled at La Malmaison-Fme, it marched to Vezilly Wood (*Bois de Vezilly*), where it bivouacked. But at 1900, it boarded lorries and was attached to Group Schmettow as army reserve, to build a rearward position on the line from Romigny to Ville-en-Tardenois, front to the south, and arrived in Aulnoy-Fme at 2300, to bivouac in a ravine south of the farm. On 21 July, the regiment moved into the area from a wood 800m north-west of Ville-en-Tardenois to the road from Ville-en-Tardenois to Aulny-Fme, where the main line of resistance was to be constructed. The security zone was south of the road from Ville-en-Tardenois to Romigny. Engineer Company 251 was attached to establish the wire obstacles. Given the greatly reduced size of the companies and the loss of experienced officers, two companies were combined into one, under the senior officer. On 22 July, the regiment began digging-in the position. At 1200, the division ordered the regiment to be ready to march west at 1300 on the road leading from Lagery. Further successful enemy attacks between Soissons and Château Thierry had made the situation there unclear. This order was cancelled at 1600 and, at 1700, the regiment bivouacked on the east side of the Five Piles Wood (*Bois de 5 Piles*) north of the road from Lagery to Igny and Abbaye-Fme.

From 23–26 July, the regiment dug various rear-area positions, among them one on the south edge of Lanaux Wood south-east of Vezilly and the Dora Position at Aougny. Every day forty men were attached to 2 Guard ID at Vezilly to conduct salvage work. On 26 July, Major Schrader assumed command of the regiment and Capt. Lademann returned from home leave to resume command of III/ 66 from Lt Menkel, who became the regimental adjutant.

At 0900 on 27 July, the regiment moved to Mont-sur-Courville to be corps reserve, and bivouacked in the ravine between the village and Courville. On the night of 28–29 July, the division relieved 2 Guard ID in the Dora Position; the regiment was division reserve. Numerous air attacks and artillery shellings during the night and the following day forced the bivouac area to be moved. At 1330 on 30 July, the regiment was alerted to move to 200 ID as the counter-attack reserve on the north-west edge of d'Aiguizy Wood (*Bois d'Aiguizy*), in anticipation of a strong enemy attack. The regiment moved at 1515 and arrived at 1700. At 1000 the next day, the alert was cancelled.

The regiment was attached to 29 ID and ordered to move by small detachments to St Gilles, and bivouac east of there. While it was in movement a counter-order arrived, returning it to its old bivouac at Mont-sur-Courville, and ordering it to dig-in the Ziethen Position on a line from the south of

Mont-sur-Courville to the south of Les Ptes–Chezelles-Fme. The position was reconnoitred that afternoon and work began at 0400 on 1 August. II and III/ 66 dug-in the first line while I/ 66 moved as reserve to the area of St Gilles. At 2000, the regimental staff occupied a command post on the high ground west of St Gilles, and at 2045 the position was occupied. 1 and 2/ 66 were outpost companies under Capt. Woytasch of Fusilier R 36. On the night of 1–2 August, RIR 32 and Fusilier R 36 withdrew through the Ziethen Position. Heavy demolitions were conducted throughout the night, and there were burning villages and camps everywhere.

The outposts were withdrawn at 1300 on 2 August to a line from Longeville to the copse north of Arcis-le-Ponsart. Lt Kenzler took over the regimental outpost sector with 1, 3 and 4/ 66 and 1/ RIR 32, with instructions to hold it until 0100 on 3 August and only withdraw under heavy enemy pressure. The enemy followed only with patrols. At 0100 on 3 August, the regiment withdrew over the Vesle, without any friction or being noticed by the enemy. The forward battalions left behind combat patrols in squad strength and with a light MG under Lts Geissler and Schröter, with instructions to only retreat over the Vesle at 0400. These also broke contact cleanly. At 0400, the regiment assembled in Révillon south of the Aisne, and marched at 1200 on a route well-known by many down the Chemin des Dames to Chermizy, north of the Ailette, where it arrived at 1630 and quartered, for the first time in three weeks out of range of enemy weapons.

The march continued to the north in oppressive heat, towards unknown rest quarters, through terrain well-known from 1917, but there were few still with the regiment who had bivouacked in the woods of Sissonne and Mauregny. We recognised the old battlefields of the Chemin des Dames, now overgrown with wild poppies, but the march north continued. In spite of long, hard marching and poor bivouacs, morale rose after so many difficult weeks. On 4 August, we reached the area near Bucy-lès-Pierrepont, St Preuve and Boncourt, where we rested for two days. Then, on 7 August, we marched to Gronard and Voharies just south of Vervins, on 8 August to Wignehies near Fourmies. The regiment already knew that it was to rest for several weeks in the area south of Maubeuge; a long and difficult mission was at an end.

39

THE FINAL DEFENSIVE BATTLES

Rest, 10 August to 1 September 1918

On 10 August, the regiment arrived in its assigned rest area, Sars-Poteries and Beugnies, two formerly well-to-do towns about 10km from Avesnes, the location of OHL. Far from enemy fire, close to the Belgian–French border, the long-anticipated rest area was initially a disappointment, consisting of mostly empty buildings that had been considerably damaged by frequent quartering. But after four weeks of combat, endless movement and humid and damp nights, and above all the serious depression everyone felt, caused by the failure of the Marne offensive, everyone was happy at the prospect of a rest for several weeks. In a few days we received materials that allowed us to make our quarters liveable, conduct delousing and maintain the equipment. The companies were far below normal combat strength, so 3, 8 and 11/ 66 were disbanded and their personnel distributed among the other companies. Each of these companies had won laurels in four years of combat, and now their traditions were going to disappear. It was a hard measure, but necessary in the light of the heavy losses of the summer and the difficult personnel replacement situation at home. In place of the dissolved companies, on 22 August we received new companies from IR 26, which had been broken up and divided among the other units in the division, along with a MG Company, a mortar squad and numerous horses, so that by the end of August the regiment had enough personnel to be combat-effective again. All necessary measures were taken to restore combat-readiness, including inspections and tactical training to increase unit cohesion. The troops also received new uniforms and equipment which considerably improved their appearance. This three-week rest, far from the front, had done wonders in restoring the troops, who on their arrival at Sars-Poteries had appeared to be physically and mentally wretched.

During this time, there were significant changes in 113 ID. RIR 32, which had fought with the division for a year-and-a-half, left the division and was replaced by IR 27, so that once again it contained three regiments of the old IV AK. The 225 Brigade commander, Col Count von der Schulenberg, was replaced by Col von Poser. In the difficult defensive battles of September and October, he would show that he was a brigade commander whose strong will and personal example supported his regiments. A few weeks later, our division commander for many years, Major General von Bergmann, who was respected by all, was replaced by Brigadier General von Passow. There were significant changes of commanders in the regiment. Major von Zepelin, from RIR 32, took over command of I/ 66. Rittmeister [cavalry captain] Freiherr von Thielmann took command of II/ 66. The company commanders were all lieutenants, who on average had been officers for two years and most had assumed command of their companies after the Marne Offensive. The only 'old soldiers' were the indestructible Borchert and Baldamns and the brave Preuss. The lack of experienced adjutants was felt most keenly, as well as the old First Sergeants, many of whom were lost in 1918.

The end of August arrived and with it the end of our recuperation period. The first indicator of our coming commitment was the transfer of all non-essential equipment. The regiment marched off to the west in the direction of the rail marshalling yards at Aulnoye, where III/ 66 quartered, with I and II/ 66 in the area of Marbaix and Dompierre. The enemy was clever enough to drop propaganda leaflets from aircraft, which preached of the futility of further resistance. On 1 September, the division mortar company was dissolved, and elements of these and the three regimental light mortar squads formed the regimental mortar company under the leadership of Res. Lt Hagen, formerly of Mortar Company 113, later under Res. Lt Sprecher. The intent of this reorganisation was to ensure the co-ordinated employment of the regimental mortars. In the following withdrawals this was not possible: what was necessary was heavy weapons working in close co-operation with small groups of infantry.

Fighting in the Siegfried Line, 2–20 September 1918

On 2 September, the regiment was loaded by battalion onto railcars. On the next day it unloaded at Rieux, 8km north-east of Cambrai. It was quartered in Cambrai in the so-called Hindenburg Kaserne, a completely ruined building. The continual night air attacks, which caused us serious casualties, removed the last happy memories of the wonderful rest period in Sars-Poteries.

It is necessary to look back at the events that had taken place while we were three weeks in the rest area. When the regiment crossed the Vesle at Fismes, during the retreat from the Marne, the French counter-attack to pinch off the Marne Bend had come to a temporary halt. A few days later, on 8 August, Haig attacked with unheard-of quantities of material and reserves on the Roman road at Amiens to Villers-Bretonneux in the direction of Peronne. During the entire month of August, the enemy continually committed fresh forces to drive the Germans step by step out of the Arras–Montdidier–Vailly salient, in spite of desperate German resistance, towards the old Siegfried Line at Arras–Cambrai–St Quentin–La Fère, from which our regiment had begun the glorious offensive on 21 March. As the regiment was committed at the beginning of September, this movement had been generally completed. Both sides were in the positions they had occupied at the beginning of the March offensive, and operations came to a halt. We gained support from our old positions, while the enemy had to catch his breath after the tough fighting in the almost impassable terrain of the old Somme battlefield.

On the evening of 4 September, the regiment left Cambrai, which had become inhospitable, towards Marcoing, with the mission of acting as counter-attack reserve, reinforced by 1, 2, 3 and 5/ FAR 225, at Ribécourt. The next day, it would occupy a delay position there, which was still in front of the Siegfried Line. In front of the regiment, on the high ground at the west side of the Havrincourt Forest, were the rearguards from IR 239, which were relieved on 6 September by elements of 113 ID. The regiment deployed I/ 66 on the front line, between Trescault and Bilheim, III/ 66 in the second position, a sunken road and old trenches close to the south of Ribécourt, and II as reserve behind them in the old trenches at the Couillet Forest. 10/ 66 was attached to the 113 ID rearguard and brought forward to Metz-en-Couture, where in the next days it fought superbly. The regiment had to anticipate that the enemy would attack soon. Initially, the regiment was involved only in local combat. Our well planned and boldly conducted patrols succeeded for days in preventing the enemy from gaining any information concerning our position, and maintained control of a deep security zone. Sergeants Wolf and Krieg and Corporals Klewitz and Brendel from 10/ 66 in particular distinguished themselves.

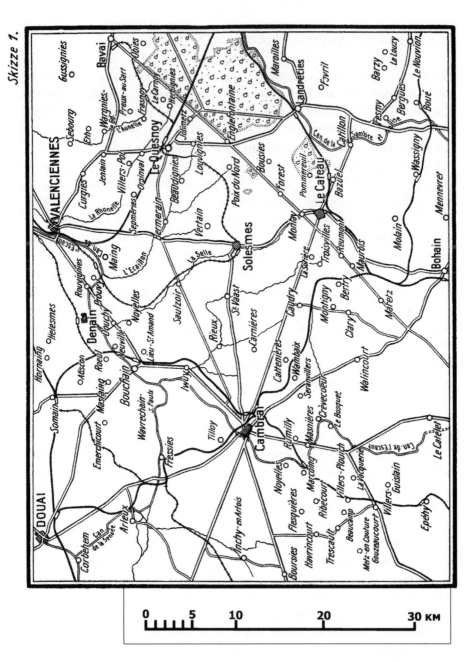

Skizze 1.

Limited contact between our position and the enemy was established only on 7 September. Occupying the somewhat dilapidated old British trenches and the dugouts with the exits facing the enemy, in the steadily increasing artillery fire, was not very pleasant, but there was no serious enemy attack. Our artillery was able to effectively shell the enemy as he slowly felt his way forward. We recognised, however, that the peaceful conduct of the British could be merely the preparations for a powerful attack. This was confirmed on 10 September with the relief of the division opposite us by the fresh British 62nd Infantry Division, and we had to anticipate an attack early on 11 September: a heavy artillery drumfire began at 0700, but was not followed by an infantry attack. On the morning of 12 September, eleven waves of British troops attacked, one after the other, supported by numerous tanks, in order to take the high ground at Havrincourt and Trescault. In spite of heavy casualties, the enemy succeeded in taking parts of the first position on the west side of Bilheim. Immediate counter-attacks by III/ 66 were only able to maintain the possession of the second position. We lost seven officers and 221 men on 12 September, with I/ 66 being particularly hard hit. Lt Peyer, an experienced officer who had contributed greatly to the development of the regimental mortars, was killed, as well as two other lieutenants. The most unpleasant development this day was that the enemy was able to penetrate relatively deeply into the sector of the neighbouring regiment to the left and continually threaten our flank. A gap about a kilometre wide developed between our left flank and the IR 27 position at the village of Beaucamp. A counter-attack by IR 27 on the evening of 13 September was not successful, and 8/ 66 had to be committed to protect our left flank. The regimental front was being held by the remains of I/ 66, intermixed with III/ 66. Only part of II/ 66 was available as a reserve. The units were thoroughly mixed together, the trenches had been flattened out, were no longer connected and the front was not continuous. The artillery could not be kept current on the situation forward, which led to many rounds falling short. The decisive factor was that everywhere small groups, even though threatened with encirclement, fought tenaciously and prevented the British from achieving greater success.

That would also be the case on the next day, 14 September, as the British renewed their attack after a drumfire artillery preparation several hours long. Due to their success in the IR 239 sector on the right, our flank there too came under severe pressure. The regiment was only able to hold its position due to a bold counter-attack by 8/ 66 under Res. Lt Nessau with the experienced Sergeants Schleicher and Kupferschmidt, and 6/ 66 under Res. Lt Schroeter, accompanied by flamethrowers, which took twenty-one prisoners. Since practically all the companies had been committed forward, a battalion of the Saxon IR 106 was attached. It occupied an assembly area in a sunken road south of Ribécourt, with the mission of preventing the enemy from breaking through to Ribécourt or turning the regimental right flank. That evening, III/ 66 took over the defence of the first line, II/ 66 was reserve and the badly reduced I/ 66 pulled back to the rear. After the evening of 14 September, a pause set in; Foch's counter-offensive from Amiens to the line Arras–La Fère, which had begun on 8 August, had in fact been brought to a halt by the old Siegfried Line.

The regiment, in spite of being under severe threat on both flanks, had for the most part held its position, and could be satisfied with this accomplishment.

Nevertheless, there was no question of us being pulled out of the line. There were no further attacks from 15 to 19 September, but unfortunately the troops suffered severely from enemy artillery fire and the poor condition of the trenches. The commander of 9/ 66, Res. Lt Nienhaus, was killed in the brave defence of his company sector against an enemy attack. Finally, the regiment was relieved by IR 24 in the night of 19–20 September and pulled back about 10km to Crévecoeur, north of the l'Escault Canal, where it was brigade reserve. It would only get two days' rest, during which, at War Ministry directive, the battalions would be reorganised into three companies. The debris of 2, 3, and 4/ 66 would be combined into a new 2/ 66; 8/ 66 was renumbered 3/ 66 and these two companies would form 1/ 66; and 11/ 66 was split up between the rest of III/ 66, so that 4, 8 and 11/ 66 no longer existed.

The Last Fight in the Siegfried Line, 21 September to 1 October 1918

By the evening of 21 September, the regiment had already returned to the front line, in a newly formed sector to both sides of Beaucamp, between IR 27 and Fusilier R 36. OHL had decided to create a new position in the rear, the Hermann Line, in general at Tournai–Valenciennes–Solesmes–Guise, to shorten the front in anticipation of the forthcoming winter defensive battles. In order to conduct the extensive work necessary, the current position had to be held as long as possible. The demands on the troops would be high, considering the poor condition of the trenches and the strain that the troops had already been under during the course of the recent battles. But the troops had, in the past weeks, already demonstrated the will to accomplish the mission. That the

regiment and the other troops were not able to hold the Siegfried Line was due to the fact that at the end of September the enemy conducted a massive attack across the entire front with fresh forces. In the Cambrai–St Quentin area alone, where the regiment was on the right flank, Foch committed forty British divisions and an American corps, all either fresh or very well-rested.

After exactly two days of rest, the regiment moved back to the front on 21 September. It was faced with the most difficult situation. The 750m-wide position, held by III/ 66, was very unfavourable. There were no dugouts, only trenches, which were under such effective enemy observation that any daytime movement to or from the rear was impossible. There were no wire obstacles. II/ 66 was the reserve battalion in sunken roads north of Villers-Plouich, with I/ 66 behind it, still in Crévecoeur. All means possible were used to improve the position. The enemy artillery and aircraft were very active, which, along with night-time lorry traffic, made an enemy attack likely. The commander of III/ 66 dutifully reported: 'The extremely poor living conditions and continual heavy and surprise enemy MG and artillery fire will soon make the troops, who are already worn-out, incapable of holding the forward position.' A company reported that on 24 September enemy aircraft had dropped leaflets encouraging the troops to surrender *en masse.* On the evening of 25 September, the British conducted a strong reconnaissance in force at Beaucamp with about fifty men that was thrown back with loss. The same night, II/ 66 relieved III/ 66. I/ 66, reinforced by 9/ 66, became the reserve battalion, with 10/ 66 and 12/ 66 resting in Crévecoeur.

On 27 September, there was an attack across the entire front. The drumfire began at 0525, landing principally on 5 and 6/ 66, so that the remnants of these companies were overrun by infantry accompanied by numerous tanks. The tanks pushed up to the sunken road south-east of Beaucamp, the location of the battalion sector HQ, where they were stopped by anti-tank rifles – Lt Kenzler knocked out two – but the situation was still more than critical unless there was an immediate successful counter-attack. I/ 66 under Lt Baldamus attacked on its own initiative from the artillery defence position, which he described:

In conformity with its mission, the company moved forward through the communications trenches. On the way to the sector HQ we could hear hand-grenades exploding, so the trench fight must have already begun. At the II/ 66 sector HQ east of Beaucamp, Captain Rieger ordered the company to take the position west of Beaucamp, which was now in enemy hands. Even before the company began the attack, a British tank, which had bypassed the I/ 66 position, inflicting heavy casualties, was knocked out by a I/ 66 anti-tank rifle. In order to roll-up the communications trench which led to the I/ 66 position from the north, a hand-grenade squad was immediately formed: it had recently conducted attack practise at the training area. The attack was conducted aggressively and succeeded completely. Initially the British fought back, but after a few waves of hand-grenades they climbed out of the trench in groups and ran over the open field to the rear, pursued by enthusiastic fire from us, some of it delivered standing. The company succeeded, with light loss, in retaking the whole 1/ 66 position west of Beaucamp and re-establishing contact with IR 27. The company's situation was nevertheless anything but rosy. The British lay in the large shell-craters in front of the 1/ 66 position and half-left behind the company was the village of Beaucamp, occupied by the British, from where they tried to roll-up the 1/ 66 trench: after some small initial success, they were thrown back again. As security against Beaucamp, a platoon occupied a communications trench leading to the rear. The British in Beaucamp continually fired into the company rear, killing the brave Senior Sergeants Kilz and Schmidt with bullets to the head.

While the regiment was successful, the enemy had made real progress in the sector of the division to the left, and that evening our division was ordered to fall back to the general line from Marcoing to Villers-Plouich. Given the heavy enemy harassing and interdiction night artillery fire, and the great distances involved, the withdrawal order arrived very late and the movement was rushed. In the sector of the division to the right, the enemy detected the withdrawal and was already pursuing. There was heavy harassment and interdiction fire in the rear area, so that the vehicles could not come forward.

Everything in the new position was more primitive than we had grown used to. Only the front-line units found anything like trenches and a few dugouts; further to the rear the old trench system stopped. The situation in Villers-Plouich, through which IR 66 and IR 36 had to withdraw, was terrible. Heavy-calibre shells landed continually in the thickly packed village. It was particularly difficult for the withdrawal of the front-line troops, since due to the poor communications, they received the order late; a great deal of valuable equipment had to be left behind. On 28 September, as the regiment began to acquaint itself with its new position, the town of Marcoing, 2km directly to its right flank, was already in enemy hands, as though to the right of the division the German front came to an end. It was lucky that the enemy did not use this opportunity to attack either on the night of of 27–28 September or on the morning of 28 September. The regiment prepared itself for the worst. All combat-capable troops (which at this time did not include II/ 66) were on the front line or immediately behind it in the Redensburg Basin. There were no reserves, so the regimental HQ moved forward to the battalion sector HQ in the Koch Ravine, where there was one of the few dugouts, which was filled with the regimental staff, the staff of III/ 66 and other personnel. We spent the night of 27–28 September with the feeling of impending catastrophe.

At 0430, a drumfire began, cutting communications. Nobody left the dugout, but a strong group of men detailed to bring forward rations entered it, filling both of the exit stairways. Orders for the men to clear the stairways brought no movement; better to be shot in the dugout than voluntarily go out into the hellish artillery bombardment. After an hour, the fire was lifted and shifted to the rear and hand-grenades could be heard exploding outside, along with cries of 'They're coming!' The mass of the troops on the stairways would not move. Lt Menkel grabbed a full food container from one of the carrying party and swung it furiously around him, pushing up the stairs. Some officers and men followed, but once outside and a few steps from the dugout entrance, they ran into a literal mob of British. Pistols were fired, grenades thrown with terrific effect, but it was hopeless: this attack had clearly been made by an unprecedented mass of men, which had put all of the men in the defence out of action, and any attempt to stand and fight was taken in the flank and rear and defeated. The men outside the dugout quickly turned around, yelled down to the occupants of the dugout and ran into the Redensburg Basin to set up a delay position with the troops there, but the mob of British had gotten there ahead of them. We saw a pillar of fire shoot out of the sector HQ dugout and thought that it had been caused by a flamethrower, when in fact it was the supply of flare ammunition exploding. The staff of I/ 66 had already been captured. The regiment disintegrated. Men could see the British in front of them and that it was impossible to get through. British troops were in the artillery positions and other British were fighting with small groups from the regiment that were still offering resistance, such as one from 12/ 66 under Acting Officer Stackmann that fought to the last.

On the morning of 30 September, a heavy fog made orientation and assembling the remaining troops impossible. Perhaps we were lucky, because an energetic enemy pursuit with fresh forces would have finished us off. In a correct evaluation of the situation, the energetic brigade commander assembled every last rifle from the trains and staffs to form a delay line on the Créevcoeur Canal. Whatever came back from the front joined them. The situation was as tense as it could be, as the great gap to our right had apparently gotten even larger. Contact to the left was not good, either, where the Jäger Division had taken heavy casualties. With great difficulty, the intermixed units of the regiment were reorganised; in general, the combat strength of the already weak companies had sunk by half: in the night of 29–30 September, the regiment had lost fifteen officers and 315 NCOs and men. Almost all of the remaining combat-experienced officers were lost; there were just enough officers from the first years of the war to fill the battalion commander positions, while the company commanders were all recently appointed officers and acting officers. The nearly complete lack of experienced NCOs was also keenly felt.

Except for some enemy patrols, 30 September was quiet: the enemy was clearly having troubles, too. That night the regiment was relieved by the Bavarian IR 7. Had the regiment remained on the front line, the British attack, launched with massive superiority on 2 October, would have made an end of us, the fate that befell the Bavarians who had relieved us. In this fighting, the regiment lost thirty officers and 1,102 NCOs and men. Eight officers had been killed.

Withdrawal to the Hermann Line, 2–23 October 1918

The Siegfried Line had been lost along the entire front, marking the beginning of the great enemy offensive with which the Allied Commander-in-Chief, Foch, intended to bring an end to the Great War. On almost all fronts, the German troops were forced out of the trench systems which they had held for four years. It was now a question of manoeuvre warfare in the open field, for us in the form of delaying actions and withdrawals, in order to win time to construct the Hermann Line and, before the expected enemy winter offensive, the Antwerp to Meuse Line as well, which would generally be located on the German border. Even after the peace offer to Wilson, leading to diplomatic negotiations on 5 October, it would be favourable if the German troops succeeded in maintaining themselves as deep in enemy territory as possible. So there was fighting in October and until the Armistice in November, which made great demands on the equipment of the regiment, particularly MG, and the infantry companies, much-reduced in strength. The enemy continually committed more men, particularly fresh American troops, and ever more material.

During October, the regiment moved in the general area Cambrai–Douai–Valenciennes–Le Quesnoy, first defending a position for several days, then falling back to a new rearward position, and was frequently used to conduct counter-attacks.

On 1 October, after successfully breaking contact from the disastrous position at Marcoing, the regiment moved to Carniers, where it quartered. There was no rest to be had here, because the town already lay under enemy artillery fire, and the regiment had to dig-in and provide local security for the town during the entire night. The regimental commander was sent on home leave for several weeks and Capt. Rieger assumed command, which he held until the end of the fighting. The next day, the regiment moved to Douchy, 15km south-west of Valenciennes, but only spent one night there before again moving forward as the counter-attack force for 22 ID at Abaucourt, 10km north of Cambrai. It ocupied a stop line on the Sensée Canal, which flowed from Arleux to

Bouchain, in case the enemy advanced from Cambrai to Valenciennes. It also had the thankless job of stopping units that had withdrawn without orders from crossing the canal. 4 October was spent in this position: it was relatively quiet during the day, but at night suffered under heavy enemy harassment and interdiction artillery fire. The next day it was relieved by a MG section and marched almost directly to the north, to quarter in Hornaing, 15km west of Valenciennes. The regiment stayed here only two days, frequently disturbed by alerts. On 7 October, we received 200 replacements and were alerted at noon. We left all of our vehicles and trains and were loaded onto lorries and driven to the area north of Douai, where we were attached to 187 ID. We occupied houses in a completely deserted town named Dorignies, with a battalion in Pont-la-Deûle, completely ignorant of the situation, distance to the enemy or our mission. After a long search, the regimental HQ found the brigade HQ to which we were attached. We learned that IR 27 had already been committed here, and two of our battalions would be attached to them, and moved forward to the rail embankment at Quiéry-la-Motte. On the afternoon of 8 October, the order arrived that the entire regiment would be committed that evening to assume the left portion of the IR 27 sector. As the battalions were moving forward, a counter-order arrived stating that the relief would not take place, but that the regiment would march back during the night to its old quarters at Hornaing. In the pitch-black night, the regimental adjutant succeeded after a desperate search lasting hours in turning the battalions around, which were already losing cohesion. After an exhausting night march, the regiment reached Hornaing on the morning of 9 October, when an order came to bivouac not in Hornaing, but in Abscon. Here the regiment found poor and crowded quarters, but were not disturbed until noon on 11 October, when the regiment was alerted in order to occupy a delay position on the line Lien–St Amand–Haspres, to cover the withdrawal of the forward line, 4km to our front. During the approach march across the heavily shelled terrain by the canal at Roeulx, we took serious casualties: a direct hit on 9/ 66 killed three and wounded seven. The regiment occupied the position in the pitch-dark night, without being able to conduct a previous reconnaissance, with I/ 66 and III/ 66 in the first line and II/ 66 in reserve in a sunken road west of Noyelles. During the night, elements of 220 ID passed through our lines, so that we were now the front-line unit. The enemy appeared immediately, and the security outposts about 1½km to the front in a sunken road from Lien to Avesnes-le-Sec were pushed back by 1200. Towards evening, the sunken road was retaken. The next day, the enemy conducted a strong preparatory bombardment and attacked. But he had been unable to identify the regiment's position accurately, most of the artillery fire landed too far to the rear and the attack was thrown back. On the other hand, the rear-area elements of the regiment took heavy losses, and the regimental staff was forced out of Noyelles. Our patrols determined that the enemy had also taken severe casualties. From 14–18 October, the enemy did not conduct any major attacks, but disturbed our front line with attacks by patrols. Various indicators, particularly heavy artillery fire during the night, pointed towards an enemy regroupment. A British patrol was thrown back in the fog early on 18 October, with a British captain from the 51st Infantry Division being taken prisoner. We avoided the impending British attack by withdrawing to the Hermann Line on the night of 18–19 October. In the process, two delay lines were occupied, one by IR 27 for a short time on the high ground at Douchy, rather close to the previous front line, behind it a second by IR 66 on the Schelde Canal between Rouvignies and Prouvy. The withdrawal began at midnight. There were extensive demolitions, as the Hermann Line was to be held for a considerable period. All the bridges over the Schelde canal and its tributaries were blown up and important areas for the enemy flooded. To screen the movement, officer patrols with a heavy MG and a horse-drawn artillery piece were left behind everywhere; in the regimental sector, this was led by Lt Lehmann. The rearward movement proceeded as planned: the regiment passed through IR 27 to its delay position.

Work on the Rouvignies–Prouvy position had been undertaken for the last few days by newly arrived replacements formed into a special company under Res. Lt Gross. The first-line units, III and II/ 66, could be rested as long as IR 27 was in front. But since the enemy had advanced through Denain on the right, and the terrain to the left was flooded, the situation was most uncomfortable. But the withdrawal order arrived in time, and the regiment moved through Valenciennes to a position behind the Hermann Line. This movement was conducted in the early morning hours of 20 October without difficulty, but in doing so crossed the road over which it had victoriously marched into France in 1914, as well as its rest area in March 1915, but there was hardly anyone left in the regiment that remembered this: by 1918, the consecutive numbers in the company rosters had risen to unimagined levels. The regiment bivouacked in Sébourg, on the Belgian border. The regiment received a meagre number of replacements, 237, few old soldiers, mostly very young men or those who had been combed out of six Ersatz battalions. Even though we had heard of disturbances during the transport of replacements to the front, the loyal elements in the companies were able to bring the replacements under discipline and order. The regiment rested in Sébourg until 23 October, then it was alerted. The Hermann Line, which had been occupied only a few days previously, was already being attacked and had been penetrated in places. Since it was to be held at all costs, the regiment again faced heavy fighting. The criticality of the situation was reflected by orders that followed one another in quick succession, sometimes one cancelling out another.

Last Defence on the Hermann Line, 23 October to 7 November 1918

The alert order arrived at 0500, followed in an hour by a brigade fragmentary order for the regiment to move to Jenlain, with no information concerning the mission. At 1345, the regiment was moved to Villers-Pol, where it arrived at 1600. A few hours later it moved forward again to become the 21 RD reserve on the rail embankment at Mortry-Fme, where it received a brigade oral order at 2200. For the last several days, the British had been conducting strong attacks against Le Quesnoy, and had succeeded in making progress on their left flank. In conjunction with Fusilier R 36, IR 66 was to conduct a counter-attack to retake Bermerain. The newly occupied position had to be held at all costs, so it was emphasised that the regiment had to conduct a vigorous attack under all circumstances. The prospects for success were, however, slim: we were in completely unknown pitch-dark terrain and had no opportunity to conduct reconnaissance. It was unclear where either the remnants of the German units or the British were located. The counter-attack would be conducted by II and III/ 66.

The result was a catastrophe. The two battalions advanced with determination, but in the early morning of 24 October collided with a renewed attack from Bermerain by superior British forces. Our attack waves were broken up. Some troops succeeded in regaining the rail embankment at Mortry-Fme, but considerable elements, those that had advanced the furthest, were captured. Another 128 men were lost, including Res. Lt Eifrig, the commander of II/ 66, and four other lieutenants. The remnants, along with I/ 66, occupied a forward line on the rail embankment. In spite of the complete failure of our night attack, it can be said that it blunted the force of the British attack and prevented a worse outcome.

The first position of the Hermann Line had been penetrated in several places, and it was unlikely that it would be held in the face of renewed enemy attacks, so, on 24 October, there was a withdrawal to a line from the south side of Villers-Pol to the west side of Orsinval. The regiment, which now had a rifle strength of 200 [there is no further mention of heavy weapons – MG or mortars], moved at 2200 to the new position. The 10/ 66 was left at Folie Fme as outpost company to screen the front and strengthen the security zone. Initially, the British did not pursue the withdrawing Germans, and it was certain that they were unclear concerning the location of the German defensive position.

The Allied command used these last days of October to conduct energetic attacks on all fronts, their goal being to push the German troops over the Belgian border and, if possible, back to the Rhine before the onset of winter. Given the active diplomatic negotiations, it was of the utmost importance for the German OHL to hold every square kilometre of enemy land that it could. If the German Army crossed the German border, the last bargaining chips that could secure some degree of reasonable peace conditions would be lost.

That the British were going to soon renew their attacks became clear from 25–30 October, with a steady increase in artillery activity and evidence of troops regrouping and preparing for an offensive. Res. Lt Fleischer was killed by an artillery shell, and command of II and III/ 66 was assumed by Res. Lt Kühne.

IR 66 was relieved on 31 October, before the British attacked. It assembled at Gommegnies and moved from there forward once again to Jolimetz between Le Quesnoy and the Mormal Forest, which became the pivotal point after the loss of Valenciennes and the subsequent withdrawal to the Franco–Belgian border. At this time, the Allies attacked in Flanders towards Ghent as well as in the middle of the Western Front towards Marle [18km north-east of Laon]; it could be assumed that the attack through Le Quesnoy towards Maubeuge would be continued with full force. In Jolimetz, the regiment was about 2km behind the front line as counter-attack force for 4 ID. This sector was particularly difficult to attack, because it was anchored on the left flank by the Mormal Forest, so that little occurred in the first days of November. The time was used to reconnoitre the area, which was cut up by hedges and offered poor visibility. After four weeks' home leave, the regimental commander returned. Capt. Rieger, the acting commander, reassumed command of II/ 66. As before, Res. Lt Baldamus led I/ 66 and Res. Lt Kühne III/ 66. Each battalion had about 350 men, so the companies were very weak and had only one officer.

The expected British attack began on 4 November at 0630. This was to be the regiment's last serious battle, which would result in 182 casualties. The British artillery drumfire began suddenly and cut the regiment's communications with the front-line regiments of 4 ID. Wounded men coming back gave contradictory reports; apparently the first line had been completely overrun, which was confirmed by the withdrawal of individuals and entire units.

Regimental HQ ordered III/ 66 to occupy the artillery defensive line, but arrived too late, as the enemy had already broken through the artillery defensive position in the 22 ID sector to the right of Jolimetz. The battalion lost a significant number of prisoners and other casualties just days before the Armistice. Initially there were no reports from ii/ 66 at all; a later report from Capt. Rieger said that he had occupied the artillery defence position on his own initiative. This was the last report we would receive from ii/ 66 and all trace of it disappeared. It was later learned that it had been surrounded by masses of attacking British and took heavy casualties. Lts Seifert and Rieger were killed. Capt. Rieger, who had been with the regiment continually since the first day of mobilisation and had only been wounded once, was captured, as were Res. Lts Rieckmann and Geisler. In iii/ 66, Lt Seelander was killed. The disproportionally high number of officers killed demonstrated that on the last day of battle the young company commanders were leading by example. The regiment, which had acquitted itself in so many battles, conducted itself in this last unfortunate fight with honour.

i/ 66 occupied the edge of the village of Le Rond Quesne and held it, in spite of strafing attacks by numerous low-flying enemy aircraft, which took any movement under fire, and the retreat of masses of stragglers, which made the conduct of the defence extraordinarily difficult. But even this would not save the situation, as the enemy had already made a deep penetration further north, and i/ 66 was ordered to fall back to the third position in the Hermann Line. The regimental commander once more fell ill and the regimental adjutant, Lt Menkel, as the senior surviving officer, assumed command. The third position consisted of poles in the ground which marked the future location of trenches, and there could be no question of occupying it, as it, too, had already been penetrated further north. The regiment had now shrunk to 150 completely exhausted officers and riflemen, but nevertheless was the only German unit to be seen between the British breaking through to the north and the great Mormal Forest to the left. A last attempt was made to hold the area near Le Cheval Blanc towards evening, but division ordered the regiment to withdraw to the area near Obies, just to the south of Bavai. The remnants of the regiment, initially fifty men, soaked through and completely exhausted, arrived late in the night, and could no longer be considered a combat unit.

Nevertheless, on the night of 4–5 November, a position at Obies had to be held, and it was on 5 November, against enemy patrols. There was no sign of the supply trains or the field kitchens, as these had withdrawn far to the rear in the face of a possible complete British breakthrough. The hungry, rain-soaked and exhausted men held a thin line in terrain in which visibility was reduced by numerous hedges. With the arrival of stragglers, the regiment again grew to a strength of 150 rifles. Late that day, the regiment moved to be brigade reserve at Audignies. On 6 November, the rearward movement continued; in pouring rain La Longueville was reached, and on the same night the march continued to Le Berlière, where the troops bivouacked in barns. Here Rittmeister [cavalry captain] Freiherr von Sternfeldt assumed command of the regiment. On 7 November, the regiment rejoined 113 ID. At 0900, the regiment crossed the Belgian border at Aulnois, 10km north of Maubeuge. For the regiment, the war was over.

In the last battles of the war, the regiment lost fifteen officers and 456 men. Six officers were killed.

40
Armistice and the March Home, 7 November to 24 December 1918

Between 7 and 11 November, the division marched east, deep into Belgium. On 11 November, the day of the Armistice, it crossed the Waterloo battlefield at Quatre Bras, and on 12 November reached the Namur–Tirlemont rail line at Éghezée, where it remained until 18 November. Early in this period news filtered down that Armistice negotiations had begun and that revolution had broken out at home. The behaviour of the rear-echelon units in the villages along the regiment's line of march reflected these developments; the regiment's order and discipline, and the confidence shown in the last battles by the men to the officers and NCOs, were untouched. The new commander, Major Rebentisch, previously the commander of the 113 ID engineers, as well as the division commander, spoke to the men about the upheavals going on at home. In accordance with a regulation issued by OHL, a Soldier's Council was elected, consisting of three men from each company, and a Senior Soldier's Council of five members from each regiment. The latter in the regiment consisted of Sergeant-Major Lagemann and other experienced NCOs and men, and worked in complete co-operation with the officers to maintain discipline in the regiment. The week's rest in Éghezée allowed the troops to recuperate from the last battles.

The march back began on 19 November, with the initial objective Cologne. It was made clear to the troops that the orderly withdrawal of the army was of the highest importance for the country; the succeeding marches demonstrated that every member of the regiment understood this and subordinated the desire to return home to this requirement.

Even though there was no enemy pursuit, the demands of these marches should not be underestimated. The roads were in very poor condition and softened by the rainy weather; clothing and equipment, particularly the boots, were in miserable condition. When the regiment arrived at what were once equipment depots, it found that they had long since been looted by rear-area units. The same conditions obtained concerning rations, as resupply had been made extremely difficult by the undisciplined behaviour of rear-area units. Continual attempts were made to revolutionise the men of IR 66. Together with the arrogant and sneering Belgian population, which decorated all the population centres with Belgian and Allied flags, the morale and discipline of the troops were put to a hard test. The organisation of the march was admirable: although every day there were several march columns on every road, and the towns were overfull, there was as good as no friction.

The German border was crossed at Michelshütte in the west side of the Hohe Venn. Our reception at the poor villages was moving, but the greatest difficulties on the march were just now beginning, owing to the icy roads in the Eifel.

On 1 December, the regiment received a festive reception at the Bonn Gate in Cologne. It was required to conduct military police duties for twenty-four hours, which consisted of holding the wild Soldier's Councils in check, so that the troops' march through the city and the provision of supplies was not disturbed. There were several clashes between the regiment's street patrols and sailors, but our men made quick work of them. During these twenty-four hours, the troops were housed in school buildings. On 2 December, the march continued, with three rest days, to reach Abbendorn in Westphalia in the area near the Lister Valley Dam (*Listertalsperre*) on 9 December, where the regiment was quartered in a 10sq. km area in villages, farms and mills. It was announced that here the 113 ID would be dissolved and the regiments would return to their peacetime garrisons by foot march. The generous hospitality of the Westphalian population, above all the unusually plentiful food, and some replacement of worn-out clothing, prepared the regiment for further marches. Some of the older year-groups were released, as well as those troops who were essential to the economy. Any superfluous vehicles and equipment were sent forward to Magdeburg, and most of the horses were sold off. Before the march began, the regiment formed a volunteer company of two officers and 120 men to be part of the State Jäger Corps to protect the state government. This was later designated 9/ State Jäger Corps.

On 13 December, the regiment continued the march. It made up for being few in number and shabbily dressed with the positive impression created by its good march formation, unbroken morale and the numerous black, white and red [the German national colours] flags on the vehicles. It lifted the spirits of a civilian population weighed down by war, defeat and revolution. They received the regiment warmly, and willingly shared with the returning combat soldiers what food they had in these hard times.

On 17 December, the Weser was crossed at Beverungen, and the march continued north of the Harz Forest through Börde towards Magdeburg. We already knew that the situation there was bad, and that the Soldier's Council had taken over the barracks. Two days' march from the city, our regimental comrade, Res. Lt Seldte, who was recovering at home from his severe wound, described to us how in the garrison otherwise exemplary soldiers had been won over to the red wave, and that he intended to establish the good soldiers in the old regiment as the basis for an association of front-line combat soldiers he was founding, the *Stahlhelm* [*Bund der Frontsoldasten* – Association of Front-line Soldiers, which by 1930 had 500,000 members, was a paramilitary organisation opposed to the Weimar Republic].

On the afternoon before Christmas Eve, Magdeburg appeared. The first to greet us were representatives of the Soldier's Council, who gave us to understand that before we entered the city we had to give up our weapons. On hearing our unmistakeable answer, the High Soldier's Council disappeared into the fog. The officers of the replacement battalion met us at the south entrance of Sudenburg, at the Hasselbach Platz the Red Cross and at Schroteplatz the heads of the military and city administrations. Accompanied by ringing church bells and surrounded by an immense sea of people, the regiment marched slowly down the Breiter Weg to its barracks, where it was met by the mayor. The regimental commander, Major Schrader, addressed the regiment for the last time, and dismissed the IR 66 men with the admonition to use all their strength for the good of the sorely tried Fatherland. Three cheers for Germany and the playing of the regimental march ended the history of the illustrious 66th Infantry Regiment.

41

DISSOLUTION OF THE REGIMENT

What now followed was sad and gloomy. The few loyal men who did their duty and assisted in demobilising the troops and dissolving the regiment, as well as the numerous reserve and replacement units, had a hard time of it. It was exhausting work, continually disturbed by the antics of the Soldier's Council in Magdeburg. Finally, this tedious and thankless job was completed in February 1919. After over a year, on 1 January 1921, the German Army was re-established, and 10/ IR 12 was designated the company honoured to carry on the tradition of IR 66.

In the Great War of 1914–18, the regiment lost 144 officers, acting officers and officer candidates and 3,067 NCOs and men killed.

We will close the history of our proud old regiment, in which so many officers, NCOs and men gave their lives for the Fatherland, and in which those of us who survived gave the best years of our lives, with the admonition that the spirit of the old IR 66, which proved itself in all of its wars, be preserved by all its members, in true comradeship and with a consciousness of our duty, and that our new army, and especially the Tradition Company, grow and enjoy a better future. May every individual member of IR 66 remember our fallen comrades and conduct himself accordingly!

INDEX